John Bascom

**The Science of Mind**

John Bascom

**The Science of Mind**

ISBN/EAN: 9783337035631

Printed in Europe, USA, Canada, Australia, Japan

Cover: Foto ©Thomas Meinert / pixelio.de

More available books at **www.hansebooks.com**

## BY THE SAME AUTHOR.

G. P. PUTNAM'S SONS, New York.

THE

# SCIENCE OF MIND

BY

## JOHN BASCOM

AUTHOR OF " ÆSTHETICS," "PHILOSOPHY OF ENGLISH LITERATURE,"
" PHILOSOPHY OF RELIGION ", " ETHICS "

———————————

NEW YORK

G. P. PUTNAM'S SONS

27 AND 29 WEST 23D STREET

1881

# PREFACE.

It has been a reproach to philosophy, generally and persistently put forward, that it makes no progress, that it lacks established elements, that it is a field of extravagant and contradictory theories. We do not accept these assertions in the unqualified way in which they are thrown out. So made, they are the result of ignorance and ungrounded contempt on the part of those who so easily utter them. So far, however, as these statements are true, they are a common reproach and misfortune, to be removed only by more patient, more protracted, more guarded inquiry. To scorn and reject philosophy as presented under its own, its metaphysical form, subject to its own conditions, is simply to deepen the difficulty, and postpone indefinitely an answer to the most fundamental and central inquiries. If more than the usual number of mistakes have been made in this department, it is because more than the usual obstacles lie in the path of progress. These are not to be removed by discouragement, or by opening ways in other directions. All success to the students of physical science: but each of its fields may have its triumphs, and the secrets of mind remain as unapproachable as hitherto. With philosophy and not without it, under its own laws and not under the laws of a lower realm, must be found those clues of success, those principles of investigation, which can alone place this highest form of knowledge in its true position. The following treatise is at least a patient effort to make a contribution to this, amid all failures, chief department of thought. If asked why I hoped this volume might reward study, I should answer, Not because the system presented is new, but because the statement it here receives is at once succinct and elaborate, is strengthened by new points, by a consistent maintenance of all that belongs to it, and by the rejection of that which, essentially alien to its principles, only embarrasses it. I trust the Intuitive Philosophy will be found hereby to have gained somewhat of that proof which springs from completeness and proportion of parts.

I have acknowledged my obligations to others in cases in which they have been direct. I here especially express my indebtedness, in the general tone of the philosophy presented, to the eminent explorer and instructor in this field, Dr. Hickok.

Holding my work amenable to thorough criticism, I shall yet expect but little profit from the facile application of previous opinions to detached points; or from any discussion of the principles involved less penetrative and systematic than that here presented. I believe this treatise to have the integrity of a system, and to call, therefore, for a joint and complete judgment. To such handling I hopefully commend it.

In the present edition secondary points are more fully presented than before, and the work is better fitted for the purposes of instruction in higher education. I have been diffident in claiming for the philosophy here offered the independence, coherence, and strength which I believe belong to it. As, however, I am zealous for the system, and have found critics easily overlooking points not forced upon their notice, I now invite attention to the clear definition given to the doctrine of the intuitions; to the care with which they are enumerated, with which their relations to each other are pointed out, and their constructive office in thought is assigned them; to the development of higher powers in connection with lower ones; and to the support which liberty receives from the spontaneity of the intellect. Herein are secured a certainty of conviction, a strength of defense, and a clearness of explanation, not otherwise attainable. The system lies in direct continuation of the Intuitive Philosophy, but is put upon advanced ground, in a form more self-sufficient and defensible than hitherto.

# CONTENTS.

## INTRODUCTION.

## BOOK I.—*The Intellect.*

### CHAPTER I.

#### THE FIELD OF MENTAL SCIENCE AND ITS DIVISIONS.

### CHAPTER II.

#### THE INTELLECT—ITS DIVISIONS—PERCEPTION.

## CHAPTER III.

### THE UNDERSTANDING.

## CHAPTER IV.

### THE REASON.

# CHAPTER III.

### THE SPIRITUAL FEELINGS.

# CHAPTER IV.

### DYNAMICS OF THE FEELINGS.

# BOOK III.—*The Will.*

# CHAPTER I.

### THE NERVOUS SYSTEM.

# CHAPTER II.

### THE NERVOUS SYSTEM OF MAN.

## CHAPTER III.

### EXECUTIVE VOLITION.

## CHAPTER IV.

### PRIMARY VOLITION, OR CHOICE.

## CHAPTER V.

### DYNAMICS OF THE WILL AND OF THE MIND.

## CHAPTER VI.

### THE RELATIONS OF THE SYSTEMS HERE OFFERED TO PREVALENT FORMS OF PHILOSOPHY.

# INTRODUCTION.

§ 1. Though a knowledge of the value of a subject is not necessary to its successful pursuit, yet it imparts to our inquiries peculiar zest. We shall never fully understand the advantages connected with any science, till we have mastered it; and it is thus natural that each should praise his own favorite pursuit, experiencing daily the enjoyment and power it confers. Nor is this commendation usually, in itself considered, excessive; it is chiefly at fault, as it disparages other investigations, in themselves possessed of rival claims. As the fashion of thought in our time is to underrate philosophy, a brief space bestowed to urging its importance will not be misemployed.

We shall not enlarge on the pre-eminent mental discipline it gives, the acuteness of analysis, the steadiness of attention, the breadth of principles. All study imparts more or less of this training, and some are willing to believe that metaphysics bestows an unprofitable subtility of intellect, a gymnastic dexterity of thought, more fit for show than service, more likely to mislead than guide their possessors. There are certain peculiar and pre-eminent considerations on which we would chiefly rest our estimate of philosophy.

The facts which it furnishes are most intimate to our own actions, to the mastery and ordering of our own thoughts, and to the influence we are to exert over others.

It is indeed possible, that there should be healthy and successful intellectual action, a wise play of the emotions and
**of the moral** nature, without understanding them. **So** may
there **be** physical **health** without hygiene; **yet** who will
deny **an** influence of the knowledge of the laws of life in
the government of life? To pick up **a** few **facts so** personal, so of our very selves, as those which pertain **to mind,**
cannot but be **of** the highest moment in ordering **our action.** Indeed, every man who has any claims to general
knowledge **is a** philosopher, however much he may deny
it, and however false and limited his conclusions may be.
It is not a question whether there shall be philosophy
among men; this there must be, if men are to think and
act at all; but whether this philosophy shall be a true
or false **one.** Yet we do not wish to dwell on the value
even of the facts which mental science gives, their direct
practical worth in affording rules for intellectual training,
and for influence over others; but rather to point out certain broader relations of philosophy, which make its acquisition yet more imperative.

§ 2. **In the first place, no true** notion of the dignity **of**
man will be **attained without it.** If we consider man exclusively in his external relations, in his physical organization, and the ministration of nature to him, though we shall
certainly assign him, if we reflect wisely, a pre-eminent po-
**sition,** we shall by no means measure his true worth. The
forces and lives of the world grade up to him, and grade
**down** from him; and while he is the highest and latest of
living things, he is nevertheless of them, ruling by a superiority, not by a complete separation, of nature. The body
of man is very perfect; but those other organisms are also
in kind marvellous. The brain of man is very large; but
those other brains are large also, and apparently thoughtful.
Having travelled in classification all the way up from in-

fusoria, the last strides of progress, great as they are, do not impress us as throwing man out of the general range and fortunes of the life of which he makes a part.

As a matter of fact, those whose attention has been most external in its objects, who have studied nature, and man in nature, have held comparatively disparaging views of the rank of the human race. They have put it in the direct line of development with the life below it; they have thought it to share its intellectual and moral endowments with the higher animals; and they have subjected it, in common with all life, to the fatalistic lock of physical forces. Approaching man from below, we interpret him from the types of power we find in nature, we limit his liberty or rob him of it, we expound his moral nature by the law of utility, so obtrusive in the acquisition of physical good; while we seem to find the germ and outline of his intellectual constitution in brute instincts, perceptions, associations. We are thus as those who contemplate in a statue more the pedestal on which it rests, the marble of which it is made, the measurements to which it conforms, than the living, spiritual power it expresses.

There is no adequate defence against this tendency, no reasoning man out of this grasp of scientific classification, from the position of bimana among quadrumana, from his rank as co-ordinate in structure with the gibbering monkey, the grinning chimpanzee, the brute-headed gorilla, except through philosophy—without reversing the process, beginning at the top and moving downward—without considering that which is internal, and overshadowing with it, transient, external conditions. Suppose, for instance, as the result of such direct, independent inquiry, it is found that liberty belongs to man, a power altogether unique, with no prediction or type in nature; that the moral intuition, the necessary accompaniment of freedom, transforming it into self-poised, responsible life, is equally independent and primary; do we not in these two pillars of personality discover supports which lift the spiritual life into an entirely new region, which cannot be broken by all the blind giants of simple, physical induction that may bow themselves against them? If also it shall appear that the intellectual action of man is throughout different in kind from that of the animal; **that** we have no proof that the truly rational elements of thought ever enter the lower field of life, ever transform associations into comprehension, then shall **we** again see, that we have reached a new plane; not **the** completion of that which is below, but the commencement of that which is above; not to be explained from the earth upwards, but from the heavens downwards.

To estimate man outwardly, physically, is to judge **a** temple from the exterior, is to decide upon it by the order of its architecture, the bevel of its stones, the greatness of its workmanship, without entering its shrine, seeing its worship, or studying its ritual. So to judge man is as if we should pronounce on the supernatural claims of Christ **by an** inquiry into his human features and Jewish characteristics, in perfect oversight of the subject matter of the question. Man is to rank according to his spiritual constitution, and that it is the office of philosophy, and philosophy alone, to inquire into. We must go within the mind, see its structure and appliances, before we can know the dignity of the race. If this is denied us, if these portals are **locked** against us, we can only remain mute till the key shall be brought us.

§ 3. The second great office of philosophy is to furnish a counterpoise, a complement and corrective to the methods of natural science. It is not because we overlook the legitimacy and practical value of these methods, nor because we disparage induction, a chief builder in the tem-

ple of knowledge, one that has commenced and is carrying
briskly onward some of its most showy and serviceable portions, that we urge the rank of philosophy; but for this end,
that the two may be seen to be truly supplemental each to
each, that the arrogance of science and its supercilious denials may be seen to so cut down the scope of human faculties and hopes as to make knowledge itself comparatively
trivial and nugatory. It is the nature of the mind that
knows that gives significancy to knowing, and if this term,
the one most intimate to ourselves, in which alone we are
deeply concerned, is to be excluded from knowledge; if the
disembodied spirit, the mind itself, is to be left wandering
in the limbo of things forever uncertain and unknowable,
then, indeed, is it a most minute and unsatisfactory gain,
that our unexplored and unfathomed powers lay hold for
a little of the things about them; a small matter that the
stream, rushing on, we know not whither, yields a troubled
reflection of the shrubs on its banks.

We claim that the knowledge that centres directly in
mind, in its moral and intellectual powers, and in the social,
civil, and religious actions that arise immediately from
them, is a full half of all knowledge; and that the methods
of reasoning employed in these departments, while very
different from the naked inductions of science, constitute
the nobler moiety of intellectual life. We urge attention
to philosophy, because the sphere of thought cannot be
complete without it, cannot be rounded into a well-balanced
and stable orb.

If there has been one development more preposterous
than all others in the growth of knowledge, that development is Positive Philosophy—a scheme that scouts metaphysics, and yet can do it on no other than metaphysical
grounds; that determines what may be known and what
may not be known, and puts among the things to be dis-

carded the knowing faculties; that uses philosophy to explode philosophy, and on the ground thus cleared builds up a cobble-house of facts, every one of whose connections must yet be as purely intellectual as those of mental science itself. This is as if the eye, failing to look backward as well as forward, inward as well as outward, should deny the existence of anything in that direction, and affirm the objects before itself to be ultimate, the only resolution of facts into ideas. To save us from such pitiful philosophizing, we need philosophy.

We are, then, in a peculiar want of this branch of knowledge, since it is a hemisphere of itself, holding in equipoise the world of truth; since in it are found new regulative ideas, new laws, new lines of order, and also the tests of the validity of knowledge, and the rational grounds on which the limits of inquiry are established. Patches of truth may be given here and there by science, but landmarks, a synthetic rendering of the whole, can only be secured by the aid of philosophy.

§ 4. A last reason we shall urge for these lines of investigation is, that intelligent moral action and religious faith must rest upon them. Fortunately, considering the premises from which they start, men are so illogical, that they find no difficulty in believing much which in consistency they ought not to believe, no difficulty in doing that for which their own philosophy can render them no adequate reasons. But in spite of the fact that there is often an interior coherence in action, in the unconscious workings of our constitution, which does not appear in our reasonings, a false, deficient philosophy will, from time to time, come to the surface in unbelief, irreligion, immorality; the ground will soften under long trodden paths of faith; and many blind pilgrims, plunged into an unexpected quagmire, will fail to reach the farther shore. All the ideas on which morality and religion rest are established and defined in the realm of metaphysics, and to deny us this branch of knowledge, or to treat it slightly, is to put us, in the conflict with unbelief, at such disadvantage that we can never maintain our ground. We may, indeed, shut our eyes, and stand fast; we may stop our ears, and run from the questionings and claims of scepticism; but we cannot maintain our position in quiet and serene conviction, without searching for those foundations of truth found in the discarded field of philosophy.

The nature of right and its obligations, of liberty and its responsibilities, of the infinite in its application to God, as well as the positive and negative knowledge we have of his existence and attributes, are to be established by an inquiry into the phenomena of mind, the truths present to it, their source and authority. To hope, therefore, for morality and religion, and yet to sink out of sight those abutments on which they are to rest, is infatuation. Those do not so hope who wittingly do this work of denial and overthrow—quite the contrary. Very many of them well understand that their mines run beneath the sacred edifices of religion, the spiritual labors and history of the race, and that, if they can be fully and successfully fired, these will sink, a mass of ruins, into a black, sulphureous chasm. We see, therefore, that the intellectual battle between belief and unbelief, religion and irreligion, must be fought, in large part, in the fields of philosophy. The truths of revelation must be vindicated or overthrown by their relation to man's constitution, his powers of knowledge and obedience, and the rational stretch of his hopes.

Simple, then, are the reasons for philosophy, if philosophy be possible. We must abandon ourselves later than all things else, consent to darkness everywhere, if we can only strike a cheerful light at this fireside of our home. Unfortunate, indeed, would **it be** to lose the reins of power wherewith we guide the forces of nature, but far more unfortunate to miss the right handling of ourselves, and that serene strength which wins the rewards of life.

§ 5. But is philosophy possible? Is there **not** rather foundation for those many taunts **and** denials, asserting the endless, hopeless round of conflicting theories, the entire want of progress, the inevitable uncertainty attaching **to** every conclusion, and all conclusions, in metaphysics? **If** philosophy be not possible, if there is ground for the scorn and incredulity with which labor in this department **is** often regarded, so much the worse for us all. Nothing can take the place of philosophy. **If we are** doomed to igno-**rance** here, our ignorance is **hopeless and pitiable.** We fail to understand the satisfaction with which **some** snuff out this light, when they have nothing wherewith to replace it—nothing better to propose than the desertion of this whole region, and a surrender of it to confusion and chaos. The injunction, "Know thyself," the revered precept **of** all time hitherto, thus becomes impossible, and to modern thinkers, ridiculous. Outside of ourselves, we move with **patient** inquiry; we may feed our senses, and through them the mind; **but** we harvest home this knowledge, we know not for what ends. We gather facts, ignorant of their ulterior, spiritual uses, as the ox grazes, letting digestion and nutrition care for themselves. We see no grounds for congratulation in such a result. If it must be accepted, it yet remains a painful and **sad** alternative, turning the key in a door which above all others we would fain open, hiding from us things which most reveal the invisible world. It is as if **some** one, moiling long and patiently and profitably in the **bowels of** the earth, knowing how to pick and blast and shovel, and sure of the productiveness of those processes, should, hearing of the miscarriages, accidents,

and embarrassments of the upper world, begin to deny this
region to himself and to others, and to make it the dogma
of his life, that there was but one form of sure, safe, and re-
munerative labor, but one unmistakable and positive good,
and that was mining. We console ourselves, in view of
such conclusions, with their entire falsity, and the utter impossibility of their general acceptance.

Other departments, moreover, besides philosophy, are to
suffer from this rejection of the philosophical spirit. The
positive sciences themselves require for their successful
cultivation something beyond an observation of facts—a
classification of resemblances. There is ever kept hover-
ing before the mind some idea of the causes, the concealed
grounds and reasons, of phenomena; and it is these
supersensual notions which guide inquiry, direct the eye,
and teach it what to observe. Without these, the classifications of science would come to little more than the
child's art in grouping its bits of crockery by size or color
or the conceits of fancy. It has been, for illustration, some
notion of the nature of light, either as a material emana-
tion, or a movement in a generally diffused ether, that has
directed inquiry, instituted experiments, and interpreted
facts. Yet there is nothing in philosophy itself more
subtile, more impossible of conception, more evasive and
evanescent than either of these supersensual conceptions,
which have presided over this department, and resulted in
most brilliant discoveries. Deny a search into intangible
and inconceivable causes, causes that in their inception are
purely theoretical, and we lose at once the clew of our
labyrinth, and henceforth wander at chance, with no forecast of thought, through its endless passages. Another
illustration is furnished by the correlation of forces. Some
notion of a hidden equivalence between very diverse
phenomena haunts the mind, of a concealed agreement

where no apparent agreement exists. This it is which sets the inquirer at work, quickens his thoughts, and leads him to new observations and experiments. An idea of a supersensible thing termed force, is present to the mind. For this force in its very diverse forms, as mechanical action, heat, electric action, chemical action, it strives to find a measure, and so to establish an equation between these different expressions by virtue of this their common term. Fruitful as this inquiry has been in science, it turns on an interpretation of things quite inscrutable to the senses.

But how vain is it to demand positive, direct knowledge through the senses of this notion itself, so serviceable and indispensable? If we are to banish, as the ghosts of past superstitions, all the disembodied ideas the mind furnishes to positive science, we shall shortly be left without guidance, deserted of these good angels of thought, in whose absence eyes and ears are of no avail. We are in science, no less than in philosophy, constantly reaching and handling supersensual notions, purely mental phenomena; we are ever making them most fruitful sources of further acquisitions, though certainly with no more full, definite, and positive knowledge of their very nature than that we possess of mental phenomena from consciousness. Indeed, the moment we penetrate a very little below the surface, Positive Philosophy is of the same nature with that which it discards, is dealing with causes, forces, and reasons which are wholly the offspring **of the** mind, and the limits of whose legitimate use must be determined on purely intellectual grounds.

Nor is philosophy itself without its fixed, settled facts, as generally admitted and as incontrovertible as those of any science whatever. The laws of recollection, attention, judgment, imagination, of the emotions, of responsibility, constitute a large department of accepted conclusions.

The principles and precepts therein involved are running hourly through our processes of reasoning, our persuasion, our judicial action, our social opinions. Indeed, no single science, unless, perhaps, we except mathematics, is furnishing so many, so constant, so undoubted guides, both to those who maintain, and to those who deny, its theoretical value, as philosophy, with its adjuncts of logic, æsthetics and ethics. Totally untrue, then, is the representation that metaphysics is a hopeless medley of contradictory and unverified theories. An appearance of truth is given to this assertion by directing attention from established facts to those skirting and partially explored fields of ontological inquiry, of the sources of our mental furniture, and of the authority of our faculties. We might thus discredit the established facts of electricity on the ground of conflicting opinions concerning the nature of the activities or physical states which constitute it.

Now, it is evident, from the nature of the case, that more of these ultimate questions, more of these points at which direct, sensible knowledge ends, must belong to philosophy than to any other branch. The postulates and definitions of knowledge are conditioned on the faculties of mind, and to state these in their safe, ultimate form ; to settle where knowing, in all its phases, begins, and to give the reasons and grounds of these statements, is a late and difficult task, and one which should not, by its laborious and partial results, prejudice a department which is highest in rank, as it is most recondite and ultimate in its conclusions.

What act more indolent and unscientific than to jump to the conclusion, that these deepest questions are unsearchable and fruitless—than to turn our back on a region that does not at once yield its secrets ? Nor are we without progress in these most obscure directions of philosophical inquiry. In some cases, the true conditions of the problem are better seen—what is to be hoped for and what not; in others, the grounds of attack and defence are shifted. Many arguments and presentations have been exploded, and, though **others have** taken their place, there has been pro**gress,** progress toward an ultimate decision. The battle surges and rolls onward, and is not endless. The doctrine **of** human liberty is an example of the first sort. **A more** consistent statement of what it involves can to-day be made **than** ever before. It can be better distinguished from every form of necessity, and set apart with proper limits, and more defensible boundaries than hitherto. To be sure **we cannot** *explain* freedom in the ordinary meaning of the **word, but we** can see why such explanations are not, and ought not, to be applicable. As an illustration of the second **form of** progress, we instance the discussions as to the sources of knowledge; whether among these are intuitive ideas. **The** doctrine, that experience is the ground of all knowledge, is a very different one in the hands of Spencer and Bain from what it was as expounded by Locke. The latter champions pronounce the earlier proofs and defences insufficient. Confessedly, then, this school has been **driven in part from its line of argument.** Herein is move**ment, looking to an ultimate** solution of the problem. **Though inner** lines succeed one another, the city cannot be **besieged forever.** The grounds of conflict **and** the balance of strength are suffering daily changes, and though the con**clusion may be yet** far off, we see that it is slowly prepared **for** by what occurs about us. This discussion is not simply **the** dogged reiteration of affirmation and denial; the striking of shadowy forms with immaterial weapons, the wounds of to-day closing against the battle of to-morrow. Quite the reverse; **old** points are yielded, new points are made; light in turn is thrown upon these, and we move forward **toward** a conclusion—move slowly it may be, but as cer tainly as when the discussion pertains to the nature of heat or light. Reid dogmatically asserted as a tenet of common sense what philosophy ever since has been defending, limiting, settling on rational grounds.

Much work, indeed, remains to be done. The grounds of reasoning are to be more definitely fixed in this higher department; the logic of philosophy to be unfolded, restraining erratic, fanciful movement, bending effort to fruitful results, and urging discussion to a speedy issue.

If the inductive sciences owe so much to a new organum, a new form of logic, and that, too, to one lacking the strict proof of previous, deductive branches of inquiry, is it not rational to expect that further modifications of method, a new estimate of the nature and qualities of the proof applicable to the unique and remote questions of metaphysics will be equally productive, will yield fresh fruits to wiser investigation.

§ 6. Before proceeding to the facts of philosophy, I wish to lay down a few of its postulates most frequently violated. First, all phenomena of mind, as facts of some order, demand sufficient causes for their existence. These phenomena are by no means of equal significance in what they indicate, are not all normal, but they are all facts, and may not any of them be overlooked by any sound philosophy. We may not select a portion, and reject a portion as the result of some vague and vaporing process which we have chosen to decry. We have disposed of no facts by calling them metaphysical or theological or any other name expressive of disapprobation. The entire facts of mind must be stated, accepted, and harmoniously covered by the theories of mind. The same test applies here as in physics, the ability of the explanation offered to expound all the phenomena that come under its consideration.

A second postulate is, that there are different kinds of

knowing, each independent of the others, each incapable of affording any light within the field of the others. The various forms of knowing show the various powers of the mind. The independence and diversity of the matter given reveal the independence and ultimate character of the faculty through which it is reached. If one knowing faculty could overlook another, the second would by that very fact be lost or merged in the first; since for the two there would be but one line of perception. We have two eyes, but only one power of sense or sight, and this sense can do nothing, absolutely nothing, to cover the phenomena of taste or of smell. The additional and independent action of each intuitive faculty is involved in the very fact of its being a faculty, a distinct power of doing a distinct work.

The reverse statement is evidently equally true, and gives us a third **postulate,** that we have as many faculties as we have distinct forms of impressions or primitive knowledge. The presence of a feeling, a perception, a conclusion, an idea in consciousness, must be explained; and if it can not by analysis be resolved into simpler forms, or by deduction be derived from a more primitive action, it must be accepted as itself primary, and the power to attain it be recognized. The question of elements is not different here from the kindred question in the physical world. Each form of matter ranks as an element, till chemical analysis **has** resolved it. The classified fruits of knowing imply as **many** powers of knowing, till the classification can be corrected by a reduction of the number of genera.

A fourth postulate is, that we have intuitive as well as reflective powers. Reflection by its deductive processes exhausts primitive material of its instructional value, and by its inductive processes combines it in forms most suitable for general knowledge. But these methods of action imply material already present. We cannot derive all things from something more ultimate ; nor combine things, till we have the things to combine, and the idea of the order we put upon them. Reflection cannot furnish its first premises. The mind must have starting points, and these must be arrived at directly, intuitively. It is irrational not to recognize the beginning, or to strive to get back of it with an explanation. What these points of commencement are it is the office of philosophy to decide, and to arrest explanation and all effort toward it, when these have been reached.

As powers are ultimate in their own field, the test of the correctness of their action in each case is its clearness, firmness, universality. This is our fifth postulate. That which is done uniformly by the mind, expresses the mind's normal power, and this normal power is to the mind sufficient proof. Though it may confirm its action at times in secondary ways, these ways will all of them involve the soundness of its permanent convictions. We may strengthen our reasonings by watching the concurrent progress of events, but we shall never allow those events to contradict a plain, logical process. We escape this result by the fresh inference that the premises in the mind and those embraced in the physical facts are not identical. Clearness in the mind's action is the first element of certainty. This clearness may be so comprehensive and complete as to enable a single mind to oppose its convictions to the general convictions of men. Pre-eminent mental power does not allow itself to be matched with majorities. Even insanity cannot escape this law, and the conclusions of the insane may even be more imperturbable than those of the sane. This fact does not destroy the value of the law. Health remains a power, though we cannot deny the existence of disease. This first clearness confirms itself by reiteration. What the mind firmly holds, under shifting circumstances, is well held. And this again is further tested by universality. Universality is in some sense the proper test of a normal power of mind, but it is one that must be applied with great discrimination. Scarcely any truth in science or philosophy could endure its heedless use. There is no average mind which is a law to mind in all its manifestations. It is only the decision of minds of like power, scope, and advantage that confirm each other. The widest experience is called for in the wise application of this test; while the mind bears with it, all through the formation of this experience, an unwavering confidence in its own clear **convictions.** This test, moreover, will vary with the power under discussion. The senses more readily contradict or correct the senses, than the thoughts the thoughts, or the intuitions the intuitions in their higher range.

A last postulate is, that what is conceded—avowedly, tacitly, or impliedly—at one point, must be freely conceded at all points. Processes which themselves assume the goodness of our faculties must not conclude with a denial or impeachment **of** their integrity. A doubt must have a premise, and if this premise involves confidence in the very reasoning by which the foundations of reasoning are disturbed, that doubt is self-destructive. An idea, whose valid possession is denied, must not be allowed to enter furtively **into those** very processes of thought by which it is professedly eliminated. If it cannot be removed in the mind's ordinary action, it must not be removed in an exhaustive scientific statement of that action.

If these postulates are truly adhered to, we shall cut ourselves off from a great deal of impossible and absurd effort to assimilate one form of knowing to another; from a feeling of dissatisfaction because our analytic inquiries are brought at **length to a** halt; from denying any knowledge because it does not assume a familiar and specified form of knowing; and from deceptively using ideas in the very attack which we make upon them, knitting together our reasonings with axioms stolen from an adverse system.

By these postulates we secure several advantages. We safely start our knowledge; we start it theoretically as we do practically in our intuitions. We prevent the trespass of one form of knowledge upon another, or the concession of an undue pre-eminence to any one process of mind. We fortify the foundations of knowledge against irrational attack. The intuitive powers which at any stage are yielded by analysis are freely accepted by us, and if there is a disposition to distrust any one of them, we are carried back immediately to the process by which its claims are to be tested. If we believe any knowledge not to be simple and primary, we have only to show it to be compound and derived. So long, however, as we accept it as a distinct, unanalyzed conviction, we must assign it a mental power, and concede its entire validity. These postulates keep our philosophy at work on the familiar mental facts offered us for explanation, and check it in any erratic speculation which is proceeding in oversight or subversion of the phenomena under consideration, the hourly thoughts of men, the knowledge current in the human mind.

# BOOK I.

## THE INTELLECT.

### CHAPTER I.

#### THE FIELD OF MENTAL SCIENCE AND ITS DIVISIONS.

§ 1. THERE is no branch of knowledge more distinctly defined in its limits than mental science. It lies in a unique realm, cut off from every other—that of consciousness. All the phenomena of this field in their separation, classification, mutual interaction and dependencies are the subjects of this science, and its only subjects. There is thus little opportunity to confound the inquiries belonging to philosophy with those of any other department. Logic and Ethics most nearly approach it; but the one considers abstractly the products and processes of thought, and not the thinking powers; and the other, the moral constitution of the mind, and is so far a branch of philosophy, adding thereto, however, an evolution of practical precepts from moral principles.

Anatomy and physiology, on the side of the natural sciences, are most closely allied to philosophy, yet, after all, deal only with the physical conditions and instruments of mental action, and, without the key and interpretation of mental science itself, can cast no light whatever upon it. The facts of philosophy lie in consciousness; here they are to be sought, and every fact therein contained is to be made the subject of consideration.

Consciousness is commensurate with all mental states and acts. It accompanies feeling as much as thinking, and volition as much as either. The only possible way in which a mental state or act can be testified to, is by consciousness; some mind at some time has known or felt it. An event that happens nowhere in space is not a physical event; an act or state that is not found in the field of consciousness is not a mental act or state. There are either facts that are neither physical nor mental, that exist neither in space nor consciousness, but in some unintelligible form in some third region, or all facts fall under these two divisions; and it remains the criterion of one class that they occur in space, and of the other that they occur in consciousness. A third state is inadmissible as unknown and unnecessary. Consciousness is neither a knowing nor a feeling nor a willing, is neither this nor that mental act, but a condition common to them all, a field in which they appear, in which they arise and make proof of their existence. A consciousness of knowing is necessary to knowing, a consciousness of feeling is necessary to feeling, and of willing to volition; and as these three cover all states and acts of mind, consciousness is involved in the very conception of a mental act or state. It is an inseparable something which defines the nature of the phenomena to which it pertains.

Consciousness gives—we use familiar language, a more careful expression would be, in consciousness is found— the mere fact of a mental state, that it is, and what it is, whether one of thought, feeling, or volition; or a complex one involving two or more of these. It renders phenomena as they exist, not analytically but synthetically, as the eye colors, or the ear sounds. To reach the primary colors which constitute the tint, the separate notes which form the harmony, calls for attention and discrimination. The mere facts of mind as facts are rendered in consciousness, and to be found there and only there by all who meet the conditions of search.

Discussion is had as to the truthfulness of consciousness. There is no ground for such discussion, since the discussion itself involves the thing doubted. Nothing can be better known than a fact of consciousness, since nothing can be known save through such a fact. Consciousness pervades all knowing, all thinking, distrust equally with trust, denial with affirmation. No man ever does doubt, nor can he philosophically doubt, the existence of a present fact of mind. To do so would rob language of all meaning. The only way in which such a dispute becomes possible is by wrongly regarding consciousness as a faculty, giving direct testimony to certain things, instead of something involved in the very fact of feeling and knowing, making them what they are, and, therefore, never present except through veritable, and, for the instant at least, undeniable, feeling and knowing. Whether the thing known has an independent existence, or the thing thought is correct, are quite other questions. A doubt of the truth of the testimony of one or more of our faculties to the various things declared by them is a scepticism by one step less central and less absurd than the distrust of consciousness. In this there is no show of rationality. There are involved in the one act an affirmation and denial of the same thing.

There can be no rational objection taken to an inquiry into the facts of consciousness, and no uncertainty can attach to them as facts which does not attach in a yet higher degree to all other facts. The phenomena of

psychology are of the most primary character and certain
order, even as compared with those of science. There is
no knowledge so direct as that which the **mind has of** its
own states; all other knowledge is indirect being conditioned on this knowledge. The phenomena of mind **are**
given truthfully and synthetically. Its facts are **evanes-**
cent in **each** mind, but they **are,** for the moment at **least,**
certain. In their several forms and their diverse lines of
succession, they are exceedingly complex and changeable.
Their obscurely synthetical character is their most striking characteristic.

§ 2. The facts of mind are confined, then, to the field
of consciousness, and there they are to be sought. In this
search there are peculiar difficulties. **It is** with most an
unusual effort of mind to direct attention **to** interior phenomena. External objects have been the chief subjects of
consideration, and to turn the sight of the mind on itself
is an unfamiliar and delicate process. It is like an effort
to reveal to the eye itself its own chambers, **by** casting
in light and by adroit reflection.

Neither are the several phases of mind observed as
transpiring, but as remembered. In the very act of thinking, the mind is so occupied with the subject matter of
thought as not to make the **process** itself the object of attention. Now memory is at best but a dim and obscure
vision, and especially so of internal **states,** which less **draw**
the mind's eye than **the** objects and facts which are the
occasion of them. If natural science were to proceed by the
memory of things, seen at periods more or less remote, its
progress would be comparatively uncertain. Nor can the
phenomena of mind be restored perfectly at pleasure, and
thus the recollection of them freshened. This is more possible in thinking than in feeling and volition; yet even in
thought, for its natural and full flow in a given direction,

the mind must be disengaged from conflicting states and considerations, and be left to the unobserved and spontaneous action of the connections and impulses peculiar to the mental movement.

This inability to hold directly the state considered before the mind, as the plant or mineral is watched and retained by the eye, is connected with another difficulty; no one can join us in our investigation with the directness and certainty which pertain to other inquiries. The object before the mind of each observer is hidden from the other, may not be of exactly the same character as that with which he is occupied, nor looked at in the same direction. This confusion of objects and observations is most perplexing. It is as if the eye were turned a little askance, and the movement and the blow, therefore, directed at an image before it, and not at the very thing itself. Much skill and time are thus consumed between different observers in drawing attention to exactly the same facts. They often, through the deceptive effect of agreeing words, seem to have reached this result, when they have not attained it, and thus fall into inextricable confusion and contradiction. The feebleness of direction and construction is akin to that experienced, when, by the sense of touch alone, groping in the darkness, we strive to understand the parts, proportions and relations of even a familiar room.

It is also incident to this search of consciousness, that no one observes more than the phenomena of his own mind, and those, too, of a comparatively recent period. It is difficult, therefore, to determine how far a peculiar balance of faculties, as individual habits and associations, may have modified the mind's action, giving prominence to certain forms and connections of thought, and obscuring others. This fact also embarrasses us in deciding how far the mind's later convictions are due to protracted association, and how far to native, inherent tendencies or powers. **Is** the normal, adult mind in forms of action the fruit of growth, or are these forms native and indispensable to it? The consciousness of **the child or of** the savage, so far as these questions may there seem to find **an** experimental answer, is beyond our direct exploration.

Another embarrassment in philosophy, though not peculiar to it, is the blended way in which its facts are presented. Not only do thought, feeling, volition unite in one state, diverse and conflicting feelings struggle for the mastery, and, in the **simplest** judgments, are interwoven perception, memory, reasoning, imagination, intuition, and the subtile effects of association, rendering analysis a difficult, yet an indispensable condition of success. Analysis of this obscure character, with phenomena in themselves evanescent and fluctuating, requires the utmost skill and tension of mind.

Another obstacle to success to be mentioned are the peculiar deficiencies of language in this department. Language, always an essential, is here a chief instrument of investigation. It is the precision of the word employed, that separates and holds **fast** the faculty, element, or relation designated. In natural science, objects exist apart, though not named, and hence do not lose their identity, are **not so** merged in **the ebb and flow of** shifting phenomena as to escape all observation. The very sense of existence is largely due in mental facts to a clear, specific, generally recognized name; since we handle the states of philosophy exclusively through their names, and without these, readily lose all traces of them. Moreover these names are applied somewhat in the dark. It is by description and suggestion that we are taught what the internal states are to which given words are set apart. The word is the same, but the internal fact which explains it is, **in every** single case, different, that is, lies in a different mind, and must be hit on as the thing meant, by the sagacity of that mind. We are as one who puts together a complicated machine by a printed description and directions before him. Careful observation is required to determine the parts referred to, and failing of this, all is confusion. Yet in this illustration the parts are fixed, separate, with a permanent, independent existence; while the parts of a complex, mental state admit of various divisions, or may disappear altogether, like some rivet in the dust of the shop. To attach words, therefore, to their objects; to unite the two so that there shall be no escape for either, is a delicate and uncertain process. The ambiguity of words embarrasses all forms of statement and reasoning, but is never elsewhere the source of so much idle discussion and fruitless inquiry as in philosophy.

A further obstacle presented by language is, that it comes to mental phenomena saturated with the imagery of the external world. Words are born amid sensible facts, and thence transferred to the mind. They come, therefore, to this new service with the images and associations acquired in the old. They subserve a popular, familiar use only the more aptly for this reason. It is when they are made the subject of careful analysis, when they are treated as the exact expression of the thing named, that their physical root and relations reveal themselves disastrously. The mind reaching this interior analogical thread of interpretation is pleased by it, and overlooks the fact, that investigation is thus sure to be led astray; to be turned entirely from true mental phenomena, and to be sent wandering among their shadows and reflections in the external world. Thus, from the very beginning, every discussion concerning liberty has been embarrassed, and in most instances has miscarried, through the application to motives and desires, in a figurative sense, of words begotten amid the necessary connections of physical things. These half-reclaimed servants, when closely questioned, have betrayed their low relations, and in so doing have lost to liberty its high, ethereal form. Like its household, it has been thought to be mud-born:

The facts before us for discussion must one and all reappear in language as a condition of their consideration ; and this difficulty subdivides itself into four obscure and shifting forms. (1) There may be no word in the language to express a mental fact or relation. Thus we are now borrowing nonmena to oppose to phenomena. (2) The exact attachment of a word may be uncertain, and different for different persons. Thus consciousness is still very vague in its application. (3) Words of fundamental importance may have several meanings, and play in a most perplexing manner between them. Thus right may designate that which is intellectually or socially or morally right. (4) The images of the physical world so pervert our psychological words as oftentimes to constitute a false connection between the things covered by them. Thus the doctrine of association has been built up on the idea of a certain coherence, affinity, or what not, between thoughts and feelings aside from the powers of mind expressed in them.

The last difficulty is allied to this, and arises from the uniqueness of the department. It refuses to receive illustrations from the analogies of matter ; or rather it refuses to accept as the exact types and counterparts of its own facts and dependencies those of a realm at the farthest possible remove from it, at the very nadir of the sphere of being. Yet the mind, familiar with certain processes, certain forms of explanation, certain couplings of thought, is uneasy and dissatisfied with all others, is only content when it has put the new matter under the old law, the new wine into the old bottles. Unable to hold it in these stiff, inflexible case-

ments, such a notion as that of the infinite perplexes and
vexes the mind, simply because it is not the finite, and
thus stands opposed to other forms of knowledge, and is excluded from them. Equally is it annoyed with liberty for
not yielding to some analogy of necessity, some interpretation drawn from the physical world; for not taking upon
itself, in a more subtile way, the iron-bound connections of
matter; and with right, because it will insist on being final,
and refuses to be merged in any other form of good whatever. To accept a new department—so new and so novel
as this of mind when contrasted with that of matter—as
new, to lay aside prepossessions, and to commence again
with simple intuitive convictions, the axioms of this field,
involve a sore conflict, and the more a´conflict in proportion as the inquirer has gained great victories of knowledge in the material world, and dwelt long amid its
methods of action. This is probably the gravest of all the
obstacles to philosophy, and the more so because it is generally entirely overlooked or forgotten.

§ 3. While the phenomena of mind are to be obtained
directly and only directly from the mind itself, there are
very important indirect auxiliaries of inquiry. Language
is one of the prominent of these aids. Language, as the
product of the mind, as the external, visible trace of the
mind's movements, reveals of course the forms of its action,
and, in the designations of mental phenomena, a part at least
of the facts of the interior world. On disputed questions
of analysis, also, the spontaneous, general convictions of
men are betrayed by the words they use; and a distinct
designation is so far proof of the general recognition of a
distinct idea. That certain words are always and everywhere floating in popular speech indicates that the thoughts
of men find rest in them, something valid, sufficient to
steady and sustain the mind as for the moment it lights

upon them. These traces of the mind, indicating its own spontaneous convictions, that which is actually woven into the web of its thinking and feeling, must be included in every sound theory of philosophy, and furnish the suggestions for its construction.

Of the same nature exactly, though not as easily accessible or explicit, are the facts of daily life and of history. The shadow of the mind is cast upon them, and we may reason thence to the powers and capacities they indicate. A theory which utterly confounds, as do some metaphysical theories, all the convictions of daily life, and makes the facts of history and those of philosophy rest on utterly diverse conceptions, so much so that no region seems so remote or even preposterous as this metaphysical dream-land to the very beings who are said to inhabit it, by that fact reflects on itself extreme improbability. History must be felt to be, and found to be, the very shadow, the intimate reflection, of that inner life which is revealed to us by mental science.

Another aid to philosophical investigation is found in an inquiry into the instruments of the mind, the physical organs which it uses; and into the incipient and rudimentary development of intellectual action shown by animals. We are thus able to give more correct weight to the purely physical element, and to separate more intelligently the lower and instinctive forms of animal life from true, mental powers. While not underestimating the secondary and inferential aid thus to be rendered to philosophy, we think that extravagant and absurd expectations of the results of investigations primarily physical have been entertained. One might look at a brain with utmost inquiry, and, without the interpretation of the facts of consciousness obtained by introspection, his observations, as initiating a science of mind, would not be of the least avail. To suppose that the divisions of mental faculties can be found either on the outside or inside of a skull is preposterous. Passing the experimental proof so fully given by Hamilton, that no such connection as that sometimes claimed between certain powers and certain localities of the brain can be shown to exist, we insist, that even if the fact of such a connection were proved, we should still as much as ever need an independent philosophy derived from consciousness. These regions are not labelled in the human subject. They contain in themselves no suggestion of the purpose subserved by the portion of the brain beneath them. The observer must have an antecedent idea of certain mental powers, and be ready to attribute one or other of these to the prominence under his fingers. Afterward he may confirm the act by observation. This first condition, however, failing him, the bump under discussion might as well be a protuberance on a potato as a projection on a human skull. The one, in and of itself, as a mere prominence on a round body, makes no more declaration of ideality, benevolence, language, than the other. Suppose we have made from consciousness a wrong division of powers, what is there to hinder us from transferring these errors to our map of the cranium? Nothing; they will rather inevitably thus reappear. The chart that is to guide us must be made out before we can begin to outline and number and name the divisions of our plaster bust, and equally also before we can attribute a faculty to a locality in the living subject. The absurd classification of phrenologists; such faculties as combativeness, philoprogenitiveness, secretiveness, are sufficient proof, if further proof were wanting, of this inability to find the invisible action of the mind in the visible form of its instrument. All the aid given to philosophy by an external fact is inferential, not direct; and that invisible faculty or force which is thus to be reached, on which our

conclusion is to land, must be given, in the only possible
knowledge of its nature, by consciousness. **The** analysis of
mental phenomena shows that firmness is the complex result of various, and of different, mental states, and no loca-
**ting of** a supposed faculty so called in **one** or another por-
**tion of the** head can alter, or throw light on, these facts.
The singleness of the name and locality imparts no **new**
singleness to the mind's action, marks no division of its
faculties. The invisible cannot be seen through the visible.
**Each** must be determined independently, and the connections between the two established by experience. It would
**be as** rational to suppose that the letters contained in the
word *will* should of themselves convey to every mind the
notion of **that power, as** to suppose that a prominent eye
should reveal the existence of a faculty called language.
Regarding consciousness, then, as the only field of the
science, whether reached inferentially, or directly under
the interpretation of the light it itself furnishes, we pass to
the general divisions of mental phenomena.

§ 4. The leading divisions of the faculties of the
mind, **so** generally accepted since the time of Kant as
scarcely to demand further explanation or defence, are those
of knowing, feeling, willing; the intellect, the sensibility,
**and the** will. **The desires are** by Kant and Hamilton included with **the will. They belong rather** with the feelings. Desire **is** employed to designate a state of feeling
toward a certain object **or objects.** We find things differently related to our happiness; we cease, therefore, to be indifferent to them; one object or line of action gets a hold
upon us; we are drawn toward it, and this emotional state
we call a desire. Language sustains this decision. Desires
are constantly spoken of as feelings, never as thoughts or
volitions; the words in the first case are used interchange-
**ably, not so in the second. We** apply the same adjectives

to them as to the feelings. We say of a desire as of an emotion, that it is strong or weak, firm or changeable, intense or feeble; and sometimes, as in the case of avarice, speak of it as becoming a passion. Our desires, also, may be directly opposed to our volitions. We greatly covet a certain possession, but our pride constrains us not to ask for it. We wish the pleasure of a given action, but through fear determine not to perform it. A state of desire, like every state of feeling, is antecedent to volition, and may or may not find play in subsequent choices. As a desire it may arise and pass away emotionally, like envy or jealousy or sympathy or love, and find no expression in action, awaken not the will at all. It may either meet with acceptance by the mind, or suffer rejection by it. Desire, then, should be included in the field of the emotions, where it arises, and spends its power. It does not, in the fact that it gives occasion to the will for activity in providing for its gratification, differ from other feelings. These also, as long as they last, are springs of volition.

§ 5. An attempt has been made to divide the department of will, into choice and volition. A color of plausibility is given to this division by distinguishing between initiatory volition and executive volition. The first is termed choice, the second volition. When two diverse lines of action are contemplated, and the mind is as yet undecided between them, the desires have free play, the sense of moral obligation is present, and the conflict awaits a definite settlement by a choice, a fixed determination, in favor of one or the other. We sometimes, at this point, use the word choice out of the meaning which should attach to it as pertaining to volition. Thus we say, " My choice would be this line of effort," though we actually accept and pursue another. Choice is thus made to express a state of desire, not one of will. The word choice, however, in its use

in the third department of mental phenomena, expresses an
explicit termination of all vacillation, a close deliberation
by an act of will in favor of this and in rejection of that.

The case thus being closed by a specific and peculiar
act, there remains a longer or shorter series of efforts to be
made in reaching the object proposed, in accomplishing the
career marked out.    There are no definite limits in analysis
to these intermediate acts.    Our division may extend to
each muscular movement, or it may stop short with each
specific undertaking.    I propose to build a house ; the
number of distinct physical and intellectual efforts involved
in the project are indefinitely great ; and while they are all
under the control of the will, we have no occasion to place
a distinct volition back of each one of them.    The will has
the power, by a few explicit volitions, to direct the current
of the vital powers in a single channel of expenditure.    A
walk once entered on, the movement becomes in a large
measure unconscious, and the mind is left at liberty to pursue any line of action it prefers.    The voluntary and the
involuntary play of physical members differ not so much in
the manner in which they are sustained, as in the way in
which they are initiated, and in the fact that the one is
momentarily open to modification, and arrest.

The distinction then made between a choice and a volition seems to be found in their position in reference to an
end, rather than in their intrinsic character.    The one is
initiatory of a line of action ; the other sustains and com-
pletes it.    Ths one is primary, the other subsidiary.    The
one is determinative and governing, the other executive.
The first gives character to an action, the second sustains
and develops that character.    The one is immediately free,
the other mediately so, through its dependence on the first.
The division thus sinks into a classification of volitions, and
removes neither choice nor volition from the phenomena of

the will. Choice, as an act of will, does not include the deliberation and the play of feeling from which it proceeds; but only that final act by which they are brought to a close, and the powers of the mind made to unite in a line of effort. Executive volitions are the secondary impulses of will, by which its primary impulses are completed; they are the prolongations of that power which is born of choice. The ball is driven in a given line, but receives accessions of force, and changes of direction, as the exigencies require.

§ 6. The relation of consciousness to the three forms of mental action is the same. Sir William Hamilton seems to have regarded its connection with knowing as somewhat peculiar. While he speaks of it as the condition of all mental phenomena, he says, "Those of the first class, the phenomena of knowledge, are indeed nothing but consciousness in various relations." The complete and expansive statement is rather that consciousness is the condition, and equally the condition, of all mental acts and states. It is merely through a deficiency, or peculiar use of language, that it seems to be more intimately connected with knowing than with feeling. To know a thing, and to be conscious of it, are used as interchangeable expressions; and, hence, we have come to regard consciousness as a kind of knowing, or as an act of knowing, and not merely and purely the condition of such an act, that which permits knowing to be knowing. It is not strange, that a constant condition of an act should, in language, take the place of the act itself. Through this interplay of the words conscious and know, we are able to say, "We know that we feel," "We know that we will;" though we can with only doubtful propriety say, "We feel that we know," "We feel that we will;" and cannot at all say, "We will that we know," "We will that we feel." This use arises through a peculiar connection in the language employed of conscious-

ness with knowing, and thus **a transfer of** the word know
to both feeling and volition. Consciousness is no more an
act of knowing than it is one of feeling, and is a condition
in exactly the same sense and way for the one as for the
other. We **know in consciousness, we feel** in consciousness, we will in consciousness ; and consciousness is neither
an act of knowing, nor of feeling, nor of willing, but a condition of them all. Consciousness is not a something, a
faculty or a light, which reveals acts, independently **of**
knowing, feeling, **willing,** to the mind ; but that which
**makes an act of knowing to** be one of knowing, of feeling
to be one of feeling, **and** volition to stand forth as volition.
Mind, by virtue of its own nature as mind, does and suffers
what it does and suffers consciously, under this simple and
inexplicable condition of being aware of **its own acts ; a con-**
dition which is no more allied to one act than to another, to
one state than to another, but is common to each in its **in-**
divisible nature. A feeling is not a feeling and a knowing
that we feel ; a volition a willing and a knowing that we
will, but simply and singly an emotion and a choice, under
the essential condition of such acts, to wit, consciousness.

§ 7.    Two allied inquiries arise in this division of mental phenomena. Are there any mental phenomena below
or outside of consciousness? Are the states of mind, the
acts of consciousness, consecutive or intermittent? Sir William Hamilton, and many other metaphysicians, recognize
unconscious modifications of mind, we think without sufficient proof. The conclusion is too purely conjectural to
command our consent. Mental and physical phenomena
are cut broadly and deeply apart by the fact, that the one
class appears exclusively in consciousness, and the other as
exclusively out of consciousness. The last are actual or
possible objects of some organ of perception, are somewhere
located in space, and thus open to the outside action of

mind through its senses; the first are within the mind, evincing their existence exclusively by their effects in consciousness. Not to exhibit anywhere, to any actual or supposable organ of sense, any phenomena, is, in the physical world, not to exist. Existence is affirmed only on the ground of some effects, however subtile, in sensible objects, and directly or indirectly in organs of perception. We never hear of physical facts above or below space, beyond all possible tests of perception; since such phenomena would be utterly unable to manifest this existence, to give any proof to it. The very notion of physical being arises from that of physical effects, under suitable circumstances open to observation. Thus also should mental phenomena be regarded. There is likewise only one known field for these—consciousness. All, aside from physical facts, that occurs outside of this, is necessarily unknowable. An alleged fact, which is to be found anywhere as a fact, has but two avenues through which it can make itself known, the senses and consciousness. These are the sole means by which we take cognizance of any class of phenomena. To assert, therefore, the existence of other modifications or changes than those which respond to these two methods of knowing, is to affirm some third field, wherein events happen whose nature is utterly unknown to us, and of whose being we can at most have only an hypothetical and inferential knowledge.

Some imperative reason should be given for the acceptance of phenomena utterly unknown, and from the nature of the case unknowable. By what principle are those unknown modifications, if thought to exist, classified as mental facts? Something it would seem should be revealed more distinctly as to their character, before they are assigned to this class rather than to that of physical facts. If these unknown modifications are acts or states of mind, are in any way phenomena of mind, we ought to have provision made for them in our classification of mental facts. The division would then run thus: the phenomena of knowing, of feeling, of willing, and a fourth class composed of certain unknowable states, acts, conditions, or whatever you please to call them, of which we have no knowledge either in perception or consciousness, and can say nothing by way of explanation. States, then, of mind may occur of which the mind itself knows nothing, and which furnish, neither in the field of thought or of forces, any direct proof of their existence. The argument for their being is thus of the most naked and inferential character.

If it be said that these modifications are modifications of the mind itself, and not of the nature of actions, I think it must be granted, that they are thus conceived wholly under the analogy of material changes, and that if they are shown to be, and to belong anywhere, it is in the physical, and not the mental world—in the brain, the instrument of the mind, and not in the very mind itself. In this last, we know, and can know, of no organic changes. Its own acts and states constitute the sum of our knowledge concerning it. Nor are we hereby rid of these alleged modifications as phenomena; nor of the consequent need of giving some clue to their mode of existence.

We are thus brought to the fundamental difficulty of this view, that it tends to confound the broad distinction between mental and physical facts—especially between mental facts and those which pertain to the brain and nervous system. No matter what relations exist in the brain itself, or what changes take place in it, an observation and knowledge of these are no part of mental science, and do not necessarily, do not alone, give a clue or explanation to any one of its facts. The organic functions and dependencies of the brain are matters of as distinct and purely physical

knowledge, as those of the liver, and no changes here can
reveal to us the nature of a mental state, or of the powers
peculiar to the mind. We can no more find the mind in
the brain—because this is the organ of thought, than we
can the life in the heart, because this is the chief organ of
life; or than the ancients could have searched it successfully
for the affections, because they regarded it as the seat of
the feelings. Listen for a moment to the words of one of
these modern philosophers, who reject consciousness as the
field of mental science.

"Not only is the actual process of the association of our
ideas independent of consciousness, but that assimilation or
blending of similar ideas, or of the like in different ideas
by which general ideas are formed, is no way under the
control or cognizance of consciousness. When the like in
two perceptions is appropriated, while that in which they
differ it neglected, it would seem to be an assimilative action of the nerve-cell, or cells of the brain, which, particularly modified by the first impression, have an attraction or
affinity for a like subsequent impression; the cell so modified and so ministering takes to itself that which is suitable, and which it can assimilate or make of the same *kind*
with itself, while it rejects for appropriation by other cells,
that which is unlike and will not blend."—*Maudsley's
Physiology and Pathology of the Mind, p.* 17.

It is difficult to treat with respect explanations like
these. Is the brain the only organ whose cells take to themselves "that which is suitable," that which they can make
of the same kind with themselves? Why then do not the
liver, the kidneys think, and unite like things in thought
by resemblance? No one thing is more separate from another than is cell-action from thought. To speak of the

two as the same is to **use words for** ideas. Who, by observing the one, could come to a knowledge of the other? One might watch at his leisure the operation **of** Morse's telegraph, and, unless his previous knowledge furnished him the solution, make nothing evident but his own vacant mind. Yet the connection **of** this contrivance with language is far more mechanical and obvious than that of **the** brain with thought. The affirmation of subconscious phenomena is especially objectionable as playing into material**istic** philosophy, **as confounding** the distinction between physical and **mental changes, and** referring real **or imagi**nary modifications of **the brain to the** mind, as if the two were equivalent.

But the views of Hamilton are **not** intentionally **open** to this objection; let us briefly **consider the reasons he gives** for the acceptance of unconscious modifications of mind. The first of these is the extraordinary power the mind sometimes shows of recalling events, and even unintelligible sounds, as those of an unknown language, long after every trace of them seems to have passed from the memory. "Extensive systems of knowledge may, in our ordinary state, lie latent in the mind beyond the sphere of consciousness and the will; but in certain extraordinary states of organism, may again come forward into the light, and even engross the mind **to the exclusion of its every day posses**sions."

In this **argument we simply meet the** old difficulty. How does the mind remember? **How does it store up** knowledge with no apparent store-house, accumulate mental vigor with no mental muscle wherein to lodge it, gain sharpness, precision, ease, with no underlying structure, **in** which these qualities may be thought of as inhering?

That memory shows unusual power under certain ab**normal conditions** of mind **does** not essentially alter the character of that power, nor introduce new conditions into the problem. Physical strength is not different in kind when exhibited in an astonishing degree by a maniac, from what it is in ordinary states of body. An ordinary act of recollection involves the whole question, involves neither more nor less than an extraordinary one. These queries — How does the mind remember? How does it subjectively acquire and retain power?—we must submit are unanswerable; questions which receive no light whatever from any supposed modifications of some supposed substance of the mind. If such modifications were granted, we should understand not in the least how they were equivalent to acts of memory, or productive of them—we should simply have two inexplicable things instead of one. The tendency to ask and answer such questions arises from the physical world, where we expect no change of powers without change of structure. The early solution given to this problem of memory, that certain films escape from objects, and are laid away in a secret store-house of the mind, is just as good philosophically as the latest; and sprang from exactly the same false tendency to carry the analogies of matter into mind. The form of mental action is not revealed to us, and we have no clue to it except this false one of reasoning from things and processes totally unlike those of mind; bringing the interpretation of physical phenomena to intellectual facts. We reject the explanation of mental power furnished by unconscious modifications of mind, because it is really no explanation, making the subject not the least clearer; because these modifications themselves are wholly hypothetical; and because they are inferred by analogy, from a field remote from the subject in hand, and alien to it.

The second proof offered, is allied to the first. It is drawn in like manner from the analogies of the physical world. The minimum object which the eye can perceive may be conceived as divided into halves; neither of these will be objects of perception, yet each of them must make a distinct, though unconscious impression on the organ of vision, in order that the conjoint effect may be perceptible. We have, then, the first conscious state in sensation secured by effects themselves unrecognized. Hence springs the inference, a conscious state of feeling or thought may be preceded by unconscious states as its conditions. We object to the analogy. The eye is a physical organ, lying between the object and the perceptive power. There may be in it action too slight to reach the mind. In the case which this fact is brought to illustrate, there is no analogous middle term between the mind and its own action. The question is, whether its own, its veritable, acts and states are always known to the mind? Now these actions are not occasioned in some intermediate substance by a foreign cause, and taken thence by consciousness, or overlooked by it, as the case may be. There is no such medium between the mind and its own acts. External, physical conditions, there doubtless are; but these constitute no part of the mind itself. Keeping the inquiry itself clearly in view, Does the mind know all that the mind itself does, all that passes in it? it will be seen that the above analogy casts no light upon the subject. If the theory is, that external forces act on the substance of the mind, or, to put the same thing in appropriate specific terms, that nervous energy animates the brain, and that a certain amount of this influence constitutes thought, while less amounts, though of the same nature, fall below consciousness, then indeed there is an analogy in the cases, and the argument so far holds; but we have reached out and out materialism. The theory on this basis offers no more explanation of the problem, How does a pure act of judgment or of memory take place, than would be found in the study of a piece of mechanism, a power-loom, or an electrometer. The brain is indeed more immediately the condition of the mind's action than any other part of the body; but the brain, the body, every machine and instrument it uses, are the conditions to one or more of its activities, and no one of them constitutes the very substance, the very nature of those activities.

A third argument is found in acquired dexterities, as those of the equilibrist, or the musician. It is asked: How shall the separate acts involved in the rapid performance of the musician, each of which was originally preceded by an act of volition, be explained, when established skill has banished from sight this directive power of the mind? One philosopher answers, "The movements of mind remain, but take place too rapidly for distinct observation and memory." A second replies, "They remain, but remain as acts or changes below consciousness." Before we attempt to judge between these opinions, it may be well to inquire for the proof, that these impulses of mind remain at all. We believe that the supposed difficulty arises from overlooking the nature of the connection of the mind and of the body. Much of the nervous, executive play of the body never passes under the cognizance of the mind, does not penetrate the region of consciousness, is purely automatic. Some of this action, on the other hand, which is usually self-sufficient, is yet open to the arrest and modification of the mind. Of this character is the process of breathing. Few will claim that an act of mind is back of each inspiration and expiration, though we can at pleasure shorten or deepen, quicken or retard the movement. I may find myself breathing in a manner that is inadequate or injurious. I may for weeks laboriously strive to enlarge and deepen the play of the lungs. I may succeed, and the improved method become habitual with me. Will it be claimed, that henceforward my inspirations are all voluntary, each preceded by an act of mind? I think not. The improved process is as automatic as the previous one, and no more requires subconscious mental acts for its explanation.

There are still other physical movements more constantly voluntary, more rarely involuntary. We thus speak of them as voluntary acts, and seem to regard them as under the exclusive impulse of the will. There is no good reason for this. The fact that I walk whither I will, and modify my movement as I will, is not a sufficient reason for requiring a distinct, mental act, conscious or unconscious, back of each muscular movement made in passing over each rod of the road I am pursuing. The will, as it were, by one volition, belts the automatic **powers**, and these run on till they are again arrested or redirected. If the play of the nervous energy to and from the nervous centres is sufficient to secure motion without consciousness of any mental action whatever, as in the case of the heart, is it not equally capable of continuing a motion the will has established? If we analyze each voluntary motion, so called, into the most single muscular movements of which it is composed, and place a mental act back of each, we have an absurdly complex result, and one not in the least testified to by consciousness, nor required by the known conditions of the problem. All the powers of life are not mental, and a great share of the labor of living is done by forces with a strength and movement more or less, as the case may be, independent of intellectual control.

In acquired dexterities, volitions are required for a time to establish and confirm the automatic movement, but this, once settled, is able to sustain itself by a purely vital power, a play of nervous energies without the direct support of the will. The difficulty of the question seems to have arisen from not marking the degree in which vital phenomena are independent of mental action.

A fourth argument for unconscious modifications of mind, is found in the association of ideas. Links of association, it is said, are frequently omitted. The mind passes from number one to number five or eight in a train of connections without distinctly recalling the intervening steps. How does this happen? Does the mind move through the entire series, though too rapidly for memory? or does the unbroken thread lie below consciousness, there traversed by the mind? The last query is thought to indicate the true solution. But is there any sufficient reason for shutting us up to these alternatives? Is it so certain that the mind never makes a leap, that it cannot associate five with eight directly, omitting altogether six and seven? Is not this also an act and a method of association, as much so as that which originally united the ideas marked five, six, seven and eight, respectively? Six scholars stand before me in the recitation room. This fact of itself is a ground of association, but it also gives occasion for fresh associations of various kinds, and so may cause the memory on the presence of one to recall any of the remaining five by some new *nexus*.

Take the case of acquired meanings. A word may have stolen from application to application along an obscure path of subtile connections, till it has reached the twentieth meaning. How many of these successive uses any one mind shall recall in employing the word will depend in part on knowledge, and in part on the frequency with which the word recurs.

The last meaning may be the only one suggested to the majority of minds in the majority of cases, though the previous ones and their connections may be known to them, in whole or in part. The word becomes at length a

literal term in its twentieth meaning, attached in this signification directly to its object; though there lie between
the first use and the present application nineteen images,
each of which has been carried in the imagination, imparting to the word a figurative force for a greater or less length
of time. What is to hinder the mind's going directly?
Nothing: association itself prepares the way for it.

The explications offered by unconscious mental acts involve facts far more obscure than those explained. This
movement under the surface of consciousness, is in itself a
most perplexing riddle, a strange something we know not
what. Nor, if it is granted, do we at all understand how
it can or does change its nature, and suddenly issue in a
movement within consciousness. The supplied links in
this theory are of an unintelligible nature, and do their
work in an unintelligible way. The whole result is more
perplexing and obscure than if we accept the naked phenomena, and suppose the mind to pass from idea to idea, now
by a more direct, now by a more circuitous route, able to
do the first, because it has done the second. The facts
presented in consciousness are more manageable by themselves than when surrounded by suppositions, which involve
phenomena unknown and unknowable. The dip of the
thread of connections below consciousness is a loss of it for
all practical and explanatory purposes in chaos and night.
If it re-appears in the realm of knowledge, it comes like a
ghost from Hades, in a mysterious method and an inexplicable guise.

The answer, then, to this proof is double. (1) New associations are constantly obliterating and overriding old associations. (2) And the intermediate steps of an association
often repeated drop from the mind. The mind is able to
unite directly the first and last terms, when these are the
only significant ones. Thus the Roman characters for four,

six, seven, eight, nine, come to designate these numbers as readily as the corresponding Arabic numerals, though at first they involve addition and subtraction. The abbreviation of mental processes by the omission of familiar steps, and by the more direct union of remote ones, is a cardinal fact in mind.

The connection of this idea of a subconscious region with materialism plainly appears in Lewes' *Physiology of Common Life.* He affirms: "that all nervous centres in action, give rise to *Sensation,* and thus furnish elements to the general *Consciousness.*" Thus we are made to be conscious of all the muscular and involuntary movements that take place in the body. This strange affirmation is thrown into the very teeth of consciousness itself, momentarily affirming the reverse truth to us all, on the purely *a priori* grounds, first, that a similarity of ganglionic structure in these nerve-centres implies similarity of office ; and second, that constant, physical impressions must be made upon them, and hence, must enter consciousness.

"Every such excitement of the sensitive organism must be a sensation. These sensations will necessarily be very various, as the organs excited, and the exciting causes, are various ; but they must all be sensations, they are all active states of the general property of sensibility. *Ergo,* they must all be elements of consciousness." Thus, this author so thoroughly identifies physical with mental states, that having established the first, he out-faces the mind itself, and declares that they must be consciously found in its record. This is only a bolder movement in the one general direction, since it pretty much annihilates the distinction between conscious and subconscious phenomena, and brushes lightly aside any testimony the mind itself may offer, as to anything that is, or is not, passing within it. If there is any mockery of consciousness more extreme than every other, it is this affirmation, that every peristaltic motion of the intestines is a phenomenon of mind. So one mind at least classifies its activities.

§ 8. There has been developed in recent philosophy, especially in Germany, an increasing disposition to extend intelligence, as a state or energy, to all forms of activity that manifest intelligence, and thus to confuse the physical acts with the mental energies from which they proceed. The strength with which the conviction has taken possession of philosophy, that certain physical states are the equivalents of certain mental ones, is very great. We must, therefore, meet it in its various forms of assertion, since the phenomena of mind cannot be profitably discussed till their independent primary character is established, and their limits laid down. A bold, firm line of division between the physical and the intellectual realms is a cardinal necessity. J. J. Murphy, in a work on *Habit and Intelligence*, presents this phase of opinion under which intelligence blends with and is lost in the physical. Sensation and thought are regarded by him as in their own nature unconscious; consciousness is quite a secondary phenomenon. "So far from consciousness being necessary to intelligence, unconscious intelligence is the rule, and conscious intelligence the exception. Intelligence presides over, as an indwelling power, all vital action—formative, motor, mental— and is as significant a term in one portion as another of the vital process."* The author does not mean by this that a conscious Divine Intelligence orders the organic process, but an unconscious constructive intelligence. There is, by figure of speech, intelligence in the steam-engine, but it is the intelligence of the machinist. This view implies something more, it identifies intelligence with physical organic processes; or with some inherent unconscious force that is

* Consult the earlier chapters of the second volume.

supposed to control them. We have, therefore, in it simply a degradation of the word *intelligence.* The conscious act of thought, and a physical fact in nerve-tissue,—or in plant-tissue—must forever remain incomparable phenomena, things most distinct, most diverse from each other. To call both intelligence, is only to lose a division in one form, which we must speedily restore in another. The things themselves we can not long confound. A physical fact, however subtile, occurring in no matter how impalpable a medium, can not be, nor in any way represent, a thought, a feeling, a volition in consciousness. Even if we were to grant that a definite physical fact is the antecedent of a mental one, it would not follow that the two are equivalent. We can not talk of shadows without light ; shadows are not latent in darkness, no more than statues are latent in marble. Shadows are to be thought of and discussed only with the light. When this comes, there are shadows ; when consciousness is present, there are thoughts. If we call any lower states thoughts, feelings, intelligence, when the true thoughts approach, we must look about us for a new and more princely appellation. To speak of unconscious intelligence is to discuss shadows, images, and reflections, with no mention of light. To speak of intelligence which is not conscious intelligence, is either to use figurative or unmeaning language. If we say of the plays of Shakespeare, that they are intelligent, we mean either that they sprang from intelligence in him, or awaken intelligence in us ; or, under human experience, we mean nothing. Things may be intelligible, they are not intelligent. Neither thought nor language justifies the idea of intelligence in things.

A feeling of which we are not aware, a thought of which we are not conscious, are simply a feeling we do not feel, a thought we do not think. We can only fall back, in connection with such a use of language into utter vagueness, or onto purely physical states.

He also says: "Sensation and consciousness are both feelings. To use logical language, feeling is the genus of which sensation and consciousness are species."* Hamilton regarded consciousness as a general term for knowledge, and here it is ranked as a specific feeling with the feelings. Hamilton would say that we know that we feel, and Murphy that we feel that we know, while the fact is that we both know and feel as simple, sufficient states of mind. Mr. Murphy proceeds to refer, in a curious way of his own, distinct states of mind to distinct nervous acts; but the theory is, in reference to every one of its significant assertions, absolutely, purely hypothetical, is semi-mechanical and completely physical; if granted throughout it explains nothing in mind proper, but serves rather to obscure and destroy the fundamental connections of thought and thought, thought and feeling, thought, feeling, and volition. These physical theories of mind are wonderful examples of explanations, fictitious in their data, futile in their expositions, and destructive of the facts expounded.

There hold against them, one and all, these objections: (1) They rest on no one known fact broad enough to sustain them. The correspondence of a definite state of brain with an exact and pure mental state has not in a single instance been made out; much less has it been shown, that the first is the invariable antecedent of the second. (2) These solutions proceed on qualities and relations which belong to matter rather than to mind. (3) They thus subvert instead of expound the phenomena to which they are applied. (4) The explanations fail at the very moment at which they should take effect. As long as the terms are physical, they are coherent, but at the instant of

* Habit and Intelligence, vol. ii. p. 13.

transition all light disappears. Nor can this failure to show how or why the physical fact is productive of the mental one be helped by the analogy of the senses. That a series of physical effects in the senses should produce effects in the mind every way unlike themselves, and so be the ground of a knowledge of the external world, is a fact of a very different order from the assertion, that certain physical states and relations are the invariable equivalents of corresponding mental ones. Two points are overlooked by the analogy, that perceptions and thoughts are sharply distinguished from each by this very dependence of the one on physical facts, and the independence of the other; and that the whole nervous structure has plain reference to, the one form of intercommunication, and no known reference, obvious or obscure, to the other form of relation.

The notion of subconscious phenomena has been one so vague, so vacillating between physical and mental facts, that it could not long hold its ground. There were three fatal objections to it : (1) It had no assignable place or form for its alleged facts. A subconscious region was as unintelligible as a post-conscious or ante-conscious or super-conscious region would have been. Indeed, it implied them all. (2) It had no means of arriving at its facts. The senses might reach physical things, consciousness might lay open mental phenomena, but what perceptive power should explore this subconscious territory? (3) These phenomena, as wholly beyond the mind's construction, could serve for it no possible explanatory purpose. They were merely verbal lumber.

As the advocates of this new tendency began to fathom more deeply the conclusions contained in their premises, the inadequacy of the old statement became apparent, and has been mainly displaced by that of " unconscious cerebration." Cerebrations, actions of brain, are supposed to have the force of mental facts, and are of two orders, conscious and unconscious. Thought is made so dependent on cerebration that if cerebration proceeds, it is regarded as immaterial whether it is accompanied by consciousness or not. The mind may be borne forward in its intellectual processes by acts of unconscious cerebration. We may travel by day or by night, waking or sleeping, to our intellectual destination. The wheels roll on without our observation. This theory of course involves the pre-eminence of the cerebral state, and the progress of thought is made incident to its progress. The sun casts a shadow on a dial; it is hidden by clouds for a time, and then again shines forth; the hands have advanced on the disk, and the index line, as if it had stolen on its way unobserved, falls at the appropriate figure. This view should recognize distinctly, and state clearly, that the intellectual movement is incident to, and controlled by, the physical one. Certainly an intellectual process as an intellectual one cannot progress in unconsciousness, any more than a shadow as a shadow can travel in darkness.

This is the fatal objection to unconscious cerebration; it subverts or obscures the true line of dependence. We do not deny, that, as the organ limits the activity of the mind, its special states enter as a factor of moment into each result. But so also does the condition of our muscles settle the effective force of the will; yet the physical energy does not predetermine the voluntary power. No more does a process of cerebration precede and causally determine the mental activity it expresses.

Dr. Carpenter, in his *Mental Physiology*, presents fully, and in its best form, the doctrine of unconscious cerebration. Many of the reasons which sustain it are those already sufficiently considered in connection with unconscious mental action. The additional points made by Dr. Carpenter we will consider. This doctrine is so generally accepted, and is so destructive of true mental powers, that we feel desirous to return to it as often as any additional light can be shed upon it.

It is a common experience, if a difficult problem, or a theme to be discussed, is called before the mind and then passed by for a time, that the thoughts revert to it later with unexpected advantage; that a certain mastery of the topic seems to have been achieved in the interval. This new power, often very considerable, is referred to unconscious cerebration, a process of thought that has gone forward, as it were, in the substance of the brain. The moment the favorite and favorable words are dropped, the argument, it will be observed, loses probability. "Unconscious cerebration," guides the mind to the conclusion more smoothly than the equivalent expression a physical change in cerebral states. We have here the trick of a phrase. These gains of thought, we think, may be much more wisely ascribed to the frequent reversion of the mind to the subject, and its leisurely consideration of it in a variety of lights, though the times of such secondary occupation, extending over considerable periods and thrown into the shadow of other events, are not conspicuous in memory; indeed, like any transient under-current of thought, may have quite escaped it. Few of these interstitial states can we recall at the close of a week. If the topic is not a familiar one, does not lie in the line of our pursuits; if it is not a habit with us to return more or less frequently to a discussion once present to the mind, we shall find the gains of delay very slight. If, however, we are accustomed to restore a theme, to recast the thoughts at odd moments, and to gather new material as the process proceeds, then the yield of the under-drift will be correspondingly large. This fact, which is the significant feature of the general fact of acquisition by delay, shows that the mind does keep its intellectual garden in growth by indirect and un-

obtrusive, though real, attentions.  **Cease** to sustain **unconscious** cerebration by voluntary **effort, and** it will cease **to
be a** noticeable fact.  Alien subjects will gain little **by de-**
lay.  Insight, following time and **rest,** is the **fruit of a vig-**
orous habit of mind.  This **result is** due to the **normal ac-**
**tivity** of the thoughts.  **It is no** matter **of surprise that the**
slight, forgotten exertions **of the passing days may, at the**
close of a year, yield a **respectable aggregate of results.**

Unconscious cerebration as **a fact is** certainly **not easier**
of comprehension than that which **it is** here brought **forward**
**to** explain.  **If** a physical activity, self-directed and self-
sustaining, can be the exact equivalent in intellectual results
of the wisest thought, then thought as **thought is no longer**
coherent, and a chain of reasoning can **be made up** of alternate links of physical and mental, **conscious and** unconscious
facts.  When we *do* understand a subject, reach **a** conclusion, **we** understand it *from beginning to end ;* **and in that**
final act of comprehension we leave no room for any merely
physical facts, facts which in **their** transpiring **were not**
**acts of** knowledge, nor are now acts of knowledge.  **The**
intellectual act of comprehension is complete, and receives
**no** known aid from a previous **unconscious act** of **cerebra-**
tion.  The conscious **act is** *the* **act, and this is** sufficient to
itself.  It is not in the least plain **how an** intellectual difficulty can be overcome in unconsciousness, ignorance or
error be flanked in the night-time.  **We must** first **say that**
physical states **determine** mental **states, and are themselves**
determined by previous physical **states, before** unconscious
cerebration can afford us any aid ; that is to say, we accept
this philosophy first, and then get what light we can from
it ; we are are not led to it by its own light.  But the philosophy takes away all coherence from our intellectual life,
subverts all its relations.

A second fact urged by Dr. **Carpenter is the sudden en-**

trance of a new idea or ideas into the mind; the return of something which the memory had struggled for in vain; the instant presence of a fortunate conception completing an invention. These facts are plainer to us as ultimate facts, as successful efforts of mind, allied to that by which we correctly articulate a sound we have long striven to no purpose to utter, than they are when burdened with facts of cerebration whose very being is conjectural, and whose mode of operation is unintelligible. A subject is not explained by two difficulties.

Still less proof is there in the inventive moods of genius, the unusual power that falls to the mind on one occasion and deserts it on another. The periods between these hours of advantage are often very irregular, and may have little to do with the direction in which the thoughts have been tending. They are preceded by no indications of an unconscious cerebration, but more frequently follow upon lassitude, indolence, restfulness, passing again into activity. Careful preparation sometimes fails of its object, and an inventive flow will at another time be present to the speaker or writer independently of previous effort. These shifting moods of mind are partially explicable by physical fatigue or vigor; but involve many conditions not traceable to uniform causes. The mind, if not capricious, takes up and lays down its strength in a way often too subtile for our analysis. Invention remains invention, a quick putting-forth of power, sometimes from restful energy, sometimes from irritable force. Observation lends no support to the doctrine that there is a slow unconscious accumulation of thought-products in the brain, which, like waters in an intermittent fountain, are suddenly poured forth. The mind, like the will, has reserved force by which it can achieve great and sudden results, and these, too, in unexpected directions.

There are some facts in abnormal states especially difficult of explanation under the idea that conscious states are
predetermined by acts of cerebration. There are those
double experiences, double **states** of consciousness, **which**
proceed each under its own impressions, and totally suspend
each other with an abrupt transition. **Can** two series **of**
physical states utterly diverse, **each** coherent within itself,
and incoherent in reference to the other, go forward in **the**
brain, arresting one another in an irregular **yet** decisive
way? Possibly, **but few** would have the boldness to affirm
that such a fact is plain enough to be offered **as the** solution
**of** any other fact, that capricious physical **states are** more
explicable than capricious intellectual ones, **so much more**
so as be able to account for the **latter.**

It may be said that **the two** hemispheres of **the brain**
take up a disconnected instead of a concurrent **action, and**
so give grounds for a divided consciousness. If this theory
is to have any weight, if the implied facts are not far **too**
obscure and uncertain to explain anything, it **must** still **in-**
volve, we think, some transfer of attention on the part **of**
the mind, akin **to** that by which we **see** through one or the
other eye. The physical states of **brain** in its two halves
are doubtless continuous, **and,** if the controlling source
of impressions, must give continuous impressions.

We ought, therefore, if states of **brain determine** mental states, to have two coetaneous mental experiences, instead
of a consecutive experience made up of alternate **parts.**
The latter fact seems **to** imply the unity of mind, **and that**
superiority by which **it** shifts its organs, calling them **into**
service or letting them drop from it. Thus, if **the axis of**
the eyes are thrown out of relation, the mind **soon learns to**
use one eye to the neglect of the other.

This idea of cerebration proceeds on that of an antecedent physical causation **of mental states, and a strict**

equivalence of these effects with their causes. Each thought, feeling, volition, every combination of these must be the exact counterpart of a correspondingly definite state of the brain. Every thought, and every possible thought on every possible topic, stand in correspondence to some form of cerebration. We think of Paris by one state of brain, of London by a second, of Pekin by a third, and of each person and thing in these cities by still other forms of physical activity. This is a complexity of conception quite startling and wholly unnecessary.

It follows from placing efficient causation solely in the physical world. Admit independent power in the mind and this reasoning at once loses its force. No definite state of the muscles decides whether the strength put forth shall be expended in lifting a pound of lead, or one of iron, or of stone; whether the person shall walk toward the north, or the south, or the south-east. A certain energy, for what purpose soever employed, taxes the muscles to a certain degree; and this fact is the simple condition of its exertion. It is not a given molecular state of the muscles which settles directions and offices, but the living agent who employs the muscles. The antecedent cerebral state may neither determine the form of the force, nor, save under general conditions, its degree. The efficiency deciding on the special kind of activity is found in the mind, not in the brain ; for the mind is something other and more than the brain and its functions, as the engineer is something more than the engine. Assigning a definite intellectual state to an equally definite state of brain, we shall be unable to account for the slight effect on the mind of accidents attended with a loss of the substance of the brain, or for the restoration of memories which have once been lost by disease. It is certainly not easy to refer this renewal to a subtile superintendence that in the passage of months slowly builds up the brain-tissue under the previous pattern, with exactly the previous action.

It may be thought that the senses, as sight, show a like complexity in the molecular changes by which facts are indicated to the mind. In this analogical example several things are overlooked. There has been a very protracted and complicated development of each special organ of sense for this very purpose, the registration of external causes. Just here lies the widest difference between perception and pure thought.

Even in the senses each impression, though complex in itself, gives a clear field for the next impression. It exists only so long as an external cause sustains it, and wholly disappears in making way for another. If we press the organ beyond these limits, as the eye by the rapid motion of the spokes of a wheel, its power of discrimination is lost. If we search this analogy, thoroughly, therefore, as we must to make it an argument, it tends to the opposite conclusion, that there are no definite lines of causation other than those manifestly laid down in the senses. **The** senses, also, work by discontinuance not by continuity. To make the analogy applicable, the eye should not merely see the new thing, but retain all previous **things.**

§ 9. We need to understand more definitely **the relation** of the mind to its immediate instrument, the cerebrum, as a means of determining the proper character **of mental phe-** nomena, and their degree of independence. The mind and the brain are reciprocally dependent on each other, the states and activities of the one affecting the states and activities of the other. We may represent this relation by that of two wheels which press each **other at their circum-** ferences, and so, in their revolutions, mutually impel each other. The moving force may be transferred from one to the other, but expends itself in either case in the revolution

of both. Indeed, a concurrent impulse may be applied to
each wheel; and in any given revolutions the eye may
not be able to decide in which the balance of force or the
entire force is to be found. The relation, however, between the mind and the cerebrum is not doubtless of that
exactly reciprocal, equivalent character implied by the comparison; the two do not stand to each other on the same
plane of causation, nor is it in their normal action a matter
of indifference by which of the two the power is applied.
Their real relation to each other is complex, can only be
disclosed by a consideration of the facts, and then but
partially.

Activity of brain always accompanies activity of mind.
(1) This is shown by the destruction of brain-tissue incident to energetic thought. A sensible increase of the
waste due to nervous tissue attends on such action. We
instantly conclude, and probably correctly, that the correspondence indicated is complete, and that all mental effort
has an exactly equivalent expression in brain-action, and
so in decomposition. (2) The fatigue and nervous exhaustion that accompany thought contain the same conclusion.
We attribute these to the expenditure of nervous energy, with its destruction of tissue. (3) The renovation incident to rest sustains the argument. Sleep is the best
restorative of mental functions, and sleep seems to bring
peculiar repose to the brain through repose of the voluntary powers, and so to make way for nutrition and refresh-
ment.

The reverse of this proposition is not so evident, that
all activity of the cerebrum is accompanied by activity of
mind. (1) We should not know what mental state, for instance, to refer to the reconstructive processes that proceed in sleep or in restful hours; (2) nor what modifications
of thought to ascribe to incipient disease of the brain that

has not proceeded to the point of overthrowing mental equilibrium. (3) The loss of brain also that has frequently attended on accidents, when a comparison is made between previous and subsequent mental states, does not show any exact equivalence between cerebral and mental activity, nor that the first, is in reference to the second, a measureable force, calling, in every variation, for a measurable correspondence. The brain may be materially reduced even in bulk with immaterial **or** vacillating results. (4) Its **en**tire automatic action, as well as organic action, proceeds also, with little or no trace on mental states.

States of **brain at all times** affect and at times control states **of** mind. (1) **The** general dependence of mental power on the size, form, quality of the cerebrum shows this functional connection. None can doubt that mental power, in its manifestation, is proportioned to the vigor of nervous action. The condition of the physical instrument is, in a large measure, that of the mental agent. This is a fact of daily observation. (2) Vivisection puts this truth beyond question. Though mental powers do not disappear in definite order and degree with specific portions of the cerebrum, they are disturbed by its injury, and lost by its removal. (3) Diseases **of** the brain complete the proof. Insanity, partial hallucinations **in** a great variety of forms, are the constant accompaniments of cerebral disturbance. Not only does such disease diminish mental power, it strangely modifies that which remains. The thoughts seem to be the sport **of** abnormal, physical conditions. If the mind struggles occasionally for self-possession, it is soon overwhelmed again, and floated on by the current. We must, therefore, grant that, **at** least in some instances, physical states seems to be the efficient, determining causes of mental ones; though even in these cases the final result combines the two series of forces, physical and mental.

The proof does not carry this conviction, that cerebral conditions establish and define mental ones, but only that they are often an immediate, irresistible provocation to them; as bad digestion to bad dreams. Physical states may overpower the mind, and the form of the hallucination still be due to the mind. The fever may induce a very diverse delirium in different persons. The two sets of causes are concurrent in the result.

The reverse proposition we confidently offer as presenting more important and more obvious truth. Pure mental states affect and usually control cerebral ones. (1) This is the manifest and unavoidable conclusion from the fact of thought. Thought involves the evolution of one mental state from a previous *mental* state, the attaching of a second conception or judgment to a former one. If it is not this, it ceases to be thought, and becomes illusion. Even imagination evokes its images one from another, unites them by a mental connection. If one thought, as in the proof of a proposition, follows another, not by an inherent connection, a mental dependence, but by the relation of successive physical states in the brain, then we are utterly at fault in the entire thought-process, and it is something quite other than we have supposed it to be. The images of the imagination even can not be shadows that chase each other on the screen by an outside, alien law, much less can the successive judgments of coherent thought be united independently of the thinking agent. Reasons cohere, thoughts coalesce, conclusions are evolved from premises, and these facts imply that a previous mental state is, in connection with the underlying powers of the mind, the efficient source of a succeeding one; that the *nexus* is a mental efficiency, and not a physical one. Reasoning, as the result of a series of cerebral states united by unknown physical forces, is utterly incomprehensible, is subversive of our most direct primitive

and constant convictions. Here is a proof that can not be
escaped without quite displacing the foundations of truth.
Argument itself is destroyed by such a conclusion, and so
this conclusion is lost in the general wreck of all conclusions. We quite deceive ourselves in argument, if conviction is only a series of states induced by causes entirely
blind, wholly alien to the process.

(2) The relation of intellectual feelings to the convictions that call them forth presents a kindred proof. **Words**
are spoken in our hearing which stand connected with our
own sentiments, actions are performed which affect our
interests; immediately there spring up decided feelings,
we accept or we disapprove the opinions or the conduct.
These states of feeling are plainly due to the mental action by which the bearings of the words or the transactions
are disclosed to us. The intrinsic order and dependence
are quite subverted, if it turns **out** that thoughts and feelings alike have been thrown in upon us in a secondary way
by the motion of physical forces interlocked among themselves, covering all real efficiency, and expounding the sequence of the shadowy states of conciousness by their **own**
independent and firm connections. Our higher emotional
life is unintelligble on this supposition, and its apparent
dependencies quite illusory.

(3) The same is true with a like startling and fatal contradiction of our daily convictions in the case of **our voli-**
tions. We refer these to the motives, to **the intellectual**
and emotional states, that precede them, while the actions
that follow them we attribute to the volitions themselves.
This interpretation, under the hypothesis that cerebral
states wholly determine mental ones, is completely erroneous, and thoughts, feelings, volitions, actions are impotent
in reference to each other; they are rolled off, as the pano-
rama proceeds, in the order in which they are there intro-

duced, by synchronous, physical agencies. Herein is the subversion of all mental processes. What matters it, what we think, if there is no logical coherence in thought? how we feel, if there are no just or unjust grounds of feeling? how we act, if there is for action, within itself, no coherent law? By this view, truly understood, intellectual and moral life are alike suspended, and are left the unsubstantial shades of their former selves. Under this hypothesis words must act as physical forces, inducing a cerebral state incident to which is a certain thought or feeling. It is not by virtue of the conception which is called forth that they are efficient agents, but the conception itself is one among the secondary states that attend on the primary sequence of forces in the nervous system. Thoughts, feelings, volitions, are as the shadows of the cars; the cars are coupled, and the links of the shadows are the images of these couplings.

(4) It would be difficult, also, under this reference of mental states to physical causes to explain the extended and exact agreements between men in their mental action. Why are the principles and processes of mathematics the same for all, except through their relation to the mind? And why are other truths so diversely viewed save through divergent intellectual conditions? These remarkable agreements and disagreements are referred, and must be referred, to the relations of the mind to truth. Truths that are simply deposited by similar physical processes, should show no such complete agreement, nor no such wide diversity. Constitutional resemblances, the physical conditions of habit and inheritance should control them, as they do the texture of the skin, the quality and color of the hair.

(5) We urge as a farther consideration—if, indeed, any farther consideration is called for—the feeling that we have on recovering from deep sleep, or a troubled dream, or a

partial delirium, of an effort on our part toward self-control, self-possession ; the taking up anew by the mind of its voluntary activity. The mind returns to self-guidance by an exertion, and false impressions are dispersed. It recognizes two states, a normal and an abnormal **one ; that in which** the mind controls its impressions, and that **in** which the mind is controlled by them ; and it asserts itself in behalf of the former. A kindred experience is often **a salient** feature of incipient insanity, and may, when a **firm will** accompanies the effort, oppose a strong barrier **to its pro-**gress.

(6) For the very reason that we ascribe delirium to the overpowering effects of physical causes are we disposed to refer rational action to the control of the mind. If insanity is due to disease, if a disordered brain brings disordered imagery, and it is an incident of this state that physical conditions control mental **ones, then we** readily believe that a healthy brain may prepare the way for the reverse action, and yield itself as an obedient instrument to the spirit. Thus cramps and convulsions in the muscular system are due to the escape of stimuli from the control of the will and its automatic relations. There is something **certainly in** the coherence of the two kinds of facts which **seems to** show these dependences. Hallucinations are fixed, obstinate ; sane impressions are flexible, amenable to influence. We seem to be dealing in the one case with a stubborn, physical tendency ; and in the other with **a** changeable, moral state. In delirium, the senses cease in part to be the media of facts ; the ways of ingress to the mind, like those of egress, are choked. In health, the movement inward and outward is alike free ; the brain is the medium, as it should be, of activity starting from either extremity.

We affirm, therefore, a reciprocal interdependence of the brain and the mind, with a **normal** government of the

brain by the mind. Each may initiate action, but in all
our high, characteristic activities, the agent is the mind itself. We object then to the statement given below from
Spencer, and to many kindred statements, as at once un-
proved, improbable, and wholly destructive of the integrity
of mental facts. "What is the meaning of the human
brain? It is that the many *established* relations among its
parts, stand for so many *established* relations among the
psychical changes. Each of the constant connections
among the fibres of the cerebral masses, answers to some
constant connection of phenomena in the experience of the
race."—*Principles of Psychology,* Vol. I. *p.* 468.

The relation of the brain to the mind is a subject un-
dergoing close inquiry and careful experiment. The conclusions already reached by Ferrier and others make it comparatively certain, that the structure of the brain and nervous system in man is one throughout of definite relations,
fitted to the double work of conveying distinct impressions
inward and correspondingly distinct energies outward. Indeed, if there are any well adjusted connections in these
channels of communication, we may well expect them to be
complete. Their value and fitness must evidently depend on
this continuity. The exact cannot pass at pleasure into the
vague, the well ordered into the unordered, and retain their
value. While these nervous connections are relatively
precise, they are by no means single, similar results may
be reached in more than one way. We may figure the
cerebrum as offering definite termini for definite impressions from the exterior world, and also definite starting
points for reciprocal energies. Here is a result like, and
yet very unlike the statements of phrenology. The nervous system, has, as an instrument, fixed relations as certainly as a type-setting machine, or an organ, though, unlike these, it conveys impressions both ways, as the recep-

tive and active powers are in close correspondence. The
definitness of the nervous dependencies of the organs of
sense carries with it a like fixedness in the means of expression. Thus by experiment and observation the conclusions
have been reached, that 'the third left frontal convolution'
is the initiative surface for intelligent speech; closely connected therewith are the starting points of that **action**
which issues in writing. The parietal region or crown of
the head constitutes the motor region of the brain, and may
be farther subdivided into specific forms of action, as grasping, clenching the fist, swimming. The temporal lobes are
centres of sensory perception, both passively and actively,
and are divisable with some certainty between the several
senses. The occipital lobes or back portion of the head are
conjecturally centres to organic activity, **as digestion.** The
frontal lobes are the surfaces for **the initiation of intel-**
lectual and moral action; of attention, inhibition and direction. It must be borne in mind, that experiments of excitation in any portion of the cerebrum can go no farther than
to indicate the nervous sources of those movements which
*express* certain mental states; the conditions of the state
themselves are not disclosed.

It does not follow, therefore, from these conclusions,
that pure thought and the communication of thought are
equally dependent, or dependent in the same way, on the
nervous system. All that the experiments **of** Ferrier,
Fritsche, Hitzig, serve to establish is the general completeness of the mechanism of expression. Indeed, the **very**
connections of thought in things belongs to the mind exclusively; even when a verbal sign is put for them, the
word of relation is no more than a sign. We may well believe that the same thing is true of that more subtile language of molecular action in the cerebrum.

Guiding or at least steadying, our thought by the im-

age of an organ under the hand of a musician, it is sufficiently plain, for reasons already given, that we cannot wisely
affirm this organ of the nervous system to be a hand-organ,
whose tunes are pricked into its revolving barrels, and whose
revolutions take place mechanically under external forces.
Nor is it probable that the tune—the pure thought and feeling—lies open, like the music above the key-board; that
the mind reads its own impressions in the molecular language of the cerebrum. In other words, it is not probable
that thought as thought has any other than an instrumental,
symbolic expression in the brain, such as it finds on a
written page, or in spoken words.

The proof of our first proposition, that activity of brain
always accompanies activity of mind, implies a close relation between the two. What is that relation? The brain
on the one hand, is the recipient of definite impressions
from the exterior world. These, offered in their last physical form as molecular charges, are not by the mind received
in that form, but are translated into states of consciousness.
These states give occasion to other more active states,
which, with a similar subtile transfer, are accompanied by
molecular changes, the agents of outgoing action. The
word, *articulation*, offered to the eye or sounded in the ear,
carries a distinct change to the brain, which becomes to the
mind the occasion of an idea. On the other hand, the mind
having occasion through the presence of an idea to write or
utter that word, initiates in the brain in a fixed way the
needed action. This translation in either direction is an
ultimate mystery, both of whose terms even the mind does
not directly recognize. Words are the counters of thoughts,
and thought can not proceed far without them. But words
are sustained in the mind passively or actively by one or
other of these molecular occasions. When the mind, therefore, is thoughtful, those incipient impressions, which are

the first terms of expression, and which are the physical
symbols of words, may well be present and take the place
in their supporting power **of** written or **spoken** language.
Thus the musician may lightly touch the **keys of** his key-
board, as a means of helping onward the inventive process.
In each case the perception of the mind **is not** in its familiar
symbols, but is simply sustained by them.

Intense thought is fatiguing, because it involves constant movement among the physical counters of the mind,
these incipient symbols of utterance in the molecular changes
of the brain.   We know what a relief it is to substitute **the**
passive for the active symbol, a **bit of paper** with its few
figures, for the vanishing figures of **a problem** worked out,
as we say, in the head.   The fatigue of extemporary speech
is very great, for all these active signs of thought are fully
present, and completely uttered, with even-paced rapidity.
Intense thought without utterance is less fatiguing, because
the process of expression is abridged,—the words hastening
by us with large representative power—and the movement
is left to shape itself to the inner impulse.   Mere revery is
scarcely fatiguing, because an indolent impulse is obeyed,
both **in** direction **and** rapidity.   Our inference then is that
the brain, as the medium of all expression, becomes, in its
definite molecular changes, a sustaining force to the language of the mind; as written words, through another set
of impressions, more passive, are an occasion of an apprehension by the mind of another's thought.   The **very**
essence of thought therefore, is no more held in the molecular type of the brain, than in the type of the printed page;
indeed hardly so much so, as the **one is** an unrecognized,
and the other a recognized, condition of the appropriate
thought.   In each case it **is the presence of pure** spirit that
evokes thought, and **carries it forward; the symbols,**
whether those of receptivity **or activity,** whether those

starting with the outer termini of the nerves and passing in, or starting with the inner termini and passing out, act simply as supports to its rapid footsteps.

§ 10. There are certain abnormal mental states that deserve a passing notice. The chief physical change in sleep is a large reduction of blood in the brain. Its external features are the suppression of voluntary action and of the action of the senses. There may always remain, and there certainly often remains, the play of the imagination known as dreaming. The mental action seems to be sympathetic with the bodily state, and to be attended with very little control. While complete sleep involves the large arrest of voluntary life incident to muscular repose, there are many partial forms of it. The senses may remain cognizant of very many events; a slight uneasiness or a gentle push may call forth a change of position. Words may be spoken; or, more rarely, words may be listened to and answered, if introduced in the line of existing impressions.

In somnambulism these states of partial wakefulness assume an extreme and troublesome form. They are characterized by an unusual acuteness of impression in some directions, with the ordinary want of it in other directions. The dividing line between waking and sleeping, active and dormant, powers is drawn with unusual decision, and in a new direction. Incident to this is also a new relation of voluntary to involuntary action, the latter taking up what usually falls to the former.

Hypnotism, mesmeric states, table-tipping, second-sight, and kindred facts, are phenomena of somewhat the same order. They involve an unusual suspension of some powers, and an unusual activity of others. Normal associations in the action of faculties are broken up, and abnormal ones take their place. They are induced and established by unbalanced tendencies, by inheritance, by habit. Revcry presents a like condition in **a very** moderate degree. A succession of images is vividly present to the mind, while the action of the senses and of the will is suspended. The degree of excitement to which an abnormal state may bring a faculty or a sense is sometimes illustrated in sickness. The slightest light or the least sound may be intensely painful, and passing events may impress themselves in quite a new way on the feelings. The nervous system under excitements or tension takes on an action quite novel to it. In hypnotism and mesmerism an abnormal state of wakefulness and of repose is induced by artificial means, the activity of certain faculties being as remarkable as the suspension of others. In the mesmeric state the patient— for we may fitly call the person subject to such disordered action a patient—becomes inattentive to the ordinary conditions of action, and highly sensitive to those which proceed from the person inducing the state. In hypnotism there is a like suspension of habitual sensations, and a kindred attention to other relations determined by previous association. We may ally the action to that by which we listen intently without seeing, or look through one eye to the exclusion of objects in the other. The states implied in hypnotism, while akin to these, are much more extreme, much more abnormal.

In these and kindred conditions unconscious and automatic connections gain ground on conscious and voluntary ones. The eye, our most voluntary sense, is least attentive, while touch, or rather the organic stimuli allied to it, may be very active. Persons who have united hands thus become the unconscious mediums of impressions passing from an active agent at one extremity to a passive agent at the other; and the latter, abnormally sensitive, marks the slightest change in the former. The least movement accompanying the recognition of **the** right **word or** the right letter on the part of the active agent, is transferred to the passive agent, and he, when allowed a choice of actions, words, or letters, reads correctly the mind of the former by virtue of impulses which quite escape ordinary observation.

In table-tipping, by mechanical tests, pressure is shown to be present when the parties to it are wholly unaware of it, and are exercising a measure of volition against it. Involuntary states triumph over voluntary ones; confused, secondary and unconscious ones over clear and conscious ones. In the planchette we have a visible record of automatic impressions escaping from the control of the voluntary life. Those who are the most coherent, rational, and self-guided in action are the least subject to these abnormal conditions, while those most impressible, excitable, weakest in their voluntary life, are especially liable to them. By repetition these states gain power with a corresponding loss of self-control. Notwithstanding the exalted susceptibility implied in them, they are to be regarded as intellectually and spiritually unwholesome. In these states, the automatic life, the life of obscure, physical impressions, gains ground on the reflective life, in a confused and confusing way. (1) There is a new and abnormal division of activities between the two; (2) in the unconscious life there is intense activity in unusual directions; (3) in the conscious life, unusual inertness in usual directions.

§ 11. We dwell at length on consciousness as including the entire range of mental phenomena, because thus only can we adequately define the field of mental science, and keep it forever distinct from all physical inquiries. Physiological facts are of incalculable interest and value, but are perfectly distinct from philosophy. Each branch is capable of independent development, nay must receive it, and neither is as obscure as the connections between the two.

Only by a double light on either hand, the mind being made known to itself, and the brain and nervous system being carefully inquired into, can we hope to trace obscurely and slowly the dependencies of the physical and spiritual worlds; even then reaching everywhere ultimate facts beyond our solution. Metaphysics, with all its erratic and fanciful reasonings, never gave explanations more absurd and inadequate than those sometimes rendered of intellectual phenomena from a study of physical organisms. The assertion that the brain secretes thought, is the crude idea out of which, with more subtile and obscure phraseology, those impotent reasonings from matter to mind arise.

This premature and preposterous union of the two realms, or rather absorption of the one by the other, is greatly aided by the admission of a region below consciousness, a region in some way attached to the mental field, though not fairly located in it. The mind thus allies in conception its phenomena to those of the physical world, taking place under a blind play of forces, and then readily unites them to nervous and cerebral action. Hypothetical, unlocated, unknowable facts are thus made to furnish a passage between the two departments; to give inlet to lower physical causes, whose service it ostensibly is to explain, but which really obscure and destroy, intellectual and spiritual powers.

We reject this region of subconsciousness as unexplored and inexplorable, either by the inner or the outer eye; **as** furnishing no ground for induction or safe deduction; as necessarily a region of myth and fancies, offering no solid explanations which can be subjected to any form of experience. Let positive science give us its positive facts, established with sufficient inquiry, located in the brain and associated organisms—facts as material and sensible as those of brass or iron, oxygen and hydrogen, heat or electricity, and as physical facts we will recognize them; let philosophy declare what the common consciousness can verify, and its statements shall be accepted as at least of equal value and validity with those which creep into the mind through the eye and the ear; but let neither form of investigation bring alleged facts from a region which it itself puts beyond the entire range of our critical faculties. Consciousness presents a distinct and independent field. On it no purely physical inquiry can enter, and in it philosophy can lie intrenched beyond the power of any form of ignorant or jealous scepticism. The students of Positive Philosophy, ready to desecrate this sanctuary of our spiritual nature, will, like the blind men of Sodom, weary themselves in vain to find the door.

Mental science will also be aided, by this divorce of the unknown from the known, the conjectural from the established, in bringing its own doctrines to a more decided test; and in expelling some of those dogmas, which, unintelligible, yet possible to a bold and blind faith, have hovered about it, and given it a superstitious, visionary, and unphilosophical appearance. Of this nature is the assertion, that one may sin below consciousness, or the belief that sin is transmitted from parent to child. If all the acts and states of mind are conscious ones, then, of course, all moral phenomena must transpire in the light.

We are ready to accept and consider any well-established dependencies between mind and matter, but many of the theories on this subject transcend by almost their entire breadth all known facts, and bring no light to what they discuss. We are now prepared to receive physical phenomena as expressed in physical terms; mental phenomena as stated in mental terms; and any relations that can be established between the two. Our philosophy is thus on the ground of experience. Data of which our experience takes no cognizance, states of mind beyond consciousness, states of matter that are in effect intellectual, intelligence outside the range of mind, are all swept away. We get back to our primitive phenomena, and satisfy ourselves with striving to analyze and classify them, and to point out their character and dependencies.

This is the true, and the only true attitude of a truly empirical philosophy. Words can never be more clear than the very phenomena which they designate. Words of mind, therefore, should be constantly and exclusively expounded by phenomena of mind, and, words of matter by the phenomena of matter. Having duly grasped and grouped **each** set of facts under their own forms, we are prepared to discuss inductively and deductively any relations between them. **To** systematically set ourselves the task of expressing the facts of mind in terms of matter and motion is to institute an effort, patient and skilful it may be, to subvert the facts of mind. Physical philosophy erred in the beginning by using words of mind to expound physical facts, mental philosophy now errs by substituting physical words **and** imagery for mental facts, presented in consciousness. **This is** the logomachy of our day.

**§ 12. The** second preliminary inquiry referred to—Is the mind always consciously active?—is closely allied to the one **now** answered—Is the mind ever unconsciously modified? **A** negative answer to the second inquiry would seem to prepare the way for a positive answer to the first. If no phenomena of mind transpire below the surface, then we should anticipate that the continuous existence of the mind would be productive of continuous activity above the surface, and that some phase of thought, feeling, or volition would be ever transpiring. The second question of course contemplates a modification **of** mind in the nature of an action, or an induced change of state, and not at all the admitted fact that the mind increases in power. The subjective method of this increase is beyond present explication; we are simply not to figure it under a material form, as if it were a substantial change. If, on the other hand, we say with Sir William Hamilton, that there are unconscious modifications of mind, we have prepared the way for denying its constant, conscious activity; since some moments of being, at least, would seem to be sufficiently accounted for by the occurrence of these subconscious facts, and the existence of such facts would prepare the way for their hypothetical occupation of the mind in periods of external repose. Yet, Sir William Hamilton answers this question, justly we believe, in the affirmative. The mind is always consciously active.

The reason which most avails in bringing us to this conclusion is one which will probably have little weight with most minds. It is of an *a priori* character. The only proof of existence is some form of phenomena. Existence without phenomena is unevinced and unintelligible. Matter that should manifest neither active nor passive effects anywhere, under any conditions, would cease to meet our idea of matter, would be non-existent. Now the sole known phenomena of mind are those of consciousness; and to suppose a total arrest of these leaves the mind, for the interval, without the proof or the form of existence. We may figure, in some vague way, under the analogy of matter, some passive state or power as belonging to the mind and maintaining for it a phenomenal existence during the hours of sleep; but here again we are in the region of pure hypothesis. We know nothing of mind save as the source of certain activities, and if these are gone, the only grounds on which we ever predicated its existence are gone. To suppose it capable of existence in a passive state, is a supposition altogether beyond knowledge, and made tenable only by analo-

gies carelessly caught up from the physical world. We
believe, therefore, in the constant activity **of** the mind, as the
only state under which we know it at all, or in consistency
with what we do know of its nature, can at all conceive it.
The notion of total rest leaves the mind as mind without
any possible manifestation or proof of existence to any
being under any circumstances. The only known phenomena of mind are removed, and with them pass away **the**
evidence of its present being.

Urging, however, no farther this consideration, we **be-**
lieve the strictly inductive proof sufficient to render the
conclusion, that the mind is always active, at least probable.
**As it is** dwelt **on at** length by Hamilton, we shall treat it
briefly.  The chief difficulty to be overcome in the affirmation, is the admitted fact, that the memory does not retain
and report the movements of the mind in hours of sleep or of
syncope.  How strong is this objection?  Much the larger
share of the thoughts and the feelings of yesterday have entirely passed from the mind, **and** yet we readily believe in
their existence.  We have no doubt of the continuity of
thought in our waking moments; **yet we arrive at the** conclusion more from our present experience than because we
can recall one in ten thousand of the feelings which have
passed through the mind in the last dozen years.  Now the
impressions of dreams, when these are known to have occurred, are of **a** much more evanescent character.  At the
very instant of waking we may be able to recall them, and
yet we lose all hold on them in a few moments.  We also
know that in proportion as sleep is sweet and sound these
impressions of the night are **fleeting, and must** be caught
almost in **the** very act of passage, or they are wholly lost.
It has happened to many, perhaps to most, to awake in a
dream, and to take delight in the images left by it, and
yet after another hour's sleep to be unable to restore them.

The memory also seems to be especially affected by physical conditions. Fatigue and nervous exhaustion for the time being greatly diminish its power; some forms of disease erase its impressions in whole or in part, while the weakness of age first betrays itself in this faculty. Since, then, physical conditions so obviously and directly modify this power, it is but natural to expect that so great a change as that from wakeful activity to sleep might decidedly affect its action. The thoughts which pass through the mind in revery or abstraction often leave very slight traces. Suddenly startled from such a waking dream by a practical claim, we can scarcely, the moment after, recall what it was which so occupied us. These facts are sufficient to overcome the antecedent improbability of continuous mental action, arising from the want of memory, and to leave the way open for proof.

The most obvious facts which go to establish the constant activity of mind are dreams. The memory does testify to a large amount of movement in hours of sleep not to be distinguished by external signs from other periods of repose. Some habitually dream: that is, the play of imagery, the dumb show in the hours of darkness, the spectral troop of the sportive thoughts pass and repass within the scope of mental vision, and the person, on waking, remains mindful of this fleet, flitting assemblage—of this masquerade of his thoughts escaping the control of the senses and the voluntary life. Now, though others rarely dream, that is, rarely recall these shadows of the mind, leaving no more visible traces on the external life than do the clouds that fly through the heavens on the earth which they darken for the moment, this fact goes but a little way to weaken the presumption, that they are not very different from their fellows; that the rehearsal of dreams is only a little more interior and close-locked in the one case than in the other.

This supposition is strengthened by the fact, that the habit of recalling and relating dreams is said to confirm the tendency to them, and to deepen their impressions. It is not probable that one dreams more as the result of reciting dreams, but rather that the deepened attention strengthens the memory of dreams.

The nature also of dreams is a proof of their continuous presence. There is shown in them a certain freedom, yet also a certain weakness, of the mind not found in the waking moments. The intellectual powers are plainly divorced from the usual restraint and guidance of the senses and the voluntary activities. Nothing seems monstrous, that is unnatural. The most incongruous events are accepted with perfect composure. The laws of nature are largely set aside, and the mind binds together, with its own fanciful connections in its own fanciful creations, the events that arise before it. The inner wheels are ungeared from the outer world, and revolve in their own rapid and irregular way. This fact goes to show that the senses are in full repose, while the mind retains this wild, free, sportive, untiring activity.

In dreams, also, the will, through the repose of its physical instruments, seems utterly powerless. Flight, however urgent the apparent necessity, is impossible. No personal exigency is met with physical prowess and strength. This seems to arise from the fact that the will finds itself thwarted by the inert, sleeping body, and not inducing its wonted effects in this torpid mass, throws back on the mind fear, faintness, and a sense of hopeless failure. Sometimes, indeed, the effort it puts forth is so great as to run, like an electric shock, through the muscles, and the awakened body is landed at a leap, startled and astonished, on the floor of the chamber. These facts all indicate that physical repose is accompanied with mental activity, and not simply that sleep is partial and disturbed. Such a state, indeed, affects the character of dreams, and deepens their impression, and thus aids us in recalling them; but does not seem to be their cause.

A third fact looking to the same conclusion is the familiar one of talking in sleep, though the person on waking retains none of the impressions which occupied the mind. In such cases, mental activity is fairly shown to exist without corresponding recollection. The dog even will bark in his sleep, tickling the motor nerves with some tantalizing image of cat or rabbit.

Allied to this is the fourth general proof furnished by somnambulism in all its forms. In these cases, the mind acquires a partial control of the body, and, while leaving the senses chiefly at rest, guides and stimulates its muscular powers. The wonderful precision and daring with which this is sometimes done evince great calmness and activity of the faculties, enabling them to reach results impossible to the frightened, swimming senses. Of this character are those familiar instances in which the somnambulist passes through positions of great peril without failure or disturbance. A student in my own college class had been greatly interested and perplexed by a difficult problem. He could not hit upon its solution. He retired to rest, and, in the night, rose in his sleep, and wrought it out on the board in the room. There, to his astonishment, he found it in the morning, the whole labor having left not the slightest trace in the memory.

A fifth fact looking in the same direction, is that testified to by Sir William Hamilton, and open to anyone's verification: "I have always observed that when suddenly awakened during sleep (and, to ascertain the fact, I have caused myself to be roused at different seasons of the night), I have always been able to observe that I was in the middle of a dream. The recollection of this dream was not always equally vivid. On some occasions, I was able to trace it back until the train was lost at a remote distance; on others I was hardly aware of more than one or two of the latter links of the chain; and sometimes was scarcely certain of more than the fact, that I was not awakened from an unconscious state."

One more fact remains of very general prevalence confirmatory of those now given. The mind is found to exercise a certain measure of watchfulness over the body in hours of sleep. We sleep, as popular speech has it, with one eye open. Anything unusual, though slight in character, arouses us, while familiar sounds pass unheeded. There is evidently a sentinel posted, who reports at once anything alarming, while he suffers ordinary events to pass unchallenged. We see something of this even in the torpor of intoxication. The mind makes an unsuccessful effort to arouse the body on the approach of danger, and, if the danger is extreme, sometimes sobers the man at once. We assign the mind a specific duty. We lay upon it as a task, that it shall awaken the body at a given moment. The mind is frequently disturbed and made nervous by the imposition, and arouses the vexed body in a tentative way half a dozen times before the hour arrives; or, better trained and more familiar with its service, it leaves the repose unbroken till the moment has fully come.

These and kindred facts of observation seem sufficiently to establish the constant activity of the mind, and to render it certain, that this invisible agent of invisible phenomena has a continuous and manifested existence, whatever the condition of its factor, the body, may be.

# CHAPTER II.

§ 1. THE first great class of mental faculties are those of the intellect. When we speak of faculties, we mean the different ways in which the one individual mind acts, rather than a combination of distinct powers under the analogy of our physical organs. The forms of knowing are treated first, not because they necessarily arise first—feeling doubtless precedes them, and chiefly occupies consciousness in the first months of life—but because, in the activity of mind, they prepare the way for emotion and choice, and chiefly determine their form. The knowing are the receptive processes, and give material to the feelings and alternatives to choice.

The intellectual powers have been divided into three principal classes; the sense, the understanding, and the reason. The first furnishes the direct facts, the forms of existence which the mind contemplates, whether of the outer or inner world. The second carries on and sustains the processes of reflection concerning these, elaborating them into knowledge. The third furnishes those necessary ideas under which only the movements of a rational mind can go on. We shall not pause to speak of these divisions, as all that we have to say under each of them is requisite for their perfect comprehension. We proceed to treat of the first of these classes, that of sense.

This term is somewhat awkward, but as it has already been used in this connection, we avoid, by its retention, one great evil of metaphysics, a perpetually shifting nomenclature. The sense includes two, and quite diverse sources of knowledge; the power of perception and the immediate cognizance which the mind has **of** its **own states. Under** an image, but very partially applicable, they may be spoken of as the outer and inner eye of the intellect.

§ **2.** In perception we shall not, as is usually done, **in**clude all the senses. A portion of **these** seem primarily avenues of feelings rather than of percepts. When the sensation is manifest, lying in the organ, and contemplated there as an occasion of pleasure or displeasure, the sense is evidently one of feeling rather than of knowing. Though we may make the peculiar character of the odor or of the taste a ground of inference as to its source, and thus of knowledge, this fact does not destroy its primary connection with the feelings. Nor is the **fact that an odor, a flavor** are, as it were, a form of knowing, a knowing that cannot be otherwise arrived at, a ground of classifying these sensations with the intellectual faculties; since the same is **true** of love, sympathy, anger. The perplexity arises, as has been already intimated, from the fact that every feeling involves consciousness, and to know a thing and to be conscious of a thing are constantly used as interchangeable expressions. As consciousness belongs necessarily to thought, feeling and volition, it is not in this common condition of their existence that their differences are **to be** looked for; but in the nature of that existence, consciousness being conceded. All, then, that abides in the organ as a distinct, local sensation, an incipient, or a positive pain or pleasure, is a matter of feeling rather than of perception, and should be classified as a portion of our emotional nature. With this distinction in view, we have but two unmistakable organs of perception, the eye and the ear. Even these, under certain conditions, may give rise to sensations.

The light may become so bright as to be painful; the sound so loud or so sharp as to be disagreeable, that is organically disagreeable, and thus these senses serve for the time as avenues to feelings rather than to perceptions. The pleasures that enter the eye and ear in painting, sculpture, music, not being organic but mental, do not interfere with the purely perceptive action of the senses.

In perception, material of knowledge, or of subjective emotions simply, is, through the medium of the organ of sense, brought to the mind. It is only by observation that we know that the eye is the means of sight, or the ear of hearing. Neither of these organs, in their healthy state, give any direct indication of their office, or excite us by any passing sensation in the performance of it. To this fact our language conforms, and we speak of perception, an acting of the mind, through, rather than in, the organ employed.

The sense of touch seems more mixed than any of the others. It declares its locality, and lodges its results as distinct feelings in the finger-ends. Its sensation should, therefore, be primarily ranked with the feelings, and it be regarded as an organ of feeling. Indeed, this conclusion language seems unmistakably to indicate, and in designation we have passed over with the same word *feeling*, from the external sense to the internal emotion. Touch, however, approaches the two higher senses, in the fact that its sensations are made almost exclusively the ground of inferences rather than of enjoyments, and when highly developed are clear and ultimate in the information imparted, and almost wholly overlooked as forms of feeling. The blind doubtless cease almost entirely to contemplate the agreeable and disagreeable in touch—indeed the tactual character of these sensations—and find in them a direct, unconscious medium of knowing. Under such circumstances, the sense is one of perception rather than sensation. A difference between sensation and perception is found in the direction of the lines of activity; in sensation it is inward, in perception it is outward. Sensations **are** converted into perceptions by making their data a subject of analysis and of inference. As the reflective element gains ground, the feeling is obscured, and the particular sense becomes **the** inlet of knowledge. Perceptions then are sensations transformed into terms of knowledge by the mind that lies **back** of them. Hamilton's statement, that perception is inversely **as** the sensation, if not mathematically true, is proximately correct.

§ 3. Taking the eye as the type of **the** intellectual senses, we ask, What do we see? Most multiform and perplexed have been the answers to this question, and most fatal, and, to the common understanding, preposterous have been the conclusions **drawn from** them. It is no part **of** our purpose to dwell on these either by exposition or refutation; but rather to state what we regard as the just view, and with passing indications of its bearings to leave this to displace them. The nature of this view, and therefore its grounds, **are so** much involved in our idea of the intuitive action of the mind as to turn upon this fundamental feature of philosophy. The full reasons of our conclusions cannot therefore at once be spread out, but will be slowly made up as we present the entire furniture and action of the mind. **The** separate parts of our structure can show neither their strength nor fitness till the survey of the whole **is** finished.

In the first place, **the eye as** an organ of perception deals with color, the ear with sound. The sources of these colors and sounds are known only inferentially. It is a necessary belief, arising under the notion of causation, that **these** organs can **become means** of cognition only through effects which have been wrought in themselves, and that unaffected they can be the medium of no knowledge. Effects not only demand causes, but causes efficiently present in them, interpenetrating them. The last, the immediate cause is inseparable from the effect. Now the vibrations of light and sound are the agents and the only agents that reach these organs, and it is a matter of experience that perception is immediately dependent on these agents as they penetrate into and work their changes on the organs of sense. Each organ is obviously fitted for the action of its own agent, and every interference with these internal adjustments destroys perception wholly or in part. While, therefore, our necessary beliefs demand an immediate effect on the organ of perception, experience clearly points out the agents of this effect, and the contrivance by which it is wrought.

The purely intellectual character of sight, the extent to which the eye is an unconscious, translucent medium of the mind, is shown by the number, delicacy, variety, and furtive character of the judgments inextricably involved in vision. The earlier years of life are evidently busily employed in learning to see, not in the scientific but in the familiar use of the word. These facts harmonize with the further recorded fact, that the eyes of one couched in mature life, seemed to report all objects under the analogy of touch; that is, as directly in contact with the organ of vision.* These spaces, greater and less, which the educated eye now reveals; this opening up and spreading out of the universe before it, this unsearchable depth, this height, this

* The case referred to is that described by Voltaire. The operation was performed by Cheselden on a lad who had been born blind. "It was long before the patient could distinguish objects by size, distance or shape. Several other like cases have been reported."—See Diderot, by John Morley, p. 54.

breadth, are not the products of direct vision, but of vision
modified by innumerable judgments, and mingled with
them. The most of them we form unconsciously, and
learned to make early in life, their accuracy and ease being
increased by every day's experience. How many things
come in to determine our estimates of the distances of surrounding objects, the clearness or faintness of colors, the
depth of blue cast upon them by the atmosphere, their
apparent size, intervening objects and the muscular adjustment of the eyes in their perception. Most have probably experienced in some moment of relative abstraction,
an exaggerated or false impression made by some object or
objects seen, but not observed, and marked the instantane-
ousness with which these flashed into their true form upon
the first distinct direction of the eye toward them. The
relative position and size of objects **are** also almost wholly
a matter of judgment; the eye itself only records their
angular separation. It reduces them to a map-surface, and
leaves their relations and distances unrecorded. Angles,
not lines, are contemplated by it. The distances outward
from the eye, and hence laterally also, are wholly **a matter**
of experience.

To these judgments are to be added those which turn
on light and shade, and from these data arrive at the most
complex surfaces. We thus see that the pure visual data
of sight are very meagre, and bear no more resemblance
and intimate connection to the world in which we live than
do the canvas and the paints thereon, as canvas and paints
merely, to the landscape represented. This saturation of a
sense by the understanding, this inflation of a single drop
by the breath of rational thought into a brilliant sphere,
and the acquired ability to do this as child's play, are the
noticeable features of this, our highest organ of perception,
quite distinguishing it from such an organ as that of taste,

from which with smack, pause and reiteration, we reach one or two uncertain conclusions.

The ear is akin to the eye, though considerably below it, in the number of judgments its habitual use involves. The direction, distance and source of sounds are plainly learned by experience; though in most cases we hardly separate the mere phenomenal fact from the judgments on which our knowledge depends. To these are to be added all the variety of feelings expressed by intonation, and also that representative power of articulate sounds instituted in language yet through familiarity employed and interpreted without thought. Here again the under-play of the understanding is very great, exploding a single ictus of sound, like a thimble of powder, into a death-warrant, or opening the gates of blessedness by the key of a monosyllabic assent. Thus does the mind work up the crude material, the physical nutrition of an organic susceptibility into the daily food and the special feasts of the soul.

The point of most philosophical interest in these senses is the approach we make to a more exact answer to the inquiry : What do we perceive ? Is it something external to the organ ? or is it something subjective to it ? or is it subjective to the mind itself ? If, in the word perception, we include all the mind's action therein, its direct and its inferential knowing, then plainly we perceive something external to the eye and to the mind. If, however, by perception, we mean only the arriving at those simple intuitive data around which these judgments cluster, and which they construct into the well-ordered and complete vision of mature life, then the mind perceives that only which is subjective to itself, and knows directly no more about the intermediate organ it uses than it does of the external object which is the joint, final product of its perceptive and reflective powers. The first spontaneous answer of philosophy has been, the direct perceptive action of the mind is confined to the circle of its own activity, to consciousness; and probably no other answer would have been sought for, had not the conclusions drawn from this earlier statement led to a reconsideration of it. These conclusions have been idealism, and have compelled those who have wished to establish the independent existence of the external world, and have had no other means at hand to do it, to re-analyze perception, and find therein a valid objective element. Overlooking the inferences of the mind, they have given it a direct knowledge of matter.

The proof of idealism runs thus : 1. " We cannot know things in themselves ; all knowledge is subjective ; it is confined to unseen states and changes.

**2.** " If this is so, then still more is what **we name the** objective, only a state or change of us as subjective, it is a *mere* fiction of the mind so far as it is regarded as a beyond, or a thing in itself.

3. " Hence we do know the objective; for the skepticism can only legitimately conclude that the objective that we do know, is of a nature kindred to reason, and that by *a priori* necessity we can affirm that not only all knowable existence must have this nature, but also all possible existence must. Self-conscious intelligence must be, according to its very definition, subject and object in one, and thus universal."

Hamilton has striven to break this charmed circle of the mind at the point of perception, affirming that a real objective element is directly recognized therein. He says, " We have no reason whatever to doubt the report of consciousness, that we actually perceive at the external point of sensation and that we perceive the material reality." " The total and real object of perception is the external object under relation to our sense and faculty of cognition."

" Suppose the total object to be twelve, that the external reality constitutes six, the material sense three, and the mind three; this may enable you to form some conjecture of the nature of the object of perception."

Is there any good ground for the very general and very stubborn conviction that the mind cannot, by way of direct apprehension, act on anything external to itself; or are Reid and Hamilton right in regarding this as a pure assumption?

It is very difficult and very important, in a discussion of this character, to be aware of the physical images which cling to our words and mislead the thought by material analogies. In and out, where it is and where it is not, are expressions applicable to matter rather than to mind, and we must not confound the intellect even with its instruments, the brain and the nervous system. The effects which take place in these are one thing, and what enters consciousness as a purely spiritual product, an inner experience, is quite another. The connection between the two, an affection of the organ of sense and an affection of the mind, is unknown, and for the present at least insoluble. They are as wide apart in kind as any two known things can be, since the one is physical and the other spiritual, classes of phenomena for which we have found no common term. There seems some plausibility in the notion of external perception, when we contemplate the organism of any one sense, as that of the eye. The light enters. A sensible, visible effect—visible to another eye—is evoked on the retina. To this compound effect to which two agencies are contributing, the eye and the light, it may seem reasonable to regard the nerve as sensitive, and therefore to suppose it to take cognizance of the immediate presence of a foreign agent. If, then, we could identify the perception of the mind with this condition of its organ, there would seem to be in it a direct knowledge of one force at least, that of light, alien and external to itself.

But even on this supposition, farther reflection would modify **our** conclusion. In purely physical causation, the cause, though entering into the effect, is not as a cause recognizable there. Indeed it seems probable that there is not invariably the same transferred force in one series of effects as in another, and that in some results the prime agency quickly disappears. A ball is struck by a bat and set in motion: after the ball has parted from the bat how much of the antecedent fact could be found in the subsequent one of independent motion? How far would the second phenomenon directly disclose the first, or what common term or force could be detected in the two? The force is not discernible aside from the results it occasions, and antecedent effects are not given in subsequent ones. Suppose the same ball to be observed falling under the influence of gravitation. How far would this new cause be discoverable directly in this new phase of movement? Again, chemical action is initiated by a rise of temperature; water is instantly frozen under certain conditions by a slight jar; the brain is quickened by a full stomach; in these and a thousand other cases of causation, what portion of the cause is in the effect, to be found there as a part in a whole, as the numbers, 6, **3, 3,** in the sum twelve. Evidently in a purely physical effect **it is** impossible for us to detect the cause **as** a cause — as a second, alien agency, entering into and constituting a distinguishable part of the new, simple state before us.

We perceive phenomena only, not the underlying forces, not the very causes; these, and the antecedent facts they may have occasioned, are matters of inference and of experience exclusively. If, then, the phenomena transpiring in the eye were, as they are not, identical with those of the

mind, it would be impossible that these should include a
knowledge of the very cause, and still less possible that
they should include a direct knowledge of antecedent, external phenomena reached only by inference through this
hidden, unsearchable force or cause. We may direct attention in this discussion to two things: the very cause or
efficiency which necessarily coexists with the effect and
sustains it, and the immediately antecedent phenomenal
effect, more often spoken of as the cause. The first of
these is not discoverable in the eye, since no causes, as
causes, can be directly known. To know phenomenally
the very cause, would be to make that cause a phenomenon,
that is an effect, that is not a cause. Pure causal being,
the being or force that lies back of phenomena, cannot be
known perceptively as a result. To affirm this is to deny
causation, and make a phenomenon its own cause.

The second of these, to wit, the immediately antecedent,
outside effect, cannot be perceptively found and known in
the eye for the obvious reason that it is not there. If,
therefore, we were to direct the attention to the eye alone,
and identify its states with those of the mind, we should
still be unable perceptively to discover anything in it but
its own phenomena, which are neither the outside object
nor any cognizable portion of it. We are not to regard the
eye with the facts that transpire in it as at once inseparable
from the mind and external to it. If its changes are the
changes of the mind, then all that is outside to it is equally
so to the perception. So truly subjective, then, is even the
organic state of the eye in sight, that were this the thing
revealed in consciousness, we should still not be able to
separate or distinguish the external element, "six," in the
sum twelve, and know it directly as a foreign agency.
The phenomenal six alone should we perceive, and still be
compelled to infer hence the causal six supporting it.

But when we pass beyond the condition of the organ as itself unknown to the mind and outside of it, and contemplate the true immaterial content of consciousness, the case is, if possible, still plainer. Perception as an act of mind does not reveal to us the instrument of sense employed, or the state of that instrument. The connection between a mental state and the physical state which accompanies it, is mysterious and unknown; it is not so much as hinted at in the very act of perception in consciousness. For aught that we can see, the last might be very different from what it is, and the first remain the same. Indeed, that there are to sight and hearing accompanying physical states, what these states are, and even where they are, constitute facts which require to be learned from experience.

It has helped to obscure the doctrine of perception, that a distinct image on the retina has been found to intervene between the object and vision. This image has drawn attention as something especially necessary and explanatory. It is, however, in reference to vision a mere accident, as much so as the possible images which may be formed within the tube of a telescope. These images one and all play no part *as images*, but simply as causal links. The image on the retina is only one term in the physical agencies, which finally express themselves in the molecular changes of the brain. If we were to examine the eye in delirium, we should find no images in it of the objects evoked by the mind.

Even in advanced life we do not always recognize at which ear a given sound chiefly enters, and tentatively test the question by turning the attention first in one direction, then in the other. The content of consciousness, then, is not of such a nature as to reveal in perception the states of the retina, or of the auditory nerve; or whether there is in them more or less of foreign action. These changes are

sunk foundations on which the visible structure rests, but
are not in the least disclosed in their nature by it.   They
are the submarine cable, neither declared in its length nor
its depth, nor in the mechanical nor electric conditions of
its structure, by the messages sent and received at either
terminus.   To introduce causes into consciousness, that
they may be there directly known, is either to assert their
supersensual and immaterial character, is to grant the assertion of idealism, "We do know the object, and therefore it is of a nature akin to thought," or it is to break
down the fundamental distinction between mental and
physical phenomena, affirming that both transpire in consciousness, and that the physical facts of the brain are the
spiritual facts of mind.   Yet having made this inadmissible
concession, we are confronted with the fact, that consciousness does not of itself indicate whether the brain, or the
heart, or the bowels, are the seat of thought; whether we
see with our fingers or our eyes; and the further fact, that
causes, as causes, are never discoverable even in purely
physical effects.

The assertion, then, that we cannot directly know things
in themselves, follows inevitably from the two assertions:
consciousness is the sole field of perceptive knowledge; no
material phenomena, as material, can appear in consciousness, interpenetrated, so to speak, by it.   Consciousness
covers all intellectual knowledge, and excludes all else;
lays down a line of demarcation impassable either from
within or from without, cutting apart matter and mind.
This conclusion we believe all experience confirms, and
that no one would have thought of denying it, save under
the pressure of certain difficulties to be evaded, and certain
conclusions to be reached.

§ 4.  How far pure idealism, that professedly knows
only mind, is entitled to these assertions which we are

ready to make in common with it, is a question of more doubt. We, in our position, arrive at them by an inferential knowledge both of matter and mind, by a discovery of their mutually impenetrable character. If we were, as idealism asserts, in every way debarred access to matter— to matter as believed in by the masses of men—it would certainly not be so plain how we could come so universally to form a distinct, uniform and controlling idea of its character, and be able also to affirm, that this most omnipresent and fixed of our notions is, in its essential features, a mere figment of the brain. Why a series of physical conceptions which is removed by the very nature of mind from even the bare possibility both of knowledge and being should nevertheless be the most uniform and universal of mental states, is not explained by idealism. How a form of thought, necessarily false, comes to be a fixed product and characteristic of mind ; how it happens that we continually talk, think and act in reference to matter—matter which by the constitution of the mind, is beyond all forms of knowledge ; how science and philosophy come to so utterly differ from each other in their beliefs, are mysteries which must ever, to the straightforward, practical thinker, reflect the highest improbability on idealism, and leave it among those strange, remote conclusions, which when not directly disproved are too far off to disturb the orbit of our daily life. When philosophy subverts knowledge, instead of expounding it, and denies the validity of the most settled, familiar and unavoidable judgments of the mind, it assumes an anarchical character, removing the foundations, if not of thought, yet of conviction.

We believe the true doctrine of perception to be, that the state of consciousness therein is purely subjective both in action and object, indeed that the action and object are inseparable. To perceive a color, is to put forth a complete, primary, simple act of knowing, complete in that something is known; primary in that no further explanation can be forced upon it, the act standing in its own light, apprehensible for what it is in itself; and simple in that it is incapable of successful analysis. On the occasion of such a perception, the mind, of its own interpreting action, under the notion of causation, infers an external source of the impression, which, as a necessary, certain and uniform conclusion, becomes to it as valid as any that it ever makes. Its validity, like the validity of all mental acts, is referable to the clearness and constancy with which it is made and repeated. We reach, then, the external world not directly by perception, but indirectly, inferentially, along a bridge of thought, whose farther abutment our rational nature supplies, and whose connections are established by varied, repeated and protracted experience. Shifting the figure we strike the shore with the grapple of causation, and by this guy we swing.

If asked why the mind supplies the idea in connection with one mental state, that of perception, more than with another, as that of thought; how it knows where and when to fling into the air its coil of rope, that it may thereby be lashed to the physical world, the answer comes: It is the fruit of varied experience. A sensation is found to be a new, distinct, sudden, independent state. As such it demands explication in an outside cause. A thought is a consecutive, evolved, dependent product, that can be renewed in the mind at pleasure, and by this fact finds explication through the mind itself. The various senses also, in their diverse yet independent reports, mutually aid and guide the mind in this reference of sensations to external causes. Impressions in distinct organs are found always to accompany each other in certain forms, under a fixed order. Thus experience is constantly disclosing the character of

phenomena, and the mind rapidly learns to distinguish
those inwardly dependent on its own action, from those
dependent outwardly on foreign agents. This class it
can not, from its own constitution, leave without this causal
reference and exposition.

The confusion which sometimes overtakes the mind in
perception, illustrates its method of education, and the
manner in which it is commenced. A pressure is felt
across the forehead, as if the band placed upon it had been
drawn too tightly. We cannot tell with certainty whether
the impression is due to this cause, or to the astringency of
a fluid with which the fillet was saturated. We test the
point by raising the hand, and determining whether or not
mechanical force is present. In the absence of this, we
refer the feeling to the condition of the nerves. Again,
we seem to hear a sound, as the anxious parent the crying
of her child. She cannot at once decide whether the impression was the suggestion of her own thought, or the
actual effect of the supposed cause. The attention is more
carefully directed, the phenomena that enter the mind
from without being discriminated from the mere play of
fancy; and by this more complete separation of its own
action from the action of other agents the point is settled.

§ 5.   It has been thought, and much has been made of
this point, that a denial of direct perception is an impeachment of the veracity of our faculties, or, as it is expressed
by Hamilton and others, of consciousness; and that the
way is thus logically opened to universal scepticism.
Idealism is certainly not a denial of the facts of consciousness. Perception as a fact of mind, is accepted, and the
first exception taken is as to what perception is, what it
gives us. Now the veracity of consciousness is only involved in the mere fact of perception, the mere rehearsal
and acceptance of its mental phenomena, not at all in the

nature and validity of its supposed revelations. Idealism does, however, set aside a most universal belief of mankind, and so far tends to scepticism. But this accusation does not hold against the view of perception now presented. The general belief of men in an external world is maintained, though a careful analysis shows the grounds of the conclusion to be somewhat different from those at first accepted. The accusation against idealism is not that it shows a general opinion to be groundless, but that it affirms simply and nakedly a general and necessary belief to be deceptive; that is, the reiterated and constant action of the mind to be delusive. We may, on like grounds, pronounce the axiomatic conclusions of the reason unreliable. These are nothing more than its inevitable convictions.

The affirmation in which the unaided powers of all men agree, which they spontaneously and inevitably make, is the existence of an external world, the opposition of matter to mind, a reference of a portion of our inner experience to outer sources or causes. Whether this conclusion is intuitive, or involves one or more of the simplest acts of judgment, most men have never so much as inquired, and have therefore no convictions concerning it. It is doubtless a matter of surprise to most persons to find, on inquiry, so many judgments mingled with the simplest act of sight. These had been overlooked, and the act of seeing regarded as more full, explicit and immediate than it is. Language favors this concealment of obscure, rapid judgments, and we are said to see the form of a sphere, when we merely infer it. Yet there is no ground for a distrust of man's faculties, because they are formed to act in ways and proportions not perfectly understood by those who accept results with no investigation of methods. To tell a man that the unlikeness of the images of the same object in each of his two eyes, is one of the grounds from

which the impression of nearness is received, may interest
and surprise him, but does not so shake his confidence in
his own conclusions as to be told that the external world,
in which he has so fully believed that he has never so
much as thought of its existence as a matter of belief, is a
mere creation of the mind, one portion of its own acts
being thrown into opposition to another portion. The one
assertion arrests and throws back in confused, eddying currents, the whole stream of intellectual action; the other
merely shows that analysis reveals more elements in mental
phenomena than those at first caught sight of. There is no
reason why the statement that there is a simple judgment
involved in a belief of the existence of matter and of mind,
should be regarded as any more destructive to the faith to
be reposed in our faculties, than the generally accepted
doctrine, that sight includes many judgments dependent
on protracted experience. The assertion of Hamilton,
" that consciousness gives a knowledge of the ego, in relation and contrast to the non-ego," even if it were readily
intelligible to all, would hardly, I think, be regarded as a
satisfactory statement of a general and unwavering belief,
when contrasted with the statement, there is found that in
consciousness from which we directly and inevitably infer
the existence of matter and mind. Most would doubtless
regard the two statements as open to consideration, as lying
alike in the line of the common belief in the external world.
Indeed, to say that the mind is conscious of itself, or is
conscious of matter, gives a shock at once to thought, and
is far from being that explicit, indefeasible statement of the
common faith which all at once recognize.

The exact ground of the general belief is certainly
open to inquiry, and one statement which accepts its validity is no more exposed to the charge of a denial of the
integrity of the human faculties than another. Indeed the

spontaneous conviction of the existence and nature of external objects involves many judgments besides this one of causation. I see the apple before me. My present impression is—the steps of my past experience being unanalyzed —that I see it to be round, to be red, to be three inches in diameter and at a distance of three feet. How does this impression agree with what Sir William Hamilton says is the real object of perception? "Through the eye we perceive nothing but the rays of light in relation to, and in contact with the retina." Who ever perceived them, or came to so much as a knowledge of them, without diligent scientific inquiry? Light, as the fruit of much research, is found to be a form of motion, and this motion to affect the retina; but no man ever knows the existence of the retina, or of the undulations of light thereon, save through an inquiry into eyes other than his own, and a careful investigation of the physical world. What is here asserted to be the sole object of perception, the mind never perceives, but only employs it as a submerged, unknown cause through which it arrives at its own knowledge, to wit: a red apple of a given size and position. In this final product of perception, there are contained innumerable judgments, and it should certainly be no surprise to find among them this one of outside existence. That the spaces of the world are inferentially given, is entirely in keeping with the fact that those of a painting are, by the previous habit and impulse of the mind, supplied under suitable suggestions of light and shade.

The crude material granted to the mind seems to be a subjective impression of redness, of angular extension and various shades. From these, by the aid of muscular and tactual experience, and the help afforded by the color and relations of surrounding objects, it constructs an apple and assigns it independent existence in a definite locality. This it now does instantly, like a flash of light, though it has acquired the power of doing it slowly, by much and forgotten experience. The primitive, intellectual elements are wholly unlike this final result, these data of sense intershot with a few firm threads from the shuttle of reason. Indeed, no instance in our later knowledge, **in** which an entire system of principles is evolved from a few facts, more evinces the astonishing power which belongs to the mind, than does this simplest, earliest, most common **case of reasoning**, that of perception.

That color is known as the motion of an ethereal medium on the retina, or that there is any connection of **the** two, or knowledge of the one in and through the other, are statements **not** intelligible even, till science by secondary inquiries has made them so. The transfer of motion at one sense into vision, at another into hearing, and in the brain itself into thought, are inexplicable transformations, whose terms we only know by independent investigation, and even then fail of their connection. To suppose **that** any portion of this knowledge comes directly in perception, is the most obvious and violent perversion of experience.

If we were directly cognizant of the **content** in the organ of sense, cognizant of it for what it is and where **it** is physically, there would be no opportunity for deception or oversight in matters of perception. **A force acting on** a machine tells, and must tell, for exactly **what it is. The** effect **is** direct **and** inevitable. So would it be in perception. We should never make a ghost of a stump, or overlook altogether the objects whose images are actually on the retina; that have actually caused the light to impinge with customary power on this sensitive medium. It is because the mind gives a frightened attention or no attention, inadequate interpretation or no interpretation, to these objects, that perception is distorted, or fails altogether. The mere physical effect in itself alone is nugatory.

It is said that those whose eyes are distorted, use either one or the other as they choose, directing the attention to the right or the left as convenience requires, the impression in the neglected organ going for nothing; and we all of us evidently take up and lay down at pleasure the physical effects on the retina, using them as means of vision only when the mind is at leisure to do so. These facts show without doubt, that perception is deeper than the organ of sense, is by no means identical with the appropriate action therein, nor is sure to follow it. It is, then, no impeachment of the veracity of our faculties to inquire into the exact mode of their action, nor any the more so because the inquiry discloses unexpected results.

§ 6. The only perfectly direct and absolutely simple form of knowing is the knowledge which the mind has of its own states and actions, because they are its own. When the state is itself simple and ultimate, we term it a sensation, a feeling; when the act is pure and simple, embracing all its terms within itself, we call it intuitive; and the mind therein is an ultimate authority to itself. The intuitive action and the consciousness of the intuitive action are one and the same thing. Thus that two and two make four is a statement that may receive illustration but is capable of no proof. The mind within itself sees and comprehends the relation expressed. It has a direct knowledge of it. When the act under consideration is one of inference, it remains known as an act directly, but is itself the ground of further indirect knowledge. Thus we see the kaleidoscope directly, but we also see in it something which depends for its form on the structure of the instrument.

All phenomena immediately known to the mind are its own phenomena, since consciousness is the distinctive characteristic of this direct knowledge. Sensations, **intuitions** are its own states and acts declared in consciousness. **From** these phenomena it may infer noumena, its own spiritual powers and the physical forces about **it**. **The** being of both stand on the same basis of valid inference. Phenomena of sensation and action being present, and **the idea** of causation present, the two coalesce reflectively **into the** conclusion of spiritual and physical agencies expressed in them.

The three terms of the problem of perception **are the** external world,—external both to mind and body—the **internal** or mental world, and the nervous organism which mediates between them. The mind first recognizes its own phenomena **of** various orders; from these it infers their sources in itself **and** out of itself; later it learns the part which the organs of the body take in this interaction.

The analysis of Hamilton, and of a large share **of the** modern school of realists, (1) confounds agent and action, substance and qualities, noumena and phenomena, causes and effects. It for the moment overlooks the facts that causes **can** not be directly known, and that all direct knowledge is a knowledge of effects. (2.) It confuses the relation of consciousness and mental processes. Consciousness can embrace only phenomena of mind, and all direct knowledge belongs therefore exclusively to these phenomena. When an act of mind gives something not existing in the mind, that act is one of inference, whose premises simply are mental phenomena. The difference between intuitive and reflective knowledge for our present purpose lies just here, consciousness holds all the terms in the one case, and only the premises in the other. Intuition is a vision of the mind that completely searches the relation before it, and is wholly held in consciousness. If equals are added to equals the sums are equals. This axiom is not the statement of one or of many known facts beyond consciousness, it predicates a relation of ideas within consciousness. This odor comes from that rose. The odor as a state of mind is directly known to the mind, but the source of the odor in the rose is an inference only. (3) The analysis of Hamilton, while designed as a defence against idealism, opens the way to it, or to materialism, as the objector may choose. The facts of matter and mind are thought to meet in one field; their identity therefore may easily be affirmed on either hand, the identity of material facts with mental ones, or of mental ones with material ones. Both it is said are known by a simple, indivisible process. (4) This analysis gets color by directing attention to one or two senses and neglecting the other senses. Take color and sound, and how manifest it is that our knowledge is made up of inner impressions, and the reference of these impressions to external causes.

(5) The stimuli run along the neural route from without inward. The interior portion of this circuit remaining complete, the loss of the exterior portion is of no moment, *provided* that the fitting stimuli can be imparted to the cerebrum. Apparent sensation remains in the hand after amputation. Hence the inevitable inference, that the molecular changes of the brain are the last and only necessary terms of cognition; that physical are translated into mental facts, not at the outer but at the inner termini.

§ 7. Each sense deals with a distinct medium, or with distinct conditions of the same medium. The eye as an organ of perception is affected exclusively by light; the ether in its vibrations is the only agent of vision. The light involves three points—gradations of intensity, color, and angular measurement. The first two are obvious, the third a little less so. It may seem to us that light gives directly through the eye a surface on which its colors are spread. These surfaces, however, in definite place and

form, are the products of experience. Colors simply have
their own character and subtend an angle. This is all that
the mind, through the eye **as** an organ, directly declares.
Surfaces are determined by distances both as to nature and
extent, and the only fixed perceptive term out of which
these judgments grow, so far as the eye is concerned, is angular measurements, which are the same for many different
surfaces, the same for solids as for surfaces, and hence directly involve no one surface. The floating muscæ of the
**eye** assume any size, according to the distance of the objects
**on** which they are cast, though their angular dimensions
remain the same. When we look out into space, the
spherical impression of the concave **is due** to partial interpretation, with conditions of vision **too** narrow to make it
complete. The stars are all thrown outward, but with differences of distances undiscernible. The corners of a room
would disappear, or the edges of a cube, were not **our** impressions of these made up of shades **as** well as angular
measurements. The two we easily translate into position
and surface. **It** is these elements that the painter deals
with, renewing the impressions of vision by colors and
**shades,** and by surfaces which act not by their absolute dimensions, but by their suggestions of distance and position.
It is true he reaches his angles through surfaces, but we do
not contemplate them as surfaces of such and such dimensions **on** the canvas, but **in** their angular force through the
eye as suggestive of the character and positions of **known**
objects. The **horse in the** foreground covers more space
in the picture than the mountain in the background ; **and**
the size of the latter is impressed upon us, first by indications of distance, and then by the angle subtended.

The earliest and most fundamental of absorbed judgments is that of distance. Touch and motion come to
initiate this judgment, and, the size of familiar objects be-

ing fixed, the eye carries forward the process by observing their angular or apparent size in various positions. Size and distance mutually contain each other; if we know the one we can infer the other.

We also judge of distance by intervening objects, themselves interpreted in their relations by experience. Again we infer it from depth of color. This test, however, is applicable only to remote objects, and, in comparative judgments, to objects quite unequally remote. The ridges of mountains, rising in succession beyond each other, are separated to the eye by the different shades of blue that rest upon them. The degree in which, in these estimates, we are dependent on our own experience is indicated by our wild conclusions under novel conditions. The pure atmosphere and the unaccustomed dimensions of high mountains make the impressions of one who visits a country like Switzerland for the first time exceedingly deceptive. Weeks and months of laborious walking must be passed before these objects assume their true dimensions, and take on their real grandeur. In like manner the inexperienced landsman loses all accuracy when called on to estimate distances on the water.

A fourth aid in determining distances is the muscular adjustment of the eyes in bringing the image to the focal point on the retina. This test affords but slight assistance, however, and is applicable to objects comparatively close at hand. We are not conscious of a readjustment of the eye, except under a sudden change of vision at ranges whose inequality is very obvious. If an object near by is suddenly thrust upon the attention, the effort to see it becomes even painful. The judgments of ordinary vision are vague, giving the general relation of objects in position more than their direct distance from the observer.

A second perceptive judgment in sight is that of form.

The conditions of this judgment are light and shade. In large and complex objects, like mountain ranges, as form involves position, our judgments in this particular are mingled with and modified by those of distance.

A third judgment in vision is that of size. Though we infer distance from size, and equally well size from distance, the former is the more common case in experience. Well-established sizes, settled by close contact, are our ordinary data. Yet it not infrequently happens that distances are known, and we thence infer the dimensions of strange objects. The variety and vagueness of our impressions as to the size of the moon are due to the fact that distance does not enter in as a measurable factor. The primitive data, then, of the eye are color, light and shade, angles ; its acquired data distance, involving position, form and size.

Two eyes in vision give us an advantage besides that of protection against accident, or even that of stronger sight. The circles of vision in the two eyes of man do not quite correspond ; the one includes portions not found in the other. Also, by virtue of distinct positions, the two alter slightly, each as compared with the other, the relations of objects. These **facts** make **the** perspective more definite, especially as regards objects just at hand, in reference to which exactness is important. We secure by two eyes a triangulation available in defining distance and position. So important is this aid that the loss of one eye is attended with considerable confusion of perspective. An intervening object, also, brings less obstruction to two eyes than to one.

The ear, the second leading organ of perception, deals with sound, with the undulations of the air within a certain range of rapidity. This range, however, is not identical in all persons, a rate of vibration being in some instances audible to one and inaudible to another. The physical characteristics of sound are quality or timbre, pitch and quantity or intensity. In addition to these primary qualities, there are secondary ones, which combine physical discrimination with rational association. Sounds are thus intellectual, emotional, and musical. The first two may each exist without the others, and the third quite modifies the two former in their combinations and force. Original discrimination and the modifications of experience enter, in a most complex and inseparable way, into the appreciation of these secondary qualities. The primary qualities of sound, like those of vision, develop a series of perceptive judgments, though these judgments are less numerous and important than those of the eye.

We infer from a sound its source, as the presence of an acquaintance from his voice. These judgments rest wholly on the associations of experience. We judge of the distance of any audible object by the intensity of the sound. This class of inferences arises under more uniform natural connections interpreted to us by experience. We also decide by sound, though with some hesitation, on the direction of audible objects. In these conclusions we derive assistance from the possession of two ears. Direction is settled by the greatest intensity of sound, it being found in the line of the wave motion.

In touch, taste, and odor we deal with matter in three forms—as offering resistance in masses, as floating in a gaseous or most minute form in the air, as dissolved in water or saliva. In the first, the condition is mechanical, in the other two chemical. The things of which these senses take cognizance are, between the three senses, incomparable with each other, and, in the same sense, very numerous, with every gradation of difference. The sensations take on the variety and changeable forms of the feelings, as opposed to the narrow and definite action of the powers of the mind. Our perceptive judgments through these three senses are

made up of the variable combinations of experience. They
retain more firmly their distinct character than in the other
senses, and are enlarged under a more directly guided effort.
Vision contains the largest amount of completely absorbed
judgments, judgments that turn on general principles, **and**
are early taken up in an inseparable way with the perception. The presence of these inferences are not only **dis-**
closed by the mistakes **we make** under them, when our data
**are** insufficient,—as in determining distances and relations
under novel circumstances—but also by various contrivances
by which we alter the conditions of sight, and so the appar-
**ent position and magnitude of** objects.

When **we roll up** a piece of paper like a funnel, and
view a painting through it with one **eye,** the perspective is
brought out more strongly. The increased effect of this
monocular vision is due to the fact, that surrounding objects
are cut off, the **actual** distance **of the** canvas, so distinctly
given by both eyes, is **obscured, and the** data of the painting alone **are present. The eye, relieved** from the contradiction of **near** objects, proceeds at once to construct the
landscape under the suggestions of the painter, with its true
dimensions. **A** mask looked at in this way in the rear may,
by **an instant,** unobserved transfer of light and shade from
**one side of the face to the other, be constructed** with **its**
features in relief, **as if seen in front.**

In the skeleton form of a stereoscope, in which two pictures of the same object **are separated by** a card, so that one
image **is** seen exclusively **by** one eye, and the other by the
other eye, the **two eyes unite to** construct the view at a
distance, as if they were looking at remote, real objects, in
reference to which the **card between the** eyes would present
no embarrassment. **The eyes being** restricted in vision,
being set free from the contradiction of surrounding facts,
each takes up its **own** representation **in a sort of** double

monocular action, and transfers it, with corresponding increase of dimensions, to the distance implied in the picture
itself. It can then unite with the impression furnished by
the other eye, and the two blend into one view. The monocular character of the effort is plain from the fact that,
when we fail to harmonize the two images, vision through
one eye still produces the desired illusion. Still farther,
the axes of vision in the eyes are made less convergent, as
when directed to distant objects. To aid the construction,
the two images are taken from slightly removed positions,
thereby, in reference to the foreground, giving the same
readjustment of objects in position as that which belongs to
double vision. This advantage is, however, immaterial,
except in connection with near objects. The lenses or
mirrors introduced into the stereoscope do not alter the
principle; they still leave the eyes to do independently
their constructive work, and to identify the images they
have removed into the distance.

§ 8. Perception is a peculiarly interesting portion of
psychology. Lying at the commencement of the study, it
imposes upon us at once a most difficult case of analysis;
the results we reach go far to settle the relations of mind
and matter to each other; we have need to determine the
full circle of mental powers and put them all in operation
in laying these foundations of certain knowledge; the automatic action of the mind, and its successive stages of growth
require immediate recognition; while historically many
questions of philosophy have been settled at this point.

Perception, in its broad meaning, includes the physical
conditions furnished by the senses, with their nervous connections; the states or actions of mind directly incident
thereto; the nature of the dependence of these states on
those conditions; the extent to which the first activity of
mind is enlarged by experience; and the character and the

certainty of the knowledge both of the internal and the external world that accompanies perception. We will rapidly review each of these points in their theoretical and historical bearings.

The physical conditions **of** sight, hearing, touch, taste, and smell are matters purely of physical inquiry. A satisfactory knowledge of the intervening means of perception is comparatively recent, as is all exact anatomical science. An inquiry into the physical incidents of perception has served to displace some crude theories of its method, and to make way for a more careful separation of the material and intellectual elements in the process, or, in the minds of some, for their more complete identification. The notion of "images," "species," "representative ideas," which mediate between the object and the mind, arose **out** of the ignorance of the organs of sense, **and** lingered in philosophy as late as the time of **Locke.** These images or ideas had one or another degree **of** materiality according to the age, the philosophy, the person, who dealt with them. Earlier, they were a physical film passing off from the object; later, **as** the immateriality **of** the mind gained ground, they shared more of its nature; but at no time could they perform their office. **To** whichever extreme they moved, they thereby **lost power to** touch the other. If spiritual, they were out of relation with matter, if material, they were disassociated with mind. A knowledge of the eye, the ear, the brain sweeps away this intermediate mechanism, establishes the complete physical character of the organic portion of perception, the complete spiritual nature of the mental portion, and leaves the interaction of the two an ultimate fact.

Descartes sharply distinguished between mind and matter, and so relegated physical inquiry to its own physical field, and mental inquiry to consciousness. All media sharing the two natures disappeared ; the separation of the two fields, though often carried to a mistaken extent, became decisive. Thus the way was prepared for sound investigation in both directions.

The second point is the states of mind incident to the organic action of the senses. The content of the sense in each instance, with its definite, discriminated qualities, in some way controls the mind, and the mind in active, constructive fashion responds to this external efficiency. If any physical force acts upon a body in reference to it inert, it is yet true that the result will turn quite as much on the qualities of the so-called passive agent as on those of the aggressive one. Every agent, physical and mental, ceases to be passive under action, and blends in the results its own activities with those of the efficient cause. We may forget this in mechanical facts, we can scarcely forget it in chemical, vital, mental facts. The mind is barely less active in a sensation than in a perception, in a feeling, than in a thought. Each is determined as a conscious state by a susceptibility called out, or a power occupied. As regards the fact of activity, the two classes are not separable, though the activity in perception and thought is more voluntary, more modifiable than that in sensation and feeling. The mind, as possessed of a definite constitution, determines the nature and efficiency of each of its states. If the mind is restricted to organic conditions for particular sensations, so are these conditions, in turn, restricted to answering susceptibilities before they pass into mental facts. Nothing but a living agent can feel. When oxygen and hydrogen combine, there are conjoint activities, conjoint properties, conjoint products.

The activity of the mind in sensation is shown not merely by the fact that sensibility is activity, but by the fact that the mind is ever interpreting and attributing its sensations. In each sense the whole complex nervous mechanism, including the external organ, the connecting nerves and the brain, lies between the mind and the **object**, as the telescope between the eye **and** the stars, the whispering-gallery or the telephone between the ear **and** the speaker. Yet it is not of one or all of these conditions that the mind is cognizant. It sees *through* them, hears *through* them, feels, tastes, and smells *through* them. **It** carries the facts of vision outward to their remote objects, and the qualities of touch or flavor to their sources. The **mind is** always taking up and using instrumentally its **organs**, and is no more subject to mere effects in them, than is the eye in using a microscope cognizant **of** its images and lenses. Intermediate conditions lie **as** submerged links in the mind's activity.

No image could well be more inapt than that of **Locke** in which he compared the mind to white paper. **As all** knowledge in chemistry **up to the** present time has been accumulating the conditions by **which** the plate of the photographer is made sensitive to light, so all evolution has joined in shaping that latest power by which mind feels. Mind is the one only agency which can so respond to the physical world. When we add perception to sensation, the marvel grows. **All** senses end **in** molecular changes. From these **common terms, so like** one to another, mind constructs, in the hidden joy of vision, and **of** every accessory sense, this universe about us, with its **immeasurable** spaces, its brilliant colors, its throbbing **sounds, its sweet** odors, its stimulating flavors, its velvety **surfaces, and its** thousand suggestions of life. If there is **any fit image of** omnipotence, it **is** this **mind in** the midst of the world which it momentarily evokes.

The third fact **is** the nature of the interaction between the last physical facts and the first mental ones. Men have struggled long and vainly with this ultimate truth, that matter affects mind and mind affects matter. They have striven to insert midway terms; they have brought down mental to physical facts, and there identified the two; they have reversed the process, and regarded perception and sensation as purely mental processes. It is well to stand with Descartes, and assert the radical division between the two sets of phenomena, so radical that facts of the one class cannot be intelligibly expressed in words of the other class. It is well to reject all explanations that explain nothing; to make no assertions of the possible and impossible which transcend experience, and imply on our part a knowledge of ultimate relations that violates their nature. It is well to stand quietly by ultimate facts, putting upon them no constructions which we cannot verify. Physical facts can be expounded under their own forms, mental facts under their forms; while their interaction, to us at least unphenomenal, is without form. The method in which a specific, organic state is transformed into a sensation, or in which a volition in turn is converted into an action, is beyond the terms of experience. So, indeed, is all transfer of forces in physics.

The fourth point is the extent to which the primitive activity of the mind is enlarged by experience. The first full discussion of this topic we owe to Bishop Berkeley. The importance attached to this secondary element in perception, these inclosed judgments, has been on the increase since his time. The organic content, or rather the activity of mind incident to this content, is the dry sponge which absorbs the inferences of experience, is expanded and made flexible and serviceable by them. There is a tendency to refer these judgments in the man as in the animal largely to instinctive action and to inheritance. As the infant and the child are manifestly for a long period employed in form-

ing these judgments, and as the process accompanies us all
the way through life, we see but little occasion to ascribe
their presence to a blind, organic tendency. Moreover,
such a movement would not prepare the way for conscious,
rational action, would not put the mind in possession of
itself, but would tend in action to anticipate order, **and** so
prevent such a result.

The fifth consideration is the nature and certainty of
our knowledge of the internal and external world. **The**
mind under any view has the most immediate knowledge **of**
its own impressions. The interior phenomenal world **is**
necessarily known to it. Here knowledge gathers its primary force. The chief difficulty is found in **the** relation of
this knowledge to real being, internal or external. The
dependence seems to us simple. We believe, with Descartes, that under the action of causation we infer decisively
and correctly external agents from fixed, involuntary **im-**
pressions. The reality and relations of these external
causes are more and more disclosed to us by perception
with its enlarging judgments, and **are** more and more completely clothed with the phenomenal impressions in **the**
mind which **are attributed to** them. This knowledge **of**
causes in their effects is all the knowledge that is proper **to**
them, and the effort to resolve the cause itself into a second
phenomenon, serves only to push the cause one step farther
back. In repeated instances this process, by which the
mind habilitates the underlying reality with its appropriate
phenomena, has, in the case of vision gained in later years,
passed on under observation. There is no element of real
doubt in this knowledge; its links are close and sufficient;
its chief mysteries lie, as is wont to be the case, in **first**
terms, in the perceptive and sensational elements, and in the
completeness with which these are made objective. This
last point is abundantly illustrated by facts **like** those of

sketching and painting. A few lines, as of a human face, on a plain surface, give us at once, under our constructive powers, form, substance, distance, character; objective throughout and thoroughly realized.

Yet around this relation of the mental impressions to the underlying facts, most of the divisions and denials of philosophy have sprung up, chiefly because the intuitive presence and the validity of the notion of causation have been overlooked, the firm yet inscrutable line between physical and mental facts been lost, and kinds of knowledge impossible from the nature of the case been sought after. If we accept these data, the separate, unmistakable character of mental phenomena, the soundness of our intuitions, and the distinct, incomparable forms of knowledge, there is very little ground for discussion. What the mind directly knows must be purely mental, for a fact becomes mental, *is* mental, by virtue of being found in consciousness. What it indirectly knows are the phenomena of space, and those of other minds, both interpreted by its own experience; and those permanent, efficient powers which underlie phenomena, known only as forces or causes, and not at all as appearances or effects. Facts that are placed in any other region than space and consciousness, or are to be known in any other way than directly as phenomena or indirectly as causes, are hopelessly unknowable, are so far chaotic as to lack any formative idea to define them, any condition of thought under which to appear.

The impressions in the mind cannot be mistaken because they are pervaded by consciousness; the underlying and the outside facts which they disclose cannot be visionary, for all the intuitions and judgments of the mind vouch for them. The external world is known as the certain cause of the fixed impressions which shadow it forth in the mind, and this knowledge is the exact equivalent of that which we have of ourselves as real persons. We allow no pre-eminence of one branch of knowledge over another; the perception and the inferences are equally decisive in reference to that which they disclose, and are **inextricably** blended.

From confusion at this point has arisen the affirmation that **all our** knowledge is relative. By this is meant, that there is ever present an unmeasured, subjective **element** which separates the convictions of each person from **those** of his neighbor, and so from absolute **truth.** This assertion has meaning and force in reference to sensations, less in reference to perceptions, and none in reference **to** intuitions, and **the** conclusions drawn from them. The sensation is more completely, the perception **less completely, involved** in a physical, organic state ; **and all** we can **say** concerning this organic element **is, that** it, under given conditions, yields in the mind **certain impressions.** The identity of the action of organs in different persons we cannot affirm, nor what forces are aside from the organs they affect. This relative knowledge, however, is real, and sufficient for **all** its purposes. We have no occasion to know matter save **as** the fixed causes of certain effects, and that its effects in **us are kindred to** those in others. **To inquire** whether **matter is** like **its** effects, or what it is aside from its **effects, are** questions out of **order** under our organic intellectual **law.** The physical element makes the knowledge of the **senses** relative without affecting its **value.** But the intuitions with their inferences have no conditional, physical element. The knowledge **of** relations is pure knowledge, identical knowledge, in all. This **is obvious in** mathematics, in logic, in all pure science. The mind **is as** capable of absolute as **of** relative knowledge, of a **movement** that goes out from itself in general principles, as of one that comes into it as specific **facts. Its** relative knowledge is of substances in their properties, those interactions by which they define each other; its absolute knowledge is one of forms, of regulative principles, which neither matter nor mind can escape. This fundamental difference between intuitive and sensational knowledge, no analysis has been able to break down or obscure. Truths of the higher mathematics rise quite above experience, and come at once with irresistible authority to it. It is strange that Hamilton should give us a direct knowledge of matter, and yet regard all knowledge as relative.

This assertion, that all our knowledge is relative, has gained great currency; yet we can look on it only as one of those false deductions which have followed the empirical philosophy, and are fitted to sustain it. If all our knowledge comes from experience, it is all tainted by the quality of the senses, and hence is all relative to their forms and powers of discrimination. Pure knowing, pure in its object, and pure in its subjective process, becomes impossible. Yet direct insight into abstract relations is evidently of this character, and evinces its nature by the uniformity and force of the conclusions incident to it. Empirical philosophy has no way of explaining axiomatic truth and demonstrative reasoning. The reference of the necessity of these convictions to inheritance is most lame. They pertain to abstract truths often very unfamiliar, and take effect at once in connection with quite novel statements. Matters of experience under the daily observation of many generations — as the rising of the sun, the blackness of crows, the whiteness of swans, carry with them by inheritance or otherwise no such necessity. That the truth of mathematics *can* be no other than they are, is a conviction that the mind takes with it to the study of nature, not one that it derives from nature. Of all branches of knowledge mathematics may advance most rapidly, and divorce itself

most completely from previous experience. This power of
the mind to deal with abstract relations, and push them
entirely in advance of physical inquiry, belongs to **it as**
possessed of pure insight. The abstractions of sensation, as
greenness, sweetness, hardness, are accompanied by no corresponding **sweep** of thought, and give no particular **mas-**
tery. The abstractions of experience can carry no **more**
force **than** the experience itself.

The complete identity of mathematical truths in different minds, and **this from** their **very first** announcement, is
**a** sufficient proof of their absolute character. They **are**
plainly not modified **by** any special qualities of special
forms **of** intelligence; **and** they stand, **in this particular, in**
contrast with all empirical knowledge.

§ 9. A farther error connected **with the doctrine of**
direct perception is the division of the qualities **of matter**
into primary and secondary. The list of primary qualities
is differently made out by different philosophers. Extension and solidity are generally recognized as chief among
them. The criteria of these qualities as compared with
secondary qualities are, that matter can **not** exist without
them, and, especially urged by Hamilton, that in the primary qualities perception is peculiarly **direct** and clear;
" the **objective** element predominates," " matter is **known**
as principal **in** its relation to mind." The distinction between primary and secondary **qualities seems on these tests**
to be untenable, and **to arise from an oversight of those**
necessary intuitive ideas involved in the **very existence of**
matter.

Extension should not be regarded as a property of **mat-**
ter, and if so regarded is not, in the form in which it exists,
a necessary property. No portion of matter is necessarily
of one size rather than another. The actual quality of extension, if it is to be so termed, **is as variable as any other**

quality. The only universality in this attribute more than in other attributes of matter is found in the fact, that all matter must exist in space, and hence under the one form of extension. Space, extension, is a necessary condition of matter. Without it, those qualities, properly so called, which constitute matter, cannot have a being. It is involved in their manifestations, that they occupy some portion of space, and this primary quality, so called, is only this essential condition for the existence of matter. We might as well say that duration is a quality of matter, as to say that extension is such a quality; since no form of matter can exist without occupying some period of time, more or less.

Nor is the second criterion any more satisfactory in its application. If there is any one direction in which the mind acts with a sense of establishing and defining its own data, it is this of extension. Odor, taste, color, are what they are, directly, through the nature of the outside cause; but the form of a body is arrived at through meagre grounds of judgment unfolded by the enlargement and corrections of protracted experience; while the notion under which alone this evolution can proceed, that of space, is furnished entirely by the mind. Perception, instead of being unusually direct and immediate in extension, is more than elsewhere indirect and enlarged by inference.

Solidity, as a primary quality, is open to a like form of criticism. That which must in this discussion be understood by solidity, is very different from the notion which the word ordinarily conveys; it is the impossibility of complete compression, complete displacement. A gas is in this sense as much a solid as a piece of steel, since, when properly confined in a cylinder, it is found to exclude the piston as certainly as the most solid substance. Compression cannot proceed to all lengths. Resistance accompanies pressure, and an increased and insuperable resistance remains as the final result. Without this capability of occupying space **to** some sense we withhold the appellation of matter. Here, again, any given degree of incompressibility is not necessary to matter, but only that there should be some degree of it, and some degree of incompressibility is necessary as involved in this method of occupying space. The general necessity, then, is evolved from this general condition of the existence and recognition of matter, that it shall **be** a space-filling force, that it shall have, in the external world, a permanent substratum to its **phenomena.**           .

As the necessary connection of extension with matter **arises from the idea of space, so that of** solidity arises from the *occupation* of space, **the ideal of a** local, fixed cause, the source of fixed phenomena. That the forces which lie at the basis of matter may in some cases penetrate each other, as in the union of two **gases, and** may in others entirely exclude each other, as in the contact of solids, are facts to be learned by experience. The very notion of matter, however, is that it involves a local cause or force, and if a cause **or** force, that it has some means of showing itself as a force.

**If it be said that** the distinction between primary and **secondary** qualities **is** valid, since solidity necessarily involves force, the substratum of matter; answer is made that **no specific form of** force is necessary to matter, but only some form of force, and that this is as necessary to color, to flavor, to odor, when these are present, as to solidity when this is shown. Solidity **has** no permanent existence any more than odor or **color, demands** like them for its manifestation appropriate conditions, and does no more than they do, in demanding as a condition **an external** force. If, then, we speak of the effects matter **is** capable of producing as the qualities of that matter, odor, resistance **are** such qualities, but neither of them **are** constant ; both are occasional, and conditioned to fitting circumstances; both of them imply that which is permanent and necessary. From taste as from touch, we may infer an external, local cause, a cause that must hence occupy space, be a space-filling force, at least to one sense, which is the entire conclusion derivable from resistance.

If it be said that the circumstances are in all cases possible under which the quality of solidity may be drawn out, while those which disclose odor are peculiar to a few bodies, we answer, this is a question of experience, is far from being proved, as in the case of ether, and, if established, could bring with it no sense of necessity, differencing the two cases. Bodies which yield no odor under one form, may under another. Odor seems to involve chemical change, and it might be found that every substance would yield it under fitting chemical conditions. This is a question to be decided by protracted and varied experience, and however decided, could only be the ground of an empirical, and not of a necessary division of qualities.

Take such a secondary quality as that of color. It seems antecedently probable, that all bodies have color. Some gases are apparently colorless, but so is the atmosphere in small volumes. Experience and theory would lead us to expect that the most diffused force in sufficient volume would affect the transmission of light.

These criteria, then, cannot be the sufficient and prevailing ground of this distinction, but we must look farther for something thought to inhere in the very nature of matter, necessary to it and betrayed by every primary quality. This necessary something we accept, and believe the notion of it to arise under the intuitive idea of cause and effect; but also believe, that this notion is called forth, as certainly by odor, by color, by taste, as by pressure; and that we inevitably put back of each of these subjective effects, a per manent force, occupying space, called matter. This permanent force is necessary to the notion of matter, and is as appropriately reached by one sense as by another, by one effect as by another; indeed, is indicated by any sensation which betrays an external world. The qualities which find entrance through one organ, have **no** more right to be called primary, that is fundamental, than those which enter at another. If the sense of muscular effort were wanting, we might still be able to arrive at the idea of matter; though its alleged primary quality should not be directly recognizable by us. We should then understand color and flavor as indications of a local force, apprehensible by sight and taste.

The second criterion more signally **fails than** the first in its application to solidity. Far from matter's coming most directly and fully in contact with mind through solidity, in many instances it is only in a secondary, inferential way, that this quality is at all arrived at. A gas makes no impression on the muscular system, offers no obstacle to movement, calls forth no sense of resistance, till closely confined; and then by that very confinement is put beyond direct contact **with any** organ of sense. We are left to infer the solidity of gases, from the fact that the piston cannot, in the cylinder containing them, be forced perfectly down to **its** bed, and recoils as the hand is lifted. Perception is not more immediate and full here than elsewhere; on the contrary, there is no perception of the point at issue, the solidity of the gas, but only a judgment to that effect. Even the solidity of a solid directly handled is inferred from the muscular effort expended in the attempt to crush it, and only admits of an estimate by an indirect method.

This doctrine of primary and secondary qualities, maintained by so large a variety of philosophers, is of interest, chiefly from the way in which it has grown out of the errors, or betrays the errors, held by them; and yet more from the indication it gives of an unconscious influence of truths not formally recognized. Thus, Locke speaks of the "inseparable" nature of extension as a quality of matter, while declining to accept the antecedent necessity of space as a condition of matter, and a knowledge of matter. Herein he grants to matter the necessity which he has denied to mind; whereas by necessity can only be meant something which the *mind* inevitably affirms, a union of things which it sees to be indissoluble. No matter how often things are practically connected, unless the mind can so far penetrate that connection as to see the one to be involved in the other, their dependence would not seem to be a necessary one. Yet this father of sensationalism speaks of inseparable qualities, when experience in many cases had neither by sight nor in any way tested their existence. Why this judgment of universal, of necessary extension and solidity? Because of a conviction latent in the mind through its intuitive ideas, a conviction independent of the complete expansion of experience.

Hamilton, again, looking at this division of qualities through the doctrine of direct perception, jumps at the conclusion that primary qualities are those more immediately revealed, whereas inquiry shows that solidity, the most undeniable of them, is often wholly unapproachable to any form of direct perception, and is arrived at by reasonings from sensations which arise indirectly from the object of experiment. The staff so quickly clutched at has become a broken reed. Thus philosophers furnish undesigned and most valuable proof to an adverse theory, by recognizing and striving to use in a disguised form the truths which it proclaims, and assigns their true position. The acknowledged necessity of primary qualities is not in *them*, but in that *intuitive action* of the mind which they call forth.

Necessity, which every philosopher seems ready **to intro-duce** at some point, is born not of experience, but of men's thoughts; not of matter, but of mind.

We briefly sum up the conclusions arrived at. Extension is not a quality of matter, but its antecedent condition, and owes the sense of necessity that accompanies it to the necessary idea of space. The same reason that makes **it,** would make duration also, a quality of matter. The actual form or extension of bodies is contingent and inferential. Solidity, or the power of exclusion, is a quality of matter, and owes its necessity to our idea of the nature of matter, an idea arising under the notions of space and of cause. It differs not from odor, color in implying a permanent sub-stratum. Every quality of matter, every **sensation** and perception involve this, though they mutually deepen and confirm it. Solidity, a sense of resistance, is felt to **be** more necessarily involved in matter than odor and taste, because, in experience, we almost exclusively use this con-stant and convenient test of its presence. This, however, **is an** empirical distinction, arising from the nature of one senses, of an uncertain character, and of no particular im-portance. The distinction then of primary qualities, while involving important points in philosophy, in its common form breaks down. **These** qualities are not more **directly** perceived than other qualities; they are not in **contrast** with them nor known to be more necessary. **If we reason** from the quality to the substratum, each implies this, and the necessity is common and complete. If we reason from the substratum to its qualities, no individual quality is seen to be necessary, neither any kind nor class of qualities as hardness, color. We can not so **penetrate the nature of the** cause as to antecedently declare what its **action will be.** The greater constancy of one quality over another is learned by experience; the intrinsic necessity of that constancy, if there be any, is unperceived. A local substance perfectly penetrable, yet having odor, color, and flavor, would doubtless be regarded by us as matter.

§ 10. Consciousness, or the inner sense, the remaining means of a direct knowledge of phenomena, requires but brief notice. Our chief difficulty in conceiving this source of knowledge, and in speaking of it, is found in the language we are compelled to employ, and the confusion already occasioned by it. Self-consciousness, or consciousness, or the inner sense, is not a method of the mind's action, is not a faculty of perception. These words are used by us simply to express the fact that the mind knows what it does; that its states, acts, experiences, are necessarily open to itself, not by any direct effort of attention on its part, but by virtue of the very fact that they are its own states. We cannot readily speak of this knowledge which the mind has of its own phases of activity without seeming to imply more than we intend; to imply an explicit form, or faculty, or means of knowing. What we wish to draw attention to, as a second source of phenomenal matter, is the familiarity of the mind with its own thoughts, feelings, volitions; and hence its power through memory to make them objects of attention, analysis, inquiry. By these processes primarily is philosophy established, the phenomena of mind separated into their elements, and the laws of their combination discovered. Consciousness furnishes only the bare data of mental facts, the perceptions or thoughts present, and is not in the least responsible for their accuracy. Its verity is only involved in rendering them as they are, that is, as they lie in the mind. Whether we perceive what we think we perceive, whether we know what we think we know, that is, the objective justness of our mental action, these are quite different inquiries. The subjective state is all that is revealed in consciousness, and this is revealed by the very nature of mind. Concerning it, there is no opportunity for scepticism in the very moment of **its** transpiring; later the question is one of memory.

Consciousness gives internal phenomena, perception gives external phenomena. Did not perception constantly involve inference, did it not reach the external world through the reflective **force of the mind, perception and consciousness would give but one and the same set of data,** and the distinction would disappear.

# CHAPTER III.

## The Understanding.

§ 1. THE understanding includes all those mental activities by which the data of sense and reason are wrought into knowledge. They are memory, imagination, and judgment. The first condition of rational activity is perception, some object given to the mind towards which it may be moved, with which it may occupy itself. The second essential condition is memory, by which perceptions gain continuity, are united into one experience, are made ready to be woven into the fabric of belief. Without memory our conscious states would be separate, incommunicable, save by direct sequence, with no more reciprocal play, unity, and growth than belong to particles of sand. Memory is involved in the coherence of intellectual life, as much as the constant interaction of its organs is included in physical life. Memory is the power of recalling the phenomena of consciousness. The experiences of the past are restored to the mind by this faculty, with a recognition of their previous existence. Like all primitive powers, it has its own simple, unique action, explained only by experience. The words *retaining, recalling,* may, through the force they have acquired in physical connections, suggest the idea that some impression of the objects remembered is held in the mind, and again restored to its observation; or that some trace or result of the first act remains with the mind, waiting renewal in memory. Indeed, looking more at the material suggestions of mental phenomena, than at the simple, primitive character of the act of recollection itself, some have inquired, Whether the very thing first known is the object of memory, or whether the mind is occupied with some image of it? We might as well inquire Whether the artist's conception of a painting is the very painting itself, or an image of it? It is certainly not the first, nor even the second in any other than a figurative sense. When I say that I recollect an event, my language is about as intelligible as it can be made. There is in it a direct appeal to the interpretation of every one's experience, furnishing like simple, original acts. In memory a new impression of the event is present, accompanied with a knowledge of its previous presence. It is merely a futile struggle with physical images, the misleading effect of physical analogies, which prompt us to inquire, with an analysis more cunning than cognizant of the true conditions of mental experience, Whether, as our language seems to imply, we actually remember the very object that has passed away, or whether some impression of it is restored to us? Each act of memory is a primitive act, efficient in itself for its own independent and peculiar end; is, moreover, purely subjective, though often involving a knowledge of the objective. Memory is not a repeated experience; it is the cognizance of a previous experience without repetition. The renewal of awakened action in the brain, if it could be shown to accompany recollection, would be no explanation of it. Of a like character are all the explanations of memory, which spring from purely physiological facts. Whatever may be the effect of thinking on the brain, the connection of these physical changes in a physical agent with the act of memory is wholly unintelligible. I might as well explain the recollection of a sword-wound by the presence of a scar on the body, as by any changes effected at the time in the brain by the suffering then experienced. That a scar constitutes memory, is as apprehensible as that a modification of a nervous tissue is memory. It is a fact, that memory, like other intellectual powers, is dependent for its exercise on the conditions of the brain, but why, or how dependent, are queries beyond the circle of knowledge. The vital play of nervous changes along nervous lines is one thing, the action of the mind a totally different thing. The one is learned as an outside fact by outside observations, the other as an inside fact by consciousness. The synchronism of the two is an interesting point, but one, for the present, barren in strict philosophy.

That memory is more dependent than other mental powers on physical states is generally believed, though we may be easily deceived in the grounds of this judgment. Memory is readily and quickly tested in its strength. A straightforward, categorical question betrays at once its weakness. We observe, therefore, failure at this point, more certainly than at others. In moments of weariness the memory fails us, but so, evidently, does the judgment. Obstacles seem disproportionately great, the occasions of fear unusual and pressing. In old age, memory is said to be the first faculty that shows decay; yet the old man, withdrawn from active life, naturally first discovers his failure here. It requires occasions of judgment to disclose the deficiency of judgment to others, while to ourselves, these failures are not betrayed from the very fact that the judgment, as weak, does not fully detect its own weakness. On the other hand, a dozen events every day expose inevitably and unmistakably the defects of memory. Moreover, the things chiefly forgotten are those of recent occurrence, a fact accounted for by the want of strong feeling, clear perception, and energetic attention. Diseases that weaken the memory by the destruction of brain-tissue, are especially unfavorable to the recollection of events that occurred in the periods immediately previous to the sickness. Remote events may be retained with distinctness, while those of intervening years are wiped away. When memory is restored, its power returns in the reverse order. The more remote events are first recalled. A simple waste of tissue would seem to be liable to interfere with one set of relations as quickly as with another. The law of mind, however, that the power to retain impressions is proportioned to their first strength and to their reiteration seems to hold in this method of restoration. These facts go to show that physiology is not prepared, I will not say to offer an explanation of the phenomena of memory, but even to point out with certainty and fulness the changes in the brain coincident with the changes of this power. A general dependence of all our powers on the vigor of this, their common instrument, is the brief summation of its knowledge. Language like the following, conveys no intelligible idea : "All that has so far been said respecting the different nervous centres of the body cannot fail to demonstrate the existence of memory in the nervous cells which lie scattered in the heart, in the intestinal walls, in those that are collected together in the spinal cord, in the cells of the sensory and motor ganglia, and in the ideational cells of the cortical layers of the cerebral hemispheres."—*Maudsley's Physiology and Pathology of the Mind*, p. 182.

What a famous stroke of explication — "ideational cells!" What a liberal distribution of recollection from the sole of one's feet to the crown of his head! Surely forgetfulness is inexcusable under such endowments.

§ 2. There are other theories of memory not so crude as these physiological ones, yet as deficient in proof, and resting back almost equally though somewhat more subtly on physical analogies. Of this character is that one elaborately and repeatedly enforced by Hamilton. He affirms "that

an energy of mind being once determined, it is natural that
it should persist, until again annihilated by other causes.
This in fact would be the case were the mind merely passive in the impression it receives; for it is a universal law
of nature, that every effect endures as long as it is not
modified or opposed by any other effect. But the mental
activity, the act of knowledge of which I now speak, is
more than this; it is an energy of the self-active power of
a subject, one and indivisible; consequently a part of the
ego must be detached or annihilated, if a cognition once
existive be again extinguished. Hence it is, that the problem most difficult of solution is not how a mental activity
endures, but how it ever vanishes." Is not this notion of
the necessary persistence of force referable exclusively to
physical forces? What is the proof of its applicability to
mental action? The facts of mind inquired into on their
own basis, seem to indicate quite the opposite conclusion.
He proceeds: "If it be impossible that an energy of mind
that has once been, should be abolished without a lacera-
tion of the vital unity of the mind, one and indivisible,—
on this supposition, the question arises, How can the facts
of our self-consciousness be brought to harmonize with this
statement, seeing that consciousness proves to us that cognitions once clear and vivid are forgotten? The solution
of this problem is to be sought for in the theory of obscure or latent modifications. The disappearance of internal energies from the view of internal perception does not
warrant the conclusion that they no longer exist." "All
the cognitions which we possess, or have possessed, still
remain to us—the whole complement of all our knowledge
still lies in our memory; but as new cognitions are continually pressing in upon the old, and continually taking
place along with them among the modifications of the ego;
the old cognitions, unless from time to time refreshed and

brought forward, are driven back, and become gradually fainter and more obscure. The mind is only capable at any one moment of exerting a certain quantity or degree of force. This quantity must, therefore, be divided among the different activities, so that each has only a part, and the sum of force belonging to all the several activities taken together, is equal to the quantity or degree of force belonging to the vital activity of mind in general. This obscuration can be conceived in every infinite degree, between incipient latescence and irrecoverable latency. The **ob**scure cognition may exist simply out of consciousness, so that it can be recalled by a common act of reminiscence. Again, it may be impossible to recover it by an act of voluntary recollection, but some association may revivify it enough to make it flash after a long oblivion into consciousness. Further, it may be obscured so far that it can only be resuscitated by some morbid affection of the system; or finally, it may be absolutely lost for us in this life, and destined only for our reminiscence in the life to come."

The view, whose salient points with large omissions are here indicated, is analogical, is purely theoretical, is beset with internal difficulties, and is unable to explain the phenomena that call it forth. (1) It is analogical. It assumes that the laws of physical forces pervade mental facts. It does not even **stop to** inquire how far or with what modifications this diffusion of forces takes place in the brain. It accepts at once the principles of physics, as applicable in the boldest way, to processes of mind. (2) It is purely theoretical, for its alleged facts all lie in the unapproachable region of sub-consciousness, whose existence is not established, much less the details of its phenomena. (3) It is vexed with difficulties of its own, greater than the difficulties it is brought forward to remove. It rests on a physical idea of force, but cannot consistently carry out that idea. If

no force, no activity can be lost, how shall an act of mind
fade out of consciousness? What is this fading away, if it
be not a loss of force? Or, again, if the mind have but a
given amount of force to bestow, and each act takes a portion, how long will it be before its stock of power will be
exhausted? Or, if this power is divided up into a multiplicity of acts, and previous acts, therefore, are weakened
in their impressions, does not this imply a withdrawal in
part of activity from earlier actions, and if a partial withdrawal is possible, what renders complete removal impossible? Again, what is meant by recalling an obscure cognition? Is it simply infusing more power into it, deepening
the action already present, or, is it a new act of mind by
which we direct attention to it, and bring it to the light?
Must this new act also, in turn, subsist forever, still farther
sub-dividing the power of the mind? These and many like
questions are pertinent to this semi-physical theory, and
show it to be unintelligible, not to say preposterous. It has
no coherence and completeness in itself. (4) Nor does it
explain the difficulties which the facts of memory present,
and which call it forth. Indeed, these phenomena are every
way more comprehensible than the solution of them thus
offered. The act of recollection still remains, and is certainly no more intelligible because we suppose somewhere,
in some out-of-sight region of the mind, is lurking a previous
act, which this new one fastens upon and brings forward.
What relation do these distinct co-existing acts, the recalling
and the recalled, the captor and the captive, bear to each
other? How do they together constitute memory? Recollection seems to be as single, simple an effort of mind, as
perception or thought in the first instance. There is no occasion, because memory is an act of *recollection*, to put either
in the mind or out of the mind, in an independent self-exist-
ent form, the exact thing recollected. A dead man can be

remembered as easily as a living one, a defunct thought **as** readily as one that has not passed **away.** Indeed, we do not see why any other needs to be **recalled. So far** as the act has not passed from **consciousness, it** calls for no recollection ; so far as it has, it is lost **to** the mind, and the power to restore it involves the whole mystery. These words, restore, recall, resuscitate, are not to be **allowed** to mislead **us** by their physical imagery. The state recalled exists anew in **the** primitive, simple, inexplicable act of memory **;** **a** movement of mind as much of its own kind, and with its own force, as **the** first act **of** perception ; and as independent, save that the occasion for it is found in the existence of previous states of consciousness. If acts of mind could be shown to the fire-flies passing from light into darkness, and darkness into light, with patient and inexhaustible alternations, it might be to the purpose ; but if there **must** still be a distinct act of recollection, either to **go in search** of other acts and restore them, or when **they are present to** remind us of their previous presence, such an act involves the entire difficulty, and to be really anything, it must be a fresh handling of an old topic, differing from the first in **that** the mind knows it to be a second state of consciousness, **and** subject to the conditions of such a state. **To re-**experience **sensations** and recollect them, are **quite different** things. **Much** is written concerning the last, which at most would be applicable to the first only. Under this philosophy, **we should** be able neither to **distinguish** between (1) the lingering of perception in an irritable organ and memory ; nor (2) between memory **and** repeated perception. **A** peculiar, primitive power is present in memory as in every other act of mind, and as a simple act, it admits and calls for no explanation. To foist on such states of consciousness, ultimate and complete in themselves, conjectural analogical explanations, is to make the simple and plain, complex and obscure, is to darken counsel with words. If we would explain memory by its own facts, it would be our true empiricism. To create difficulties by the introduction of physical analogies into a field alien to them, and to seek their explication by a farther importation of imaginery states is a palpable violation of the principle of original, simple induction in each department of inquiry. It is a most vicious *a priori* method, disguised under the form of empirical investigation.

§ 3. We need to distinguish memory from certain things with which it is in result allied. Association may restore facts to the mind with no direct effort of recollection, indeed, in hours of idle revery, with scarcely a distinct observation of their previous presence. This indolent flow of thought, mingling past, present, future, blending the real and the fanciful, submitting itself to the native cohesion of events and desires, is remembering, precisely as it is thinking. It is neither the one nor the other, consecutively, tensely, clearly; but is merely a succession of mental movements, holding on to each other, under a feeble impulse of pleasure, by accidental connections of thought, memory, fancy, acting the part of nimble servitors in this feast and repose of the desires. Association in large part rests upon memory, yet this easy natural movement of the mind, along certain trails of imagery which have been established by previous experience, serves to disguise the action of memory which underlies it. A certain sequence of impressions may be the result of many previous examples, yet directly recall no one of them, when, in the lazy flow of thought, the mind passes this way, using once more groups of conceptions which the entire past life has been combining. Much therefore rests upon memory in which its action is so far from being prominent, that its presence is hardly discerned. Much is thought to be origi-

nal which is not so, because the memory has restored it
stripped of the time, place and circumstances of its acquisition.

Habit, a permanent union by repetition of certain states
with certain acts, often closely unites itself with memory.
Words which have been very frequently uttered in a fixed
order can be repeated with a rapidity and slightness of
attention which hide the act of memory. We are said to
recite them **by rote.** There is here doubtless muscular
and nervous training as well as recollection. The facility
gained in any lengthy process by repetition is of this
double character. The memory itself, however, seems in
most cases to require the lapse of a certain time, and a
certain frequency of recurrence, to make its action rapid
and spontaneous. We readily repeat in the morning **what**
was recited with difficulty the evening **before,** and few
can acquire a literary composition for easy, accurate rehearsal in the period immediately preceding its delivery.
The same effort, scattered through several days, is far more
effectual.

The growth of the mind is also to be distinguished in
its effects from the action of memory. Mental phenomena
**are** so blended that the predominant is by no means the
exclusive element. Later movements of mind are not **mere**
counterparts of earlier ones. A better grasp of premises,
and more insight into them; conclusions more complete
and decided, belong to the thinking powers, as they are
strengthened and enlarged by use. This fact of growth is
an ultimate one. We know it, and through familiarity it
seems simple to us, without our understanding its grounds.
It is something more than memory. We are not merely
wiser, with more acquired knowledge; we are stronger,
able to make an increasingly effective use of what we
know. Memory and growth are very closely related. The

accumulated stores of the mind are the condition of its expanded action, and this increased action gives new significance to its acquisitions. It is not easy to say how far
present soundness and shrewdness of judgment are the
product of increased strength, and how far of increased
knowledge. Our reasoning powers, by easily evolving conclusions from premises, by renewing, rather than by recalling previous processes of thought, may closely resemble the
memory in their action. We may seem to recollect an
argument, to remember a proposition, when in fact we are
merely tracing again the steps of reasoning of which it is
constructed. Historical facts also, as our information is
enlarged, cluster together, and are held in the mind with
less tension of memory than while they remained comparatively few and scattered. A knowledge of their dependencies enables us to reach one from another, to mingle
reasoning with memory, and hold the entire group by the
double ties of deduction and recollection.

Memory is the simple power of recalling the past in
our intellectual experience. We have no occasion for the
double division of a conservative and a reproductive power.
We know nothing of any conservation save as we choose
to infer it from reproduction. The first, without the last,
can give no ground of inference even wherewith to establish its existence. Reproduction is the only process that
comes under our observation. We do know that the mind
recalls its previous states, but how this is done, or whence
these states come, are inquiries either impossible of answer,
or impertinent to the subject. Indeed, the tendency to ask
them, we regard as an unphilosophical one, pushing back
of simple ultimate action, and this under the analogies of
the material world. Of course those who enter on the
wholly theoretical ground of the manner of the mind's possessing its phenomena may find occasion for a theoretical,

conservative faculty, to do the theoretical work assigned it.
Of the presence and action of such a faculty, we directly
know nothing, and find its existence a matter of inference.

If then we confine our attention to actual phenomena **of**
mind, and believe it quite as intelligible that the mind
should repeat states in the interim inexistent, as to recall
states that have hidden themselves in some region of **de-**
funct ghostly impressions, we have only occasion **for one,**
to wit, the reproductive faculty. What becomes of a
thought after we cease to think it, of a feeling after we
cease to feel it? From what quarter of the universe do
they return to us when recollected? are inquiries whose
only **gleam** of meaning comes to them **from** material
fancies. A power, that should simply hold without being
able to recall facts, would be an odd power, a power not
powerful enough to show its own existence, an activity too
indolent to give the least scintillation wherewith to indicate
its whereabouts; a gratuitous and ridiculous faculty.

§ 4. The two qualities of a good memory are said to be
strength and quickness. These are thought to be separable,
to exist in various degrees in different persons. **Is not**
this conclusion somewhat akin to the double division of
the power? and does it not arise from not directing attention exclusively to **the** action of memory? A strong
memory is a quick memory, and a quick memory is so far
forth a strong, retentive one. We sometimes fully recall
things which at first we could not remember, the mind
struggling with obscure recollections till the facts one by
one come to the light. This result is only partially the
fruit of memory; it is largely reached by reasoning, by
closely questioning the facts that are retained, and making
them witnesses for the recovery of the remainder. When
the reflective, philosophical habit of mind predominates,
memory may have the appearance of retentiveness without

celerity; but it is an appearance rather than a fact. The weakness of the memory is covered by the strength of the elaborative faculty, and results are at length reached which the memory vouches for, but could not alone have plucked from oblivion. The action of simple memory is aided by other powers and facts of mind. Our recollection fails us, and we strive to grapple the lost fact by inference. We say it must have been so and so, because these were the preceding causes, and these the accompanying circumstances. A clue thus given to memory, the detached fact lays aside its disguise, comes forth from its hiding-place, and confesses itself found. Or the mind keeps in the region of the lost fact. It directs its attention to every resembling or adjunct object, hoping by some thread of association to restore to consciousness the furtive event. The mind thus, in the weakness of retention, avails itself of the logical cohesion of thought, betakes itself from one position to another, lingers in the neighborhood of the lurking impression, to see if from some vantage-ground, from some sudden disclosure, the memory may not again seize it. This, however, is not recollecting, it is trying to recollect, bringing other powers and attitudes of the mind to the assistance of memory. Such a memory is neither strong nor quick. The one quality, therefore, of memory is strength, indicated by quickness; while what has been termed strength of memory, as opposed to quickness, is to be referred to reflection.

Memory presents different phases of power. Some persons recall one class of things easily, other persons another class. Some have a verbal memory, while others are very deficient in this respect, finding it perhaps much easier to retain figures than names. The idea alone is treasured by one mind, while the exact expression is borne away by another. These variations seem chiefly due to different degrees of strength, and the different degrees of interest attendant on diversity of powers. The memory that refuses to retain the precise language is relatively a feeble one, while the thought itself is lodged in the mind as **much by** the force of the truth, by logical connections, by the interest of the statement, as by mere recollection. The power of recalling words, especially proper names, is a good test of the strength of memory, since these, detached from all connection, are thrown as a dead weight on the mind. Weakness of memory may sometimes exist in connection with considerable ease in the retention of figures, since a mathematical habit of mind and general interest and power in this department may concentrate attention on its data, and increase the ability to retain them. The diverse forms of memory are chiefly to be ascribed to diverse tastes and habits, and the interest and attention which accompany them. A tendency once established toward a given pursuit reacts strongly on all the faculties engaged in it, making them peculiarly vigorous and effective in that direction.

Though memory looks for aid to all those mental powers which unite and correlate ideas, it is by no means dependent on them. Its most vigorous and characteristic efforts are almost wholly independent of association. It is when its native strength fails, that association comes prominently forward. If the memory could act always with entire vigor, it would pick up at random, by any arbitrary, **momentary** law, the **facts** of **past** experience, not collocating them by any of the accepted connections of thought. This, in cases of rare power, it freely does. A person has been found, who, after a single rehearsal, could recite hundreds of words thrown promiscuously together, could repeat them backward, could **give** every fifth, sixth, eighth word, could deal with them exactly as if they lay before the eye. Herein is the perfect, the typical power of memory, and it derives no assistance from association. Even when the influence of association is most manifest, it is only the order of the conceptions which can be accounted for by it, not their actual restitution to the mind. The power to do this work still remains simple and primitive. We need, therefore, no doctrine of latent states to account for the remote character of two facts reported by the memory; nor a belief in a great crowd of thoughts, always present to the mind, of only a small number of which we are distinctly conscious, in order to explain the celerity with which memory produces an appropriate event, or matter pertinent to our state of feeling, or to the argument in hand. The conception that the memory has already partially evoked from limbo a great crowd of facts, and is moving among them as so many *personæ dramatis*, making ready by various laws of association to produce the next fit player on the open stage of consciousness, entirely transcends the facts, is no more intelligible, is less simple, than the statement nakedly accepted, that memory, under the suggestion of a direct question put by a stranger, or at the intimation of the thoughts with which the mind itself is occupied, can directly reach and repeat pertinent previous experiences, and thus enable us to regain, without constantly maintaining, former phases of activity. In many of the connections of association, there is no potency whatever wherewith to restore a missing member, except as memory gives them that potency.

Strength of memory depends much on original endowment, though this faculty is as readily cultivated as any of our powers. It comes to do what we patiently insist on its doing. The acquisition of a few names in botany or in ornithology may at the outset be very difficult, yet in the end memory may retain many hundreds with comparative ease. In extemporary discourse the line of thought comes by practice to be recalled with scarcely an effort; yet when the occasion has passed, **it at once** and entirely slips from the mind. To insist early and strenuously on the tasks assigned the memory **is** necessary to its efficiency. Yet in spite of cultivation, there will be very striking differences in this power. Some will retain lengthy discourses **after one** or two readings, while others **can scarcely repeat with accuracy** the shortest production.

A powerful memory is **a great aid to** other faculties, though its strength **does not** seem necessarily connected with the strength of any other portion of our intellectual endowments. Memory **is** liable **to** usurp the office of reflection, **and** to overshadow the native growth of the mind with the luxuriant **products of other intellects.** Indeed, there come these compensations **to** a memory comparatively weak, that we are thrown **back** more habitually on our own resources; that the thoughts find free play, the statements of others on the same subject, and their methods of treatment not being vividly present; **and that we** make all acquisitions minister to the **vigor and** growth of thought, to **its** nutritive processes rather than to those formal posses-**sions** which are **held in** a somewhat lifeless way in the **memory.** We are thus compelled to enlarge and develop our strength by consumption and digestion rather than by retention. **Yet with a** truly vigorous mind, that cannot be overborne and burdened by the thoughts of others, a strong memory is **a most valuable power.**

Memory is cultivated in several ways; first, **by persist-**ency and vigor of purpose **in** its use, by requiring *positively* what has been *distinctly* committed to it. If its burdens can be made wise, definite, and reasonable, and the mind return patiently to the effort of bearing them, the memory will take up its tasks **with** increasing ease, and become **more** and more trustworthy. **If, on** the other hand, ma-

terial in large quantities, in an unanalyzed, vague form is
put upon it, and then its delinquencies are passed carelessly
over, it will become increasingly slovenly and unreliable in
its work.

The second method of increasing the strength of the
memory is found in deepening the original impressions
which objects make upon us.  Lively attention, active
thought, sincere interest, these are the conditions under
which the mind truly receives, and so easily retains the
matter before it.  Inertness, sluggishness, and wavering
attention, in weakening first impressions, weaken also the
memory.  As, then, our interests is not likely to be universal, a concentration of it, an exclusion as well as an inclusion of topics, are needful, lest in dividing we weary and
waste our forces, and make our faculties negligent.

The third aid to memory is reiteration.  Facts which
we are determined to retain, we must return to frequently,
till we thoroughly possess them.  The paths of memory are
to be made smooth and hard by use.  If we pass on to new
material without returning often to the old, a process of
separation and disintegration follows rapidly upon growth.
We need to integrate and re-integrate our material by re-
sorting often to first principles.  Thus, while we build
layer upon layer around the core of knowledge, we are not
to allow the circulation of thought to desert this heart-
wood, till it is compacted in perfect strength, and lies within, an insensible presence of power.  The memory above
other faculties demands reiteration, repeated integration of
its material.

A fourth and yet more fundamental condition in the
cultivation of memory is that our knowledge shall be made
logical, coherent, and fairly complete in the departments it
covers.  The logical relations of truth greatly support the
memory.  If the topic is incapable of close connections, yet

many facts near to each other in one field, as in any portion
of history or of science, are more easily held fast than a
few. It may be doubted whether a wise progress in knowledge, notwithstanding the rapid multiplication of facts, is
not a relief to the memory. One truth unites itself to another, and all are knit together by so many and so rapidly
increasing relations, that we have various approaches to
each distinct fact. Nothing is of more moment in reference
to its own value than this interior coherence of knowledge,
nor in reference to the mastery of the memory over it.
Detached facts are like sand. We may fill the hand with
it, and firmly grasp it, yet it begins at once to ooze out at
every crevice till the palm is left empty. Moisten it, till
it coheres in a ball, and the open hand will hold with ease
twice the quantity.

Mnemonics, or artificial associations as aids of memory,
is not to be commended, as its application is at best limited,
and tends to divert attention from those inherent dependencies an observation of which should accompany us everywhere.

§ 5. The second faculty belonging to the understand-
**ing** is that of imagination. By the imagination we mean
the power which the mind has of presenting to itself vividly
**all** phenomenal forms. Whatever has assumed, or is capable of assuming, this **phenomenal** character, whether in the
external or internal world, is an object of imagination. A
landscape, a melody, **a state of** consciousness, a character
may all be imagined, that is, vividly presented to the mind
under their own appropriate forms. As sight is the most
full, elaborate and distinct of the senses, giving many particulars, and cutting them apart by sharp outlines, the pictures which arise under this form of perception are especially clear and impressive, and hence have given the
name imagination to the faculty which paints them, and

have furnished the general type of its action. Nothing however seems unapproachable to the imagination which is capable of phenomenal existence, that is, of appearing and hence re-appearing in consciousness. Thought, let it be observed, enters the imagination as it enters consciousness, merely as a phenomenon. The moment we begin to think, that is to judge, we renew thought as a fact, and do not restore it as an image.

Imagination is simply a general, representative power, and can not therefore work alone without working at random. The powers which direct it, which employ it in their service, are memory, appetite, desire, the æsthetic and the moral taste.

By its aid we restore vividly, that is under a living form, the past; we intensify the present, filling it with the imagery of pleasure; we reach toward the possible, the future, in a higher conception of achievement and character. Imagination is so blended with memory in a portion of its action, that we should hardly separate the two, were it not for other fields independent of recollection on which it enters. It, like memory, is instrumental, and waits the use and guidance of other faculties.

§ 6. A theory of the imagination accepted by philosophers so diverse as Hamilton and Bain, is expressed by the latter in these words:

" *The renewed feeling occupies the very same parts, and in the same manner as the original feeling, and no other parts, nor in any other manner that can be assigned.*" (The Senses and Intellect, page 344.) " The imagination of visible objects is a process of seeing. The musician's imagination is hearing, the phantasies of the cook and gourmand tickle the palate." (Page 352.)

The statement of Hamilton is not so unqualified, and to that degree less objectionable. Both of them, however, go much beyond our knowledge. **When a** statement so purely theoretical as this explicit, italicized dogma of Bain's, is made the foundation of a complete explanation of the faculty involved, **an** explanation resting entirely upon its truth, **we** see that metaphysicians of the old school are **not** the only ones who can put foot in air, and mount to the stars. **An** act of imagination and memory thus becomes with **the latter** another—as **indicated by the** clause, "**nor in** any other manner"—unmodified perception, lingering **or** reawakened in the organ of sense.

The proof of their explicit assertions is found by Bain and Hamilton in the fact, that the organs of action are evidently affected by the images present to the mind in imagination as they would be by the objects themselves, only in a less degree, and **that with a loss of any** of the senses the power of imagination disappears in a corresponding direction. The examples adduced under the first **ar**gument are of **a** kind not leading directly to the conclusion in issue; but are quite as explicable on other grounds. "A dog dreaming sets his feet a going, and sometimes barks." "Some persons of weak nerves can scarcely think **without** muttering—they talk to themselves." "Anger **takes** exactly the same course in the system, whether it be at a person present, or at some one remembered or imagined." Suppose **our** fancies **to** be pure intellectual acts, independent of the senses, should we not expect these results? The nervous flow outward on the active, related powers would naturally be secured, though the senses were quiescent, if that state of mind were present which occasions this result. These examples furnish no proof, that the organs of perception are affected, and are the source of this tendency to movement.

Farther examples are quoted from Müller. "The mere idea of a nauseous taste can excite the sensation even to the

production of vomiting," We think the more correct statement would have been, the mere idea of a nauseous taste
can produce vomiting. In this form, it loses all pertinence
as proof. The active results follow from the idea, the
action in the brain, and not from the sensation. We do
not in such cases suppose that we taste the disgusting food,
but only that we conceive its taste. "The mere sight of a
person about to pass a sharp instrument over glass or porce-
lain, is sufficient, as Darwin remarks, to excite the well-
known sensation in the teeth."

Now the setting of the teeth on edge, is an effect of
nervous action, and may as fitly follow that action when
coming in connection with the imagination, as when occasioned by the senses. The fact that fancy affects the nervous system, and hence the muscular system, in a manner
allied to that of the senses, no more proves the identity of
imagination and sensation than a fright at a ghost proves
the existence of a ghost. These examples do not reach
deep enough to do the work required of them. They only
show the results to be in a measure the same, whether the
object be imagined or perceived, whether the initiative is
from within or from without : whereas, they ought to show
the organs of sense so affected in what we call imagination
as to be a sufficient cause of the effects which follow.
Against this, mental and physical experience testifies. (1)
We distinguish easily between acts of imagination and perception, both in the character and locality of the activity.
An impression that lingers in the organ, or renews itself
there, implies disease. The organ shows its power by a
quick, exact response to external conditions only. (2) We
observe, also, that the action occasioned by the images of
fancy in most men is slight and ineffectual when contrasted
with the results of real perception. Great diversities in
character hinge just here, on the predominance of the senses-

or of the imagination; the latter type being peculiarly divorced from action. Action may arise directly from stimuli in the senses ; or indirectly from the states of mind evoked by sensations ; or again **from states** of mind called out by memory or by imagination. **This** partial agreement of effects does not imply an identity of the causes involved in them.

Neither do we find that that which paralyzes the organ **of sense** necessarily and immediately destroys the power to imagine **objects which enter** through that sense. A deaf Beethoven **can compose** music, a blind Milton, blind by disease of the nerve, can write an **epic.** That there should **be a slow** decay **of** the imagination **in** connection with the early loss of a **sense** is natural, **almost inevitable.** The requisite material ceases **to be** presented **to the** mind; present possessions, impressions, fade out, and the objects of the remaining senses **usurp** the place of the lost sense. The doctrine, as stated above, would require that blindness, when an affection of the nerve, should be followed by the instant and entire loss of the images of visible objects. The facts signally contradict the theory, and the theory fails. The blind man deals with all the imagery of the eye, walks the streets, and uses, to the full, the language of vision. Indeed, **in** the strict form in which it is stated, this dogma approaches **an** absurdity. If I imagine a visual object on the retina of the eye, **"in the** same manner " in which I see it, my imagination should be confined **to the** open eye, and **be** identical with the impression of objects actually seen. Otherwise it must be conceded, that in one case the agency affecting the retina acts from without, and in the other from within, in itself a grave difference. The imagination of feelings, tastes, odors, should also be as clear and deci-sive as the conception of the objects of sight. Quite the reverse is true, **a** fact entirely intelligible on the ground

that imagination is an intellectual power independent of
the organs of sense ; as the intellectual element decidedly
predominates in sight, while the lower senses are single and
emotional in their character, and thus yield less matter to
the fancy.  We take a certain pleasure in drawing attention
to the airy strides of one who so thoroughly sympathizes,
as does Bain, with Positive Philosophy.  Not having set
to ourselves the task of preparing the way for the insensible
growth of intellectual out of physical phenomena, we can
accept the impression of consciousness, that an act of imagination is one of imagination, quite distinct and distinguishable from every form of perception, clear or obscure.
We feel no more interest in discussing imagination under
perception, than perception under imagination.  In honest
induction, we can take what we find.  Nor is the intelligibility of our philosophy any the less in thus regarding the
mind as an independent first cause of its own action than
in filling it with echoes, and mild vibrations, and the lingering, trembling, sobbing, swelling cadences of sensation,
as of a harp unable to part with the harmony that has
once run along its strings.  These transferred analogies are
the most inexplicable of all explications.  Mind and matter
present plain phenomena, each in its own way cognizable ;
but mental movements that are semi-physical, and physical
movements that rise into and are productive of thought,
have no organ whatever for their apprehension.  Seen with
the eye, they become purely material ; known by consciousness, they become at once and completely transcendental.
Two things known as unlike, each by its own faculty, are
far better known than when affirmed to be alike, with no
common ground or common origin for their comparison.

§ 7.  Whatever is thought of the nature of imagination,
its influence and office are not doubtful.  It is a great in-
tensifier of emotions.  Acting under the impulse of desire,

it brings vividly forward the means of gratification, and kindles the passions into a flame. **The** mind occupied by furious lusts, becomes, till imagery is displaced by reality, the lodgment of a Tantalus. Unreal phantoms provoke the eye, stimulate the appetites, and, in the grasping, sink back into tormenting shadows. The mind is consumed momentarily in the red heat of its own passions, which **it can** neither quell by authority, nor quench by indulgence. **Mis**ery in all forms uses the imagination as a means wherewith to irritate and exasperate itself. Discouragement and fear evoke troubles beyond the reality. Not only is the ship battered by the waves about it, the vista of a yet more angry ocean is opened up, and it plunges on from shock to shock, the heart sinking in despair more in view of what is to be, than of what is. Disappointment aggravates the evils it suffers by exaggerated pictures of the good to have been attained. One feels the heat of the desert, and thinks of cooling streams.

On the other hand, pleasure owes its hilarity, its intoxication very much to the imagination. It spreads the rosy, blithesome atmosphere of the present to the very horizon, and makes the distance gorgeous with a play of light, beyond what approach will verify. The eccentricity, the boldness, the poetic inspiration, the enthusiasm of the mind find expression and play chiefly in the fancy. **By it we** cease to be roadsters along the regular route of existence; we dart ahead, or fall behind, or turn to the right, or to the left; we rise upward, tread paths of air, and return only at intervals to the actual, where the foot-sore senses and judgment are plodding on.

It is evidently this faculty that is yoked to the car of the mind in sleep, and wheels it, in ranging fashion, through possible and impossible scenes, through weird imagery, recollections interlacing fancies in **strange and** monstrous guise. The very fact that the senses find such complete repose in sleep while the imagination is so bold, dashing and wayward, would seem to indicate that the action of the two is far from identical. The same is true in reverie, in day-dreaming. The mind closes its senses, takes out these airy steeds of fancy, throws the rein on their necks, and gives itself up to the luxury of motion along ways in which the friction of ruts, the jar of collisions, and delay of wheels lifting slowly in the mud are not experienced.

The imagination also greatly aids our thoughts. The judgment and the fancy are frequently regarded as faculties somewhat opposed to each other in their action. The ease and certainty of the first, in some of its most severe and logical processes, depend very much on the clearness and precision of the second. In solid geometry, in many branches of the higher mathematics, in mechanics, in astronomy, a first condition for the ready and safe movement of the thoughts, is a clear unwavering image of the solid, or of the objects and their relations, involved in the problem. If the subject of contemplation cannot be easily evoked, and quietly held in the field of imagination, the judgment is at once at fault in establishing its connections, and gropes in the darkness, like one blindfolded. Scientific inquiry also, the tracing of analogies, the observation of resemblances, are greatly aided by a vivid imagination, presenting distinctly to the mind a large circle of objects. The memory is but very partial in its action without this faculty, and the mind, in the weakness of representation, is compelled to take up objects singly, to the oversight of dependencies which might furnish the key of success. The imagination, then, is as essential to philosophy as to poetry. The difference, lies in the two cases, not so much in the number of objects presented, as in the manner and purpose of consideration.

Most immediate and powerful is the influence of the

imagination on action. The pleasures, disappointments, regrets, admonitions of the past, keep company with the mind in that living way which makes them effective counselors through this faculty; and, as the wisdom of the present is chiefly the gleanings of the past, our immediate purposes its ripened conclusions, the pictures of the fancy are as the reflectors which gather the otherwise diffused, fugitive light, and pour it all in on the working-point. But **it** is in the ideals of action and character, which are always distinctly present in noble minds, and hardly wholly disappear even with the lowest, that the most constant and valuable function of the imagination is seen. Through a conception of that which is more desirable in ends, more skillful in means, more wise in action, more graceful and winning in method, more **pure and holy in** purpose, more benignant and beautiful in presentation, imagination furnishes an embodiment of the truth nearest **us, becomes an** angel of light running before us, guiding our steps, scaling for us every steep of excellence, dropping back upon **us** words of encouragement and hope. To be destitute of **an** ideal, is to want the best motive of effort, is to lose direction, **is** to lack momentum, is to be dead, passively preyed on by the forces that have clutched us. Evil and death admit this inertia, goodness and life do not; and an imagination that looks out on fields of light that open vistas into the paradise of hope becomes an essential to all high resolve **and** cheerful effort. If the imagination is captivated with the past renewing **its** life with an art more cunning than that which first spread its **colors, we have** the poetical temperament; if the imagination **keeps close** at home in the present, it gives the practical disposition; or if it pushes out with a noble impulse of exploration and improvement into the future, it discloses to the full the spiritual force of man.

§ 8. The strength of the imagination, aside from original gift, (1) depends on exercise. This faculty cannot fail to be called forth ; the point of interest is chiefly the direction and degree of its employment. When made to minister to the judgment chiefly, it seems to be somewhat overshadowed by that graver power, and its action oftentimes appears to be less than it really is. Philosophy may be as impassioned as poetry. When, on the other hand, the fancy is left to construct its imagery at the beck of desire, bound down to no useful artistic end, it leaves the mind extravagant in its conceptions, wayward and fickle in its purposes. Persons characterized by the unguarded, ungoverned action of this faculty, are inefficient and visionary. The most perfect and exclusive training of the imagination, is found in the fine arts. Here it is put to its boldest, yet most restrained and governed efforts. The sense of the beautiful calls it forth, and guides it, and the combined vigor and poise of its action yield the highest works of art, the statue, painting, cathedral. The energetic exercise of our intellectual powers, especially elicit this faculty. All forms of expression seek its lustre. (2) The power of the imagination is also increased by a cultivation of the senses. These give it material. If physical and mental phenomena are appreciatively received in the first instance, the imagination will restore them with corresponding clearness. The imagination is thus closely associated with the sensitive force and sportive freedom of the mental life.

There is, in this connection, a very misleading use of the word conception, to which we wish to draw attention. That an idea is conceivable or inconceivable, is constantly brought forward in philosophical discussion as a reason for its acceptance or rejection. There are other uses of the word to which we shall revert later, but the use which connects conception with imagination, and calls that conceivable which can be imagined, and that inconceivable which does not respond to this faculty, is a frequent and deceptive one. As the imagination deals only with the phenomenal, to say that a thing is inconceivable, is only to say, that it is not of a phenomenal character, not presentable in its essence under a phenomenal form. This may very well be, and yet the idea be one that is to find acceptance. It may be offered and urged as one that is not phenomenal, but is of a direct, intuitive character. To say of such an idea, that it is inconceivable, is simply to restate what is avowed, indeed insisted on, concerning it. It is the essential character of an inner intuition, that it should not be an object of experience, and therefore not capable in the fancy of assuming this form. In this sense of the word, the truth of a judgment even is inconceivable. The act of judging is conceivable, the objects to which it pertains are conceivable, but the truth itself of the judgment is inconceivable. If it were so, we should require no judgment. The act of conceiving or imagining, would be sufficient, and would include in itself the entire process of reaching the truth. The judgment is superadded to the imagination for the very reason that new matter is and may be amenable to it. Not to be able to conceive a thing is simply not to be able to imagine it, and the field of imagination is, in the outset, put down by us as a limited one. When, therefore we are by claim and concession talking of that outside of this field, the assertion disproves nothing, that the subject is inconceivable. Of course it is; if it had not been, we should not have offered it as an intuitive notion, a necessary and universal idea, but as conforming to our observation. The true stroke of overthrow directed against such notions as that of liberty, of the infinite, would be that they are conceivable, and therefore of a phenomenal character, not deeper nor more necessary. To say of such ideas, that they are inconceivable, and therefore not true, is to make that a ground of inference for their non-existence, which is in fact the result of their peculiar and permanent character. The blind might as well say, colors have no existence, because they are neither tastes, odors nor sounds, nor are they conceivable as such.

§ 9. The third power of the understanding is judgment. This is, in some sense, the most fruitful and important of all our faculties. To it, the others seem especially to minister, and, in connection with it, to fulfil their purpose. By the judgment we rationally combine and use the material furnished in perception and intuition. It is that action of the mind, by which the phenomena of sense are taken up into the light of reason, there interpreted in their necessary relations, and presented as a system of things. The judgment is the power by which we unite subject and predicate under some appropriate regulative idea. The exact meaning and force of this language may not at once be obvious, but will be unfolded by farther discussion.

Abstraction, generalization, conception, classification, analysis, synthesis, are all processes of thought, requiring no peculiar powers beyond those now mentioned. They are the results and the attendant methods of judgment, judiciously employed. The faculties of perception are not left to perceive all things promiscuously and indiscriminately. The judgment does not judge blindly, satisfied with the link of each copulation, no matter whether it lies apart, or is united into a chain with others. This power is set at work in the service of certain intellectual impulses, and works therefore consecutively with selection and rejection, with directed and conjoined effort towards the desired results. Separate judgments are thus thrown into trains of reasoning, and those judgments sought which can be made the parts of such a train. Those objects are considered, and those qualities in each object, which are, in the present connection, points of interest. Agreements are sought as links of thought, to the dismission of differences. Thus we have abstraction, the separation of one quality or relation in attention from every other; generalization, the detection of one quality, one form of action, one relation in many diverse objects; conception in its limited sense, the uniting of several qualities under one generic or specific word, to the exclusion of individual distinctions; classification, the uniting of conceptions into a complete system, covering some department of knowledge. Analysis and synthesis are the same processes differently expressed. The first process, that of abstraction, which is the foundation of the other three, is analytic; while the remaining three are synthetic. By analysis we separate concrete wholes into their intellectual **parts**; by synthesis, we recombine these parts in new ways for intellectual ends. These, then, as the various methods and fruits of a fertile judgment, require no farther attention in a discussion of faculties, but belong to logic, which treats of the laws of thought, of the several forms of activity which the one power, the judgment, presents. The extent of field and the complex results which belong to this faculty are evinced by the fact, that a distinct science is set apart to it, and the laws of thinking or judging are discussed in a separate and complete form as logic.

Very simple sentences are a *plexus* of judgments. They are primary statements in which many other statements are included. A brief affirmation has the same involution of judgments as a simple perception. The central assertion only assumes the full form of a judgment, while every adjective, adverb, conjunctional and propositional clause, every inflection, modify the primary affirmation by a subordinate statement. The giving of a name, the application of an adjective, the change of a prefix or affix are judgments. The abstract noun in its formation and in its use involves a judgment. One quality or relation is distinguished from others, and affirmed separately in its associations with them. Generalization is a similar judgment, the ascription to many things or actions of one quality or relation. Conception is the grouping of several qualities, as the *differentia* of species, genera, classes. Classification is a formation of groups in reference to each other in a field of knowledge; these groups mutually excluding each other, and conjointly covering all the facts before them, and marking their relation to each other. It involves, therefore, very many judgments, is made up of a series of judgments. Classification is the final result of inquiry into things, and if it rests, as it must ultimately rest, on the relation of forces, it is the summation of knowledge. Abstraction leads to generalization, generalization to conception, conception to classification. Analysis and synthesis accompany the entire movement, analysis being foremost in its earlier, and synthesis in its later stages.

We should observe how thoroughly the action of the judgment is a construction of relations; how exclusively the concrete fact is considered in its invisible dependencies. The whole process opens in abstraction, which is a breaking up of the concrete experience, a consideration of it in constructive parts or elements which have no separate existence. This abstraction is not only not an act of the senses, it is impossible to them, and must commence and proceed in a purely mental region; one in which relations, not sensible qualities, are the objects of consideration. Each successive step involves this same abstraction in an increasingly extended and complicated form. The conception is made up of a group of qualities which the mind is constantly shifting for purposes of more exact classification, and which have no detached existence in experience. Classification involves an extended consideration of relations that abide only before the inner eye of the mind; and thus the entire web of knowledge is spun out of a material wholly impalpable to the finest senses. Analysis yields a tenuous thread of thought, and synthesis weaves it into the invisible connections of knowledge. The material of the senses remains after observation and inquiry precisely what it was before, but perfectly new relations have been disclosed between its parts. Supersensual forces and dependencies have been put back of the visible facts, and so they are understood. The judgment, then, can do nothing with mere phenomena. These are declared by the senses. It is not till a new approach is opened up in a process of abstraction, that the relations of things are separately discussed, and the judgment combines them in an independent way for its own ends. A getting out of and beyond the senses into relations abstractly considered, is the first condition of the exercise of the judgment. But this condition involves two others, the presence to the mind through the senses of concrete material, and the power to analyze this material by the intuitive discernment of its dependencies, its primary intellectual elements. Reasoning, a series of interlocked judgments, arises from the same clear and exclusive in sight into relations, and the same ability to deal with them, both independently of concrete things, and as associated with them.

§ 10. The mind of man uses the contents of the senses simply as the raw material of knowledge. It constructs for itself many systems of arrangement, and by analysis and synthesis works up these subjects of inquiry under them. Though the world is already an orderly and beautiful thing as offered to the senses, it is none the less treated by the mind as material roughly gathered into a museum, there to be sorted and put in its place. Language is the medium of this great transformation under the constructive force of the judgment.

No sooner in the use of language was a name annexed to an object, than, by virtue of resemblances discerned though not defined between this object and other objects, the word began to enlarge its application, and to include many things within a vague circumference of likeness. This movement is so normal to the human mind, that many nouns doubtless never had a very distinct use as proper nouns; and many proper nouns began at once to expand into common nouns. The fixedness of the proper noun grows up with the fixedness of the common noun. It is quite too much to assert that all common nouns have been proper nouns, simply because this expansion in the beginning would be the prevailing line of growth. Trees seen in a grove, birds seen in flocks, and animals encountered in troops, would be named collectively or rather as a class. As words enlarged their meaning, other words would be called for under the wants of men to designate things more narrowly, and so a counter movement of restricted definition would arise. Classification would thus proceed by accident, under the variable interests and inclinations of men.

But no sooner is the mind awakened to its own processes, than all this is altered. Classes are distinctly formed and put in definite relations to each other. Among all comparable objects proper nouns are extended, and each held fast; and thus the purposes of thought and expression are subserved with increasing clearness and thoroughness. Much discussion has been had as to the precise significancy of this growth of knowledge by the mediation of language. How far are the results in the things themselves, and how far in the mind? What are the things expressed by words? If we take any common noun, as stone, the discussion is

brought to an issue by asking, What does it designate? In
an obscure form the controversy was included in the
"ideas" of Plato, those intellectual prototypes of classes.
Plato putting the constructive force of mind in the foremost
position conceived of individuals as only the variable expression of a controlling idea; as the Madonnas of Raphael
of a conception in the mind of the artist more perfect than
any one of them. Aristotle, more empirical in his bent of
mind, did not accept the idea as preceding the individual,
but as found in it. He explained things from the position
of the critic rather than of the artist. In the scholastic period this discussion gathered heat, both because of its own
subtility, and because of its relation to doctrines such as the
trinity and headship in Adam. It developed three leading
opinions, with minor shades of difference under them. The
realists, at first the more prevalent class, asserted that the
generic name expressed real generic being, of which **individuals** are variable manifestations. Thus the same water
reappears in many different waves. The nominalists, whose
earliest representative was Roscelin, and ablest representative was Occam, affirmed that we have in classes only
words and individuals. The conceptualists declared that we
**have** the general word, the conception back of this word,
and the individual things grouped under it. Though the
controversy lingers to our time, the nominalists and conceptualists prevail. The empirical school inclines to the first
opinion, and the intuitional school to the second. The
reasons are obvious.

The empiricist works up his mental facts out of the
impressions of things. Imagination, on its passive side, is a
supreme fact with him. Things repeat their impressions
and these impressions grouped by association become the
substance of knowledge. The common noun is simply a
word backed by many **images instead of** by one image.

While the statement of the conceptualist seems to most minds simple and sufficient, the nominalist succeeds in obscuring the subject afresh by an appeal to the imagination. When we use the word *horse*, it is said, we cannot realize the idea back of it, save under the image of some individual horse. The word then differs only from Bucephalus in calling up many images instead of a single image. But this is the difference between the names, John Smith and Martin Van Buren. It seems plain that the mind can and does proceed without the accompanying imagery of the imagination, and that the fact of images is not the entire fact of classification, nor the very gist of it. If we know things only by perception and imagination, the nominalist is correct; but the entire reconstruction of the world through language, by which the thoughts pass away from and transcend the senses, is in contradiction of the assertion. It is sometimes said, that we cannot think without language. This would be true under nominalism, since words and things make up the sum of being, and we must handle either one or the other. Yet it is not true, the thought always precedes by a little the word, and words follow on to hold the ground gained. There is no more certain distinction than that between words and the meaning of words, the one giving occasion to the other. If common nouns have meaning, and that meaning is present to the mind, the conceptualist is correct. The by-play of the imagination does not alter the primary fact. The mind passes rapidly through page after page of abstract terms, and scarcely reverts once to any illustrative images. It has not, therefore, been unoccupied, or occupied only with words. The mind in judgment gets as certain a hold of single qualities, as it does in the senses of concrete groups. Take such a relation as that expressed by the conjunction in the sentences, You or I must do it, You and I must do it; the mind notes them at once, and shapes its apprehension to them at once, without the aid of any image. Indeed, no image exactly covers them. The whole question resolves itself into the reality and validity of the processes of mind, expressed in abstraction, generalization, conception. Have we here a power of mind, or only the grouping of images?

§ 11. Before proceeding to speak more fully on the exact office of judgment, I wish to draw attention to one or two erroneous views becoming increasingly prevalent concerning it. Says Sir William Hamilton, "Consciousness, necessarily involves a judgment; and as every act of mind is an act of consciousness, every act of mind consequently involves a judgment. A consciousness is necessarily the consciousness of a determinate something, and we cannot be conscious of anything without virtually affirming its existence, that is judging it to be. Consciousness is thus primarily a judgment or affirmation of existence." These assertions are much too broad; especially so for the philosophy of Sir William Hamilton, that we directly know the object of perception as external. All matter in consciousness may become a subject of judgments; if it is thought about, it must become such a subject. But there is no absolute necessity that it should, by the judgment, be made an object of attention; that this faculty should play upon it; that it should more than quietly flow through the organ of sensation without producing any action of mind beyond simple perception. To say that mere, pure perception is a judgment, that "consciousness is primarily a judgment," is an affirmation wrong in form, since consciousness is the condition of mental action, and not the action itself; and erroneous in idea, since it virtually merges all mental acts or powers in one. If perception is primarily a judgment, so is feeling, so is memory, since out of each of these acts, by the same method, a judgment can easily and instantly be constructed.

Perception as perception is distinct from judgment, and may exist without it. There is nothing in the one which necessarily involves the other; though in the rational mind the one gives constant occasion to the other. Moments of perception may be moments in which objects come and go with no thoughtful attention directed to them; they are left to expire in the sensual impression they are for the instant making. In the case of the brute, is not this the habitual attitude of mind, the field of consciousness occupied with sensations with no reflection on them, or interpretation of them? Why speak at all of the power of perception, if, in later analysis, we purpose to resolve it into judgment? What may instantly spring from an act and the act itself are very different.

What also becomes of Hamilton's doctrine, that "perception affords us the knowledge of the non-ego at the point of sense," under this farther assertion, that "consciousness is primarily a judgment or affirmation of existence." Is such a judgment involved in the perception of an object? If so, we have not the doctrine of direct, external perception, but rather the view given by us of the inferential existence of the outer world. The two views would be identical, save that we do not affirm, that each single perception compels, or in that sense involves, the formal or actual inference to real, outside existence. It only gives a ground or occasion for such conclusion, which may, or may not, in a specific case, be made. If, however, we do perceive simply and purely "the non-ego at the point of sense," then that act of perception or of consciousness is not a judgment, does not include one as its primary element; or the distinction between judgment and perception disappears, and we infer, and do not in the

ordinary sense perceive, the existence of the external world.
If an act of perception, as such, gives **us** the "non-ego,"
we find no occasion for an act of judgment to do the same
thing.

The actuality and externality of the phenomena are
already present as a fruit of perception. Does not the difficulty lie here, that Hamilton has given to perception a task
impossible to it, and then, in later analysis, for a moment
forgetful of previous assertions, has made it to involve a
judgment, thereby easing it of its burden, though at the
same time losing the distinction between these two acts of
mind? The simple content of a perceptive organ is knowable, for perception is a power of knowing. It is not, however, while it remains in the sense simply, thinkable,
because thought is an additional action of judgment, nor
is it wordable, because words are **the** instruments of thought
and imply it. The only confusion here arises from the
fact, that the above assertions apply rather to the primitive
data of perception than to its acquired elements. These
have been added as the products of judgment.

A very limited and objectionable statement of that in
which judgment consists, has been much dwelt on by Herbert Spencer, and distinctly enunciated by Alexander Bain.
"What is termed judgment," says he, "may consist in discrimination on the one hand, or in the sense of agreement
on the other: we determine two or more things either to
differ, or to agree. It is impossible to find any case of judging that does not, in the last resort, mean one or other of
those two essential activities of the intellect."—*The Sense
and the intellect p.* 329. Says Hamilton: "What I have,
therefore, to prove is, in the first place, that comparison is
supposed in every, the simplest act of knowledge: in the
second, that our factitiously simple, our factitiously complex,
our abstract and our generalized notions, are all merely so

many products of comparison: in the third, that judgment, in the fourth, that reasoning, is identical with comparison."

That resemblance, or, stated on both sides, agreement and disagreement, is the sole ground of connection between subject and predicate in a judgment; that comparison is the only act of mind involved in reasoning, are conclusions quite consonant with a philosophy that derives all the data and the conditions of thought from the phenomenal world, from perception and consciousness; but is wholly at war with a philosophy that accepts those ideas which illuminate facts and make them intelligible subjects of thought, as of supersensual origin, furnished by the mind itself as adjuncts of its comprehending powers. If we deal purely with phenomena, we can only compare them, discover and assert their agreements and disagreements. If, then, we do more than this in judgment, this limited statement should recoil against the system that puts it forth, whose ultimate and consistent product it undoubtedly is. That all judgments do not rest on resemblance will appear in the analysis of the action of the mind in predication—in the office which thought performs.

We believe a judgment always to involve the direct or indirect application of a regulative idea to the phenomena included under it, and this is its peculiar feature and occasion. Using an undesirable word, judgment is the rationalizing of sensations, it is completing them in thought, through those ideas which the mind furnishes in making them objects of rational contemplation. The full force and proof of this statement can not be easily seen previous to a detailed statement and establishment of these native forms of thought; yet a little analysis may render it intelligible. Every single perception admits of a judgment, which is the product of the first action of thought upon it. This statement has no two perceptions to deal with, and therefore no ground for a comparison between them. It is simply an application to the phenomenon of a regulative idea. The finger is pierced. A single, sharp feeling is present. We say, it is painful; a judgment which, restated to give its substance distinct expression, becomes, Pain is. Here the specific experience is taken under the general notion of **ex**istence, and we call the result a thought, a judgment that may be offered to another mind. Between the idea of **ex**istence and that of pain, there is no resemblance, for I could have as readily affirmed it of a pleasure, of a color, an odor. This judgment, the type of a large class, a step by which any experience whatever receives a form of statement and becomes an intellectual product, is bringing to a phenomenon one of the regulative, formative notions pertinent to it

But I might have said—The pain is **one,** The pain lasts, The pain is here. In each of these cases, I should have brought forward a different idea, and affirmed its application in a given form to the sensation. Now, if these ideas are themselves previous sensations, then the doctrine that resemblance forms **the** substance of every judgment holds good, but not otherwise. If for instance the idea of duration be entirely distinct from the whole and every part **of the** sensation that evokes it, and is ready to be furnished by the **mind** to each of twenty or twenty thousand sensations that endure, in order that they may singly or collectively be made intelligible in this relation of time, then this judgment, **It endures, is one whose** predicate and subject are totally distinct **in** kind, received through diverse powers, and united in another relation than that of agreement by a third power. In this example **we** suppose a mastery of language, which does indeed in its acquisition imply comparison. This fact, however, does not weaken the analytic proof, since we can suppose the judgment to be present without the words to express it, **or** a present mastery of

words independent of the training which leads to it, is
essential to it, though not to the very act of judging. The
belief which identifies comparison and judgment must make
the notion of time derivable from a number of sensations ;
something in the sensations themselves, rendered discernible
and comprehensible by repetition. It would thus follow
that a single sensation could not be made the occasion of a
judgment, since there is in it no opportunity for comparison. It is a unit. The mind has nothing to bring to it,
and it abides barren in the organ of sense alone. The feeling could then no more be said to exist, than it could be
said to be unusually intense, since both assertions are alike
relative. How Hamilton, who has given his authority to a
statement so alien to the intuitive philosophy, would dispose
of the fact, that the mind puts a single perception in the
form of a judgment, a point he especially insists on, going
so far as to say, that perception necessarily involves judgment, is not evident. In the first act of perception, there
is no material present to the mind, between which to institute the comparison said to be involved in the judgment,
itself involved in the perception. To initiate such a movement Hamilton would be compelled to make his comparison between the pain and the idea of number, the
idea of time, the idea of space, the idea of existence, and
affirm at this point a resemblance, a complete abuse of
the word comparison. The objects compared are unlike
in kind, belong to alien fields, and do not admit the notion
of similar and dissimilar. In fact they must admit similarity if either, since the two are coupled in a conjunctive
judgment. Only as we regard the time, the unity, the
existence, as in some way in and a part of the sensation,
and also in and a part of the other sensations present to
the memory, can we make these judgments examples of
comparison. That these ideas cannot be thus directly dis-

covered as parts of sensation, as Spencer, Mill, and others affirm, will be further seen in a later discussion. In this class, then, of judgments, which are statements concerning single states of consciousness, it is evident that a regulative idea is united to a phenomenon, and the content of the lower organ, so to speak, taken up into the intellect. To this class also may be added those judgments in which the same idea, as existence, place, time or number, is affirmed of several phenomena; and we have our first division of judgments, those which directly unite to facts a regulative idea.

§ 12. Another form of judgment unites two distinct objects under a regulative idea. Of this character is the statement, This apple is like that apple. Under the notion of resemblance, two objects, the products of distinct sensations, are united. Here the thought-process **consists in** bringing the two together under a comprehending form or rational notion. It is to this kind of judgment, that Bain and Spencer would analyze all thought, omitting even here the essential feature of the act, that a notion is intuitively seen by the mind, under which the movement goes forward. A sensation is complete and independent in itself, and does not necessarily lead to any farther state of mind. This **it** may or may not do according to its connections. In reflex action, so-called, an inward current, that may not affect consciousness, is followed by a physical force, by an outer motor current. This inward movement may, as a sensation, enter consciousness, and may thence go forth in certain, involuntary, automatic actions; or, as a sensation, it may be taken into the processes of thought, be merged in the intellectual movement, and reappear as a voluntary act, a new and independent impulse. Now **the** sensations occasioned by the presence of two apples, may simply and directly, as in the case of a brute, draw forth

action; or they may become the occasions of thought, and
the inquiry be instituted, whether they are of one kind, or
of different kinds. For the first result there are necessarily
present appetites and senses; for the second, rationalizing
power, which is no other than the power to furnish an idea,
in this case, that of resemblance, under which an inquiry
can be instituted and a judgment formed. It is the exact
office of the judgment to apply discriminatingly, in reference to an end, these notions to the objects before the mind.
The sensations, as sensations are complete. They are not
halves; they are not uneasy, nettlesome, looking out for
mates; nor adhesive, linked, dragging something after
them; nor are they dove-tailed into thoughts, making their
succession inevitable. They might lie forever perfectly
quiet, nothing coming of them, were it not for the appetites
below them, into which they sink by physical connections;
for the eye of reason above them, into whose realm of
thought they rise, by the dropping down upon them of
judgments, through tentative inquiries prompted by its own
perception of invisible, unheard, unfelt relations. This
working up of sensations, this vitalizing of them in processes of thought, needs solution, as much so as the activity
of chemical elements previously dormant, when heat is
applied.

We know an object as red, as sour, as fragrant, through
our respective senses of sight, taste, and smell. A judgment has nothing to do with this knowledge. The first object received in any sense imparts to it a form of knowing,
in itself ultimate and inexplicable. When we meet with a
second object of a like kind, we have no new sensational
knowledge; yet we have an occasion of a judgment, which
we did not have, as regards the quality, the flavor, or odor,
or color in the first case. We say of the two, They are
the same. Now how happens it that the second sensation

has in it more than the first, to wit, this occasion **of a** judgment? As sensations they are alike; one is no more stimulating than the other and, to the sense, should yield no more than the other.

The solution lies in the fact, that the mind is able to furnish an idea, that of agreement and disagreement, infusing rational order and relations into a plurality of objects, and brings it forward for immediate application, on this the first occasion. Here the judgment finds its function and office to run between phenomena, and marshal them under notions. Of phenomena alone it could make nothing. It must have its men, and its plan of rank and regiment, and then it can construct an **army.**

Of the same character are the judgments, This is higher than that, This event is more recent than that. **In each** case objects of perception are thrown into relation with each other, by means of a regulative idea. Many, accepting the intuitive nature of the idea of space, would easily recognize the character of the judgment, This house is nearer than the mountain, who would yet fail to see the transcendental element in the kindred statement, This stone is like that rock. Evidently the mind furnishes the ground of the judgment,—the idea of the relation, as much in the one **case as in the other.** The present division of judgments **in**cludes all acts of classification, and **is a most numerous one.**

The statement, This action is right, may sometimes be one of classification, assigning **the** act by its form to a kind or class previously recognized as right. More frequently, however, it is a judgment of the first class, in which a single act is stated and interpreted under an intuitive notion. The notion right is not perceived in the action, but brought to it, discerned as a spiritual factor in it. If it had been redness that had belonged to the object, the mind must needs have waited for a second, **third,** fourth instance before it

would have said, This is red: and then the assertion would
have been one simply of classification. The perception
gives the quality, and the judgment remains quiescent till,
by repetition, it is called to the act of classification. In the
case of the right action, however, the action enters through
the senses without this quality, simply and nakedly as an
action, and the reason bringing forward a farther idea for
its explanation as the act of an intelligent and free being,
the judgment at once finds play in applying it, and says, It
is a right action. This it might do should the mind never
know another, if this act in its motives and consequences
were plainly before it. In the first class of judgments, one
limb of the predication rests on the phenomenal, the other
passes over into the purely intellectual, the transcendental.
In the second class, both abutments of the arch press back
on phenomena, but the spring and crown of it rests in
the air; the connection strikes into and returns from the
region above.

There is a third class of judgments of which the expression, The heat melts the wax, is a type. Here, under the
notion of causation, we grapple by a judgment that which
physically exists, yet never directly enters the phenomenal
world. The mind walks as one who travels on a morass,
the points of support are hidden a little below the surface.
The foot, under the quick suggestion of the eye, and the
inference of reasoning, dashes at the more stable ground,
which it never sees, and is yet able to find. The mind
could not move, did it not believe in causes, yet it never
sees a cause, or knows causes save through effects constantly
attributed to them, safely expected from them. It is not
sufficient that the mind should weave the visible into a
firm fabric of order by invisible connections it alone can
grasp; it is made to stand, and must forever stand, and all
it beholds stand with it, on invisible, intangible supports

of forces, whose existence it can verify by no sense, and must leave with its own assured conviction. Deny these supports and it must yet seek for them, and believe in them, and talk about them every moment of its life. These judgments by which we spread the phenomenal over the actual, by which we search out the streams of force, and feel the under-flow of divine power, are among the most constant and radical of any we ever make. It is evident, however, that they do not rest on resemblance merely, since the cause is never in any way phenomenally known, save through its effects, and therefore furnishes no hold for a comparison. Of course we mean the actual cause, and not the phenomenal cause, that is the effect just previous to the effect under consideration. We mean the very heat and not the taper, which is itself in its visible form an effect, and not a cause. In the third form of judgment we unite the sensible and the transient to the insensible and permanent through **a pure** intuitive movement of mind. What was understood to be, also understood in relation **to** other things that are, is now referred to hidden sources or causes. We do this under two notions. That of causation and that of spontaneity. In this third class of judgments we refer effects to causes and acts to agents. It is then the general office of judgment to unite the phenomenal and the intuitive, the perceptive and the purely intuitional elements of mind, in the rational apprehension and use of the former. Reasoning is the interlock of these judgments, a chain of these conclusions by which remote points are united, and discloses therefore no new power.

§ 13. Before passing from the judgment, we wish to mark a second use of the word conceive, leading to further obscurity. By a statement, that an idea, for instance that of infinity, is inconceivable, seems sometimes to be meant, that the judgment cannot grapple it, that it can not be

wrapt about sufficiently with logical relations, worked up as
material in the processes of thought. Very well; the judgment deals with the phenomenal under ideas, and therefore
a notion not phenomenal, and not calling for the interpretation of a farther idea, is not material for the judgment.
The judgment ought not to be able to handle it; if it were
able, a phenomenal element would therein appear, destructive of its pure intuitional character. The query still remains, however, whether such an idea may not be validly
presented to the intuitive power set apart for its apprehension, given to perform this very service? The 'incogita-
bility' of a thing may be proof of its nature, though not
necessarily of its reality or want of reality.

We are now able to see something of the relation of the
understanding to the entire mental furniture, and also of
the three powers which compose it to each other. The
understanding plays between the intuitive parts of our
nature, the physical perceptions on the one hand and the
spiritual intuitions on the other. With no absolute final
comprehension of either, it interlocks them, and comes to
a definite knowledge of their relations. This knowledge
of connections seems to us more satisfactory than that of
qualities in perception, or of ideas in intuition. We try to
make a color, an odor or the notion of existence, an object of
reflection, and can do little or nothing with it. As simple
and primitive, it eludes those relations which we are so
diligent in establishing between objects, and the mind,
perplexed by its inability to fasten and weave the web of
thought, is ready to feel that there is here no real knowledge; forgetful that an organ of sense, or an intuition gives
a new and final form of knowing. All knowledge is good
and adequate, if we know enough to recognize and accept it.
The understanding furnishes us a knowledge of relations.

The judgment, like a busy shuttle, flies between the

loose, parallel, independent lines of phenomenal being, bears with it the interlacing thread of intuition, and shortly weaves all into a firm, coherent fabric, a system of things. The steadfastness and permanence of the work are secured by memory, while its brilliancy, the vividness of its coloring, arise from imagination. We thus seem to see some reason why these faculties, and no others, are called for. The judgment, under the eye of reason, knits together facts into relations, which make them significant and intelligible, which show them to be a system of things; the memory stands by to proffer the facts, and store the fabric; while the imagination dips again in living colors these shadow products of the mind, as the sun saturates the cloud with its own hues.

§ 14. There are very important laws of thought in connection with the understanding of which but slight mention has so far been made, those of association.

Association is brought forward to explain many processes of mind; we believe that association is rather the result of these processes. Ideas, images are not associated in the mind otherwise than as it itself binds them together. Reflections in a mirror gain no coherence, have no power to restore each other. Aside from the analogy of physical habit, which is of narrow, indirect application to mental **phenomena, we** have no reason to believe that ideas as ideas can maintain a **sequence among themselves, the first idea** bringing with it the second, the second the third. It is judgment, memory, imagination that separately or in combination restore ideas and images; in these faculties, not in themselves, are found the laws of coherence. Involution, causation, resemblance are the primary connections of judgment, and time and place of the imagination and memory. When Hamilton resolves the laws of association first into simultaneity and affinity, and then into the one law of re-

dintegration he is not stating an ultimate force acting between ideas, but is falling back on the memory and judgment, and later on memory alone. Things once together in
the mind are restored again to this first relation by virtue of
memory. This restoration is memory, and is not to be explained by a power of images over the mind, but of the
mind over images.

Association, greatly enlarged as an explanatory doctrine
by Heartly, has been increasingly brought forward by later
writers as an all-inclusive law of mental phenomena. Taine
goes so far as to speak of the anterior and posterior portions
of an idea, and ideas are made to arrange themselves and
adhesively drag themselves through the mind, quite passive
in reference to them. Spencer, in his Data of Ethics, p. 109
makes this concise restatement of mental processes. "The
first of these elements, originally an excitement, becomes
a simple sensation; then a compound sensation; then a
cluster of partially presentative and partially representative
sensations, forming an incipient emotion; then a cluster of
exclusively ideal or representative sensations, forming an
emotion proper; then a cluster of such clusters, forming a
compound emotion; and eventually becomes a still more
involved emotion composed of the ideal forms of such compound emotions." Mental powers have disappeared in behalf of some assumed coherence among the molecular con-
stituents and movements of ideas; and obscure physical
images have taken the place of clear mental facts. This
power of association among images can in no way be explained except by referring it to cerebral states, that in some
way collocate and continue themselves. But these alleged
facts are unknown, obscure, inexplicable; far more so than
the facts they are brought forward to illuminate. We
know of no distinct coherence of nervous states that can be
plausibly offered as the exact equivalents of logical pro-

cesses. The connections between stimuli, sensations and muscular action are not of this order. Nor, if we were aware of such special dependencies, could these be presented to explain the connections of thought. Ideas manifestly cohere as ideas in the mind by the mind's action; they are not seen to follow each other by a physical link. There are in this doctrine of association, as very generally held, a wonderful displacement of plain facts by obscure ones, an astonishing assumption of facts, and a strange **in**sufficiency in the expositions offered.

The law of association, now so omnipotent in philosophy, has grown up slowly in connection with that empirical tendency which more and more divests the mind of power, and accumulates within it a series of impressions that carry with them their own connections. This philosophy should be able, first, to show clearly and certainly that a given cerebral state is the precise equivalent of a given mental one, and its immediate cause. Nothing approximating this has been done in a single instance. It should then show that these cerebral states have cerebral laws, by which they combine with and follow each other; and, third, that these physical connections are the exact equivalents and causes of the various relations of thoughts, feelings, and volitions to each other. This work has not been so much as entered on. The law of association is left regnant when no sufficient ground of connection has been disclosed between cerebral facts and mental facts, and even while the cerebral facts themselves are purely theoretical. If all this had been done, we should have simply a physical or organic philosophy in place of a mental one; but it has not been done. Ideas, thoughts, feelings, volitions are intangible, have no power over each other or relation to each other save those intangible ones which the mind itself, in evoking them, imparts to them. The mind makes a feeling to be a feeling, and so gives it its energy. The logical insight discloses the logical relation, and so welds the conclusion to its premises. Thus also the memory renews those impalpable, vanished relations expressed by place and time, and, in doing so, sets things once more as they were.

The primary powers in association are memory and judgment. Memory restores things as they have been phenominally offered to us under the connections of time and place. Judgment unites images and ideas by the relations of resemblance, causation, involution. The imagination, working with both these faculties, combines its images under all applicable ideas. We have thus, as expressing the relation of ideas to each other under the force of memory, the law of contiguity; and under the force of judgment, the law of affinity or congenesis; and under the energy of the imagination, the law of congruity, a combined and softened application of the other two. The laws of association are convenient as forms of expression, as rendering relations on their objective side which are due to the hidden energies of mind. But when these laws are spoken of and applied as ultimate, they become another of those many disguises of words by which sequences are put for forces, and statements for reasons. The question involved is one again of the nature of mind. The seat of energy is transferred from mind to the products of mind.

# CHAPTER IV.

## The Reason.

§ 1. WE have now reached an action of mind, a faculty, whose existence is strenuously denied. Most able and thorough thinkers, patient inquirers within the field of philosophy itself, with a host of scientific investigators who bring with them predilections and reasonings suited to other departments, regard this furniture of intuitive ideas as wholly fabulous, as an unnecessary assumption in the explanation of phenomena entirely intelligible without it. Yet there is in philosophy no point of more importance, of more wide-reaching influence than this; and that, too, not merely in the department itself, but in its social and moral and religious bearings. It is vain to strive to disconnect social and religious issues from mental science. The institutions of society and the commands of God have man for their subject, and neither their defects nor their excellences can be understood without a knowledge of his nature. Indeed, the very character of those notions on which duty turns—of **right and** of liberty—are here brought under discussion; **and** also the validity of those conceptions and that reasoning on which the existence and government of God repose in our thoughts. The past attachments of our nature, its present powers **and** future hopes, are all involved in these investigations of philosophy, and more especially in that branch of them which settles the original endowments of mind, and the **degree of** its dependence on the external world. Indeed what **is** meant by the external and internal worlds, and whether either or both of them can furnish a valid proof of their being, are inquiries that are now to find settlement, or to be left unsolved doubts, unexplained fears, ultimate mysteries, drifting athwart the mind, restricting its spiritual vision, and displacing its cheerful surface-life with the shadows of deep, despairing clouds.

Yet these discussions are as subtile and perplexing as they are important; and moreover are looked on by patient plodders amid facts—most influential and serviceable men —as hopeless and futile. They regard these labors as the mere money-maker would regard another expedition to the North Pole. The whole region, to the purely scientific mind, seems one of chimeras, not dire only because increasing wisdom enables us to laugh at them. Ghosts are always unproductive, and to men ridiculous. The only touch of kindly sentiment that the student of natural science has on this subject, is the regret that so many are still found to waste a hope or a fear on such airy existences; are yet unwilling to confront daylight with open eyes, instead of owling in invisible regions for invisible things. In these fields of difficult and abstruse inquiry, we shall need to work our way slowly and patiently, confronting our adversaries fairly, ourselves convinced of the importance of the truths here hidden; sanguine as to the power of the mind to push and answer the questions most intimate to its own destiny, and repelling the scorn of ignorance with the silence of settled conviction; knowing that if ours or another's keel shall ever touch the distant shores of truth, shall ever add to the hemisphere of matter that of mind, the question, Who are fools? will be easily settled.

The ideas in dispute have received various designations. They have been termed innate ideas, regulative ideas, intuitive ideas, *a priori* ideas, categorical ideas, and also have been regarded as forms of thought, entirely independent of the objects or matter of thought. Some of these are very faulty methods of expression, especially if adhered to as complete in themselves to the exclusion of other methods. Indeed, no one word or expression is perfectly applicable to any one of these ideas, and the relation of the mind to it; much less is such a word sufficient to characterize all of them, varying as they do, intrinsically, and in their connections with the phenomena explained by them. One seems to inhere like a quality, as right in action; another to be a condition, as space to the objects in it; another to be the manner in which the mind regards the things to which it applies, as number in connection with the objects numbered. No single expression, therefore, can be analyzed, no particular words tortured to disclose more exactly what is meant by an intuitive idea. In each case the relation itself must be contemplated, and the word be shaped to the fact, rather than the fact be learned by the word.

We do not understand by this doctrine of innate **ideas,** that the mind finds in itself a notion as a realized mental product, and applies this to the facts before it; nor that there is in thought certain forms or directions of movement from which it cannot depart, and under which it works up the material brought to it. We understand rather that in the facts, on the occasion of the facts, the mind, not the senses, discerns relations by which it is able to explain them, to think concerning them, and this by means of a certain rational power which it brings with it, or finds evoked under the conditions of the problem before it. Nor do we affirm that these notions come necessarily and at once **to** every mind on every occasion intrinsically fitted for them; but that they each and all do find, sooner or later, an occasion on which they do arise, and that there is in them a furnishing by the mind itself of other and higher material of thought than the senses alone can supply. In

other words, there is called out, in the intellectual handling
of the facts of the world revealed in perception and consciousness, a new power of mind, which we term the reason,
furnishing rational ideas and grounds of procedure, and enabling the judgment to operate on the otherwise stubborn,
irreducible sensations present. The existence and office of
a portion of these ideas all philosophers admit; they are at
variance only as to their source and nature—a variance
which leads to the denial of the remaining and most essential ones. The notions of space and of time, traced to
an empirical source, prepare the way for a denial of right
and liberty in their transcendent character.

The term, *innate*, was an early and unfortunate one, as
it seems to imply an inborn product rather than a primitive
power. The word, *regulative*, as also the word, *categorical*,
find application to these ideas as bringing with them into
knowledge fundamental lines of order. The adjective, *intuitive*, indicates the directness with which they arise, like
an object of sense; while they are termed *a priori* as logically preceding the experience they expound. An occasion
being given, each idea arises at once as the condition of its
apprehension. These ideas are either denied by the empiricist, as that of liberty; or differently referred, as that of
space; or modified, as that of right.

We shall now proceed to take up these ideas one by
one, both to establish the whole class and each member of
it singly. In doing this, we shall not hesitate to repeat the
argument in each case, so far as it presents any new features.
The general doctrine of intuitive ideas is maintained if any
one of them holds its ground, though for its successful and
thorough application, the exact number and nature of these
notions must be known.

§ 2. The first of them is that of existence. This has
drawn forth less discussion than some others, and does not

therefore afford the best ground on which to meet the opposing views. The affirmation is, that in the presence of sensations, perceptions, the mind comes at some moment to say, These are; or, involving another idea, that of causation, to say, The object occasioning them is. When this act of mind does take place, there is proof in it of a double activity aside from that of the judgment — an activity furnishing the perception, and a second activity supplying the predicate. Can the judgment be made without both of these conditional activities? Can the three be resolved into two, or one? We answer, no. The judgment can do nothing with a naked sensation. It is to this higher faculty, lumber without tools. The sensation can yield nothing but mere feeling. Feeling, as feeling is complete in itself, and may as well repose in the sensational structure of an oyster, as in that of a man. The judgment alone can add nothing to that which it is to handle; for if it does, you therein assign it a double office, that of reason and judgment, that of calling forth the predicate, and of coupling it with the antecedent.

A sensation and the notion of existence involved therein, or better, evoked thereby, are very different. I see no reason why the one may not be experienced indefinitely **without, in and** by itself, giving rise to the other. Indeed we, with our rational powers even, are constantly enjoying or suffering sensations without affirming, or thinking of their existence. This notion is present only as the mind from time **to** time is brought directly to contemplate them. There is no latent judgment of their existence in clearly experienced, but not definitely thought of, sensations, in any other way than that the mind may, at any moment, have its attention directed to them, call them before itself for contemplation, and then be led to affirm their existence, under this mode of regarding them. A cloud is above the earth, and the mind may so decide at any instant : but there is no latent decision to that effect in the simple act of seeing a cloud, only the possibility of one.

As the opposite view has not here received that complete and exhaustive statement which we shall find of it under space and time, we can not to the best advantage, controvert it. We merely remark, that it seems to confound the sensation with the idea. This it does partly perhaps through the ambiguity of the word consciousness. It is not an unusual or very harsh form of expression to say, I am conscious that the odor exists, while the affirmation, I smell that it exists, is obviously inadmissible. Yet for philosophical purposes the last expression has all the breadth that can be allowed the first. Consciousness only reports the sensation, is as broad as the sensation, and this is fully expressed in the verb, *smell.* We are not then conscious of the being of an odor, unless we smell that being. The words *conscious, consciousness* have so enlarged their meaning as to be regarded as the ground of that which is known, when that knowledge springs from a judgment, and is thus referable to a reflective and not intuitive faculty. We are conscious of a sensation in no other sense than that we are conscious of the sensation, and also of the intuition and judgment by which existence is referred to it. These three acts are separate sources of separate elements in the joint product, This odor is. Consciousness is nothing in itself, nothing additional, but is the common and pervasive condition of each of these acts as of every act of mind. No knowledge can be referred to consciousness which is not farther, more explicitly, referable to some given specific power of mind, and the power of mind yielding the notion of existence is the one here insisted on, the reason.

Says Bain, " The sum total of all the occasions for putting forth active energy, or for conceiving this possible to be put forth, is our external world." (*The Senses and the Intellect, page* 380.) In this and the accompanying passages, the sensations of resistance, rather than the suggestions and interpretations of those sensations, are kept uppermost, and thus the action of the reason concealed under that of the senses and the judgment. But "occasions" are occasions to the mind, and thus become the conditions of a knowledge not found in the simple sensations which compose them.

The judgment of existence does find its chief significance in connection with the experience and exercise of force, since here, united with that of causation, it leads to the telling affirmation of the noumenon, the permanent being, underlying the phenomenal, material world; and also of the spirit, the abiding source of changed and changing mental states. To affirm phenomenal existence seems a merely formal act beside the doubly pregnant one by which we go deeper than consiousness inward, farther than consciousness outward, and fill supersensual regions with supersensual forms of being. Phenomena are known directly, and thus directly yielded in consciousness; but now the conditions of a judgment are found which penetrates beyond appearances, and affirms permanent and unphenomenal existence, a fact incapable of experimental verification, and thus of appearing directly in consciousness. We are conscious of judgments, not of their truth.

We refer then this idea of existence to an independent faculty, the reason; because it is not in the sensation as a sensation, nor to be secured by a passive flow from sensation to sensation, each equally destitute of it; but is found first and fully in the incipient action of mind, when it begins to deal with and handle its hitherto unobserved experiences. This judgment is too habitually involved in our experience to be ordinarily significant, but to one

waking from syncope, it may become a most momentous
conclusion.

§ 3. The second regulative idea is that of number.
This, like that of existence, is so simple and direct, so constantly merged in the very perception to which it is attached, as to have called forth little discussion, and made
but slight claims for explanation on sensualistic schools of
philosophy. Language also favors this oversight. I see
one apple, I hear several sounds, I feel three distinct points,
are examples of familiar expressions. We cover directly
by verbs of sensation, their objects and the numerical relations of those objects. Yet it is evident, that we do not
see an object to be one. The numerical notion is brought
to the mass of colors before us as one of the ways in which
the mind may regard it. Indeed, the same object differently
contemplated, yields a great variety of numerical relations,
the sensations remaining exactly the same. It may present
several colors, and while, therefore, we call it one in cohe-
sive connection, we may separate it into a multiplicity of
parts by diversity of shades, or by outstanding members, or
by relative position. An object of regular outline and
uniform color may still yield a plurality of parts through
the unit of measurement we apply to its lines, angles,
surfaces. The mind plays upon it with standards of its
own, divides it with various linear and solid measurements,
finds with each a diverse numerical expression, and terms
it now one, now many, as suits the purposes of thought.
All this is not a simple action of the senses; nor any more
is it when the incipient step of the process is taken by
roughly calling the whole one thing. The color is seen,
the hardness is felt, the odor is smelt, and the sources of
each are regarded as one object, or more than one, as the
mind chances to contemplate it, bringing to it one or another of various combining ideas. There is no object of

sense which is not in some relation one, as a tree, a grove, a forest, a world, a universe; and none which may not be divided and thus yield plurality. Now this action of the judgment and attention must all go on under the notion of number, and, till this is furnished, all objects must remain undistinguished either as single or manifold. Objects of sense may reach the mind without drawing from it a numerical estimate. One may gather berries without regarding the number taken or left, though both be clearly seen. Distinction in the senses is not distinction in the intellect, and does not necessitate it; any more than distinction in existence is distinction in thought. A dozen calls may bring a dog, though he has taken no note of them as a dozen. Articulate sounds may convey the designed thought to the mind, a thought dependent on the exact number of elements, without attention directed to them as twenty, less or more.

This separable character of number from the objects perceived, is seen in the fact, that two impressions on the senses, as on the eyes of men, or many, as on the eye of an insect, become one object in the intellect; and still more strongly in the fact, that numbers are treated independently in arithmetic and algebra, are accumulated in amounts entirely beyond experience, and are divided and compounded by processes not founded on observation, or proved by it; **but** which belong to the necessary character of numerical conceptions. Our powerful algebraic solvents are general formulæ, are wrought out wholly independently of things, and are brought to explain outside facts otherwise numerically unintelligible. Thus most evident is it, that in the more abtruse application of numbers, as to curves and to complex motion, phenomena receive their solution from the numerical conception and do not, through the senses, yield it. Moreover, these estimates are reached by an arbitrary supposition of an equality of units never found in experience. One pound is regarded as absolutely equivalent to every other pound of the same denomination; one foot, one mile, to the like measurements elsewhere. To fix on standard units, in which the approximation to equality is sufficiently close to enable us safely to neglect errors, is a large share of the difficulty in mixed mathematics, and only when we deal with pure conceptions, as with that of space in geometry, do our numerical processes show their full power, stretching an unimpeded wing in realms as airy as themselves. Existence and number are among the most general of our notions, finding inherent, and, to a rational mind, necessary, application everywhere.

We regard the idea of number as one brought by the mind to things, (1) because the thing considered remaining the same, numbers may be applied to it in many different ways; (2) because distinctions in the senses which are naturally an occasion for the notion of number do not necessarily call it out; (3) because it is applied to things not objects of sensation; (4) because it assumes an absolute equality of units; (5) and because abstract numerical processes wholly transcend experience.

§ 4. The next regulative idea we offer is that of resemblance. This idea, though recognized by Plato, has been very frequently overlooked, and with great injury to the arguments sustaining the Intuitive Philosophy. It has been quietly assumed that resemblance is a matter of sensation only, that in it exclusively are given the data of this category, that one color is seen to be like or unlike another; one taste tasted as like or unlike a succeeding one. We might as well claim the judgment in which this relation is expressed to be an act of sense. Green, red, sweet, sour, are known as qualities by sensation, and here the sense pauses. The eye sees a green color once, twice, thrice,

but it makes no comparison, institutes no judgment, recalls
no impressions. These, the labors of other intellectual
powers, must commence and go on in the light, and this
light is that of an interpreting idea. What is resemblance?
It is not the red in the apple; no more is it the red on the
leaf; no more is it these two sensations united in time and
place. It is a specific relation between the two, intelligible
as a given case of a general notion. Can the specific relation be first reached, and the general idea be deduced from
**it? No!** As a relation it is an intellectual product, an intuition, two sensations explained in their bearings on each
other under an idea. The sensations alone do not contain
in their sensational matter the relation,—if they did, each
should contain it entire, or each a part of it—and can not
furnish it, nor can the intellectual movement proceed without the forecasting apprehension, the head-light. Moreover,
the specific relation must express the general relation, or
that relation cannot be deduced from it. Resemblance is
intellectually involved in the first instance of it; and, as it
is not a sensation, it must be involved for the direct apprehension of the mind there present for its interpretation. It
**is not the result of** the judgment which expresses it, but an
element and ground of that judgment. There are sensible
and supersensual data for the declaration, The leaf is like
the apple.

The frequent over-sight of this fact has greatly embarrassed the discussion between the two schools of philosophy. The idea of resemblance has been quietly appropriated. The observation of agreements and disagreements
has been allowed to proceed as if it were purely a matter of
perception, and thus a play of mind has been secured, a
germ of judgment, a nucleus of thinking, with no recognized *a priori* material. From the elements of intellectual
action thus secured, it has been comparatively easy, by pa-

tient composition and slight oversight, similar to that which characterized the first step, to broaden the grounds of thought, and to surreptitiously include one after another of its essential conditions. This process is arrested at the outset, if we reclaim, as we should, the idea of resemblance. No generalization can go forward without it, and the fictitious growth of regulative ideas is checked at once. We can not, for instance, compare sensations as co-existent or as successive, and under the one agreement smuggle in the idea of space, and under the other that of time. We are left, as we should be, standing on sensations alone; knowing color, odor, taste, but with no opportunity for comparison, classification, generalization, as we have no luminous idea under which a movement of thought is made visible.

There must be a little play given to thinking somewhere, in some direction, under some notion, before it can work out anything whatever; before it can acquire momentum, institute a process, and, in the superficial movement established, give apparent ground for the true connections of thought. The sensations are indeed present as the material of thought, the judgment is waiting as the agent of thought; but there is no plan of thought, no direction of thought, no space or orderly way wherein thought can find exercise, till some notion, most frequently this of resemblance, is furnished. The axe cannot cut while it is pressed close against the timber; tools are of no avail packed tightly in a chest. Give the hatchet the play of an inch, and with patience and an increasing sweep, it will at length hew for itself a broad path. Scope must be granted for wielding a weapon. One after another the implements must be loosened from their lodgment, and to initiate this movement, *room*, the ground and condition of effort, must be granted. So must room, an *idea* under which to move, be given to the very first judgment, before generalization is possible, and the one stolen for this purpose, is that of resemblance.

Resemblance is an intuitive idea, (1) because the likeness in two things compared is not in the first, nor yet in the second, as objects of sensation; (2) because the direction of the comparison must be indicated before the comparison is made; and (3) because each case of resemblance, though holding between specific qualities, is yet only a particular application of a general idea. The general here expounds the particular, and not the particular the general, as in generalization under the senses.

§ 5. A fourth intuitive idea is that of space. This has drawn much attention and been one of the centres of discussion between the different schools of philosophy. Space, as immaterial and exterior to the objects of perception, can not be directly referred to the senses, or lost sight of in that which is furnished by them. It is not, like existence, the very thing itself as it were, or like number, the inseparable form of it, but stands an antecedent and independent condition of the objects it contains. The derivation of this idea has therefore been assiduously labored over by philosophers who accept no intuitive faculties beyond those of perception. Herbert Spencer has given this subject a statement considered highly satisfactory and conclusive by those who share his general view. We will take from his *Principles of Psychology* sufficient matter fairly to present his conclusions. Those who wish the entire argument by which they are supported we refer to the above work. It is impossible for us **to** do more than present its initial features.

"Imagine that an immense number of fingers could be packed side by side, so that their ends made a flat surface; and that each of them had a separate nervous connection with the same sensorium. If anything were laid upon the

flat surface formed by those finger-ends, an impression of
touch could be given to a certain number of them—a number great in proportion to the size of the thing. And if
two things successively laid upon them, differed not only
in size but in shape, there would be a difference not only
in the *number* of the finger-ends affected, but also in the
kind of *combination*. But now, what would be the interpretation of any impression thus produced, while, as yet,
no experiences had been accumulated? Would there be
any idea of extension? I think not. To simplify the
question, let the first object laid on these finger-ends, be a
straight stick; and let us name the two finger-ends on
which its extremes lie, A and Z. If now it be said that the
length of the stick will be perceived, it is implied that the
distance between A and Z is already known, or, in other
words, that there is a pre-existent idea of a special extension, which is absurd. If it be said that the extension is
implied by the simultaneous excitation of B, C, D, E, F,
and all the fingers between A and Z, the difficulty is not
escaped; for no idea can arise from the simultaneous excitement of these, unless there is a knowledge of their
relative positions; which is itself a knowledge of extension.
By what process, then, can the length of the stick become
known? It can become known only after the accumulation
of certain experiences, by which the series and fingers
between A and Z become known. If the whole mass of
fingers admits of being moved bodily, as the retina does;
and if by virtue of its movements, something now touched
by finger A is next touched by finger B, next by C, and so
on; and if these experiences are so multiplied by motions
in all directions, that between the touching by finger A
and by any other finger, the number of intermediate
touches that will be felt is known; then the distance between A and Z can be known—known, that is, as a series

of states of consciousness produced by the successive touching of the intermediate fingers—a series of states comparable with any other such series, and capable of being estimated as greater or less.   And when by numberless
repetitions the relation between any one finger and each of
the others is established, and can be represented to the
mind as a series of a given length, then we may understand
how a stick laid upon the surface, so as to touch all the
fingers from A to Z inclusive, will be taken as equivalent
to the series A to Z—how the *simultaneous* excitation of
the entire range of fingers, will come to stand for its *serial*
excitation—how thus, objects laid upon the surface will
come to be distinguished from each other by the relative
length of the series they cover, or when broad as well as
long, by the groups of series which they cover—and how
by habit these simultaneous excitations, from being at first
known indirectly by translation into the serial ones, will
come to be known directly, and the serial ones will be
forgotten, just as in childhood the words of a new language,
at first understood by means of their equivalents in the
mother tongue, are presently understood by themselves;
and if used to the exclusion of the mother tongue, lead to
the ultimate loss of it.   The greatly magnified apparatus
here described, being reduced to its original shape — the
surface of the finger-ends being diminished to the size of
the retina, the things laid upon that surface being understood as the images cast upon the retina, and its movements
in contact with these things as the movements of the retina
relatively to the images — some conception will be formed
of one part of the process by which our ideas of visual
extension are gained."—*Pages* 221-2-3.

The difference between the view we wish to enforce,
and that presented in this passage, lies here: Do we interpret the experience here detailed by a notion of space, of

extension—for the one involves the other—*at some instant*
evoked by it, or do we, *at its conclusion*, as *its result*, finally
eliminate such a notion? This may seem a slight difference, yet it is a fundamental oné. We give a further quo-
tation in completion of the above. "How, through experiences of occupied extension or body, can we ever gain the
notion of unoccupied extension or space? How from the
perception of a relation between resistant positions, do we
progress to a perception of a relation between non-resistant
positions? If all the space attributes of body are resolvable
into relations of position between subject and object, disclosed in the act of touch—if, originally, relative position is
only thus knowable—if therefore position is, to the nascent
intelligence, incognizable except as the position of something that produces an impression on the organism, how is
it possible for the idea of position ever to be disassociated
from that of body? How can the germinal notion of empty
extension ever be gained?

This problem, though apparently difficult of solution, is
really a very easy one. If, after some particular motion of
a limb, there invariably came a sensation of softness, after
some other one of roughness, after some other one of hardness—or if, after those movements of the eye needed for
some special act of vision, there always came a sensation of
redness, after some other a sensation of blueness; and so on
—it is manifest that, in conformity with the known laws of
association, there would be established a constant relation
between such notions and such sensations. If positions
were conceived at all, they would be conceived as invariably
occupied by things producing special impressions, and it
would be impossible to disassociate the positions from the
things. But as, in our experience, we find that a certain
movement of the hand which once brought the finger in
contact with something hot, now brings it in contact with

something sharp, and now with nothing at all; and that a
certain movement of the eye, which once was followed by
the sight of a black object, is now followed by the sight of
a white object, and now by the sight of no object; it results
that the idea of the particular position accompanying each
one of these movements, is, by accumulated experiences,
disassociated from objects and impressions, and comes to be
conceived by itself; it results that as there are endless such
movements, there come to be endless such positions conceived as existing apart from body, and it results that, as
in the first, and in every subsequent act of perception, each
position is known as co-existent with the subject, there
arises a consciousness of endless such co-existent positions;
that is, of space."—*Pages* 233-4.

We find, in our criticism of this passage, fatal defects
of method involved (1) in the assumption of the idea of
resemblance, and (2) that also of time, the experiences considered being known as serial; also (3) in the fact that **in**
putting these experiences on different finger-ends, Spencer uses a significant feature which is yet without significance in the experiment contemplated since the mind is sup-
**posed** to be unable to note the relation involved; and (4) in
**the** fact that **in** making the simultaneous excitation stand
for and represent the serial excitation, he is merely substituting a section of time, already assumed, for that of space.
The force of the third point will be seen, if we consider a
circle of an inch between the shoulders. Touching successively such a circle in various parts, we not being able in
sensation to distinguish its parts, would give us no clue to
the extent of the surface involved.

We hold that these experiences must call forth at some
point the idea of space, as the light under which comprehension must commence and proceed, and that they can not
**close with** a half-formed generalization waiting farther ex-

perience to grow into knowledge. Till this idea is evoked, every movement will, in its special relations, be utterly unintelligible, provoking indeed no attention; after it is evoked, these movements will but make it the more definite and precise in its application. Take the illustration offered by Spencer. Let a stick rest on imaginery finger-ends, by its two extremities, designated A and Z. Can that fact alone call forth the idea of space? We think it may, provided the mind is ready to know it as a fact, and to recognize two mutually excluding positions in sensation. It would evidently be thus interpreted at once by the adult mind, and a farther movement of the fingers would only be be sought after as giving confirmation to the fact of two mutually exclusive sensations, and as furnishing a distinct estimate of the distance between the two points. The objection expressed by Spencer in the words, "If now it be said that the length of the stick will be perceived, it is implied that the distance between A and Z is already known; or in other words, that there is a pre-existent idea of special extension, which is absurd," has no particular force; for it only holds against the assertion, that the space A Z is not merely recognized as a space, but accurately known in its dimensions. This knowledge, our latest adult experience fails to give us, and certainly a general notion of some space must go before this, its careful estimate. Spencer confounds intuitions with generalizations of the senses. In these the particular does precede the general, the sweetness of honey or of sugar the notion of sweetness. It is not so in intuitive ideas; here the general precedes the particular, the notion of space that of a given distance, the notion of time that of the time of day. Here is a fundamental difference between the two, which Spencer overlooks.

If the points A and Z are recognized as distinct, according to the comparison on distinct finger-ends, or in the

sense of sight, which these multiplied points of **touch are**
intended to illustrate, at different parts of the retina—then
this simple experience **of** sensations, at diverse positions
excluding each other, can only find apprehension by and
through the comprehending idea of space. Only under this
fact of space can the phenomena occur; only by it can they
be understood for what they are, and there are no possible
steps toward their solution, till this first idea is present, as
an apprehension of the conditions of the problem. If the
sensations are not known as in position, and in distinct positions, then there is not yet the germ of suggestion, the
rudiments of inquiry; if they are so known, there is already present the initiatory knowledge of space.

Let us suppose, with Spencer, this notion to be wanting,
that we have sensations at A and Z, and at such other intervening points as we choose, and yet have not any suggestion therein of position or extension. The mind remains
perfectly quiet.

The sensations as sensations merely lie in consciousness,
but in their space-relations no attention is directed to them,
or evoked by them. Exactly the same mental state might
remain when the sensations should change by becoming
serial, by alternating backward and forward on successive
finger-points, by furnishing in any way farther data of that
exact knowledge which the first data had done nothing to
call forth. The images in a mirror may lie still, or move
among themselves, and in neither case is any comprehension
of them made necessary to the mirror. No more would
there be if the mirror were simply and permanently conscious of them as sensations. Suppose, however, the attention of the mind is awakened and directed to this movement. How alone can it *begin* to understand and explain
the facts before it, except by applying the notion of space,
**now** so strongly plucked at among its comprehensive sol-

vents? If "numberless repetitions" are requisite, that is, if an entire series of movements can be closed and the mind still remain without the idea,—remain quiescent, dead, mirror-like, holding distinct sensations in distinct special relations without knowing them as distinct, reaching no judgment—then a second, a third, a fiftieth repetition, as mere repetition, having the light of no new idea cast upon it, may leave the mind, nay, must leave the mind, unless at some point it be awakened to a new method, as quiescent and dark as at the outset.

The only ground on which any other conclusion is possible is, that space is not an idea, but literally a series of sensations; or at least a sensational fact or quality generalized from a series of experiences, as sweetness is a quality separated clearly by repetition from other qualities, red, a color distinguished by repeated observation from other colors. In these cases the reiterated sensation enables us to distinguish and abstract its peculiar quality.

Absurd and impossible as this view of space, that it is a quality of sensation, seems to us to be, we believe that it lurks in the arguments and statements of the sensational school. Thus, in the passage given above, it is " the serial excitations," which are identified with the notion of space, and are made by association to underlie and explain " the simultaneous excitations." In fact, however, the one set of phenomena no more requires the explanation of the idea than the other, no more contains it than the other. It is merely because there is in the first a variation of the sensations, that they give or rather seem to give, a foothold to explanation not found in the second. Yet this change must be observed in the very quality of the sensations and not in the relation of the sensations, or no ground of exposition is afforded by Spencer. Relations are intellectually seen, the qualities alone are a matter of perception. Elsewhere Speneer speaks of the " sense of *ability to move*," " the sense of *freedom for motions*," as a constituent in our idea of space. Observe that this ability, this freedom, are not spoken of as something explained *under* the idea, but as a *constituent* of the idea.

Bain says yet more explicitly : "Extension or space as a quality has *no other* origin and no other meaning than the association of these different sensitive and motor effects." Mark the words *quality* and *no other meaning*. Again, " The mental conception that we have of empty space is scope for movement, the possibility of potentiality of movement ; and this conception we derive from our experience of movements."—*The Senses and the Intellect, p.* 378. How is it as to the interstellar, or the intermolecular spaces ? What has experience to say concerning these ? Do we in them derive our belief of space from the changed sensations of motion ? Bain proceeds still farther. " By such **steps** as I have endeavored to describe, we derive our notion of extended things, of extension in the concrete. And from this we can obtain an abstract notion of the extended in the same manner as we gain any other abstract notion, as color, heat or justice." This can only be true if our knowledge of space, like our knowledge of heat and color, is a sensation ; and this belief, not explicitly stated, underlies logically the sensualistic philosophy. The doctrine that space is a sensation or "quality" of sensations, or a series or concatenation of sensations, or in any way an immediate product of sensation, we are willing to leave without argument to the refutation of simple statement. It would thus sink wholly from the intellectual field, and, if allowed to drag other kindred ideas with it, would leave neither occasion nor opportunity for any other faculty than that of perception. Sensations lie together, and need no conjunction by the judgment ; and as for any notions wherewith the mind is to comprehend and classify them, there are none; those thought to be such, are themselves sensations. Feel your way, feel on and feel ever, would be the comprehensive direction to a being—we can scarcely say mind, for the mind is now resolved into mere sensibility — so formed. Feel space, feel time, feel number, and look to your finger-ends for liberty and right, or eternally lose them.

Let us carefully guard against one point of misapprehension. We say nothing as to any definite time in the progress of the infant in which the idea of space will arise. Sensations as sensations may come and go, we know not how long, without evoking the idea; but when it does come, it will come at once from within; not in an abstract, discriminated form, but in a concrete, obscure application, and prepare the way for a new series of intellectual actions. All precise estimates and measurements are, of course, the sole fruit of experience, and give the infant mind abundant occupation under this regulative idea.

One may study geometry with little or no abstract consideration of space as space, yet the idea is tacitly present everywhere. The child may come to a knowledge of the position and dimension of its own members, with no direction of the mind to the notion of space as such, though that idea quietly informs the whole process.

In the second of the longer quotations above given from Spencer, we have the notion of space, empty space, derived from a vacant organ of sense. Direct the mind steadily to this point. An organ, as the finger-end, or the eye, with no content of sensation in it, a simple blank, is one thing; and this fact accounted for and explained to the mind by the idea of empty space is quite another. If the first, generalized in any way he pleases, is Spencer's idea of space, then that idea consists in the mere absence of sensation, and should exist in the highest degree in connection with paralyzed organs. A recognition of blindness, or even deafness, should be one of space. If, however, the fact of a vacant organ becomes significant only in connection with a process of mind, we wish to know under what guiding clue that process proceeds. What is brought to the explanation of the fact of motion without sensation ? It seems **to us** that but one answer can be given—space. This conception as absolutely simple must come, when it comes, in (1) a complete form; coming completely, it must come (2) suddenly ; and, (3) till it comes, no experience is intelligible under it.

Spencer, with the marked approval of Bain, makes, in another phase of the argument, the notion of space dependent on co-existence, and co-existence the fruit of experience.

" Not only is it that the idea of space involves the idea of co-existence, but it is that the idea of co-existence involves the idea of space. Fundamentally space and co-existence are two sides of the same cognition."

" On the one hand space can not be thought of without co-existent positions being thought of; on the other hand co-existence can not be thought of without at least two points in space being thought of. A relation of co-existence implies two somethings that co-exist. Two somethings can **not** occupy absolutely the same point in space. And hence co-existence implies space. Space can be known only as presenting relations of co-existence ; relations of **co-exist-**ence can be known only as presented in space."

" If now it should turn out under an ultimate analysis— that a relation of co-existence is not directly cognizable, but is cognizable only by a duplex act of thought—only by a comparison of experiences ; the question between the transcendentalists and their opponents will be set finally at rest. When after it has been shown as above, that our cognition of space in its totality is explicable upon the experience hypothesis, and that all the peculiarities of the cognition correspond to that hypothesis, it comes to be shown that the ultimate elements into which that cognition is decomposable —the relation of co-existence—can itself be gained only by experience—the utter untenableness of the Kantian doctrine will become manifest."—*Pages* 243-4.

Herein our author hardly agrees with himself, having insisted that the co-existent points, A, B, Z, can not give the idea of extension, though it now turns out that a knowledge of their co-existence would have been essentially a knowledge of space. We believe (1) that the notion of any simple position involves that of space, is explained under it, and therefore that a single sensation of touch, complex indeed, yet regarded as simple, might call forth the idea. This we do not care to dwell on, as it is doubtless in connection with many simultaneous and serial phenomena, presented in several senses, that the notion actually does arise. We can not accept the statement that the ultimate element into which the cognition, space, is decomposable, is co-existence. On the other hand, (2) the notion of external, material co-existence is subsequent in the order of thought to that of space. Nor are the two by any means the same. I may have the idea of empty space. I may put one object in it, or two or three objects in it, but the idea of space has preceded each and all before they became to me external objects, or the images of such objects. Indeed, (3) simple co-existence, as of an act of memory and a thought, of a thought and a feeling, does not involve the idea of space. The contrast of the inner and the outer, of the ego and non-ego, may or may not go forward; but the *first* step in such a contrast, the initial stroke of light in handling a local sensation, is the localizing idea of space. How often, and how long I may have one, two, three sensations, and not expound them, is simply the question, How

long do the senses ante-date in development the other
intellectual powers? When these come, they come thus,
not otherwise. The fact of co-existence is a mere blind
datum of sensations, until contemplated under the idea of
space. The (4) *actual* co-existence of two things is not
involved in space, but only its possibility. The extension
of space as the possibility of such a co-existence is the **no-**
tion of space, is in and of the very idea. Actual co-existence alone rests on sensation, the possibility of it on the
intuition. Mr. Spencer is not to think and speak of the co-
existence of two positions as if it were identical with the
co-existence of things. The first is in no way a datum of
sensation. If he tries to make it so, he is thrown immediately back on to his former proof, and loses his present
foothold.

We have made no distinction between extension and
space. We regard the first only as a specification under
the second. The extension of particular objects, and the
duration of particular events, are forms under which the
mind applies the intuitive ideas of space and of time. A
knowledge of actual spaces, a measurement of material
objects, are the fruits of experience; but these estimates
proceed always under the prior notion of space, which
makes them intelligible.

Space, **in its** analytical contemplation, furnishes a variety
of intuitive conceptions which are the basis of the demonstrative reasonings of Geometry and Trigonometry. Such
a notion **is position, a line,** a surface, perfect curves, figures,
solids. A circle, in its accurate form as a ground of demonstrative truth, is an intuitive conception, as are the propositions which flow from the immutable relation of its parts,
and of the lines which define, and are defined by them. A
surface without thickness, a line without breadth, a point
without dimensions, are all intuitive conceptions under the

primitive idea, and are the elements of a purely intuitive science. The most marked of those secondary conceptions is that of position. It is to be entirely distinguished from an infinitesimal body; as the infinite of the metaphysician wholly transcends the infinite of the mathematician. Position is not arrived at by the futile sub-divisions of the fancy, is not the result of the dogma of divisibility. There is here absolutely no length nor breadth, and the idea is reached directly by the grasp of the reason. The imagination may falter in struggling by additions to reach the infinite, and by subtractions to arrive at pure position; but the reason easily and at once accepts both notions, and rids them of those measurable parts by which the imagination baffles itself in the pursuit. Position is absolutely without measurements, and hence without parts; the infinite is absolutely beyond measurements, and hence also without parts. There is no whole, therefore no division of that whole.

§ 6. The ideas of existence, number and resemblance belong equally to physical and mental facts. Space, on the the other hand, is the peculiar formative idea of physical phenomena alone; while the idea we have now to offer, that of consciousness, is the exclusive characteristic of mental experiences. There has been no debate concerning this idea, because it has not been presented as belonging to this department of our intellectual furniture. If, however, it shall appear that consciousness exists as a form rather than as a substance or quality, that it is therefore directly arrived at by the mind, and also that it furnishes the distinctive feature of a class of phenomena, the transcendent predicate of a series of judgments, it will be plain that it belongs properly to the class of regulative notions. Consciousness is often spoken of as if it were a faculty, a form of knowing; yet a little thought at once shows that it is not. I see a ball. I say in farther enforcement, I know that I see it. This lan-

guage has divided the first simple act into two, an act of perceiving, and one of knowing directed toward that of perception. Yet this is merely a convenience of expression. The
one single act of seeing the ball is all that is present. **If**
there were a second act of knowing, this also would require
sub-division in order to reach the element of consciousness
in it. Thus analysis must go on indefinitely, unless we
finally accept an act of knowing which is simple and indivisible. There is no double faculty, or double movement
of one faculty, in thinking, feeling, willing. A thought is
a thought only as it is known; a feeling is a feeling only
as it is felt. They do not first find existence, and then an
added quality or element of consciousness; but consciousness **is** the condition and form of their existence. Consciousness, then, is not, like judgment, a power; nor like
pain or pleasure, a quality of certain states; it is not a feature or a relation of a sensation, but involved in the very
notion of a sensation. This idea, therefore, as neither **a**
faculty to be known by its exercise, nor a quality of mental
states to be learned by observation,—indeed every act of
observation must itself contain it—must be evolved by the
mind as an explanatory idea, or conditional notion in considering the phenomena to which it is applicable.

It is not only unphenomenal itself, it is introduced as the
antecedent condition of a large class of phenomena, to wit:
those of mind. What space is to material facts, consciousness is to intellectual facts, the interpreting light under
which they occur. The words we constantly apply to it,
recognize this relation. We say, "the field of consciousness," "transpiring in consciousness," "coming up into the
light of consciousness," "the flow of consciousness,"—that
is of thought and feeling in consciousness. These and like
expressions are shaped under an image in which consciousness is presented as an arena of mental movements, as is

space of physical events. The peculiar nature of knowing, feeling, willing, is not understood till the idea of consciousness is present : yet these facts remain in their integrity possessed of all the elements that analysis discloses in them, without accrediting any one quality to consciousness. Consciousness thus shows itself to be to the inner, invisible world, what space is to the outer, visible one ; the condition of its existence, the only canvas on which its colors can appear. To occupy space is to have physical existence, to occupy consciousness is to have an intellectual existence, to occupy neither is not to exist, is to present no one of the known forms of existence. The idea is seen to be regulative in the large class of propositions which arise under it. I know ; I see the book ; I feel the pain, are of this sort. Each of them is comprehended by virtue of the notion of consciousness, which expounds their several predicates.

This view also finds support in the difficulties which attend on the ordinary explanations of consciousness. What is it ? is a question that has greatly perplexed philosophy, and has seldom received a very definite answer. Some have striven to conceive it as a faculty, yet this faculty must be present in the action of every other faculty, and that other faculty would be absolutely null and void without this. To divide an act of knowing into one of knowing, and one of consciousness, each taking a distinct moiety, is impossible. Hamilton has said, " Consciousness is the genus under which our several faculties of knowing are contained as species." But our faculties of knowing, no more require it than those of feeling and willing; and what exactly is a genus in distinction from the species it contains? Nothing but a word. Certainly an effort to make definite this view, prepares the way for regarding consciousness as a general idea, under which all specific acts of mind, in themselves complete, find recognition. J. J. Murphy, in his work on Habit and Intelligence, has united consciousness to feeling, and made it and sensation species under that generic term. The conclusion is on the opposite side to that of Hamilton, but no better than his; since consciousness belongs equally to thoughts and feelings. Others figure consciousness under the image of an internal light. This is virtually to decline the inquiry, What is it? since the illustration can reflect no explanation on this point. Others speak of consciousness as that power by which we refer acts to ourselves. This is to let the eye wander altogether from the subject, since the explanation overlooks the facts to be explained. Consciousness has also been divided into common consciousness and philosophical consciousness, and into consciousness and self-consciousness. These are divisions which pertain to the phenomena in consciousness and not to consciousness itself.

It occasions confusion in some minds that consciousness should be spoken of as an intuitive idea, when it is obviously something more and other than an idea. The language merely indicates the manner in which the mind arrives at the relation expressed by consciousness. In the same way we speak of space as an idea, and of a landscape as a perception, and of a general term as a conception. A man may have an idea of himself, that is be an idea to himself; yet he is something more than an idea. The recognition of consciousness as a distinct category cuts apart physical and mental facts with the deepest possible division. They lie in two incommensurable and incomparable realms, that can never overlap each other.

§ 7. We now pass to time, a regulative idea, like that of space, which has attracted much attention as obviously open to a super-sensual reference. It is the idea which unites all events, whether physical or mental. The sensations occasioned by phenomena into which the idea of time most

obviously enters are diverse in their relations from those
chiefly suggestive of space: or rather, things are viewed
in distinct bearings in the application of the one or the
other notion. In each case, nevertheless, the diversity is
only understood by an *a priori* recognition of the controlling idea of the relation under which it arises. Some objects
can be contemplated indifferently in one order of succession
or in a reverse order. We may move from A to Z, or return from Z to A. Others, transpiring in time, confine the
attention to one direction. We pass from A to Z, but cannot retrace our steps. The cars enter the field of vision
at the left, and pass out at the right. In these facts there
is an occasion, though not an explanation, of the notion of
time. The mind cannot, under the influence of a mere series of sensations, discover this relation; since it is not in
and of the sensations, but that which expounds them. Nor
can it institute a comparison between the two relations of
objects which shall issue in any comprehension of them,
without itself supplying the essential conditions of that
comparison — the notions of space and time. We must
either hold that time is an order of sensation, or we must admit it to be that transcendent idea which expounds that order, and is therefore supplied by the mind.

Says Spencer, "As the ideas of space and co-existence
are inseparable, so also are the ideas of time and sequence.
It is impossible to think of time, without thinking of some
succession; and it is equally impossible to think of any succession without thinking of time. Time, like space, can
not be conceived except by the establishment of a relation
between at least two elements of consciousness, the difference being, that while in the case of space, those two elements are, or seem to be present together, in the case of
time they are not present together."—*Principles of Psychology, page* 247.

This statement, so far as it is admissible at all, is so as a statement of the circumstances under which the idea of time arises, and not of the nature of that idea itself. Used for the latter purpose, the author legitimately reaches the conclusion that time *is* "relativity of position among the states of consciousness." The process of arriving at this result is farther explained thus : " Gradually, as by the accumulation of experiences, there are found to be like and unlike sounds, tastes, smells, sizes, forms, textures ; the relationship which we signify by these words, like and unlike, will be more and more dissociated from particular impressions ; and the abstract ideas of *likeness* and *unlikeness* will come into existence. Manifestly, then, the ideas of likeness and unlikeness are impossible until multitudes of things have been thought of as like and unlike. Similarly in the case before us. After various relations of position among the states of consciousness have been contemplated, have been compared, have become familiar ; and after experiences of different relations of position have been so accumulated as to dissociate the idea of the relation from all particular positions ; then, and not till then, can there arise the abstract notion of *relativity of position* among the states of consciousness—the notion of time.

Thus so far is it from being true that time, as conceived by us, is a form of thought ; it turns out contrariwise, not only that there *can* be thoughts while yet time has not been conceived, but that there *must* be thoughts, before it can become conceivable "—*Page* 252.

Our objection to the above conclusion is double. The comparison itself cannot go on without a regulative idea, that of resemblance, under which it can be instituted ; and that in which it is said to issue is not the notion of time. That which is explained by time is very different from time itself. If the first were the second we should have no need of an independent explanatory notion, the phenomena would be complete and intelligible in themselves. The sequence of events provokes the notion, but is not that notion. Sequence and time do not mutually contain each other, but (1) time is that *idea* without which the *fact* of sequence is unintelligible. That time is not identical with succession is seen in our measurement of it. (2) A succession of events may be completed in a shorter or longer period, and if time to us were their mere relation in sequence, we should insist on its identity in the two cases. (3) We distinguish time from any given sequence, indeed from all sequences, longer or shorter according to the forces at work. We do not identify it with that series of events even by which we measure it. The conditions for its exact estimate and general apprehension are different. (4) The notion of time, with no actual events transpiring in it, is quite consonant with thought. Moreover, many sequences are simultaneous. (5) The relativity of which one of these is it that constitutes time? It cannot be one to the exclusion of the remainder, for no one has such a pre-eminence over every other. Neither can it be all, since they are constantly varying among themselves. What effect has it on time, that one drives faster than he has been driving, that a railroad train has stopped at a station, that the thoughts have been quickend by danger? The quality of sweetness may exist in many things, and have shades of diversity in each ; is this also our conception of time ?

(6) The prior notion of time, moreover, imposes sequence, when there is no sequence in the states of consciousness, but rather alternation. The mind may pass from A to B in contemplation, and back again; it may vibrate between the two in alternate thought : yet it does this as certainly under the idea of time as if it had simply passed on to Z. Motion in a circle is felt to be motion as much

as movement in a straight line. Bare contemplation without conscious progress is felt to occupy time; it is for the measure, not for the fact of time, that we revert to external events at the expiration or change of a single absorbing feeling. There is doubtless some succession in every phase of mind, but it is not necessary for us to contemplate these minor and obscure transitions to be aware that every act, the very act of attention, occupies time. We might as well endure an intense, absorbing pain for an hour as for an instant, if we were not able to distinguish between the two cases. That which we urge is, that the notion of time imposes the sense of sequence where there is no proper sequence in the sensations as sensations, and the alternate consideration of A, B, like the beat of a clock, marks distinctly the flow of time. Indeed all consciousness is made sequential, no matter what the order of its states, by the very notion of time in which they transpire. We can not escape the inner succession of impressions, because we cannot elude the interpreting idea, that of time. The position of "states of consciousness" can be only that of succession, whatever their character or the number of times they are repeated. The inner law overrules the outward appearance, and imposes the notion of sequence.

Suppose, on the other hand, with Spencer, that we could pass from A to Z, without the idea of time. In that case we should not only be destitute of it, but have made no progress towards it. We should simply have experienced sensations without interpretation. No repetition of this process, however frequent, could make it fruitful of a new notion. The simple idea must be present to open the inquiry. Time must be a sensation, like that of green and red, or its distinct abstraction can not follow from repetition. The sensation green is given in each particular instance, and then, by distinguishing attention, assumes the abstract form. This process is possible only to sensations, —and even then involves more than sensation—not to relations; since a relation is addressed to the intellect, and not to the sense, and can only be understood in connection with an idea under which it arises and is defined as a relation of place, time, dependence. On no supposition is the closing statement of Spencer admissible. "So far is it from being true that Time, as conceived by us, is a form of thought, it turns out contrariwise, not only that there *can* be thoughts while yet time has not been conceived, but that there must be thoughts before it can become conceivable."

As a sensation, time must be experienced in each sensation from which it is to be abstracted; as a relation also it must be discoverable in each series or it can not be generalized from all; and as an idea disclosing a relation it must come at once. Time must be a sensation, or it must be a specific relation under some general idea, or it must itself be a primary idea, the condition of actual, individual connections. The first supposition is plainly false, while the second is as unacceptable to the empirical school as the third, since it also implies original, intuitive action of the mind. Yet I see no escape except in the assertion that a relation of no specific order or kind can be discovered, and this is not an escape, since such a relation could not be generalized into one of a specific order or kind, to wit, that of time.

§ 8. The seventh regulative idea is that of cause and effect. This is one of the most undeniable of them all, and is either greatly restricted in its statement, or entirely rejected by those who refuse to accept the reason as a source of knowledge. Indeed an adequate presentation of the notion as it lies in the general mind, shows it at once to be beyond sensation, generalization, or any action that these processes can verify. The convenience of expression has led to the extension of the term cause, not merely to remote agents, but even to the conditions of their action. Any one of all the circumstances necessary to an effect is spoken of as its cause, though no direct efficiency proceeds from it. In a stricter sense, the word cause includes only those antecedents which are active in the effect, and in a yet closer sense, the sense which belongs to it in the present discussion, the forces *immediately* operative in the fact before us. *The* cause is strictly contemporaneous with **the** effect, underlies it, momentarily occasions it. The antecedent effect had its antecedent cause, and though this cause may have been identical with the cause now operating, it remains a cause by virtue of its present activity. The effect is the immediate evidence of the cause; and though the last is prior in thought to the first, neither can exist an instant without the other. The sound of the steam-whistle is remotely attributable to the distant locomotive, is more immediately to be referred to the movement of the air and the tympanum, but finds its causes exactly in the forces which sustain the movement, and the living powers which receive and interpret it. In this sense the cause is always and necessarily transcendental, out of the range of the senses, incapable of verification by any other than the very faculty which in the first instance yields the idea.

The statements of empirical philosophy are quite different from those now made. Says Bain, "The successions designated as *Cause and Effect*, are fixed in the mind by contiguity. Belief in external reality is anticipation of a given effect of a given antecedent; and the effects and causes are our own various sensations and movements." More clearly still does Mill speak of the notion as one of simple antecedence; while Spencer treats of it under the caption, "The relation of sequences." If these and other kindred statements are correct, then there is no veritable idea of cause and effect in the precise, intuitive sense, since a sequence finds explanation under the notion of time, and requires for its statement no other form of thought. That there is any sufficient knowledge or idea of the ground of such a sequence is simply denied by this class of philosophers. There is in this attitude an abandonment of the idea of causation as irresolvable into experience, and a substitution for it of a certain application of the notion of time. The ground of debate, therefore, is narrowed down to the correctness with which the phenomena under discussion are stated by the respective parties. If it be shown, that simple sequence does not, in the common mind, cover the entire ground of causation, there is in the empirical philosophy a surrender of one actual, universal idea as inexplicable; a superficial substitution for it of the fragment of another, and this for no other reason than that its own theory can find no place for this fixed conviction. It is the facts of the mind's action that philosophy inquires into, and the above proof being given, there will here be left a form of action as universal and persistent, and hence as ultimate and authoritative as any, uncovered by materialism.

The universal conviction, if it can be arrived at, is not to be pushed aside, to be left unexplained, nor to be regarded as an accidental, invalid movement of mind, without a reason rendered, distinguishing this from kindred affirmations of our faculties. We may not impeach the action of the mind at one point, without at least separating this point broadly and decisively from every other. These universal convictions are not to be obnoxious, merely because, as otherwise inexplicable, they demand the intuitive insight claimed for them. There is here really *a priori* conviction brought to disprove *a priori* truths; for what

but an *a priori* bias of mind, is this antecedent reluctance
to admit the possibility of regulative ideas?

What then is the fact? Which statement best conforms to the universal conviction, that of fixed antecedence,
or of present underlying power? There can be no doubt
on this point. The case is a plain, almost an admitted one,
against empirical philosophy. Language is full of this
notion of inherent, sub-phenomenal connections between
events. The word *force* distinctly expresses this causal
link, and few words are more familiar, or play a more important part in speech. Of the same kind, are the words
*power, influence, energy, strength,* and more or less markedly
most of the words which express physical **action.** *Pull,
push, press, pry, lift, lug, labor,* the entire vocabulary of
effort are saturated with this causal notion of an invisible
efficiency, which expends itself in all forms of activity.
Behold any striking display of force, the blasting of rocks,
and every mind is impressed with the power of the invisible agent. To look upon the lifting of detached masses,
the seaming of the solid bed, as a mere sequence of disconnected events, is impossible to any mind, in its spontaneous action. No descriptive language was ever applied to
such events, that regarded them simply as a sequence. The
popular and the universal conviction is unmistakable, that
**here is** force, invisible power.

Equally present is the idea to all science. Gravitation,
cohesion, chemical affinity, the correlation of forces, the
various theories of physical facts, like Darwin's theory of
gemmules, or Spencer's of physiological units, involve the
notion of inherent power, working the results under consideration. Science could **not** carry forward its investigations without this recognition of force. To discover the
traces of its presence, and the lines of its action, is the constant triumph of knowledge. To confound fixed antecedents

with efficient force is impossible to successful inquiry. The shadow of an object approaching us from the light, would thus be its cause; the effervescence of lime and water, the cause of the heat; the dissolving of salt in the water, the cause of the cold. The first fact, in each series of associated effects, would be the source of the remainder. No sequences are more fixed than those of day and night, summer and winter, yet there is no direct, causal connection be tween them, and no one ever so conceives the dependence.

Philosophy likewise reverts constantly to insensible, unapproachable causes. A large share of philosophers admit their existence and the grounds of it; and those of them who through their denial of the latter are content to sacrifice the former do not, and can not, use language, except in a few guarded passages, consistent with their own statements. They must, with Bain, in each inadvertent moment, speak of "active energy," of "mechanical powers," of "rousing the dormant energy," and to deny themselves these and kindred expressions, to forego the ideas back of them, would be to take away the opportunity of composition, or to make language most cumbersome, and untrue to our convictions. The generally accepted dogma, that the mind can not know anything beyond its own modifications; a dogma insisted on by many of the empirical school, finds its ultimate support in this notion of cause and effect. The existence of the object perceived outside of the perceptive organ, independent of it and removed from it—at least by insensible distances—has determined the large majority of philosophers to deny the possibility of direct perception. If, however, the connection of cause and effect is one of antecedence merely, then this separation of the object perceived from the organ perceiving it, should oppose no obstacle whatever to direct perception. A fixed sequence can be established between things remote and wholly unlike, as easily as between things, like and occupying common ground. If, therefore, this connection of sequence is the deepest, nay the only connection between things thought to act on each other, it would seem to suffice for knowledge at all distances; or if not, to make knowledge impossible. How shall even successive states of mind lie fruitfully together in simple sequence, if sequence after all is a barren connection. If it fails to unite remote, how can it unite proximate objects? If one set falls apart, all must.

The general point is too plain for farther statement. Evidently the doctrine of simple antecedence does not express the universal conviction, does not cover the phenomena under explanation, does not accept and expound the affirmations of knowledge which every mind is constantly making.

Quite a different explanation of cause and effect has come from another quarter. Sir William Hamilton applies to it what he terms the law of the conditioned. The notion of causality is thought by him to arise from the weakness of the mind, its inability to conceive a beginning. The mind, he affirms is unable to conceive events without a beginning, nor yet with a beginning. "We can conceive neither the absolute commencement, nor the absolute termination of anything that is once thought to exist; nor any more the opposite alternative of infinite non-commencement, of infinite non-termination." Herein is given the the principle of causality: "When an object is presented phenomenally as commencing, we cannot but suppose that the complement of existence, which it now contains, has previously been; in other words, that all that we at present come to know in it as an effect, must previously have existed in its cause." This is a most inadequate explanation for several reasons. In the first place, it inverts the order of dependence in our mental action. We can not conceive of anything as absolutely commencing, because of this notion of cause and effect. The existence of the notion is the ground of our embarrassment, not the embarrassment the occasion of the notion. What would be simpler, were it not for causality crowding us backward, than merely to conceive any landscape, any personage, any event, with no thought of what has preceded it? The present act of the imagination is not conditioned on the past, neither should we be compelled to evoke the present from the past, any more than to carry it forward into the future, were it not for causation. Any cross-section of the events of time could be as complete as a single pebble on the shore.

Thus, often in dreams, when the imagination finds unrestrained phenomenal play, the judgment not being sufficiently active to impose the check of this purely sub-phenomenal idea of causation, we in a great measure disregard it, and, with no sense of jar, suffer the unexplained presence of unexpected persons, and an incongruous order and issue of events. The ideas regulative of space and time relations are present, while cause and effect, regulative of consecutive thought, is in whole or in part overlooked. A city makes its appearance suddenly, the ship moves unobstructedly across the land, the facts and figures of fancy come and go freely, bound to no ordinary sequence.

A second objection is found in the fact that the theory affords no explanation of the alternative adopted by it. We can neither conceive, it is said, the commencement, nor the non-commencement of anything. Very well, but how is this dilemma to be escaped by the present notion of causation. The conclusion accepted under it of "infinite non-commencement" remains as inconceivable as ever, and, therefore, as far as conception is concerned, presents as many difficulties as would the opposed alternative of an immediate, independent beginning of events. If the mind is as open

to one of these conclusions as to the other, and can properly
be satisfied with neither, what reason has it for preferring
one to the other? The difficulty is met only when causation is made a positive notion, compelling us in the one direction. Accompany this acceptance with a denial of our
right to direct the imagination in explanation to that which,
according to our very notion of it, is sub-phenomenal, and
we have at once the ability and the inability of the mind
explained. We have a reason for its convictions, and also
for their inconceivable character.

Again, this theory is a concealed theory of antecedence,
**and** fails to cover the strict idea of causation. The efficient
cause is present with the effect, immediately underlies it,
and sustains it. Thus the substance, the force, which constitutes matter, each instant gives occasion **to** its qualities.
The power which is in mind, is the groundwork and source
of its thoughts, feelings and volitions. The stream of
causation flows under the stream of events, and momentarily floats them, as the surface of the ocean is supported
by its invisible depths. Simply to insist on an antecedent
event to every event, is to throw up the phenomenal path
along which the imagination travels, but is not a recognition of the true force and nature of causation. The imagination, exploring the past, does indeed require that distinct,
tangible foot-stones should, in due order, link its steps ; but
that which impels the mind in thus sending it to search its
way backward, is a sense of an unbroken series of causes,
and that which the mind finds everywhere beneath the phenomenal supports of the imagination is the permanent
power and flow of forces. This theory of the weakness of
the human mind signally fails to account for so positive and
pervasive a notion as this of cause and effect.

If we accept this notion in its full, universal application, leading us to those invisible energies which thread to-

gether the phenomena of the universe; if we do not deny
or limit the facts presented to us in our own spontaneous
beliefs, in universal action and universal language, it is at
once evident, that this idea must have an intuitive origin.
Admittedly it transcends all experience, is wholly unapproachable by the senses. The presence of such a notion,
evinced by language, by science, by philosophy, by our
spontaneous and inevitable interpretation of events, is undeniable; to discard it as a purely fanciful notion superinduced on the facts, is to deny and not to explain the phenomena of the mind ; is to construct our theories in neglect
of facts too broad for them ; is to invalidate an action of
mind, as universal, as strong in the confidence and spontaneous trust of the mind itself, as any of its processes. This
is to make our several forms of activity, intuitive and
rationative, contradictory and self-destructive ; is to bring
one form of knowing from its own field into that of another
faculty, and, because it fails to understand the diverse action
of a power given on purpose to do a work different from its
own, to expel, as fictitious and fanciful, conclusions wrought
out by a native force of mind. Daily life pursues its hourly
labors ; natural science accomplishes its great achievements,
following the clue of causation; and yet a speculation
termed philosophy steps in to declare the light under which
these processes proceed, false and deceptive. It seems to be
light, and does marvelously well the work of light, and all
men insist on using it as light ; yet evidently it is not the
waxen taper we are after. This, then, can not be our predetermined light, and as there is no other, it follows plainly
that this is not light, but darkness rather. Correct ideas
must come from experience, and be capable of its verification ; this is not so reached, and cannot be so explained ;
therefore it is no valid notion. In all this there is a fla-
grant begging of the question. We thus put the grounds

and tests of validity in the faculties that directly concern experience, and then deny validity to ideas that must confessedly, if they exist at all, transcend experience and the judgments which unfold it.

The notion of causation is well fitted to be a test of the two schools of philosophy, because of its plainly transcendental character, and because knowledge can not be gained without it. Deny causation and we deny reasons of all sorts. Mere continuity of impressions in the mind can not be the ground of any expectation, unless this succession tends to repeat itself, that is unless there is in it some causal energy. All thoughts equally with all things must fall apart, if there is no coherence between them; apparent order would be no more significant than apparent disorder, as both would be accidental.

A cause is **a transcendental,** co-existent, co-extensive force, underlying **its effect.** The effect is its only proof, its only measure, its only expression. The cause is neither less nor more than the effect; no portion of a cause can exist without an effect; no portion of an effect can exist without a cause? While the word in its most explicit use **is equivalent to the** noumenon underlying the phenomenon, **and is the source of the conviction** of real being, the noumena and phenomena, at any moment present, imply previous facts, facts from which they have sprung. This **second** application of the notion is of quite as much interest **as** the first, since events **and our** control of events turn upon it. Valid **being is the statical force of the** idea, and evolution its dynamical force.

Every **section of a river is** referred to the **one** next above it. **Language suits itself to** the convenience of use as certainly **as to the facts** expressed. In speaking of a river, we divide **it, though it is in itself** continuous, into portions easily **designated by changes in** its banks, or by features which interest us in the stream itself. Thus we refer to the bend, and the stretch above the bend; or the rapids and the level below the rapids. In like manner in the coherent flow of events, we select the causes which interest us, and we name them by the effects through which they are expressed. Thus the death of a man is said to be due to the premature explosion of a charge, and this to the hasty firing of the fuse, and this to a reckless temper. Thought lays hold of those causes and conditions which are of moment in reference to the control of events. The mind is, therefore, even more likely to be attracted by secondary and variable conditions than by the fixed lines of forces, since it is through these conditions chiefly that it modifies events. An engine on a railroad fires the barns along its track, it is complained of as being constructed without a sufficient defense against scattering sparks. The defect is said to be the cause of the conflagrations.

Causes are divided into efficient causes, conditional causes and final causes. Strictly efficient causes are the forces which, interesting each other in the effect, occasion it; or these forces in some previous form. Thus the flying of the rocks is due to the expansive force of the gases imprisoned in the charge. The gunpowder is an efficient cause. The food which a workingman has eaten, and the weight and temper of his axe, are efficient causes in the felling of a tree. Evidently many lines of force may unite in an effect. Conditional causes are those things, actions, relations, which, without constituting a part of the efficient forces, determine the presence of these forces in the effect in an efficient form. Conditional causes are of quite as much practical interest as efficient causes, and may not be easily distinguishable from them. Drilling the hole, charging it and firing the fuse are conditional causes of blasting the rock.

Final causes are not causes. We mean by a final cause

the motive which prompts an action. Thus the final cause of removing the rocks is the construction of a railroad.

The doctrine of intuitive ideas is often damaged by its advocates. It is asserted that consciousness testifies to much not referable to this source. The direct matter of consciousness, sensations, thoughts, feelings, volitions, are undeniable. There is no ground for dispute when any fact is **a** product of consciousness, that is, belongs to mental states. It is quite a different question, What is involved in the data of consciousness? The validity of our judgments, the ideas under which they proceed are to be arrived **at** by analysis, by reasoning, and are not directly vouched for by consciousness.

It is sometimes said **we** are conscious of force, and therefore of a cause in putting forth voluntary effort. The true statement would rather seem to be, we are conscious of volition, and of the subsequent sensations which accompany action, but not at all of the hidden link of power which unites them. Indeed, it is not always possible for us to tell whether the intended muscular result will follow the volition. Some paralysis may have intervened, arresting **the** flow **of** energy, and the interior connection lies **so** wholly beyond consciousness, that we can only determine the presence or absence of suitable muscular conditions by a tentative effort at movement. If we were conscious of force, force itself would be phenomenal, and lose its subphenomenal character. It would cease to be a causal idea and would become a sensible fact or effect.

The simplest statement of causation is, Every effect must have a cause. In this is involved the expectation of the perpetuity of nature, since every change in the effect, as itself an effect, would demand a new, specific cause. With no apparent change in causes, we anticipate previous results, since these must follow from the unchanged forms and conditions of action. A prolonged duration of the present physical system is expected by us, unless we see, or think we see, reasons for change in the government of God, or grounds of change in the system itself—an introduction at some point of new forces.

§ 9. Causation is the law of connection between physical facts; spontaneity, the idea we have next to offer, is the ground of connection between purely mental facts. These two sets of facts are as distinct in their dependencies as in the fields in which they occur. Confusion may easily arise from blending physical and mental phenomena in the nervous system which lies as a medium of interaction between them. All physical facts and facts immediately dependent on them come under the law of causation. Causation involves the presence of forces, definite in quality and quantity, which, in transition from form to form, give rise to events. These forces have always some mode of existence which exactly expresses them. A power of mind can not so be conceived. It is not a realized patent or latent force of a given order, waiting on a proper occasion to pass through another form termed thought. The law of thought, that of truth, can not be maintained on such a supposition. Truth would become a simple effect, and lose its very nature. The mind must, as a power, seek, discern, and embrace the truth, otherwise it is not truth. This search implies spontaneity on the part of the mind, a self-guided power that moves toward its own ends. The laws of thought, of feeling, of volition do not abide as forces in this power, but are the product of the rational insight involved in the power itself. Language constantly regards this distinction, but not with the firmness it might. Over against forces should stand powers; against effects, actions; against causes, incentives and motives; against instruments, agents.

While spontaneity is the cardinal fact of mind, so much
so as to be essential to any apprehension of mind as mind,
it has more frequently been discussed as liberty. Proof of
the actual possession of liberty **by man** as a voluntary
agent, and a precise statement of what is involved therein, will be presented later. Liberty is to be distinguished
on the one side from those necessary connections which
are causal in character, and on the other from chance, **the**
denial of all dependence on antecedents. Indeed, strictly
construed, there can be no chance events. The positive
notions of causation and liberty, which cover the entire
phenomenal field, do not permit them. It is only under a
qualified form, as events with unknown or incalculable
causes, that chance ever appears in the field of facts.
Liberty allows the influence of motives, but not their
measured, definite, irresistible influence. We admit and
deny in the same instant the application of the word influence, admit the word in its substance, deny it in the
form which its connection with causal events has given it.
Herein is the peculiar and primitive character of the conception, that of a connection which is not necessary, of
persuasion which is not imperative in either branch of the
alternative, of influence which does not push with a fixed,
determinative force towards a given volition. The will
is neither capricious, nor mathematically calculable in its
**action.** It is free, and submits freely, so far as it *submits*
to the motives before it. There is no great difficulty in
this conception so long as we let it alone. It is when we
begin to compare it with other conceptions, that its peculiarity appears, and this we are liable to mistake for intrinsic absurdity, falsity.

This idea of liberty—the motives lying before the will,
not back of it; persuading, not impelling it—is primitive,
**and** brought **by** the **mind to the** explanation of a class

of facts that require it, those of choice and responsibility. The sense of obligation, with the subsequent feelings of virtue and guilt, of approval and condemnation; the facts of government, of reward and punishment, the mind can not understand or fully accept without the interpretation of the idea of liberty; without making the connection between choice and motives, between personal action and the circumstances under which it takes place, one of freedom. Hence springs the notion of liberty, and the obstinate defense and maintenance of it by so many, in spite of faulty definitions, in spite of this inability to render any explanation of it satisfactory to the purely scientific mind.

We are not conscious of liberty. If we were, there would be no room for discussion. We no more know the exact nature of the connection between the motives and the will from experience simply, than we do the connection between the volition and subsequent muscular action. In view of the accepted fact of accountability, and the absence of all sensible constraint in motives, the mind predicates of the connection liberty—itself supplying the idea, and applying it to the phenomena; exactly as to another class of facts, it, in the same independent way, brings the idea of causal interdependence. In each case the mind proceeds to meet and expound the facts with its own independent notion, seen by itself to be applicable to the conditions of the problem. The movement is exactly that which takes place in the explanation of other experiences under the notion of space; and of still others under that of time. The supersensual nature of the idea of liberty must be admitted by all, certainly not less by those who deny its intelligibility, and ridicule the assertion of its existence, than by those who accept both. It seems quite evident, that if freedom does exist, it is the regulative idea presiding over the facts of choice; the form under which the connection of the

will with the causal forces about it is to be conceived.
Indeed, philosophers of the empirical school usually deny
the existence and notion of liberty, at least as insisted on
by Intuitive Philosophy. No one can reach, or has striven
to reach, the notion of liberty through outside experience.
It has, when accepted, been referred directly to consciousness, or to an intuitive power.

§ 10. A ninth intuitive idea is that of truth. Truth is
the law of thought. It is the agreement of the judgments
of the mind with the facts and principles to which they
pertain. It is thus the goal of all intellectual inquiry.
Truth may seem to be a special application of the notion of
resemblance. More careful thought will distinguish the
**two**. Between the intellectual statement and that **to** which
it pertains there is no resemblance, as between one color and
another, one form and another, one feeling and another; nor
is the correspondence of truth that of identity, the van-
quishing point of resemblance. The two terms, the one an
immediate product of the mind, the other a fact of some
order in the Universe about us, are in every way distinct
from each other in the formal elements of being; they coalesce only in that single relation which we express by the
word truth. The power to discern the relation is a peculiar power of mind; and that it is an intuitive power is
seen in the fact that at least one of the two terms brought
together is an intellectual product. The senses therefore
can not pronounce on truth, while the judgment simply
affirms that true which is seen to be so.

§ 11. We have now reached an idea, whose nature and
origin have been the occasion of much diversity of opinion.
The conclusion we arrive at as to the nature of right, will
profoundly affect our intellectual and practical life. The
phenomena that call forth the discussion, though often
narrowed by the theory adopted for their explanation, are,

in a general way, accepted and agreed upon. They are
these. Certain forms of action are known by us as right,
others as wrong; a sense of obligation accompanies the
former when urged upon us, and of satisfaction and approval when performed by us. The latter, on the other
hand, when distinctly contemplated as wrong, deter the
mind from acceptance by a minatory sense of duty, and
punish the commission by a clear feeling of guilt. Of the
presence and operation of these facts, history and language
are full. Neither the speech nor the actions, the laws nor
the religion of men, are intelligible without them. The
testimony of individual experience is repeated in that of
communities and nations. From the beginning men have
been dealing with virtuous and vicious acts, with right and
wrong courses of conduct, with innocence and guilt, responsibility and irresponsibility, honor and shame, praise and
censure, rewards and punishments. These ethical ideas
grow in the race as it advances. Our legislation, our social
institutions, our daily actions, our religious beliefs are full
of them ; and new labors of reform are constantly putting
them into more pithy and pungent shape. Ethical science
commands a large share of attention, and takes under its
survey more and more broadly the actions of men. The
shades of feeling involved vary from remorse and despair
to the slightest uneasiness, from the triumphant self-justifi-
cation of the martyr to a transient thrill of delight. Sin,
wickedness, guilt, duty, right, righteousness, integrity, justice, holiness, are a few of the weighty words under which
these grave thoughts take their way.

The facts involved being thus comparatively bold and
salient, in a measure admitted by all, what is that theory of
intellectual powers which best covers and expounds them ?
The perception of right and the feeling of obligation are
inseparable ; they are the intellectual and emotional sides

of one mental state. An obligation can not be felt without
some direction or line of action to which it attaches. An
obligation must be of a specific, definite character. An
obligation without attachment to any act, is unintelligible,
is no obligation. The quality right, seen in an act, is that
which at once calls forth the feeling of duty, and directs it
into a particular channel. No more can the intuition be
separated from the feeling than the feeling from the intuition. Indeed, it is chiefly through the strong sentiment
that accompanies it, that we discover the distinct character
of the intuitive act. Language abundantly recognizes this
double bearing of ethical insight. We have the word right
as expressive of the intellectual recognition of moral law ;
and the words ought, obligation, duty, presenting the emotional element.

The theories which do not accept the original, simple,
inseparable character of the idea right, explain the intellectual element by the generalized notion of utility. This
is done with very different degrees of success by earlier
and later writers ; but the empirical school agree in making
utility the intellectual ground of ethics. We have appetites, sensibilities, tastes, affections to be gratified. Any
thing or action which affords pleasure to any one of these
is useful. This common power, which belongs to so many
objects and relations, of furnishing some form of enjoyment, or some condition of it, is abstracted under the word
*utility.* The inquiry which guides the conscience, it is
said, is this inquiry into pleasure, into immediate and
future enjoyment ; and that, if fairly and thoroughly pushed
and made to cover all gratifications high and low, it is an
exhaustive statement of all that takes place in ethical research. While this is an inadequate theory of the intellectual grounds of duty, it is difficult to disprove it. What is
affirmed by it does take place, and is a most apparent and **a**

most necessary part of the process by which we arrive at a practical conclusion as to a line of action, whether it be right or wrong. The usefulness of an action, in a broad and deep sense of the word, is a correct criterion of its moral character; it becomes, therefore, very difficult to show, that it does not cover the entire ethical element.

The quality right, like the quality beauty, is seen in an intellection, that is, in an act whose relations and bearings backward and forward have been inquired into and settled. What are the results which flow from it? What are the feelings it expresses? How will it work forward in the world of facts? How does it work backward on the emotions? These are the inquiries which disclose to us the intellectual bearings of the action, and prepare us to pronounce wisely on its character; they are also those which determine its utility. So far the ground is common to the two theories, sensualistic and intuitive. At this point they diverge. Says the one philosopher, these facts exhaust the grounds of intellectual action; says the other, they prepare the conditions of a final, intuitive act overlooked by you, pronouncing the action not useful or otherwise, but right or wrong. The last words are not, and can not be measured by the first. In the intellection which we have reached in part at least as you have reached it, we discover a farther transcendent relation to ourselves, which we term right, and from which springs all our ethical action. In this we affirm we have the testimony of language with us, which by no means confounds, or allows us to confound, these two notions of the right and the useful. Nay, it separates them in clean and clear division from each other, reserving an emphasis for the one which it never thinks of bestowing on the other.

It is, however, when the emotional element is considered, that the utilitarian theory is seen to be most obviously

inadmissible. It does not satisfactorily meet the question,
Whence arises the sense of obligation which is the salient
feature of the right? It strives **to** make answer by affirming that the feeling of duty is conventionally imposed **by**
the community in satisfaction of its own sentiments, and in
view of what is advantageous to itself. The obligation of
ethical action is thus referred to education, to social **and**
civil institutions, in their own behalf laying the pressure of
duty on their subjects. Says Bain, " Authority or punishment is the commencement of the state of mind recognized
under the various names—Conscience, the Moral Sense, the
Sentiment of Obligation. The major part of every community adopt certain rules of conduct necessary for the common preservation, or ministering to the common well-being.
. . . . Every one, not of **himself disposed to** follow the
rules prescribed by the community, is subjected to some infliction of pain to supply the absence of other motives:
the infliction increasing in severity until obedience is attained. It is the familiarity with this *régime* of compulsion, and of suffering, constantly increasing until resistance
**is** overborne, that plants in the infant and youthful mind
the first germ of the sense of obligation."—*The Emotions
and the Will, p.* 481. His definition of Conscience is, " An
**ideal** resemblance of public authority, growing up in **the**
individual mind, and working to the same end."

The **community** grounds the law of action partly on
utility, and partly on the transient sentiments which possess it, and so, with a variety of sanctions, trains the child to
obedience. " A certain dread and awful impression is thus
connected with forbidden actions, which is the conscience
in its earliest germ or manifestation."

This theory derives **a** force which does not belong to it
from the very fact that social law, appealing, as it often
does, to our moral nature, acquires thereby a prescriptive

power which would not otherwise be attainable. If there were no foundation for custom and law in our moral constitution, the results of social instruction and discipline would be much less than they now are. With this grave advantage afforded by the frequent coincidence of our moral constitution and social customs, the theory still plainly fails to cover the facts. It should be observed, moreover, that man's habitual disobedience to moral law weakens its authority, obscures its phenomena, and thus greatly aids the effort to confound it with conventional rule. Notwithstanding these causes of obscuration, we believe a better theory still remains visible in the facts.

(1) We have repeated examples of what general agreement and enforcement can accomplish, and the results are of another kind from those arising under true moral force. Take again, from another point of view, the illustration afforded by fashion. A kind of censure to which the masses of men are exceedingly sensitive, is constantly and unsparingly inflicted on those who disregard fashion. Yet the most infatuated devotee of the fickle goddess would hardly venture to regard scrupulous obedience as a virtue. Such an one is quite content if she escapes positive censure in her fashionable follies. How very different, also, the feeling arising from a violated fashion, from wearing a proscribed coat or hat, from that which affects the sensitive soul under the sense of wrong action. Allow each violator to be equally appreciative of the law whose precepts have been infringed, and we have, in the one case, mortification, and in the other guilt. The most scrupulous observance of the details of fashion, of fashion enforced by two thirds of the community, can not, does not, bestow the sense of virtue; nor disobedience the feeling of vice.

Take again the standard of honor enforced among certain classes, as among soldiers, or gamblers, or on the Stock

Exchange. The penalties here inflicted on disobedience, are as unsparing as the parties can make them. Yet such a custom as dueling is broken down by a purely moral sentiment, based on the individual conscience, struggling with and at length conquering the general consent of the community. It may be answered: Yes, but the sense of utility is with those who favor reform. Granted, but it is not, under the theory as presented in its present form, the notion of utility that imposes obligation, but the concurrent, educational force of **the** community, and this is fully pledged to a custom which nevertheless calls forth on the part of a few a staunch condemnation, finding at length such response in the consciences of all as to lead to the abandonment of the censured act. Now, if the question were one merely of wisdom, there would be no mystery in the formation of a new opinion, and hence in a change of action. The difficulty under the **theory lies** in explaining how moral obligation, which rests on an educational basis, which arises from the enforced sentiment of the many, which is the volume of sound made by a multitude of voices, can be brought to bear against an overwhelming majority, to the breaking down of those **very** beliefs whence it springs. How can **one, two,** three, outshout the crowd? How can there arise **a** counter-sense **of** duty, when this sense is simply the concurrent opinions of **men, sustaining as** sacred the censured institution. Duty would thus be like respectability, like popularity. They do go, and must go with the dominant party, and can not be used as an incipient force against themselves.

(2) The thief, the gambler, the speculator, rest their laws on an educated sense of honor peculiar to themselves, and while they **do secure** obedience, sometimes more self-sacrificing and implicit than much of that which arises under moral law, it is notoriously with little or no reference

to such a law. They do not mistake their precepts for morality ; they are scrupulous, not conscientious, in their obedience to them. Occasionally to throw a slight coloring of morality over their actions, is the most they aim at. In a community in which slavery for many generations has been the law of the land, we find, nevertheless, an independent moral element getting a foothold. Conscience is appealed to, and a vigorous moral warfare springs up in the teeth of uniform custom. Nor do those who justify slavery do it on the ground of uniform practice, except so far as this is regarded as an expression of opinion on the part of those who have thus held their fellows in bondage. Other grounds than the mere fact of custom are sought, grounds which, so far as they exist, have a true justificatory element in them : the good condition of the slave ; his inferiority ; the general social order ; the exigencies of the case. I may almost say, that never is the appeal directly made between intelligent parties in an ethical discussion to naked custom and its penalties, for the defence of a line of conduct. This is a fact very damaging to the explanations offered. Men are never reverting to the bare fact of enforced law, as the ground and justification of law : yet this after all is made the source of the sense of law. Moreover, in the very face of such enforcement, there does spring up, in single minds, a moral sentiment, which with pure moral power breaks down institutions hitherto unanimously sustained. We thus see what prescriptive force can do ; that it is by no means identical with morality, and that it constantly comes in conflict with the power this manifests, and yields to it.

(3) Again, this theory fails most signally in cases in which the moral phenomena are most distinct. In the explanation of mixed conduct, of actions assuming an ethical form, disguising themselves under moral sentiments, it prospers somewhat ; but when the moral element is promi-

nent and pure, it comes short. A conscientious man becomes a martyr to his convictions of duty. He stands
against the community, and confronts its authority, its alleged line of duty, with his own independent convictions,
his own sense of what is right. All the explanation of
these most startling and pregnant facts in the world's moral
history, facts that above all others catch the rational eye,
and disclose the new force that is flaming up in them, is
that of the "Self-originating or Idiosyncratic Conscience."
It is an instance of "the transfer of the sentiment of prohib-
ition from a recognized case, to one not recognized." That
is to say, with no notion of obligation but the enforced one
of education, the individual may, nevertheless, transfer it
so strictly to his own independent, unsustained speculation
as to oppose these serenely and unhesitatingly to the utmost stretch of the authority of the community over him.
This is a transfer indeed, a transfer that is a transformation,
that discloses a sentiment in kind and quality totally unlike that with which it commenced. It went into the co-
coon a worm, it comes out a butterfly. This is no explan-
**ation**; it is a confession of defeat. Better would it have
**been** to have left the phenomena unexplained.

(4) Further, we do not day by day impose duties on
others in the manner that would be indicated by the above
theory. Scarcely anything could be more adverse to the
methods of those who are constantly using moral force,
who are addressing and stimulating the conscience, than an
appeal to the common sentiments, that is popular sentiments, of those approached. Indeed, to such persons it
would seem unworthy, sometimes even absolutely immoral
to urge action on others primarily on the ground of the customs and censures of general society. Nor could these censures often be made to subserve the purposes of morality.
The apostle of moral truth expects more frequently than

otherwise to confront this public sentiment. and his appeal is not to what has been or is, but to the individual idea of what ought to be. The practice therefore which would flow logically from this theory of enforced morals, is not at all the practice of the actual, ethical world; it is rather that of those classes who are feared and warred against, as always careless of the law of right, and often disobedient to it.

Kindred expositions, insufficient to cover the facts to which they are applied, are found everywhere in the works of philosophers who advocate this theory of morals. "By remorse, we understand the strongest form of self-reproach arising from a deep downfall of self-respect and esteem." *The Emotions and the Will, page* 106. This definition applies to a conspicuous act of misjudgment, and most plainly does not reach the fact of remorse. Again, love is said to be "as purely self-seeking as any other pleasure, and to make no inquiry as to the feelings of the beloved personality." This assertion leaves out the entire moral element which belongs to love as an affection, and is true of it only as a passion. The peculiar effect of "signal generosity" is referred to the "shock" given to the "mind totally unprepared" to see kind offices rendered to an enemy. Mill makes our sympathies with others in their injuries the basis of our sentiments of justice, a condition of feeling, certainly, which as often perverts justice as secures it. These and kindred solutions show the weakness of utilitarianism in handling striking moral facts, and how greatly it abridges and mars the facts themselves by a forced, belittling estimate of them.

Nor is the sense of obligation any more satisfactorily accounted for under this theory by referring it directly to the idea of utility. At times, Mr. Mill seems ready to do this. As the useful, in the concrete, is the pleasurable, this reference would involve the assertion, that pleasure, as pleasure, is felt in human experience to be obligatory. This would farther include the statement, the stronger the pleasure the greater the sense of duty; and, as our own enjoyments are more distinctly conceived than those of others, that these are pre-eminently enforced in practical morals; and farther, as present gratification yields more intense feeling **than** anticipated indulgence, that the pleasures of the hour **are** especially watched over by conscience. Each and all of these conclusions are in exact contradiction of the facts. If there is anything in reference to which we feel ourselves **left to our own** unrestrained choices, it is our pleasures. The moral nature has not laid upon it the superfluous task of enforcing these; but rather that of restraining them. By playing cunningly between the two, public sentiment on the one hand, and utility on the other, some embarrassments may be evaded by the theorist; yet neither nor both can be successfully made the source of the sense of duty. When we are brought face to face with any, the wisest statement of the utilitarian law, as for instance that we are to seek the greatest good of the greatest number, how is that statement to gain any authority with us? Evidently by our rational penetration into its inmost quality. Enforced in any other way on us it loses power to bless us. Its intrinsic fitness does not save it, if we do not see that fit**ness.** Enforced obedience is slavery for all the parties in**volved** in it. Insight is the only refuge of manhood. Ultimate, honorable guidance must come to us through our own powers.

While these failures of explanation rob utilitarianism of all claims to acceptance, is there not in it a yet deeper difficulty in supposing that a simple notion, like that of obligation, can be other than primitive and independent of the action of society? What would be thought of a philos-

ophy that should refer compassion, love, hope, as induced
feelings, to the influence of others over the mind. Evidently all extraneous action is of no avail to awaken a feeling not given in the emotional constitution itself. A sense
of duty, of obligation, is as simple as any emotion can be
and if we acknowledge its presence, we must look on it as
primitive in our constitution. But a sense of obligation is
not intelligible as a general unattached feeling, indicating
no definite line of conduct, haunting the mind as a vague
premonitory fear, ready to be seized on by the first foreign
force, to be applied as an alien impulse, having no necessary existence in the individual nor office for him. The imposed opinion of others can not create a feeling; the feeling
of duty, like every feeling, must have a deeper basis than
this. A general notion of obligation, with no intellectual
element, no specific direction given to it by the mind whose
it is, is as incomprehensible as would be a general impression of truth, or delight in truth, with nothing presenting
itself as truth; or a vague satisfaction in beauty, with no
object regarded by us as beautiful. What can be found
in our constitution, allied to such an unattached, unelicited
emotion? The vague feelings of fear sometimes present to
the mind nevertheless disclose to more careful inquiry some
occasion and ground of attachment in past experience and
existing circumstances.

There are but two open, plausible theories of our moral
constitution; the one which recognizes it as an original, independent part of our constitution; and the one which,
through generalization, explains its manifestations by the
facts of our physical and social position, making utility and
public sentiment the germs of its intellectual and emotional
elements. The last, in its pure, naked form, produces a
far off semblance of the facts, replacing love and duty
with fear and interest, and mistaking the forces at work in

a selfish, immoral world, for the true constitutional links of a higher, a holier, state.

There are, however, theories which strive to combine these two, and while, in the last analysis, they are utilitarian in their principles, they keep aloof from the avowal, and include elements which only logically belong to an intuitive philosophy. Utilitarianism relies on the happiness afforded by correct action as the sole motive to it, and falls short of ethics in not being able to impose any line of action with authority, or to enforce one form of enjoyment in preference to another. Indeed, it has no sufficient standard by which to decide between pleasures, and to prefer one class above another. The question of the actual satisfaction experienced by different persons in different lines of action must, like that of physical tastes, be left with the individual, and if he prefer physical, to intellectual and social enjoyments, one cannot, under a mere law of highest gratification, impose on him the opinions of others. I do not need to inquire of a philosopher as to which apple is sweet and which sour, which agreeable and which disagreeable; nor shall I much respect his view if it differs from my own. Thus, in all questions of pure pleasure, each man has his bias, and is not likely to yield it to a speculation that runs counter to his own experience, the final interpreter to him of the nature and quality of enjoyments.

An effort to obviate this difficulty has been made by affirming the superior character of moral pleasures, and from this supreme quality reflecting back on the actions which secure it a sense of obligation. Herein is found the stolen element of a better theory. If we rely on the good which diverse lines of conduct produce to define and enforce our action, then we are entitled to these several kinds and degrees of satisfaction to direct and establish conduct, and to no more. Let all the sources of pleasure, making the

catalogue as discriminating and exhaustive as you please, be
represented by the letters A, B, C, D, E. Let each one
choose between them as he, under the guidance of his own
tastes and capabilities, is able, in kind, degree, duration, difficulty of attainment; and thus mark out for himself the
path of prudence. He can not now go farther, and add to
the motives urging any one proposed line of conduct a peculiar blessedness which is to crown it as right above all
others. This is to establish again in our constitution a moral
law, to restore to it intrinsic obligation, and thus secure the
unspeakable satisfaction of obedience. All that our quiet,
careful reasoner, overlooking the various sources of pleasure,
and choosing between them, is entitled to, is, if he select
wisely, the satisfaction of sagacity. He is always right when
he is prudent, and the rewards of right sink to those of
prudence. The self-congratulation of shrewdness, takes the
place of the blessedness of a law implicitly obeyed, clung
to in darkness and in light. No peculiar happiness can
follow obedience to right, till we have recognized it as an
antecedent, supreme, self-enforced law. As long as it remains a line of conduct resting for support on its pleasurable results, it must look to these exclusively, adding nothing to them save the satisfaction of sagacity. The right
must come before the satisfaction which springs from obey-
ing it.

Herein is revealed a difficulty which more or less embarrasses every presentation of the utilitarian theory. We
grant, that what is right is always ultimately in a broad
sense useful, but the moral nature, itself an independent
means of gratification, a pre-eminent source of good, is
often the necessary condition of its being so. The martyr
sets this one pleasure over against all other pleasures, and
wisely; yet he never would have done this, if he had started
with the idea that the right action is only the sagacious

choice between enjoyments other than those which belong
to the moral constitution. We are not in our theories to
have, and not to have, at the same time, the law and the
rewards of the moral intuition. We are not to make ethical pleasures to arise simply from the successful pursuit of
other pleasures, and yet allow them themselves to be furtively included among these pleasures between which we
are deciding. Many lines of action are obviously useful
when accompanied with the gratification of our moral sensibilities, which are not so, when these as independent
sources of good are left out of the calculation, as they must
be in any honest evolution of a utilitarian theory.

Spencer, in his Data of Ethics, falls headlong into this
error. He affirms that life is for the sake of pleasure,
and therefore that "that conduct is good which subserves
life." If we suppose perfection of character, he argues,
to lead only to pain, then that perfection itself disappears.
He herein overlooks two obvious relations. Virtue can not
be separated from the satisfaction that virtue occasions.
This is to cut into parts a living thing; this is to destroy
the very notion, and of course if the notion becomes something other than what it is, the results will be correspondingly different. Nor does it follow that because satisfaction necessarily attaches to virtue, that that satisfaction, as
a new pleasure, is the motive of virtue. A disinterested
act as disinterested is peculiarly pleasurable. If one "is
blessed in performing an act of mercy," he is blessed
because he did it as an act of mercy in oversight of personal interest. Confusion at this point ought not to be any
longer possible. The word pleasure is also plainly of a
very generic order. There are the most marked differences
in pleasures in kind as well as in degree. Yet if the utilitarian grants this, all his weights and measures are at once
broken.

Nor is the intuitive philosophy, rightly presented, at all open to the repeated taunts of Bentham, that each individual by a blind irrational power may thus pretend to decide what is right, and capriciously lay down a law absolute for himself and for others. All the investigation that Bentham or any other philosopher may bring to the practical effects of action, to its immediate and ultimate results, finds a place in our moral judgments. It is in full intellections made up by exhaustive inquiry, that the reason sees the right. We might as well say, because the judge authoritatively decides a case, it is of no avail for the lawyers thoroughly to present it, as to say, that because conscience adjudicates between right and wrong, it is of no moment that the action to which the discussion pertains should be fully understood. It is the intellectual conception of this action which is declared right, and if this conception is incomplete, then a verdict intrinsically correct is practically false, as pronounced on a hypothetical case and not a real one. The last decision, that of conscience, we believe to be correct; the presentation of the case, that on which this decision is made, to be often incorrect. Here enter the full fruits of investigation and protracted experience, an opportunity for a broad, honest, faithful survey of the facts of the exact case to be made up and presented at the judgment-seat of the ethical sense. This merely gives the weight of law to what the other faculties have pronounced prudent and wise. There is no more opportunity for caprice and individual assumption here than in any debate concerning the qualities and bearings of actions.

We designate in common language as conscience that action of the reason which discovers the right, and this is the ground or centre of our entire moral nature. Any theory which regards obligation as simple and ultimate, therein accepts the intuitive and independent nature of the

right, in the meaning in which we have employed it. Obligation must arise in *view* of something, and in view of it
in a *moral relation*. The two are as indivisible as the flavor and savor of a peach, the perception of the one and the
enjoyment of the other.

The system of ethics to be evolved from the above view
is briefly this. All moral emotions, the entire moral nature
is conditioned on a moral intuition, which we term that of
right. This relation of rational acts, arrived at by a simple
stroke of the eye of reason, in grounds previously unfolded,
and which uniformly relate to the actions of free, intelligent
sensitive beings, involves as an inseparable element the feeling of obligation. Here is the final authority of morals in
the moral intuition. A reason can be given for the decisions of conscience in this sense, that the character and bearings of the acts pronounced right can be given; not in this
sense, that the intellectually discerned relations of **these ac-**
tions are, aside from **a** distinct action of the moral faculty
upon them, a ground of obligation. No " good," as a good
**can give** a law, can give a moral basis of action, since to do
this it must go beyond its own appetitive range, and reach
into the moral field of authority. It is to account for *authority* that we invoke the moral **nature.**

§ 12. The third idea regulative of our intellectual life
**is that of beauty.** Concerning the existence at this point
of peculiar phenomena that require explanation, there is no
discussion. **Yet results of analysis are** quite different; some
reaching **a simple,** original idea; others resolving beauty
into utility, or unity and variety, or making it the product
of association. That beauty is intimately connected with
utility, that it is always accompanied by unity and variety,
that taste is strongly influenced by association, and, in some
cases overshadowed by it, are undeniable; yet that these
explanations, in conflict among themselves, fail each of

them to cover the entire facts, seems equally plain.  Beauty
is not proportioned to utility, is not always attendant upon
it and exists sometimes with little or no utility, save that
which the gratification of taste itself affords.  Unity and
variety are frequently present with no corresponding beauty,
belong to structures which do not pertain to the fine arts,
and thus show an independent existence and range.  Association explains many of the judgments of those who give
little attention to intrinsic beauty, who under the influence
of others yield their opinions to be swayed by the prevalent
sentiment; yet just in proportion as the presence of taste is
manifest, as the perception of beauty is developed, as the
phenomena to be accounted for are obvious and declared,
this explanation fails.  The leaders in fine art have no
higher association from which to derive their estimates of
excellence, while the different, external, accidental pleasures, that may for them incidentally find connection with
works of art, are no sufficient ground for their uniform estimates, singling these forth in all generations as objects of
peculiar power and value.

But this theory of association, of character transferred to
objects of beauty from the relations in which we find them,
is met by the fact that we have a pertinent example of what
association can do in this same direction in affecting our estimates of things; and that it wholly fails to sustain the
explanation here offered of the facts of taste.  The admiration the general public express for a new fashion is almost
wholly due to association, and what are its characteristics?
This esteem is fickle, contradictory, and wholly destitute of
standards of judgment.  Though in the present, unanimity
may be complete, successive periods differ greatly in the
forms rejected and accepted.  Fortuity and the most extravagant fancies reign, and are equally imperious in their contradictory commands.  The whole realm of fashion is one of

unreasoning association, and it stands in conspicuous contrast with that of taste, refuting the explanation offered of
its stable phenomena. The uniform admiration bestowed
by different nations and generations on objects of beauty ;
the first high estimates which give direction to public opin-
**ion ;** the word beauty, accepting in careful speech no syn-
onym ; the fine arts, a distinctly bounded territory, eliciting
the most skillful and prolonged attention ; and the well-established principles of this department, show that the fickle
fanciful connections of association furnish no sufficient the-
**ory of taste.**

That the quality, beauty, accepted as unresolvable into
any other, is of intuitive origin is seen in the fact, that it is
not directly a quality of things, but of intellections. An
intellection is the product of the mind. The qualities,
forms, and relations of an object—its expression—are by
studious observation brought before the mind. This estimate which the intellect makes of all that unfolds the character, the emotional power of an object, is an intellection,
and in the object thus conceived, thus unfolded in the
thoughts, beauty is seen to inhere. As beauty thus does
**not** belong to a flower, a tree, a landscape, a bird, a man,
merely as a sensible object, **but to them** as products of an
**arranging,** vitalizing, perfecting power ; **as** it is seen not
in the thing simply, but in it as conceived by the mind,
it must be the object of an interior, intuitive faculty, which
can take into its contemplation the appropriate intellection.
An act **of** exposition more or less complete, has followed
perception, and thus the object has been taken from the
senses into the mind, and there awaits the insight of the
reason. The qualities one and all which make up the
expression pronounced beautiful are not the very beauty
which we attribute **to** the cathedral, the painting, or the
**statue.** The skill, proportion, height of the towering edifice

may be discerned separately from that final effect, that joint and supersensual power, that more than analytic pleasure, which we term beauty. This is not the craft of the workman, the single nor the combined excellence s of the work, but an overshadowing power through which these have their chief value, by which the seal of a fine art is put upon them. The intellectual relations of an object, capable only of an inner presentation, are that in which, as substance, the reason sees beauty to inhere. Beauty is not these simply, though it comes and goes with their varying combinations.

§ 13. It only remains to speak of the infinite, the last of the intuitive ideas, and one that has recently given rise to much discussion. It finds application in several directions, and perhaps, in the development of the mind, as early to space as to any other form of thought. The notion of space cannot be dwelt on without soon suggesting this idea of the infinite. The mind soon sees the inapplicability of any measures, limits, finite relations to space, and that, in the very moment of establishment, they are swept away by the on-going movement. Space lies without, as much as within, any line we choose to run, and the nearer has no advantage over the farther side. The mind under this new necessity laid upon it, with this new occasion given to it, grasps the idea of the infinite, of unmeasured and immeasurable extension. This conception is not the result of mere weariness, is not the affirmation of an inability to proceed farther, does not spring from repeated and reiterated failure ; it is rather the force and insight of the mind that disclose it. It is seen that there can be no advantage in pressing the imagination to its utmost flight, that the conditions which are now present at this point of space, must recur everywhere, no matter what the position attained by us ; that one point and one position here or there, that each

bound longer or shorter, are *fac-similes* of every other, and
therefore contain the solution of the problem as perfectly
as if it had been raced after with the most wearisome
efforts. The mind does not then distress itself in search of
a limit, and fail; it discovers that there *can* be no limit; it
penetrates the conditions of the problem, and brings forward the notion of a true infinite, which it sets over against
the finite, and is at rest, as it knows that nothing other or
more is to be found elsewhere.

Thus the mind hits upon the true infinite, not by experience, not by exhaustive effort, but by its own penetration
of relations; and through this idea it understands another
of the conditions of its experience, and declines exertion
which it sees to be necessarily futile. Standing, not moving; by insight, not by baffled effort, it grasps and henceforth uses this notion, so super-sensual in character, so
necessary for the exposition of the being we possess, the
universe we inhabit. Space, as infinite, admits of no division. No plane can cleave it, no line pierce it. In strict
language, it is without parts, at least so far as these imply
remainders. The true infinite is subject to no addition,
subtraction, multiplication or divison. These are processes
which find play in the finite alone.

A second point at which this notion arises early is in the
contemplation of time. Here, too, the mind discovers that
the conditions of conception are not in the least varied by
movement, and that the years which beheld the laying of
the foundations of the world were no less central than those
which now are, or those which shall behold its overthrow.
Geologic æons lie lapped in eternity, with no more power of
measurement than the point which defines pure position on
the board before me. Here again there is no opportunity
to take aught from, or add aught to the infinite, to eternity.
Indeed we may not strike it into two infinite halves by this

fleeting moment the present, as if it were a node jointing
the past to the future. A hemisphere is not a sphere
because it meets on one side the conditions of the definition. A true infinite must be immeasureable in all the
directions in which measurement can be applied. A forward or a backward stretch, leaving a definite, finite period
in the opposite direction, constitutes no true infinite; the
lines which pass out from any given point are not infinite,
they lack an essential feature of the infinite, interminable-
ness. They are limited in one direction. We are always
to distinguish between the indefinitely great and the infinite. Mathematics deals with the one, metaphysics with
the other. A series of figures increased as you please, can
never *express* an infinite amount, and therefore no infinite
can be twice or thrice as great as another infinite. This
borne constantly in mind, and we shall easily dispose of
a portion of the perplexities Sir William Hamilton has
thrown around the subject.

"A quantity, say a foot, has an infinity of parts. Any
part of this quantity, say an inch, has also an infinity. But
one infinity is not larger than another. Therefore an inch
is equal to a foot." Neither an inch, nor a foot, nor any
other definite quantity, has an infinity of parts—parts that
are parts, that have any size, will exhaust any dimensions
short of the infinite, and the quotient still remain finite.
"A wheel turned with quickest motion; if a spoke be prolonged, it will therefore be moved with a motion quicker
than the quickest."

This example and similar examples, are mere riddles
arising under a play of words. There is no absolutely
quickest motion, and no motion that is infinitely rapid.
The perplexity in these cases does not all spring from the
notion of the infinite, but from the effort of the imagination to transcend its own conditions in a false search by a

false method after the infinite, or the infinitesimal. The imagination must have finite, phenomenal quantities to deal with. These, therefore, are always capable both of multiplication and division. The fancy may carry on the process till it gets weary; confounded with the results, it may mistake its own embarrassments for those of the entire mind. It does this only by overlooking and denying the true nature of the infinite, and the source whence alone it can be rationally looked for. It should not distress the mind, because the end of a circle can not be found by chasing round and round it. No more should it, because that which has not dimensions cannot be reached by cutting down, and at the same time saving, that which has. This is striving in the same instant and act to hold on to the finite, and to take it away, to keep it and to get beyond it to the infinitisimal. It is no more a startling and discouraging fact, that the imagination can make nothing out of nothing, nor give limits to that which is without limits, than it is that the body can not be suspended by a spider's thread. Remove the support beyond a certain amount in either case, and there must be a downfall.

A third direction in which this notion is applicable, is to the attributes of God. God is infinite in power, in wisdom, in goodness; that is there are no limits to these attributes within their own nature. All that power can do, the power of God is able to do. The infinite in space presents itself under other forms from the infinite in time, and both **of these in a way yet different** from the infinite in power. The nature of power is not altered by the affirmation of its infinite extent. This merely removes its limits. It can no more do now than before what is not pertinent to its nature, what must be the product of wisdom or of grace. The notion, in its application to God, comes to assume those personal relations, that independent perfection of existence, which we designate by the Infinite the Absolute. God is thus lifted above the reflex action of causes, as well as above their antecedent action. Not only is nothing back of Him, there is nothing before Him, giving condition and law *ab extra* to His nature. God as infinite is not limited in action; as absolute, he is not straitened by any reaction. The material with which man works, limits the work; no limitations reach the labors of God save those contemplated and established in his creative thought. The infinite in this form, in these its various applications, we must defend as a positive, intuitive idea—indeed, if it be an idea at all, it must be an intuitive idea.

The first objections against the positive, valid character of this notion which we shall consider, are those of Sir William Hamilton, presented under what he terms, *The Law of the Conditioned.* It is claimed, that this impression, like that of causality, arises from the powerlessness of the mind, not from its insight. The line of argument is much the same as in the case of causation. The following with omissions, is his presentation of the subject. It is found in the *Lectures on Metaphysics, p.* 527.

" We are altogether unable to conceive space as bounded, as finite; that is as a whole beyond which there is no farther space. · · · On the other hand, we are equally powerless to realize in thought the possibility of the opposite contradictory; we cannot conceive space as infinite, as without limits. You may launch out in thought beyond the solar walk, you may transcend in fancy even the universe of matter, and rise from sphere to sphere in the region of empty space until imagination sinks exhausted; with all this, what have you done? You have never gone beyond the finite. · · Now then, both contradictions are equally inconceivable, both are equally incomprehensible; and yet, though unable to view either as possible, we are forced by a higher

law—that of excluded middle—to admit that one and but
one only is necessary." He then treats in the same way
the minimum of space, the maximum and minimum of
time, and proceeds, "The sum therefore of what I have
now stated, is: that the conditioned is that which is alone
conceivable, or cogitable. The unconditioned that which is
inconceivable or incogitable. The conditioned or the thinkable lies between two extremes or poles." Later he says,
"These poles are the absolute and the infinite; the term
absolute expressing that which is finished or complete; the
term infinite that which can not be terminated or concluded."

The doctrine of the law of the conditioned is the most
characteristic feature of the philosophy of Hamilton, and
is open to obvious and fatal objections. It does not explain
(1) why the mind is thus embarrassed in its conception of
the maximum and minimum of space and time; nor (2)
why it is ever led to vex and torment itself with these im-
possibilities, forsaking the conditioned where traveling is
comfortable and profitable, to scale cloud-heights which
never give foothold to the foolhardy assailant; nor yet,
most strange omission, (3) why of two impossible conceptions equally perplexing, we are called on to accept the one,
that of infinite space, infinite time, in place of the other,
that of bounded space and time. A better theory is able
to offer an explanation of these difficulties. The mind is
baffled in a conception of a maximum and minimum of
space, because a faculty is set to the task which deals exclusively with the phenomenal, and it is no more curious or
surprising that the imagination can not attain to the infinite, than that these limbs of ours can not mount a sunbeam,
and so reach the heavens; or, more aptly, than that we can
not see, hear, smell the infinite; since the senses are the
analogues of the fancy, both covering in a different way the

same field. We have given the imagination a work to it impossible and preposterous. Why are there these excursions of fancy into impracticable regions? Because overlooking the direct, intuitive grasp of the mind, and still haunted by the notion of the infinite, we put spurs to the steeds of the imagination to see if we may not in this way overtake it. The sober, plodding judgment turns aside from the thinkable to the unthinkable, in hunt of a ghostly conception which is real enough to bewilder the eye with strange appearances, but too unsubstantial to be grasped and handled in physical fashion. To pursue spirits or flee from spirits on horseback is of little avail, though, with man's belief in the spiritual world, the nature of the pursuit and its philosophy are sufficiently plain to the quiet looker-on.

A most fatal failure of this theory is to explain why we uniformly and certainly accept infinite space which has no advantage to the mind over the supposition of finite space. This embarrassment at once disappears, if we suppose the notion a positive one, provided by the mind to be placed in explanation and comprehension over against the finite. The theory of Hamilton succeeds in eliciting the perplexities of the subject, but brings to them no solution.

But it will be said, the intuitive theory has its own and yet more fatal difficulties. How can the infinite be a positive idea? Very easily, if we assign it to the right faculty, and make it simple and ultimate; as easily and intelligibly as red is red, or sweet, sweet. In neither case can we go beyond the ultimate fact, and we have fortunately learned in the more familiar instance to give up the effort. This objection may come in the form of a second theory of the infinite, to wit, that the notion is a negative not a positive one, involving a denial merely and not an affirmation. That the word is negative in form is a fact of no significance; so are inhuman and indecent. If the word infinite simply set forth the fact of non-existence, we should at once lay aside the article, and no longer speak of *the* infinite, any more than of the nothing. It is because it stands over against the finite, embracing the sum of possibilities and powers not expressed or measured therein, that we call it *the* infinite. If its negative form contained the true secret of the word, it would occasion no more perplexity, would contain no more profound depths, than does the finite. Nothing is as intelligible as something, the termination as the extension of physical objects, and if the mind did accept the word as a mere denial of anything more, it would accept it contentedly, without this endless bother and perplexity, this groping on for something not yet reached.

It is said, in proof of this negative character of the notion, that it is inconceivable. This we grant, and have given the reason why it is inconceivable. It is not an object for the imagination. No more is the notion of causation, nor of liberty, nor of right, nor of beauty. Nothing which is not phenomenal, nor under the immediate form which phenomena are assuming, is a subject for the imagination. It is further said, The infinite is not thinkable. "To think is to condition," is to throw into finite relations, is to destroy the notion of the infinite. The same answer as that already made is still open. The list of our faculties is not exhausted when we have marked off the imagination and the judgment. It is possible that the reason was given to us for this very end, to reach ideas *not* otherwise present to the mind. We hardly see why it should be present, or thought to be present, to furnish thinkable and conceivable objects, that is, objects arrived at by other faculties.

In what sense, however, is it true that the infinite is not thinkable? It is true in this sense only, that it can not be approached by explanations grounded on resemblances, that it can not be made the subject of judgments, at least, of those which limit it under finite analogies. And why should we expect it to be? Do we not antecedently see and say, that this process must be destructive to the very nature of the notion? Why then proceed to allege the fact against it? We can do this rationally only by involving the assertion, that the judgment and imagination are our exclusive faculties of knowledge; and this begs the question at issue. To reject the reason because it does not do the very superfluous work of giving an idea capable, by likeness and relation, of falling into the list of previous ideas, is to misunderstand the object of the faculty, or to assume that its existence is impossible. We might as well object to the validity of our knowledge of an odor, because it is not thinkable, or, forsooth, conceivable under color or sound. In this sense, then, we admit the infinite is not thinkable; but all thinking is not under limitations and conditions. Sometimes it is quite the reverse. To say that God is infinite is to deny conditions of Him. To say that The Infinite is, that He is free, that He is holy, is not to condition, to limit God, rather the reverse. The fact that we cannot go farther, and conceive the acts in and by which His liberty and holiness express themselves, except under a finite form, does not destroy the meaning or significance of the antecedent assertion, it merely presents another case of a familiar difficulty, that of getting from one province of knowledge to another. Different tracts of cognition do not lie together, like the provinces of one empire, the transition one of movement only.

Here springs up another modification of this theory, that of Herbert Spencer. He regards the notion of the infinite as of an illusory character, shown by the very fact that every effort to give proportion and definiteness to it, baffles us, and results in driving it into more remote re-

gions.   We admit the perplexity **which a portion** of our
faculties, whose action we are most familiar with, and from
which we are accustomed to receive most of our conclusions,
experience in handling, or rather in striving to handle, the
infinite.   This fact presents to us no difficulty; we see the
reason why these faculties are not adequate to the labor laid
upon them.   Indeed, our belief in the infinite would be
overthrown by a successful presentation of it, either by the
imagination **or** by the judgment under its own forms, and
is established by this very failure on their part.   The objection of our adversary is proof with us.

On the other hand, the opposite view, that the notion is
wholly illusory, is involved in difficulties that it cannot
evade.   **How can** Spencer insist that any presentation of
the infinite is not adequate, when he has no notion of what
the infinite is?   **How can a** notion be shown to be illusory,
except by a growing intuition?   How can Hamilton require
us to accept by faith that which is unintelligible, absolutely
and completely so.   Here are real contradictions.   There
can be no general denial of the applicability of any and all
conceptions of the infinite, without postulating thereby
**some notion** of the infinite with which these are compared,
and, as falling short, are pronounced wanting.   One notion
of an utterly unknown thing is as good and as adequate as
another.   Neither can faith make that an object of belief
which is utterly unknown to the mind.   The faith of Hamilton, and the vanishing conception of Spencer, are both
self-contradictory, as being alone able to arise under the
furtive, **but** real light **of an idea** present and ruling in the
mind.   No false conception of the Deity can be set aside
except by one which is better, or is deemed better; no faith
can be expressed except toward a Being thought to be.
These perplexities find no removal.   To escape, therefore,
difficulties whose reason is forthcoming by difficulties that

find no solution, is to forsake the light for darkness, is to employ exposition with a loss of expository power.

Nor are formulæ of thought which are inadequate, in a limited sense false, unserviceable, if their deficiencies are clearly seen by the mind that uses them. The expressions, infinite power, infinite wisdom, infinite goodness, contain as statements two things : the qualities indicated by the nouns, *power, wisdom, goodness ;* and their unlimited degree, pointed out by the adjective, *infinite.* Our ideas of the first may gain in precision and clearness without affecting the applicability of the adjective which sweeps away their limits. We may inquire experimentally into the nature and forms of power, and yet well understand that these precise manifestations are swallowed up in, included under, infinite power. We thus use in mathematics the first term of an infinite series to define and represent the remainder ; or we make the rule for the area of an inscribed polygon that of the enclosing circle, on the ground of the constant approximation of the one surface to the other with each increase of the number of sides. Yet the one never absolutely conforms to the other. The intellectual formula for the infinite is, This and more. The noun gives that which is to be expanded, the adjective, the law of its expansion. The *this* of the formula gives room for inquiry and growth, the *more* cuts us off from regarding a part as the whole. This is a movement of thought practically simple and safe ; no more inexplicable, no more dangerous than the use of suppositions in mathematics which reach toward the exact truth without finally covering it, which put one thing for another on the ground of constant approximation. Conceptions are habitually employed in mathematics which are inconceivable. We regard circles as perfect, yet the description of a perfect circle is to the imagination an impossible task, for the same reason that it is to the senses. Start

with a describing point. If it move for the least interval
in a straight line, so far the line is not curved ; if it begins
to bend before it has traced the least portion of a line, it has
nothing from which to bend or curve. It must begin to
move and curve at once, and an image of this the fancy can
not form. Even a point, in order that progress may be
made by passing through it, must have some breadth, and
this breadth, if it is to give an initiatory direction from
which the curve is to depart, must be straight. In analytic
conception we resolve the descriptive process into motion
and departure, or bending from that motion; we can not
conceive these two to be absolutely and constantly synchronous, yet without this the circle is imperfect. The imagination follows after the hand and eye, and as these are not
exact, neither is it.

§ 14. Having presented the twelve intuitive ideas which
constitute the mind's intellectual furniture, and also the
grounds of proof in each case, we propose further to draw
attention to some considerations which belong to all of
them, establishing their character, and separating them
from generalizations. Necessity and universality have been
fixed on as the criteria of these notions. The two tests are
liable to be mistaken for one, and **are** so under a certain
rendering of them. To distinguish these from each other,
we should understand by necessity, that certainty of conviction which attaches in all minds to truths purely dependent on intuitive ideas. Thus there are in the definitions
and axioms of Geometry many secondary intuitions, referable to the primary intuition, space. From these there
spring convictions, in the certainty with which the mind
receives them, wholly unlike those dependent on experience. That two straight lines, lying in the same plane, and
for a space equally distant, will remain so through their
**entire** length, is an assertion which the mind accepts at

once, as a necessary truth. Nothing, probably, but the exigencies of a theory, would ever lead one, with Mill, to strive to trace a conviction like this to experience. Certain it is, that no mathematician ever thought of establishing it by induction. Experimental truth never imparts such immediate and perfect belief. Of a like nature is the instant and unavoidable assurance that the changes taking place before us have a cause. Whenever a statement is solely dependent on a regulative idea, it becomes a necessary or demonstrative truth.

Universality, remaining a separate criterion, must refer to the constant presence of one or other of these ideas in every judgment; to the fact of the impossibility of distinct, declared thought in any mind without them. These universal antecedents of thought cannot be furnished by thought itself. Thought cannot supply its own conditions. The universality of their presence in each act of mind and in all minds becomes thus a proof of their supersensual nature. It seems to us, however, that it is a careful analysis of the processes and growth of thought, that is to establish each idea by itself; to lay open its transcendental character, as in the case of the infinite and liberty; or its necessary, antecedent presence to a certain class of judgments, as right to ethical judgments, consciousness to the apprehension of mental facts. The three criteria, the necessity of the involved truths, the universal presence of one or more of those notions in all judgments, the transcendental nature of the conceptions themselves, are not applicable all of them with equal clearness to each of the twelve ideas, and must be applied and sustained by a distinct discussion of the mental phenomena involved.

A more analytical application of criteria would involve five tests of intuitive ideas, (1) immediateness, (2) necessity, (3) universality, (4) identity, and (5) transcendental character. These are not distinct tests, but different applications of the same test, that of a simple idea, disclosed as such in intellectual analysis. A simple idea must come, when it comes, abruptly, must carry with it absolute conviction, must be the only solvent of the facts it expounds, must ever be identical, and transcendental. The absolute identity of space, of time, of number in all their applications is noteworthy. Resemblance, though it may lie between different things, is yet ever one and the same relation; right marks the one fact of a rational law of action.

§ 15. Another vital point in this discussion is whether these ideas are to be regarded as purely subjective, as mere mental forms brought to the object-matter of thought, or whether they pertain as external, necessary forms to that matter itself, thus possessing an independent being. The first belief, as advanced by Kant, that intuitive ideas are the mere moulds of thought, becomes the initiatory term of idealism. It is as contradictory to the universal opinions of men as any philosophy well can be. We do not say, that it is contradictory to consciousness, for it is not, but that it sets aside as wholly invalid and without foundation the universal convictions of men, thereby casting great improbability on its own conclusions.

Cause and effect constitute the notion by which we more especially establish the existence of the external world. Not to accept as just and safe the inference to which this idea of the mind lead us, is (1) to deny the integrity of our faculties, and to introduce a fatal scepticism to which no after limits can be set. It is a fundamental principle of sound philosophy, that the integrity of no faculty can be denied, nor its guarded, normal action be set aside. If, therefore, we recognize the universal presence of the notion of cause and effect, we have no more right to treat it as illusory, than we have thus to regard vision or memory. Spencer justly says, "That Space and Time are 'forms of sensibilities,' or 'subjective conditions of thought,' that have no objective basis, is a belief as repugnant to common sense as any proposition that can be found." This conclusion is reached in philosophy by rejecting without reason an action of mind universally present. We do not, indeed, know the objective world in perception, since consciousness is a condition of mental phenomena only, and these are not identical with the physical phenomena which they represent or accompany; but we do know it inferentially under causation. The action of the mind herein, as clear and constant and universal as any action, implies a power or faculty whose office is to make these disclosures.

It may be said, that this view is as open as the opposite to the criticism of disregarding the general conviction, since this is not merely that we know, but that we actually see and feel, the outside world. The cases presented by the two theories are very diverse. The one rejects entirely conclusions universally accepted; the other, in careful analysis of a complex operation, refers them to an obscure element, easily and frequently overlooked. The popular mind regards sight, touch, as simple operations, and so ascribes to them our knowledge of the external world. It is deficient in analysis, not erroneous in its reference. Philosophy resolves sensation into distinct operations, and assigns to one of these, that of causal inference, the immediate proof of outside existence. It is to be claimed that the general action of the common mind should be regarded as normal; it is not to be claimed that analysis may not go farther than ordinary concrete judgments.

The mind soon learns (2) to distinguish between sensations and thoughts, between phenomena which come and go at its own bidding, and those which are entirely independent of its will. It necessarily assigns the one a different source from the other. (3) As sensations in different organs are found to be connected with the same object, this fact, in an additional and confirmatory way, establishes for the mind its external and independent existence. Touch and sight aid each other in fixing and locating the source of the impressions in each sense. The sensations and perceptions are found to come and go together, and are therefore inferred to spring from a common cause, external alike to each organ. The location of the senses themselves, the gradual apprehension of the objects, distances, and relations of the external world, are processes of which we shall have occasion to speak more fully. It is sufficient for our present purpose to observe, that under the notion of cause and effect sensations and perceptions are distinguished from other facts of mind as having an independent origin ; that these external causes are slowly confirmed by repeated experiences, entering through a variety of organs, and that as a result of this normal movement of mind, men do everywhere arrive at, and believe in an external world, the same to them all. The cause is as real as the effect, and to accept a sensation as actual, is virtually to accept for it an independent cause, and, under the instruction of protracted experience, an external cause, external not merely to the mind, but usually to the body also. This movement as spontaneous and universal cannot be invalidated without an overthrow of the credibility of a portion of our faculties.

(4) Observe also that the result is the same for all ; men move in *one* external world. One set of objects, one relation of objects belong to them all, and they harmonize their actions by the validity of this their common experience. Make the world subjective to each individual, and you virtually deny for each the existence of all others. The preposterous conclusions of pure idealism could only

be made to rest on the most undeniable proof; nor on that, for the effect even then would be one of general confusion; of speculations wholly at war with practical conclusions; of the discord of knowledge rather than of sound, settled, consistent belief.

A similar line of proof has been carefully applied by Dr. Hickok to the notions of time and space. The reality of space has been shown to be the only condition on which the phenomena of the physical world can be the same for us all, included in "one whole of all space," open to common knowledge and common use. (5) Moreover we distinguish imaginary space—space which the fancy furnishes as a setting for its pictures—from real space. The space of the senses and that of the imagination are entirely different, showing that space as a form of thought is at once distinguishable by us from space, an external form of real being.

We may advantageously distinguish between formal entities and real entities. The substance of a pillar is a real entity, the appearance under which it presents itself is a formal entity. An event is a real entity, the time and the space in which it occurs are formal entities. Formal entities share the fortunes of real entities. The mere image of a pillar in a mirror has neither, in actual existence, the substance nor the form of the pillar. If a thought exists so does the consciousness in which it arises. If the one is imaginary, the other is imaginary also.

Other ideas have been offered as intuitions, and great patience and skill of analysis are requisite in settling these first forms of thought. Relation is one of these notions easily presenting itself as intuitive. It is obscure generalizations that are especially open to such a reference. Relation does not express any one specific connection, any one form of dependence, but many and most diverse forms. It is one of the most vague and broad of generalizations.

Resemblance is a specific form of connection, not so relation. If relation expressed any intuition, it would express
a large bundle of them. Moreover, other regulative ideas
involve in different forms this idea of relation, and can not
maintain their integrity without it. Resemblance, causation, liberty are specific relations; number, time, space, include many relations. Hence we must regard relation as a
generalization, whose various concrete forms are found in
other regulative ideas, and the combinations of phenomena
under them. An intuition always involves the essential
unity or simplicity of the idea, as that of time; a generalization involves the variety of the quality or relation, like
that of sweetness or of usefulness.

§ 16. An effort is made by empirical philosophy with
increasing distinctness to strengthen by inheritance the
processes by which it supposes the general mind to have
reached among its convictions those expressed as intuitive
truths. Especially is it thought that the necessity that is
attributed to these ideas is to be explained in this way.
Fundamental convictions once reached by the mind are
passed over, confirmed and enlarged by descent, till they
assume an instinctive, intuitive character. Spencer, in his
Data of Ethics, enforces this view in explanation of the
right. A sense of obligation is due to "preferences and
aversions rendered organic by inheritance." "The intuitions of a moral faculty are the slowly organized results of
experience received by the race while living in presence
of the conditions of the highest life."

To this opinion there are plain and decisive objections.
(1) Knowledge proper, clear mental conviction, does not
pass by inheritance. The father does not transmit to his
son his skill even, much less his mental acquisitions.
Knowledge which is of the nature of training, which has
a large physical element, and is closely associated with in-

stinct, may in a measure pass by descent; as a modified form of nest-building with a species of birds, or hunting qualities in a dog. The more, however, that acquisition partakes of the nature of knowledge, the less is it transmissible. That our highest, most penetrative insights, like those of morals or mathematics, should owe anything directly to physical inheritance, is quite opposed to the laws of heredity.

(2) Such descent would also reverse the general order of progress. Instincts precede knowledge, rather than knowledge instincts. Intelligence bases itself upon the organic, instinctive life; rather than itself issues in these foundations. Habit or skill, though somewhat beyond thought, is yet thoroughly permeated with light, is something quite above instinct. The field which instinct properly covers, it tends to occupy to the exclusion of knowledge. The region of instinctive activity is a dark, opaque one. It is the deficiencies of instinct which knowledge is called on to supplement; while instinct anticipates knowledge, and, in its own direction, renders it unnecessary. The true order of growth is overlooked by this theory. Organic forces and instinct, not knowledge, initiate life; while knowledge holds its own in possession more and more perfectly. An insight that should lapse into an instinct would tend to deaden the intellect; but nowhere is our knowledge so luminous, so complete, as in our intuitions. This knowledge is at the very farthest remove from a blind, half-organic under-current. Its certainty it wins not from instinct or inheritance, but from insight.

The constructive order of the world is this: purely physical forces support and minister to organic forces; organic forces expand into and nourish instinctive forces; these in turn make way for associative processes; while associative processes prepare the ground for and find their

interpretation in rational activity. By instinct we mean
subtilé constitutional connections, through which actions,
having the form of intelligence, are automatically accomplished. It is simply an extension, as in the spinning of
the spider, of organic *stimuli*. By association we mean,
the union of facts of experience in *quasi* judgments by
memory.* Each higher stage in this series will react on
and modify **that below it,** but the fundamental dependence
is the one indicated. Any other relation would make the
higher endowment the preparation for the lower one, and
its condition in development. Instances may easily be
given **in** which **the** later gift modifies the earlier one ; but
this is quite a subordinate fact that must itself find explanation in the previous relation here presented.

Intelligence will work its way in a limited degree into
instinct, and secure transmission **by** descent ; **but this** will
take place only in lower forms of life, and is **a wholly in-**
sufficient theory of interpretation when applied to man's
highest powers, powers that are not instinctive but intuitive. These must be accepted in their supreme quality,
and their action upward and downward sought out.

Intelligence, in its higher forms, holds beneath it a
large constitutional automatic region which it can penetrate
as voluntary power, and ultimately possess and control as
habit. Instinct and habit are allied to each other in form,
but quite distinct in origin and office. Instinct is an expansion from below of automatic action ; habit is the higher
life finding its way into the lower.

(3) Moreover, the first knowledge, on which inheritance
is made to rest, remains to be explained, and adequately
explained leaves no room for inheritance to add anything.
Inheritance can do nothing unless there is something to in-
herit. Whence comes that incipient perception of right, or

---

\* For a farther discussion see Growth and Grades of Intelligence.

those first convictions of necessary truths, which have been confirmed by descent? We are to remember that descent obscures rather than makes clear the rational element, these earlier insights, therefore, must have been as bright as the morning light, and are still to be explained.

(4) Farther, these intuitions are now with us as insights, not as instincts. They express mental powers, not organic processes. The truths of morals, the axioms of mathematics, indicate the clearest and most decided action of the intellect. It is strange that these latest convictions should be likened to the organic impulse with which a bee builds its comb.

(5) These higher truths also, as those of mathematics, have not been with the race to be confirmed by descent. They have come late and suddenly, and have come with full force.

(6) Nor does uniform, empirical truth gather by inheritance this sense of necessity. The world would still be perfectly willing to find a white crow.

§ 17. The twelve ideas now presented are capable of being grouped in various ways. Space and consciousness are the two diverse and complementary fields in which all phenomena occur. The higher plane has, as ideas peculiar to itself, consciousness, spontaneity, truth, right. The only ideas peculiar to physical events are space, and cause and effect. The infinite, on the other hand, is an idea that keeps aloof from the phenomenal, comes in only to comprehend the finite, and, in its personal form, to give the investigations of the mind a final goal,—one from which they may start, and to which they may return.

Existence finds its chief significance in its resemblances; space, in its numerical relations; time, in the causal sequence of events. The first couplet gives us the facts of being, and their character; the second, the most abstract

relations of things in co-existence; **the** third, their relations
in sequence. Cause expresses **the law of** evolution in the
physical world; spontaneity, that of the spiritual world.
Forces are installed in distinct measure and form in space,
their initiation is an act of mind. Liberty in actual choice
forecloses liberty, and henceforward realized force moves
with a necessary impulse to its goal.

These ideas admit of a collective grouping in reference
to the method in which they cover all phenomena.

Existence.
Number.
**Resemblance.**

Space.

**Time.**

Consciousness.
Spontaneity.
Truth.
Right.

Causation.

Beauty.
The Infinite.

We start with existence as the fundamental affirmation
in connection with all facts. This is followed by a recognition of their plurality, and this—we are speaking of logical
order—by their variety. Plurality and variety, number and
resemblance, tend at once to emphasize each other, though
**the latter,** in its discrimination, is an advance on the former. These three ideas are **common** to all phenomena,
whether of matter or of mind. At this point the stream of
events divides, though its facts flow forward in each branch
alike under the idea of time. **Physical events, arising in**
space, and impelled by forces, take up the notion of causation. Mental phenomena show themselves **in conscious-**
ness, and are linked, so far as they are purely mental facts,
by spontaneity. The law of pure mental action is truth.
This connection constitutes the logical coherence of thought.
**But** rational conduct includes liberty, and liberty as choice

necessarily involves an alternative, a law from without, from above, to be obeyed or disobeyed. This law is given in the intuition of right. To this intuition the mind adds that of beauty, lying in somewhat the same direction, and expressing a certain supreme recognition of, and pleasure in, the thing that is aptly done.

Beauty embraces two terms, form and spirit, and is found in the perfect union of the two. It thus arises at the junction of physical and intellectual facts in perfect expression. From the flow of either series of events there comes the suggestion of the infinite, as the all-encompassing thought. As causation changes not, neither waxes nor wanes, while liberty alone can make a beginning and shape events to a purpose, the idea of the infinite united with that of personality gives to us the Infinite, the completely comprehensive Being, from whom all things flow and to whom they return. Efficient causation backward brings events to rest in God; final causation forward does the same thing, and so the force and thought of God interlace all things.

§ 18. We have no such complete oversight of the conditions of human knowledge as to be able to say, that the formative ideas now offered exhaust all its relations. We can only say, that no others seem to be needed, save these and those involved in them; and that the general correspondence of these twelve ideas with the directions of human thought is very plain. A complete system of categories outlines all forms of human knowledge, and gives the subphenomenal links of thought which bind these forms together.

In testing the sufficiency of such a system, we must remember that these ideas, in their application, give rise to many subordinate ones; as time includes past, present and future; and space, here, there; above, below, in short all the words of relation under this pregnant notion. Under existence are shaped some of the primary axioms of logic ; A is A, A is not not-A, A is or is not. In the development of resmblance, we meet with agreement, disagreement, antithesis ; and under number with unity, plurality, totality equality. **In connection** with causation and time, we have succession, continuity, identity, action and reaction. Identity here means the oneness of a substance or a form with **itself.**

Identity, as the complete correspondence of a thought with a thought, arises under resemblance and spontaneity. Under space we have quantity, and under causation and space we have the subordinate notions of substance, actuality, necessity, fate ; and under consciousness and spontaneity, possibility, liberty, **chance—as an** event not ordered in reference to an end. Under truth, beauty and right, appear the secondary ideas of the false, the imperfect, the wrong ; and on the other side, the perfect. With the infinite arises its **correlative, the** finite. We do not strive to give all these subordinate **forms, but simply to** indicate a few of them and their relation to primary ideas.

We subjoin the categories of Kant :

| | |
|---|---|
| Quantity. | Unity,<br>Plurality,<br>Totality. |
| Quality. | Affirmation—agreement.<br>Negation—disagreement.<br>Limitation—partial agreement. |
| Relation. | Substance—internal relation.<br>Causality—dependence.<br>Reciprocity—external relation. |
| Modality. | Possibility,<br>Actuality,<br>Necessity. |

These are chiefly subordinate forms of primary ideas,

and by no means exhaust the list. They neglect the primary categories, and even include, as in quality, a partial generalization under the senses. In relation and modality, we have generalizations of dependencies involved in primary ideas. These categories have therefore but little claim to attention from a psychological point of view, being constructed to express the logical forms of judgments rather than the ultimate ideas under which they proceed.

# CHAPTER V.

§ **1.** WE are to speak in this chapter of the growth **and** interaction of the intellectual powers, of the dynamic states of the mind. The Intuitive Philosophy has been censured, not without reason, by the Sensualistic School for contemplating the mind only in its maturity, with no sufficient allowance for the results of previous conditions upon it,—for the effects of growth. This criticism we so far respect as to find a conspicuous place for truths which have been chiefly urged by such men as Spencer and Bain, always shaping them, however, to a new position and purpose. We are not prepared to admit any hereditary influences which vary the fundamental conditions of the problem of our intellectual nature. The varieties of character, the growth of national and race distinctions, find explanation here; but no sufficient proof has yet been given to establish, or even to render probable, the transformation of species by the accumulated changes of descent, with no increments of power. The past is not equivalent to the present. We must still regard each normal individual as the type of the race in its essential features; nor are we ready to look upon any one of these faculties as the product of simply external conditions, the sum of growing, hereditary tendencies.

When, on the other hand, we contrast the infant with the mature man, it must, we think, be admitted that the complete activity of the latter, is very different from the tentative, partial movement of the former. It is to this development of intellectual power that we first direct attention.  (1) The earliest distinct mental phenomena are doubtless those of sensation, are physical feelings.  These should be conceived as perfectly pure, that is as simple states or activities of mind—for our present purposes there is no difference between a state and an activity of mind; both are activities.  These first sensations may be of one kind or of another, but are more likely to enter through the general sensational system than through a specific sense, to be sensations of pain, local or pervasive, demanding relief, and rising with acute, jagged certainty into the light of consciousness.  It matters not what are the first sensations, since it is a changing series of sensations that invites attention. These are each simple, single, mental states known in the very fact of their existence as sensibilities.  Separately, they are capable of no analysis, no division whatever.  A pain, a taste are as individual as any objects of contemplation can be.  To suppose these to reveal directly an external object, would be to suppose that the phenomena of matter become the phenomena of mind, and are known directly as such. We can only allow, then, that sensations disclose themselves directly in consciousness, all beyond this is inferential. At this stage of growth, possessed of sensations merely, the infant is as ignorant of his own physical organs as of the world about him.  He absolutely knows nothing save the varying pains and pleasures that flit through that unlocated region called consciousness, itself more often hidden under the cloud of dreams than open to the new light of waking perceptions.  A tongue, a hand, an eye, a foot, are wholly beyond the scope of his knowledge; nothing physical, external to consciousness, is as yet recognized.  In adult years we so instantly locate each sensation, that it seems to us that it itself declares its position.  We are doubtless to conceive of the mind as using the entire body, as making it directly and immediately instrumental in reaching and influencing the external world.   The brain is the chief seat of power, but is no more the mind, is no more a condition of its activity, than the nervous system generally, spreading through and through the body, and perfectly possessing it.  But this instrument of the mind is not directly known to it.   The mind uses the body and controls it unconsciously, in the dark, not in the light.  Its shape, form, and members even, are all to be learned by experience.  We may hesitate at first to admit this, but a little thought will compel the concession.

If the mind in sensation itself knows and locates the instruments of those sensations, then ought the mind to know its internal organs as well as its external ones.   These are often independent sources of pain, and in the nervous system are as indispensable means to perception as the special senses ; yet the existence of the stomach, the brain, the liver, the interior formation of the eye, the ear, the **nervous** fibres and their ramifications, have all to be learned, must all be made objects of examination, and declare nothing to us directly of their own existence.   These do not differ as regards our original knowledge of them from the tongue, the finger-ends, except in the fact that we necessarily learn the existence and form of the one set of organs much earlier than we do of the other.

We return to the consideration of our first intellectual states—the flow of simple, subjective, unlocalized sensations.  (2) General sensations would be quickly accompanied by more special sensations, arising from appetites and from special senses.   That special sensations follow general sensations is evident from the fact, that those senses which are peculiarly full in their primitive data, as the eye and the ear, are called latest into action ; and also from the fact, that these senses in the earlier forms of animal life are fitted to give only general distinctions. Appetite, taste, touch concur in the first wakeful experiences of the infant, and these are organically united as instinctive stimuli in the act of suckling. The coming reason finds its first conscious experiences in this border ground of appetite and instinct—in sensations still obscure and mainly automatic in their action. It has been thought that the elephant owes much of his intelligence to the delicacy of touch in his trunk, and to its extended mobility. These facts certainly give him an unusual command of the conditions of inquiry.

(3) General and special sensations would immediately give rise to voluntary action in their gratification. The first conditions of life are met by automatic connections, but the rational consciousness begins at once to build its own constructions on these foundations. The limited number of sensations are at first distinguished as pleasurable and painful, and each class is accompanied by more or less of spontaneous muscular effort, gradually changing into voluntary effort, fitted to retain the enjoyment or escape the pain. The pleasures of touch and taste are especially concentrated on the tongue, and the infant first spontaneously and then more consciously seeks the breast in gratification of its sensibilities. Later, the feeling awakens in the hands, and the child is not at ease till these are laid on the mother. In these earliest, tangible sources of pleasure, secured and maintained by muscular effort, the infant rests; wanting these it worries, and moves inquiringly till they are regained. Later, other forms of sensation succeed; the hand grasps more definitely, and seeks a greater variety of objects; the ear is cheered by the voice of the parent; the eye is delighted with the brightness of the lamp-light, or with the sun-light. In these last cases, it is evidently more as sensations than as perceptions, more as organic impres-

sions, than as distinct cognitions, that the new objects find admission and confer pleasure. Slowly **the** eye learns to separate objects just at hand, and distinctly discern them, though possessed of no peculiar brilliancy. **It** recognizes the face of the mother, and at length follows, even into the distance, her retreating form. Still, its range, for a considerable period, seems limited, scarcely passing **the** verge **of** the cradle.

(4) The mind is now ready to harmonize in action **its** different senses. Taste and touch are united, and each object **that** can be handled is subjected **to** the double test. The hand also follows vision, and strives to lay hold of each **new** thing. The ear learns to direct the eye, and the dis-**tant voice wins the attention of both organs.** The process of acquisition goes on till a definite mastery of each member is secured, its **peculiar** impressions discriminated, and the visible world unfolded and rolled out in its marvellous complexity of forms and relations.

This movement, from the beginning, takes place under an objective form. The sensation is not enjoyed subjectively, dreamily; but objectively, really. The pleasures are attached at once to an object and a state; thus also the pains. The spontaneous, muscular effort with which they are **connected** facilitates this external form of experience, by attaching enjoyment to objects independent of the senses themselves, to things momentarily lost and momentarily regained. Distinct, muscular exertion aids in distinguishing different states, in marking their attainment, maintenance, **and loss.**

The objective character of early experience is also heightened by the degree in which it is composed of sensations—often the definite rugged sensations of pain—as opposed to perceptions, and later, of external, as contrasted with reflective pleasures. Language presents the mind as

especially passive and receptive in feeling ; and attributes
the efficiency to the exterior occasion of the emotions.
This we observe also in uncultivated, immature persons.
Their attention is particularly directed to the objects and
sources of pleasure. Their appetites and passions lead
them inevitably to this objective life, to this hanging upon
the external conditions of pleasure, this clinging to the
bosom of nature. The notion of cause and effect—its own
momentary enjoyments the effect—attaches the mind, as
yet little more than a bundle of sensations, strongly and at
once to the external world. Slowly it unfolds the facts of
this world, the avenues and dependencies of its own pleasures, its senses and the things which minister to them. The
internal rather than the external is overlooked. The senses
are separated from the objects which affect them, but the
attention of the mind is much later referred to itself, as
truly subjective to them al'

If we were to neglect the objective character of experience from the outset ; if we should suppose the mind for
a time floating from sensation to sensation on the inner,
tidal movement of its own phenomena, we should find increasing difficulty in making the transition, and in justifying it when we had made it. We are rather to regard the
mind as at once borne outward toward the sources of its
enjoyments, and as realizing these in and by their causes.
We should likewise observe the great aid which muscular
effort gives in interpreting and locating sensations. By
this means the child at first automatically, later voluntarily,
renews and discontinues its physical impressions, till the
mind has matured its knowledge of them, their diversities
and conditions. The relations of space are especially dependent on movement for their determination. The eye
and the hand work with each other in exploring surrounding bodies and intervening spaces, while a series of sensa-

tions record the motions of the arms and fingers. By movement we repeat at pleasure the problems offered by extension, and secure varying conditions for their solution.

In this growth of the mind into the possession and handling of its instruments, into the rudiments of experimental knowledge, the appropriate regulative ideas are present doing their work, though of course they are unrecognized by the mind, as is the fact of sensation itself in the first feelings, or the fact of judgment in the early perceptions of likeness. It is the substance of experience, not its forms, the facts of experience, not its conditions, that occupy the attention. Experience is not for this reason destitute of form, or without conditions. The first when and where, though as yet unanalyzed, involve time and space, as certainly as the last.

(5) One of the great labors of childhood is ready to follow the steps now taken, the conversion of sensations into perceptions by virtue of associative judgments. This change takes place chiefly in seeing and hearing, though the movement reaches the other senses somewhat, and, in the absence of the higher senses, may thoroughly transform them. This remarkable conversion takes place so early in life and so rapidly that we may readily overlook its extent. The ear and the eye, though more frequently indicating instantly the directions and relations of objects, obscuring the judgments of the mind by their rapidity, are sometimes so slow and uncertain in their decisions as to make the presence of their reflective processes conspicuous. We frequently have occasion to listen attentively in order to judge of the character and distance and nature of an unfamiliar sound. An object seen across the water deceives us, is farther off than we think it to be. Our estimates of the height of a cloud are very uncertain; or of the size of unfamiliar objects, especially when our ordinary standards of measure

ments are taken from us, and the proportions, as of a cathedral, are grander than those to which we are accustomed. The incomplete state in which the work still remains here reveals the fact, that size, form, direction, are to the eye solely matters of judgment.

The eye may also be deceived. The fans of a windmill may seem to revolve in a direction opposite to the real one. We explain this as an error of the accompanying judgments, induced by an unfavorable position. The same form of error occasionally occurs in touch. The fingers being crossed, and the hand placed behind its possessor, he is often not able to decide which one has been touched. The ordinary accuracy of judgment is lost on account of the unusual conditions under which it is exercised. The vast majority of our localizing power being manifestly of an acquired and experimental character, we are inductively led to the conclusion, that all of it is of this nature ; and the more so when we find that the most steadfast and stubborn conclusions are occasionally at fault, when formed under changed conditions of judgment. The patient whose limb was to be removed, returning to a state of consciousness, can only determine by observation, whether it has been amputated. Indeed his sensations may lead him, through the accustomed reference of pain to the accustomed quarters, to feel the limb in its place, and this though weeks may have elapsed since it was lopped from the body.

Touch is the sense whose localizing power is regarded as the most immediate, while its acquisition of this facility is most concealed from us by remoteness of time. The dependence of this sense, in common with others, on experience for its localizing power, is seen in the fact, that on the finger-ends, where it exists most perfectly and in most constant use, we distinguish much more completely and accurately than on other parts of the body. A considerable space must intervene between two points applied simultaneously to the person elsewhere, **before we** can discern them as two; they may approach very closely, and **yet be** separated in sensation by the fingers. **This sense can, by** special cultivation, **when** other senses are wanting, be made so much more perfect than **it now is,** be so filled and rounded out with instantaneous judgments, as to have but a slight resemblance to its former self. The raised letters **of** the blind are distinguished by most persons slowly and with the utmost difficulty, while the trained touch glides rapidly along them, almost as the visual nerve moves over the printed page. The blind in some instances acquire a power and precision of touch **inexplicable** to us, and are enabled to carry on employments, like engineering and warfare, **from** which **we should regard them as** entirely **excluded.** Ziska **was among** the more distinguished of generals. When the entire mind is directed to this avenue of communication with the external world, it brings it by included judgments to an unthought of perfection, and widens it into a wonderful inlet of information.

The most remarkable development of this lower sense is offered in the case of Laura Bridgman. " In 1837 a delicate, light-haired girl, nearly eight years old, who at the age of twenty-six **months had lost** sight, hearing, and to a great extent the senses of smell and taste, from an **attack of scarlet** fever, was brought from her home in New Hampshire to the Perkins Institution for the Blind, in Boston."* A mind of great vigor was here cut off almost wholly from the external world; by walls of separation unpierced by the ordinary senses. In spite of these difficulties, her powers were awakened to complete activity, and put in comparatively full communication with the outside world by means **of** the one remaining sense of touch. Nothing could better

* See an **article on** Mind, No. 14.

disclose the relative independence of the mind of any particular sense, its own large contributions to every sense, and
the very secondary weight in intellectual development of
simply organic and hereditary forces, than the very wonderful triumph, on the one side, of instruction, and, on the
other, of native power. The identification of physical and
intellectual unfolding incident to normal growth quite disappears, and we find the mind reaching its goal by means
peculiar to itself.

(6) In connection with this development of perception,
—a work which is never quite finished—those acquirements
are made which combine in harmonious exertion mental
and muscular action. Here belong graceful and dexterous
movement, all forms of skill and art, and above all the
learning of language. The perfect mastery in articulation
of any speech is so great an attainment, that it is very
rarely successfully accomplished but once in life. The
thorough acquisition of a foreign tongue in middle and
later life is deemed impossible. The following of the letters on the printed page with the eye, and the easy, instant
and exact utterance of them with the rapid and complex
play of the muscles involved, is, indeed, the acme of accomplishment in a combined mastery of body and mind. This
work, which the child does unconsciously, the laborious
efforts of later life fail to repeat. Most busy and fruitful
are these early years of childhood. Scarcely again do we
learn so many and so perfect lessons in so brief a period.
What the painter by slow analysis is able to reverse, presenting spaces, directions, distances, forms, on a plain surface of varying colors; rendering the landscape, with an
area of many square miles, on a canvass of scarcely more
square inches; the child of a few years has learned to do
with far more perfection, opening up and out the simple
vignette of the retina, till it fills in every part the magnifi-

cent stretches before and about us. **Nor** does the growing mind stop with understanding the things about it. It finds, in a marvelous way, those harmonized powers by which **it** moves among these objects, modifies them, and **reproduces** them in articulate **speech.**

(7) With these acquisitions partially made, **the mind is** ready for the ordinary work of what we formally recognize **as** study—the acquisition **of** knowledge. **This process will** receive farther **attention.**

(8) The last step in this rational movement **is** the clear recognition of regulative ideas, allowing each its due position and force. This makes the **rational** process rational to itself.

Regulative **ideas are not first present as** objects of distinct recognition, **but as unthought-of** principles which guide our consideration **and apprehension of** the phenomena before us. They may **sooner** or later, or **not at all,** be analyzed out as distinct **elements** of thought, though **as unconscious** ingredients they are, in some one or other of their forms, present from the very beginning. It is not till **the** class of phenomena to which it pertains are brought forward, **enter** into the experience, and call forth **the** attention **and judgment, that any** one of these ideas, as that of beauty, **of liberty, or of right, will find development, application and,** latest of **all, comprehension.**

§ 2. The **mind, once in possession and use of its** faculties; its perceptions **and sensations made complete and instant** in their action **by** the absorption **of the needed judgments;** the intuitive notions all **present, aiding to expand,** locate, relate, and **expound** the **several objects and events** of experience, **and give** form and **rational coherence to** thought, is ready **for** the acquisition **of what is more commonly** known as knowledge. This mastery of **conditions is so early, so spontaneous, so** inevitable, **that we more fre-**

quently overlook it, and regard the complex result as immediate and direct. For the same reason we hardly expend a thought on the ways in which spoken language is secured by the child, and look upon education as commencing with the learning of the letters—the written alphabet. Yet the first acquisition, though imitative and spontaneous, involves a more fundamental training and penetrates deeper into the physical powers by far than the second.

The intellect, once in possession of itself, finds chief occasion to expand its knowledge under the notion of resemblance. It is through this that it traces and interprets the lines of force; and by these that it gains power. Yet we cannot accept the statement, that all judgments can be analyzed into resemblance, into agreement and disagreement; and yet more do we not assent to the assertion, that these resemblances are sought for their own sake. Each regulative idea furnishes the ground of a distinct predication, not to be resolved in its very essence by the most subtle analysis into any other. Moreover, resemblances are of value, and only of value, as they are the indices of agreeing forces, as they are the surface marks which disclose the concealed lines of connection between objects and events.

Power is the fundamental element of knowledge, that which makes its search pleasant, and its acquisition profitable. The desire for knowledge which gives no power is like avarice, the morbid play of a just impulse. To know the exact number of leaves on a tree, their position and form, the precise way in which some ancient but insignificant event happened, the very words in which some second-rate poet expressed himself, is to know to no good purpose, is to have the semblance, not the substance of wisdom, the shell, not the kernel of truth. Resemblances which are accidental, which betray no relationship, as the size and form of a boy's marble when compared with the pebbles on the beach, or the agreement of sounds and signs in unrelated languages, have no interest and subserve none of the purposes of knowledge. A resemblance which is a mere resemblance, which casts no light on the past, and gives no clue to the future, which discloses none of the forces at work in the world, is unfruitful, and the knowledge of it of no value. That which makes the search after agreements so unremitting are the axioms of causation: that Like causes are followed by like effects, and that Like effects **in**dicate like causes. These transform a knowledge of real central agreements into power, put us in connection with the plan of the world, enable us to bring new forces into **it,** and take new and coveted effects from it. Resemblance is simply the key to the storehouses of forces.

Uncultivated minds, so far as they pursue knowledge at all, do it under this form; an observation of resemblances with reference to an ulterior possession and control **of** causes. The savage distinguishes between the different kinds of timber, because he expects the same external indications to remain the accompaniments and marks of certain interior qualities of strength, weight, elasticity. A bow of the same material he believes will exhibit the same good points **with** which he is familiar; a spear of like wood possess like pliancy and toughness. Language comes in to mark and hold together for the mind-these agreeing things, by which the implements of man, and his successive wants are to be supplied.

Science, the advanced and complete movement of thought, is but a more rigid separation of like with like, a more careful selection of central qualities, a complete and interdependent classification of objects, both that the resources of the globe, in all its ministration to human life, may be laid open, and also, that the concealed chart of laws, according to which the events of the present come pouring

down from the past, and go forth to occupy the future,
may be disclosed. While our experience, then, finds its
first efforts directed to resemblances, these lead to pro-
founder inquiries into causes, those links of force which
lengthwise and laterally bind together the physical events
of the world.

At length the purely objective character of knowledge
passes somewhat away. The mind gives heed to the agent
as well as to the instrument. Having acquired power, it
learns to value itself, the possessor of that power. With
more pure reflection and subjective attention, it inquires
into its own faculties, and the laws of their control. Now
come forward new intuitive ideas, liberty, right, beauty,
disjoining philosophy from science, and setting the first
over against the second as independent of it, and complementary to it. This change and jar of transition constitute the great danger attendant on the acquisition of this
form of knowledge. The forces and notions of the one
field are intruded into the other, and those who suppose
themselves the most patient of inductive philosophers are
really visionary theorists, adopting a disguised *a priori*
method; since they bring to a new department methods
and conceptions alien to it, and refuse, vacating the mind
of prejudice, to examine and classify these fresh phenomena
according to their inherent characteristics directly observed.
There is thus more or less of vibration between the two
fields. Now the philosophical, now the scientific conceptions rule the inquiring mind. The present, passionate,
physical researches and methods of thought are sure to
be followed by a recoil against forms of inquiry so one-
sided, so unscrupulous in their application. The deductive
method was never more arbitrarily applied to science, with
less correction from experience, than is the inductive
method now to philosophy, bringing with it the forms and

forces of physics. Induction transferred from one field to another, without fresh starting points and new limitations, is really disguised and unsafe deduction. Knowledge stalks on with alternate strides, and, in the rhythm of **progress,** the swing of one limb makes way for that **of the other.** The movement is in truth somewhat more complex than here indicated. In the earlier periods of thought, the notion of spontaneity crowds upon that of causation ; physical events are displaced by spiritual ones, or are referred to supersensual causes. Hence come the endless throng of superstitions. These at length are driven back by science, and the reverse error commences. Causes take the place of powers within the domain of mind itself, and an unreasonable skepticism displaces unreasonable belief. Later the mind learns to **balance** its convictions, and make them proportionate within themselves.

The mind measures all things by the scope of **its own** powers too much to rest on the naked facts of the world. The forces which they disclose and the plan which they reveal, with the wisdom of its conception and the kindness of its execution, push the thoughts farther back to the source of these truly intellectual and moral elements. The progress, also, which is discovered, together with that irresistible claim **which the** mind institutes for completion, for ends reached and fruits acheived, push it forward in thought, and lead it willingly to gather up the issues of existence into the hand of **Him who** gave it. That this movement **may be final,** that a true compass and circuit, source and conclusion of the actual, the finite and the necessary, may be found ; that **the** mind may rest in one last stroke of comprehension, it brings forward the highest of its intellectual solvents—the Infinite, the Absolute. A free and holy personality is to be made to the mind and heart, the cause and compass of the universe. This movement becomes complete and assured in connection with revelation, an outer voice, which takes hold on inner powers, and gives steadfastness and certainty to their conclusion. The mind is not left alone to travel these outlying highways of thought.

In this growth of knowledge through science, philosophy and theology, deduction and induction play intermingled and inseparable parts. Deduction from necessary ideas, from definitions and axioms intuitively conceived under them, gives us first principles, the ever present instruments of inquiry. Induction is nothing without a theory, a conception of some sort, running side by side with its classifications, guiding and interpreting them, and ready deductively to furnish shining strokes of exposition. The theory with its derived conclusions is most impotent and misleading, save as induction presides at the birth and growth of it. The wise mind is always laying up the facts of nature, like stones in a building; but laying them up under a plan which it has caught by penetrating beneath the surface; by interpreting signs and relations unintelligible to the merely physical eye. Here, then, in the growth of general knowledge, we have the counterpart of that which we find in the individual mind. The elaborative faculty, the understanding, is ever playing between the sensations and the intuitions, weaving them into a rational experience. In like manner the philosophy and the science of the world are bringing downward, deductively, the theories of the mind; are bringing upward, inductively, the phenomena of nature and mind, and slowly uniting them into one compact web of knowledge; the exposition running as light through the facts, and the facts embodying and presenting the exposition. The one process is as necessary as the other, the woof as the warp.

§ 3. We wish to mark briefly the means by which the mind advances in acquisition—the instruments of intellec-

tual growth at its service. Sensations, perceptions, the data
of consciousness enlarge for it the material of thought, and
are themselves simple, ultimate forms of knowing. Nothing
can replace them. **Colors,** sounds, odors, flavors are appre-
hended exclusively through the organs by which they enter.
Further, they give us inexhaustible material for inquiry,
facts to which the mind may bring its explanatory processes,
and which it may work up into knowledge. Intuitions
without these, as mere intuitions, would remain empty formulæ, intellectual solvents with no mysteries to resolve.

Next come judgments. These are the steps in the rationalizing, comprehending process. To be able to form a
judgment, is to be able to put forth true intellectual effort ;
is to turn the key in locks that **guard** all knowledge. It
implies completeness of mental **furniture, the entire** material of growth. Simple judgments are the staples of knowledge; while they **may** be formed under any idea, that **of**
resemblance assumes chief significance. All classification
proceeds through this, and is a first and last step in progress.
It is by a comparison of qualities that our knowledge of
the objects about us becomes serviceable. Much, perhaps
the larger share of our progress, is made by simple judgments, related indeed to one another, but not interlocked
in reasoning. By a series of inquiries, we place objects in
their appropriate classes, and furnish them ready both for
our intellectual and physical uses.

Reasoning, or interlocked judgments, follows simple
judgments as **a means** of progress. There **is considerable**
disagreement as to the forms and character of reasoning,
arising largely, we think, from a different use of words.
One form of procedure is covered by the words *reasoning*
and *logic* as used by Hamilton, **and** another as used by Mill ;
while others combine, with more or less confusion, the two
uses. Hamilton, by a definition, confines the province of

logic to the necessary laws of thought, or practically to the demonstrative evolution of conclusions from premises that are given. He does not inquire into the manner of obtaining the premises, but only into the certainty and safety of that purely intellectual process by which, as verbal propositions, they are found to hold those other verbal propositions known as conclusions. The whole movement is thus detached from facts as facts, and, according to the general use of words, is, when reasoning at all, deductive reasoning. That is, the conclusions are wholly contained in, and demonstratively taken from, the premises. Hamilton gives a technical and peculiar application to the words inductive and deductive, regards both forms of reasoning as equally demonstrative, and leaves wholly out of his logic that true induction, usually so-called, to the elucidation of which Mill has given his entire strength. Induction in its commonly accepted meaning, the establishment of a general principle through a limited number of specific examples, is all the reasoning which the sensualistic school can consistently recognize. What others regard as deductive reasoning, they are compelled to look upon in ultimate analysis as inductive. Deduction can be nothing more with them than the re-statement of a specific case already included in the establishment of the general principle, or major premise, from which it is now taken. No conclusion is strictly demonstrative, since it is in advance of the premises on which it rests. The degrees of evidence for new statements, statements not confirmed by direct observation, vary with the amount and character of experience on which they rest.

The entire system of logic, therefore, as presented by Hamilton, has for them comparatively little value. It is a cunning play upon words, rather than an estimate of facts. They are interested in the growth of laws, principles, out of those separate instances which are only to be gathered and interpreted by patient, careful, and often doubtful induction. Each party thus neglects a valuable field which the other exclusively cultivates. All that Mill regards as reasoning, Hamilton scornfully rejects from the province of logic as invalid, as not presenting with certainty the conclusions in the premises from which they are taken. Mill, on the other hand, can only look on the complicated syllogisms of Hamilton as a cumbersome restatement of work already done, of knowledge already gained.

Much is undoubtedly included by Hamilton, in the formal expansion of his terminology, as reasoning, which would generally be regarded as simple statement, as the fruit of single judgments, as the results of perception. This desk contains this drawer: This drawer contains this paper: Therefore this desk contains this paper. These propositions form a syllogism under one of the forms into which he divides deductive reasoning. Most would regard them as in no proper sense reasoning, but rather as a formal, unservicable statement of a fact, learned by observation. So also his inductive reasoning is made up of cumbersome formulæ of classification. "Gold is a metal, yellow, ductile, fusible, and so on : These qualities constitute this body (are all of its parts) : Therefore this body is gold." Here is no argument properly so called, but the rendering of the results of the experimental test of a bit of metal, with the accompanying act of classification. There would seem to be room in a logic, covering all the forms of reasoning, and those of reasoning only, both for deduction and induction, using the words in their more general and generally accepted meanings. An important branch of logic finds representation in Hamilton and Mill respectively.

What is reasoning? It is the reaching of a new conclusion, certain or probable, by means of two or more interlocked judgments. We would lay stress on the word *new*, and on the words *certain* or *probable*. Our necessary ideas and our theories suffer expansion by a purely deductive process. Geometry is a deductive science, derived from intuitions, definitions, and axioms. Astronomy and mechanics are full of pure deductions, resting on conceptions of force confirmed by experience. How much is involved in certain, simple statements, we often only learn by a series of related judgments. This is one of the earliest forms of scientific reasoning, and presents in mathematics, pure and mixed, its most extended and serviceable results. The certainty, and, when fitting data are found, the celerity of its conclusions, abundantly explain its fascination, and the position it has held in investigation. The introduction of a mathematical unit, and application of number to a subject, have usually been the signal for a rapid advance.

This deductive reasoning rests on intuitive steps, and will readily fall into a syllogistic form. The syllogism is perfect ; for the premises as premises, in their very statement, are seen to contain the conclusion. No outside circumstances affect their relation.

Inductive reasoning, on the other hand, deals only with probabilities, because it pertains to things imperfectly known and to facts whose conditions are ever changing. It rests at bottom on the intuition of causation, the simplest statement of which is, Every event must have a cause. Its corollaries are, that every effect measures its cause, that the two are exactly commensurate, and, that sameness in one is proof of sameness in the other. These spring from the original, independent conception of causation. Proof under this notion, would be as certain as under the ideas of space and time, were we always dealing with perfectly fixed and perfectly known premises. We do not by observation so penetrate the nature of objects, and the character of complex phenomena, as to be sure of the elements present, and sure, therefore, of the effects that may be expected. We do not know exactly how far one wood differs from another, one metal from another, one element, so called, from itself at a former period. Much less do we know all the circumstances which affect the complex problems of life, which influence the growth of a tree, which are concerned in the health of a man, in the welfare of a community. We here, therefore, advance from one case to another along uncertain links of likeness, not knowing positively whether the agreement covers the essential points of the two cases or not. The various degrees of likeness are identity, sameness, resemblance, analogy.

In induction, by which from several examples we infer a general principle, we are proceeding on a resemblance more or less obscure, hence more or less uncertain. Different cases stand on their own independent merits, and the probability in each is in proportion to the certainty with which the agreement in the example covers the force or forces involved in the causation under consideration. That all magnets attract iron, **is** a conclusion on which we rest with entire conviction, having by such uniform observation traced this result to this cause. Yet it is not an impossibility, that some new substance or combination of substances should exhibit the other properties of a magnet with the omission of this. We cannot say, how new conditions of action may modify the force termed magnetism. **Now, by far the** larger part of the reasoning of natural science and of every-day-life is of this character, creeping from resemblance to resemblance, and unable to affirm of its best conclusions, that they are demonstrative. To this reasoning, the syllogism is not applicable, since the premises as premises are partial, and do not contain the law in its full breadth which is to be evolved from them. This phil-

osophy of experience, therefore, can lay no great stress on
the syllogism. The only service it can assign it, is that of
a convenient re-statement of conclusions already arrived at,
and this, not in the exact line in which the first, the real argument lay. This was on the road upward to the principle,
whereas the syllogism lies in the way downward to a specific
example included under it. When inductive matter receives syllogistic statement, either the statement is defective, or the general principle is assumed, and then the case
in hand is taken from it. The argument by which we mount
to a general law, does not suffer a syllogism; the seeming
argument by which we descend to a particular fact is but a
restatement of previous knowledge, and yields a syllogism
deductive in form. Of the defective, inductive syllogism,
the following is an example; The metals A, B, C, represent
(not are) all metals; A, B, C, expand under heat; therefore
all metals expand under heat. This result is proximately
not absolutely true. If the law had been established by
sufficient observation, that all metals expand when heated,
the following would be the deductive syllogistic statement
of a single fact covered by it. All metals expand by heat:
A is a metal; therefore A expands under heat. The confusion which has arisen in the various estimates of the value
of the syllogism seems to find its sources in the language
employed, in two restricted definitions, and, more than all,
in failing to estimate the influence of different philosophical
systems on the respective methods of logic.

The two forms of reasoning differ (1) in their data.
Deduction starts either with intuitive data, or with statements of facts regarded as complete; induction rests upon
facts and statements obviously partial. (2) The connections
between the premises in the one form of reasoning involves
axioms only; in the other it includes one or other of all the
shades of resemblance contained between perfect identity

and mere analogy. Between these **two** there is a continuous series of weakening agreements, **which** we have divided into parts by the words, identity, sameness, resemblance, analogy. Identity is a secure basis of reasoning, but
we cannot absolutely affirm it ; sameness, a close agreement
in qualities, admits considerable doubt; resemblance, a less
close agreement, renders the argument insecure ; while analogy, **an** agreement in relations, may only call out a presumption. (3) The two forms of reasoning differ, therefore,
broadly in the force of the conclusion ; in the one it is demonstrative, in the other **it has** every shade of certainty
**less** than the highest. (4) They differ also in form. The
syllogism belongs to deduction only ; if applied to induction, it is either incomplete or assumes the thing to be
proved. Life is thus permeated with both elements, with
certainty and with doubt. Wisdom and strength are found
in handling the two conjointly.

We have followed the ordinary division of reasoning,
though we doubt its completeness. We prefer to regard reasoning of three orders, according as it deals with pure intuitive data, with empirical data, or with these data assumed
as absolute. Mathematics is the chief example of the first
order. Pure mental conceptions are unfolded through long
trains **of** reasoning into appropriate formulæ and propositions. The connection under which this **is done** is that of
equality or equivalence. The reasoning proceeds by affirming—or denying—an exact equality. The conclusion is
identical with the premises as clearly understood. This reasoning may be termed production, the leading onward of
data from one form of expression to another. In dealing
with things, we are constantly embarrassed by the want of
perfect insight. We hesitatingly reach a general conclusion by combining under it few or many examples. This
is induction. Such a conclusion being reached, and ex-

pressed as a class, we may, either in extending our knowledge or in reviving it, reason from the class to any one of
its subdivisions. This is done under the Aristotelian principle, that what is affirmed of a class is affirmed of each
member in that class. This is deduction, and its logical
formula is A is A.

§ 4. The intellect being thus furnished with faculties,
and stored with their fruits, we inquire into its control
over them, its directing influence. We speak first of the
government of the thoughts. The mind can direct the eye,
the ear, to any object it chooses, and command their prolonged attention. (1) It can make any object the subject
of protracted contemplation, and confine the analytic and
reasoning processes to it. It can intensify and guide its
mental activities in degrees varying with the power which
previous practice has given it. This voluntary direction
and handling of faculties is attention, and is referable to
that personal force from which all the faculties as separate
directions of action spring.

The number of objects which can at once be made the
subjects of attention has been a question vigorously de-
bated. The mind seems to be single in what may be
termed its line of movement, its chain of connections; but
to be able to unite in this movement many diverse things.
Our thoughts braid into one experience, link in one argument, diverse subjects; they proceed by junction and inclusion, evening and strengthening the thread with material drawn from the right hand and the left.

The reason why it has been doubted whether the mind
can attend to more than one object is in part found in the
fact, that the very effort of the mind to decide the question
serves to occasion that fixed, full, complete attention which
is concentrated on a single object, and leads to the partial
exclusion of other objects. Of course we cannot give the

entire attention to **two** objects as **two,** struggling in the
same instant to contemplate them **with** distinctness separately. Failing **in this, we have** hastily concluded that the
mind can attend to but one thing at a time. Let the
thoughts move freely, and it seems obvious that we do consider **several** objects at once, **some** of us more, some less.
The shepherd counts his flock as they pass before him or
stand around him. He will more likely do it by threes or
fives, grouping the numbers by a stroke of the eye. One
practiced in dividing paper into quarter quires will instan-
taneously, on the ruffled edge, select the number six, and
**with** astonishing rapidity run through the pile. This tendency in enumeration to divide objects into greater and
smaller groups, according to the degree of skill, plainly reveals the power of the mind to contemplate at once several objects. Indeed, were the mind limited to absolute
singleness of attention and direction, its states would **suc-**
ceed each other in a disconnected and independent form.
Every judgment involves two terms and a relation between
them.

A **more** important question arises, (2) as to the power
which the mind possesses in introducing to itself the objects which it may afterward consider. So far as these are
external objects it may open for them the avenues of perception, and then select among them those which it will more
carefully observe. It may also seek the locality of remembered or described objects, and thus prolong their consideration. **In** this direction, the mind is limited, first to things
that are; second to those among these known to it and accessible to **it. A** large share of the government we have
over our thoughts is found in our mastery of the external
conditions of life, of situations and circumstances. A
deeper inquiry lies in the questions, (3) How far does the
mind control the order of ideas **that** are passing through it?

and How far is the flow established and maintained by independent connections?

The doctrine of association has been the occasion of ascribing a dependence and passivity to intellectual connections which we deem wholly false. The association of ideas has been accepted as an ultimate fact, and itself without explanation, been proffered as an explanation of every other fact. This solution has proceeded under physical analogies, especially those of habit in the body. A form of activity, often returning to the muscles, so interlocks the nerves and muscles, so passes over their connection from the voluntary to the automatic region, that the mere fact of repetition becomes a reason for many movements not directly intended. Under the suggestion of this fact, ideas are spoken of as associated, and this association seems to be often thought of as involving some direct, almost mechanical connection of one idea with another; as if the first evoked and drew on the second by an immediate force. Thus we have such expressions as the " cohesiveness of ideas," " the principle of cohesiveness," " the property of plastic adhesiveness," " the tenacity of association." Those who thus use the law of association, refer the order of ideas in the mind to it, and give the mind itself but little control over them, beyond that of hastening or checking their movement.

It is the living power of the mind, rather than an intrinsic coherence of ideas that combines them into thought, and locates them in revery. The memory proceeds along the connections of place, time, resemblance and causation, because these are the forms under which objects are principally presented to it ; and the groups of memory principally determine the connections and dependence of conceptions, when they return to the mind. One object tends to restore in memory, more or less distinctly, the entire group of which it forms a part, and its earlier and later relationships are renewed, because the memory is by it directed to that portion of experience in which it has played a part. Ideas are thus interlocked in memory, and return to the mind surrounded more or less completely with their adjuncts, their companions in previous knowledge. A second ground of association is that of the deductive dependence of ideas. The logical power of the mind on the presence of a part expounds it by reference to the whole; or on the presence of a whole unfolds it in its parts.

These two forms of association correspond to the two methods of acquiring knowledge. Observation, induction present objects as physical wholes, and the memory so retains them; analysis, deduction unfold **ideas,** and the memory and the logical faculties combine to repeat, on fit occasions, these processes. The cement of ideas is the living forces that use them, not a dead adhesiveness belonging to them as ideas, or dependent on the nervous conditions of their presence. It is not a reverberation of tissues, but of thoughts, **to** which attention should be directed.

We see at once, then, that the power of the mind over its trains of ideas is greater than many are willing to admit. **Take** any one moment, with the tendencies and memories **of the** past fixed, the circumstances of the present established, **the current of the desires strong and declared, and** thoughts and conceptions may seem rather to sweep independently through the mind, a deep, uncontrollable current, than to be called forth and used by it. Take, however, a longer period, let the mind desire to assume control, and this appearance of helplessness will pass away, and our impressions will be reversed. Times are set apart to definite inquiries. The passing hours bring each its suggestion of its part of the plan. The memory is more and more stored with material suitable to the investigation

or to the effort in hand. External circumstances favorable
to the inquiry, are secured. The desires, quickened by exercise, lend their aid in constraining and spurring on the
thoughts. The purpose, kept in view, evokes from the
memory on each new exigency, every fitting idea in the
increasing circle of its information, while the logical connection of ideas guides the pursuit along the right trail.
Under these conditions, we shortly behold an intellectual
power which works as intensely, as directly, as uninterruptedly toward its end, as the engine whose valves and pistons
and wheels are driven by a mechanical agency. A wayward pleasure of vagrant connections may turn the thoughts
for a moment aside, but not more frequently nor more un-
fortunately than the flower or the fruit the wayside trave'ler
steadily pursuing his journey. States and powers of mind
are not indeed instantly determined, immediately gained;
but tendencies are established, and control acquired as certainly here as in any form of effort. The person himself
may determine within the limits which the surrounding
world presents him, what shall be his resources of thought,
and what the motives calling them " into act and use."

The whole movement is a living one, under a living intelligent power, and is no more to be expounded as a dead
process, an adhesion of one thought to another, than is the
life of the plant or of the animal to be traced to simply
chemical forces. The very secret of life is to combine material into living organs ; the very knack of mind is consecutive, coherent, self-supporting thought and self-directed
action.

If we look upon the phenomena of mind as passing on
under its observation, its immediate power over them is
found in its ability to select any one, and to intensify and
prolong its consideration. This is attention. Its second
more comprehensive power over the flow of experience lies

in the introduction of new terms by memory, by following
out logical relations, or by altering external conditions.  But
the full sweep of its government, embracing long periods is
found in shaping distinct lines of inquiry and of action,
and in adjusting circumstances to their accomplishment.
The whole stream of experience may thus be turned into
new channels.

§ 5.  The last point on which we have occasion to speak
under the dynamics of the intellect is the difference in
mental endowments between the brute and man.  We are
necessarily somewhat theoretical in handling a subject so
much beyond direct knowledge; but trust our theory will
commend itself as the simplest explanation of the facts,
with the least assumption and the fewest forces.   There
seems to be no proof, that any animal, **the most sagacious,**
possesses any intuitive ideas, and consequently that it forms
any judgments properly so-called.  There is no conscious
estimate of the value and bearings of sensations, no classification of them inductively, no conclusion deductively
drawn from the premises as such.  Sensation, perception,
memory and imagination evidently belong to the higher
animals, and by these faculties, we believe, all the intellec-
**tual** phenomena they present can be readily explained, while
**the** ascription of fuller powers than these to them brings
difficulties which cannot be easily met.   **To those who**
doubt the possibility of presenting the appearance of reasoning processes with these limited and elementary powers, we
would commend the works of Bain, and kindred philosophers, who, with patient and adroit analysis, think themselves successful in resolving the phenomena of mind, in
their most exalted forms, into the play of sensations and
perceptions.  They at least render this service to true philosophy, of enabling us to explain brute life, without ele-
vating it in gifts to a rational platform.  Those who do not

believe that the races of men could have sprung from one pair, may be referred to Darwin; those who cannot explain the sagacity of the dog, his apparent sense of shame and approval, without endowing him with the entire circle of · human powers, moral and intellectual, may well find profit and conviction in the works of the sensualistic school.

The truth is, memory and perception can present, with close agreement through quite a wide range of conduct, an image of rational and moral behavior. Memory can unite impressions and their appropriate accompanying actions in permanent associations, exhibiting results as safe and sagacious as if the union had taken place by judgment. We constantly interpret the conduct of animals under the analogies of our own experience; an act more unphilosophical even than for the accomplished and sensitive man to infer the exact counterpart of his own feelings in the clown from an agreement of external actions. The aspen trembles without fear: the dog skulks and crouches in apparent shame without a sense of guilt. The severe tones of voice, the sharp eye, punishment associated in experience with like action, are a sufficient explanation of conduct which we often hastily regard as showing the germs of a moral nature.

Indeed, this inferring the same sweep of thought and feeling from coincident actions in man and in animals leads constantly to the most insecure and unfortunate conclusions; unfortunate when they are made the grounds of cruel exactions, and the tyrannous handling of domestic animals. Says Professor Whitney, in his treatise on *Language and the Study of Language:* "A dog, for instance, as surely apprehends the general idea of a tree, a man, a piece of meat, cold and heat, light and darkness, pleasure and pain, kindness, threatening, barking, running, and so on, through the whole range, limited as compared with ours, of matter within his ken, as if he had a word for each. He can as

clearly form the intention, ' I mean to steal that bone, if its
owner turns his back and gives me a fair chance,' as if he
said it to himself in good English.    He can draw a complex
syllogism, when applying to exigencies the results **of** past experience, and can determine ' that smoking water must be
hot, and I shall take good care not to put my foot into it ; '
that is to say, ' water that smokes is hot : hot water hurts :
this water is hot : ergo it will hurt my foot,' "—*page* 414.

While making no objection to the spirit of the passage, we regard its philosophical implications as all wrong.
Keen perception and quick association by an active, retentive memory offer a complete explanation of the facts involved, and of kindred ones, without supposing the presence of a single act of judgment, of one thoughtful junction of premises and conclusions ; nor the recognition of any
general idea or general principle.    The fear of the master
is present, and the desire of the bone ; withdraw the first,
and the last comes into unobstructed operation.    The sight
of steam and a delicate sense of heat, associated with pain
under exposure, apply as direct a restraint to action as the
shutting of a valve to the ingress of water.    The difference
between the two cases lies in the fact, that in one instance,
the restraining power appears in, and works through, consciousness, and in the other it does not.

That association is sufficient to explain the apparently
thoughtful action of brutes, is seen, in the first place, in
the way in which their sagacious tricks are acquired.    A
cow learns to open a gate ; but how ?    First, by acciden-
tally or impatiently rubbing her head and horns against it,
and thus loosening the latch.    This process, repeated once
or twice, establishes a connection between the act and its
results, and later, when she wishes to be free, she worries
**the** gate open.    A change of fastening relieves the difficulty, not because the new method of reaching the latch is

necessarily impossible to her, but because it is not accomplished by the same blind movement which removed the previous one from the catch. The horse learns to untie himself; vary the knot, and his skill disappears. That the protracted experience of the brute must yield to it not very unfrequently a repeated concurrence of the same cause and effect, and thus enable it to reach the one through the other, in those cases in which appetite impresses on the memory the connection, is obvious. Indeed, that this happens so rarely, is quite as much a matter of surprise as are the few cases of apparent skill. We know the cunning, vicious tricks which a street animal acquires; but we also know that in a keen appetite on the one side, and much persecution on the other, it has under the law of association the most unwearying and vigilant instructors. The restive horse, scorning the restraint of fences, has compounded his education of short and easy attainments. The spiteful nag, grazing on a village common, has learned the ins and outs of advantage, the safeties and dangers of provender, by many a sharp thrust and sturdy thwack, and it is not surprising that it has quite a store of ideas pricked into its tough, retentive hide.

The same truth is seen in the methods of training—as of the dog and the horse. The first effort is to establish a definite association of reward with the action to be done, and one of suffering with the action to be avoided. Says a skillful handler of horses, " The difficult point is to secure the right action in the first instance. Every approach to it should be at once recognized and encouraged. The animal should be petted and rewarded at each repetition, till the thing required becomes habitual"—that is, till the right association is established. On the other hand, the wrong action is painfully and peremptorily checked, till the tendency to it is corrected. In the meantime, the fitting words of command uniformly accompany the discipline, and it re-quires no intelligent apprehension of language to lead the horse to stop at the word *whoa*, when it has been repeatedly accompanied with a severe jerk of the bit.

A change of masters always interferes with the training of animals, as for instance of a yoke of oxen, because there is a breaking up of associations, a diversity, and hence a confusion of methods. Passion and hasty punishment like-wise retard the education of an animal. The reason is obvi-ous under the princple of association. If the brute were in a measure rational, he might interpret aright the flogging, and profit by it; but, acting under association, his con-sciousness is simply flooded with suffering and fears, and henceforth, on the like provocation, he becomes restive and excited in anticipation of a similiar, painful experience. Punishment that is not proportionate to **the wrong, or** does not immediately follow it, and spring as it were out of it, is of no avail. The association is lost, and no reasoning process is present to take its place. All the facts of skillful and successful discipline in animals come in to corroborate the assertion, that action, with them, follows the appropriate perception under fixed associations.

But it may be asked, why is not the opposite sup-position of reasoning faculties an admissible one? We answer it involves at once the entire circle of regulative ideas, postulates more powers than are needed to explain the phenomena, and it is not consistent with the fact that brutes exhibit no such growth as should, in some instances at least, follow the rudimentary possession of such high en-dowments. If the animal reflects, there is no reason why he should not occasionally express by language, at least by signs, the results of that reflection. One rational thought is not possible without the possibility of two, of three, of **many** thoughts. One syllogism carries with it the entire logic, and such powers would quickly command expression. This utterance of judgments we should the more anticipate, as the most sagacious brutes are in constant company with man, and might learn from him, in some instances, vocal language, in others, sign-language.

The fundamental difference in mental action between the brute and man, incident to the absence of intuitive ideas, is the fact, that man alone deals with abstractions, generalizations, conceptions. The animal has to do directly with things and their images. All analysis proceeds under an intuitive idea, and no sooner reaches an abstraction than it calls for a sign, a word to express and hold fast the product. The animal can not be taught language, because it has no occasion for language, lacking abstractions either of qualities or of relations; and the animal never is taught language, no matter how many words it is made to repeat, or how many sounds it associates directly with concrete feelings and actions. Without the demand occasioned for language by an incipient act of abstraction of some sort, language is impossible, and with this demand it is unavoidable. Contemplate things solely as present and in the concrete, and the senses quite suffice.*

The only way in which a brute does show intelligence is in action, and this may as well spring from association as from reflection. The utmost efforts of instruction expended by man on animals, even when it has reached to the mechanical repetition of words, has only secured results in conduct readily referable to slow, established, and patiently confirmed associations, the varying perceptions of the animal putting it, in connection with accompanying pains and pleasures, on the clue of the behavior designed for it.

* For a fuller discussion see Comparative Psychology, or Growth and Grades of Intelligence, Chap. VII.

Moreover, if rational ideas are conceded to the brute, they must be granted in a more powerful and perfect form, rather than in a less perfect form than to man. The chicken, the young of many animals, almost immediately begin to successfully estimate all the relations of objects in space. They evince more mastery over them at the end of a few hours or days than does the child at the close of as many years. If, therefore, any judgments intervene in this process; if the perceptions do not directly, by an immediate transfer of stimulus, secure and guide the motion; if there is not the same spontaneous completeness in the action of the mind that there is in that of the body, what a marvelous, unaccountable rapidity of development should we have here. We must exalt in accuracy, ease and celerity the reflective processes of the animal far above those of man. This seems, to us at least, a *reductio ad absurdum.* But, if the sport of the lamb, its leaping and running; if the flight of the bird, and the ease with which it hits and rests on the spray, indicate no conscious recognition of space, the presumption is that other less astonishing powers have no basis in reasoning or in intuition.

We object, also—though this consideration may have little weight with some minds—to the character which this idea of reflection ascribes to the consciousness of the brute. A thoughtful animal would be one of the most unfortunate of beings, the incubus of its physical structure weighing down its destiny. Rational hope and fear to a being like **this** would be an unnecessary and cruel source of suffering; nor do animals often show apprehension and alarm except in the immediate presence of danger.

But it will be said, there are examples of sagacity on the part of animals which candor forbids us to refer to association, to anything short of reflection. To this we answer, these examples require more searching inquiry as to their exact form and value than they have received, as the shades of action that distinguish association and reflection are unobtrusive and delicate; and few are aware of the extent of results easily within the scope of association alone. Farther, we are not considering what would be referred in man to reflection, but how much is possible to quick perceptions, strong appetites, and a ready memory, when they are left to act alone, and are not therefore superseded or embarrassed by reasoning. Says the writer last quoted, "It has often been remarked, that the crow has a capacity to count up to a certain number. If two hunters enter a hut, and only one comes out, he will not be allured near the place by any bait, however tempting; the same will be the case, if three enter and two come out, or if four enter and three come out, and so on till a number is reached which is beyond his arithmetic." How far are we to give credit to these current statements is very uncertain, but granting their accuracy, they do not require for their explanation a distinct recognition on the part of the crow of numbers, a conscious subtraction and the acceptance of a definite remainder. Concede these, and the sagacious bird would quickly find in the objective teaching of the rowed cornfields before him, an express provision for a grander arithmetical procedure. Within narrow limits, groups of two, or three, or four, or five objects are directly and readily distinguishable in perception aside from numeration; beyond these they do not so vary the impression as to make the difference easily observable. Groups of twenty and of twenty-one persons will hardly be distinguished by a stroke of the eye. Certain separable sensations, therefore, may be associated in the experience of the crow with danger, while others inseparable have made no such impression. Let, however, one of the twenty men always remain, and doubtless the crow would soon attach danger to this number also, and the philosophers find in the new fact proof of a growing power of calculation. The crow learns by experience **to** fear man, that is to connect danger with certain perceptions. In rare cases, under protracted experience and varied discipline, he might carry this association two steps farther, to three definite, closely united impressions; a hut, the entrance of three, the departure of two. This experience, provoking alarm in him, would extend by admonition to others, and would at once receive the interpretation above given. We find it very difficult not to attribute to such actions the same degree of thought and intelligence which would be indicated by them in us. Yet this tendency should be easily overcome, when we remember that we are compelled to cover up by the word instinct actions which in man would show the most **wonderful** knowledge and skill. It is certainly no very strange thing, that three perceptions should, in the ready memory of a crow, alert and watchful, by life-long instinct and habit directing its attention to like facts, find at length a fixed association with danger.

It is narrated, that a raven hit upon this method of defrauding a dog of a portion of his dinner. The raven would approach so near and so annoyingly as to provoke pursuit. This pursuit would draw the dog from the dish, and the **raven, quick** of wing, would immediately rise and pounce down on the unguarded meal. Observe how easily such a series of associations would be formed, the acts constituting it finding union and undesigned repetition in experience till they became a habit apparently shaped on a rational purpose. Impelled by hunger, the raven would naturally approach the dog as near as he dare venture; the dog as naturally would resent the intrusion. The raven, pressed by pursuit, and rising on the wing, would see the unprotected dish, and at once pluck a portion of the coveted food. This process would repeat itself a second and a third time, till, connected with the desired result, it would become direct and constant. What shall be said of the reasoning of the dog who repeatedly suffered from such a form of depredation ? It matters little whether the above instances are true, others like them are true, and admit of similar explanation. The fear and caution of a dog when he has committed an offence, the cunning and skill of a fox, the pliancy of a horse, are not surprising, when we consider their quick senses, sharp appetites, retentive memories, protracted, varied, and severely enforced experience, and inherited tendencies. Knowledge, moreover, is communicable between animals by inheritance and by transfer. The obedience, docility and training of the horse are readily imparted to his yoke-fellow, and the fear and sagacity of a fox help to awaken like qualities in his companion.

The practical value of the above conclusions is very great, in teaching us how to handle, and how to estimate, brute life ; and still more in establishing a fitting barrier between it and rational life. If this difference exists between them, then is man unapproachable by the animal. He stands on another platform of being. It is not an accident of physical structure, the absence of language, less fortunate or less protracted development, that divide the two ; but entirely new endowments, bringing with them a new and exalted sphere of being. Man shares consciousness, a perception and retention of external events, with the animal; but not his intuitions of the invisible, nor his rational apprehension and government of action, nor his moral and spiritual endowments.

# BOOK II.

§ 1. We have now reached the second class of mental phenomena, that of the feelings. These have received less attention than the intellectual faculties. They are far more numerous and complicated, and have been more recently regarded as a distinct division. **The** three classes, recognized by Kant, have since his day been generally accepted. **Knowing,** feeling, and willing, are each forms of action so simple, that it is easier to perceive, than to state their differences. Indeed, expository definition of each is impossible **in other than** synonymous terms. Each is known and only fully known by experience. There are, however, **certain** diverse relations of these several acts, or states of mind that may be pointed out.

Though the feelings were late in receiving attention as a distinct portion of our mental endowments, popular language has so far severed them from our thoughts, as to refer them to a separate part of our nature. It is a method of expression still somewhat unusual to common speech, to talk of the emotions of the mind; we more frequently hear the words, **the** sentiments, **the** emotions, the feelings of the heart.

A first distinction **to** be marked between knowing and feeling is that one proceeds under a double, the other under a single form. The thought and the object of the thought lie in the **mind,** distinguishable **parts of one process; while** the feeling **is a** simple **mental state. This has been ex-pressed by saying, that the processes of thought are more objective, those of feeling more subjective. This language,** however, seems not quite explicit. In one point of view, the feeling is more objective than the thought. To be sure the thought attaches itself necessarily and distinctly to an object, but that object itself becomes a subjective one, something grasped and held by the mind as an object of contemplation, so that the entire movement maintains a subjective character. On the other hand, a feeling is often occasioned by an action or an object external to the mind, under whose influence the emotion is suffered. This object, in connection with our stronger and more well-defined feelings, evokes especial consideration, is seduously sought after or avoided, and thus imparts a peculiarly objective turn or tendency to emotion. Take such passions as love or hatred, such sentiments as admiration and contempt; consider the appetites and the desires, how objective are they in the frame of mind and cast of action they produce. Indeed, the first condition of contemplation, a quiet, subjective handling of a topic is, that the feelings be hushed, that these restless children of the household be put to sleep, and the thoughts be left to move uninterruptedly within their own circle. On account of this ambiguity of the word subjective, and the marked external tendency given by feeling to action, we prefer to speak of thought as *bi-partite* and feeling as simple. Neither method of presentation holds equally well in all forms of the phenomena concerned. Sensation most distinctly separates itself from perception by its more definite and local action in the organ involved. In speaking of a feeling as subjective, reference must be had to the emotion itself, and not to the contemplation of the object which may call it out.

A second diversity in thinking and feeling is found in their dependence on volition; the former is more, the latter less immediately the result of voluntary effort. The thoughts are more directly reached and guided by the will than are the feelings. Indeed the most of these are so occasioned by the immediate and unavoidable presence of external conditions, that it is only indirectly and with considerable delay that volition can reach and modify them. Our thoughts, our subjects of reflection are the primary objects of volition, while the feelings are slowly changed with a change in their physical and intellectual conditions.

While the thoughts are more directly subject to the will than the emotions, the emotions more immediately influence the will than do the thoughts. Here is found ·a third difference of relation. The state of feeling is the direct ground and occasion of choice, while our opinions govern the will only as they first govern the heart.

The only opportunity of confounding knowing and feeling seems to arise from their common relation to consciousness. We express the fact that our feelings, as our own, are present to the mind by the language, I know that I feel, I know that I am angry, I know that I have sympathy with the suffering. We thus seem to underlay feeling with knowing as if the one were but a peculiar form of the other. The same reasoning, however, would apply to volition, and the difficulty springs only from the defect of language. We express the simple and single fact of a feeling under the form of a double act, one branch of which is an emotion, and the other a cognition. A better analysis has enabled us to see that the expression, I know that I feel, no more implies a double act than the kindred assertion, I know that I know. An act of knowing is distinguished from one of feeling or of volition in involving a disclosure of something beyond itself. The three, in involving consciousness, stand on common ground. Herein is the *bi-partite* character of knowing apparent. A perception that encloses no judgments is undistinguishable from a sensation.

§ 2. The feelings may be divided by their intrinsic character, or by the objects or conditions which draw them forth. The first would seem the more just ground of distinction, yet the second finds easier application, and closely allies itself to the first, since different grounds give different emotions. Our first division into physical, intellectual and spiritual feelings proceeds on the conditions or occasions on which they are respectively called forth. The physical feelings are located in the body, have a physical source, and pertain to the states of physical organs. The intellectual feelings arise in connection with the judgments of the mind. It is the perceived relations in which we stand to objects about us, and especially to other men, which call forth these emotions. Their ground then is an intellectual one; since if we were destitute of thought, forethought, if we could form no conclusions concerning the effect of things, their approach or their possession, the effect of the actions and character of others upon ourselves, we should be left destitute of these feelings, and only subject to the immediate play of physical forces upon us.

The third class of feelings is the spiritual. The word spiritual is not so definite as the other two. We employ it to designate the highest portion of our nature, that by which we have a rational and responsible life as opposed to a merely intellectual one. Now it is our intuitions, more particularly a limited portion of them, which confer these higher powers, and put us in these higher relations. The sentiments elicited by these more profound revelations, this deeper insight into the rational world, the truly spiritual world, are the spiritual feelings. More concisely, the spiritual feelings are those immediately conditioned on the intuitions.

Of these several classes, the first may belong in feeble form to the lowest animal life, and in full form to the highest. The second belongs chiefly to man, though in a few of the nobler animals, it finds partial presentation in connection with the tacit anticipations, the informal conclusions of association. The dog does, through the education of a retentive memory, permanently interlock what, for want of another word, we must call conceptions, and is, therefore, ready for the feeling of joy or fear in view of anticipated results. Yet, in fullness and variety, these emotions do not compare in the most sagacious brute with the corresponding class of feelings in man. Indeed, much that we regard of this character in the animals below us, is but the false, the flattering interpretation which we bring from consciousness for the explanation of acts, in their external form alone, like ours. The dog licks the hand of his master, and that master conceives it, not as the act of a blind, instinctive fellowship, worth intellectually no more than the good-will of the cow that cards with her rough tongue the hide of her gratified companion, but as a distinct expression of a clearly defined attachment. The third class, from the nature of the case, belongs exclusively to man, and, in its full forms, to the cultivated, the developed man,—one who has been ripened out of physical sensations, out of the halfway ground of the simple connections of thought into the habitual and active play of his intuitive powers.

The words by which we designate the emotions are, for the most part, very loose in their application. Of these the word feeling is the most general. It ranges through the three classes. The pains and pleasures of the body are feelings ; equally so are the fears and hopes of the prudent, the delights of the artist, and the satisfaction of one obedient to moral truth. The word emotion, is applicable to the feelings of the two higher classes, hardly to those of the lower ; while the word sentiment finds at least its fullest meaning in the third class only. We designate as sensations, physical feelings exclusively; as passions, intellectual feelings exclusively,—though only a part of them reach the intensity indicated by the term;—and as affections, the higher, the moral emotions exclusively. That, however, which is especially confusing in the language of the emotions, is the different states included under one word, for instance, love. We love the food that pleases us, we love the wealth that gratifies desire, the scenery that delights the taste, the person whose character meets the approval of our moral sense. We have occasion, therefore, to put feelings covered by the same word, into entirely distinct classes, and to regard love as an appetite, a passion, or an affection, according to its several objects. The word now shows a decided tendency to withdraw from the lower field, and take up its abode in the higher one.

# CHAPTER I.

## *The Physical Feelings.*

§ **1.** THE physical feelings are distinguished from others by arising directly from the body. They have a physical source and locality somewhere in the body, or, like nervous debility, are diffused through it. They are divisible as regards general quality, into **pleasurable**, indifferent **and painful feelings.** By indifferent **feelings** we do not mean complex states of mingled pain and pleasure, but states declared to consciousness, but neither as yet agreeable or disagreeable. The three divisions, if we look at them in reference to action, may be termed the stimulative, the indicative and the repressive feelings. The condition of certain organs indicates **a preparation, or want of** preparation for activity. Thus an appetite gently aroused prepares the **way for** indulgence. Simply as **an appetitive** movement, **as yet** neither balked **nor** gratified, it **is hardly** an occasion **of pain** or pleasure, but merely gives suggestion of a line of gratification.

As we begin to indulge the appetite, a sensible, declared pleasure sets in, stimulating farther indulgence, and this continues till the present power of the sensibility is expended. Then a second indifferent or indicative feeling succeeds, dissuading, without pain, from further indulgence. If this limit, however, be over-passed, positive discomfort follows, decidedly repressing activity. These three states may be regarded as a series of alternating cycles through which the physical feelings tend to move, and in one or other of which, when active, they remain for the time being.

There is a farther connection between the three states in the fact that they arise successively in one organ or set of organs.

§ 2. The earliest of these physical feelings are general sensations. These may arise either from conditions which affect the body extendedly, as those which occasion lassitude and unusual vigor, or the sense of pressure, or of heat and of cold, or of numbness; or they may indicate the condition of some one organ or set of organs, as nausea, tooth-ache, or irritation in the eye. This class of feelings it is not easy to enumerate. Some of them approach in character very closely the special senses, while others appear but rarely, and subserve a very limited purpose. There is, perhaps, no organ, or portion of the human body, which may not become the seat of a peculiar feeling, more especially a painful feeling, indicating difficulty and demanding relief. As a class, the sensations which disclose states have more frequent reference to some repression or modification of action than to its excitation; and present themselves under the form of suffering instead of enjoyment. The reverse is, however, many times true. Buoyant life declares itself in physical impulses, at first obscure, but leading when fully developed to the intense pleasure of sportive action. Redundant power tends to explosive efforts and renders such exertion very enjoyable.

Feelings which indicate states of the body or of its special organs are for the most part present only as they tend directly to affect action, and through the will to secure either exertion, repression, or changed conditions. The stimuli that regulate involuntary action do not usually come into consciousness. Respiration, in its safe and measured movement, is secured by nerves and muscles that act and react on each other automatically, with no direct cognition of the mind. Let, however, some unusual state arise;

let the air be restricted, or become very impure, and distinct sensations follow, provoking in extreme cases the most
**violent** exertion. The larger **portion, then,** of those sensations which spring from some unusual condition of our physical organs, are present to indicate a line of action; at least
to compel inquiry, and set the reflective powers to the **work**
of guidance and correction. Thus are the nature and limits
of the physical, physiological laws under which we live declared to us ; the times of activity and repose, the forms and
bounds of indulgence, and the necessity of remedial measures. As most diseases find their true remedy in some form
of rest or of restraint, we see that the pains which indicate
them are not only directly repressive of effort, but indirectly
also through the increased advantage which arises from an
appetite denied, from labor laid aside. On the other hand,
the power to do begets corresponding effort, and is rewarded
with a pleasure which in turn stimulates the body through
the mind, and tends to make the exertion nutritive **of the**
faculties to which it belongs. We cannot go to the extent
of the view presented by Bain, which makes pleasure and
pain automatic, the one stimulating, the other arresting
action, much like the opening and closing dampers of a
steam-engine. Such direct effects they frequently have, but
more often they incite or correct action through the intervention **of** thought and volition. Indeed pain may momentarily quicken action, and pleasure may ultimately exhaust
the strength, and so slacken effort. The sensations stand
in too living, too complex a relation to our vital, intellectual
and voluntary powers to submit easily all their relations to
a single statement. Pleasure and pain alike exhaust power,
but the one with, the other without compensation. An
half-hour of intense suffering takes away not simply the
strength,—play would have done this in part—but leaves the
nutritive powers depressed. The exertion of enjoyment, on

the other hand, while expending the present store of power, re-acts favorably on the vital forces. Intense pleasure at its consummation trembles on the verge of pain, and intense pain, when not utterly exhaustive, passes back at its expiration into intense pleasure, occasioned partly by contrast, and partly by the flowing in again of vital power to its normal channels.

Spencer's assertion that "Every pleasure increases vitality, and every pain decreases vitality" * is also too sweeping. Both pains and pleasures may tax vitality; both may be remedial; and both, may be unfortunate. This relation to vitality does not explain the peculiar character either of pains or pleasures, nor exhaust their intellectual offices.

§ 3. The second source of distinct physical feelings are the special senses, the organs of sensation. The chief of these, at once recognizable, are touch, taste and smell. Sensations and perceptions should be distinguished, and these classed with cognitions, and those with feelings. Perceptions have with some clearness a *bi-partite* character; the object and the action directed towards it at once appear. The seeing, and the object seen, are necessary complements to each other; whereas by taste and smell we only indirectly and inferentially reach the source, given under another sense, that of sight. Evidently in sensation, we are engaged with the feeling; in perception, with the source of the impression. Perceptions also differ from sensations in having so little of a declared local character, that, though physical in their sources, they no more reveal their physical connections than does pure thought. Sensations, on the contrary, disclose themselves as a certain peculiar state of a given organ, and are therefore to be ranked as feelings. Of all the senses, touch occupies the most intermediate ground; while its phenomena ordinarily present the phases of feel-

* **Data of** Ethics, p. 87.

ing, it may in the absence of the higher senses of sight, **of**
hearing, become **so** far intellectual **as** scarcely to direct attention to the sensation.    **It thus becomes** the unobserved
medium of knowledge, the **matter** revealed being the only
object obviously before **the** mind.    Any sensation may be
the occasion of a judgment, bearing the mind outward to a
particular object ; the peculiarity of touch is, that **often by**
habitual use for **this** end, the sensational element **is lost**
sight **of,** sinks **from** observation, and the perceptive **ele-**
ment rises in its place, making this ordinarily over-shad-
**owed** sense a not inefficient substitute for sight.

These special **senses,** all **of** them, stand closely connected
**with the** intellect, **and** have thus **been** more frequently
united with the **organs of** perception, **and** fallen into the
first **class** of **mental** powers.    The distinction now made
seems, however, fore-shadowed in the physical fact, that
the senses of sight **and** hearing are so immediately connected with the cerebrum, the seat and instrument **of**
thought, that a removal of this destroys them, though **leav-**
ing the other senses unimpared.    Touch, taste and smell,
however, while primarily feelings, are used constantly as
**means of** discrimination and guides to action.    They very
**frequently draw after them** conclusions, set in motion the
judgment, and thus return on the will through the mediation of the mind.    **This is the** ordinary action **of a pure,**
well-defined, **special sensation.**    Taste may be so pungent
**or so** nauseating **as to** produce a direct, involuntary action
of ejection; but odors and flavors are **usually,** in their effects on action, simply grounds of discrimination by which
we are guided in accepting or rejecting the object before
us, in assigning it a definite position among the things used
by us.    Our sensations thus start from the central, the perceptive, the indicative point, and then become either stimulative or repressive, according to their nature.

Sensations are also three-fold in their relations to enjoyments. From the midway ground of indifference, they pass into pain and pleasure. Their double office is here again very obvious. They are means of independent gratification as well as of guidance. They are sources of abundant physical pleasure, and find a primary purpose in this their direct character as feelings. In this connection, they act more immediately on the executive powers, stimulating the effort necessary for their gratification, and checking any movement that gives rise to pain. Sensations then, are in a double sense stimulative by their direct character as feelings, by their indicative character, revealing to the intellect the nature of the objects about it. It is, however, in the first aspect alone, that they can be divided, as feelings, into the three classes, stimulative, indicative and repressive. Those sensations are chiefly indicative which, in reference to pleasure or pain, are indifferent. Things inimical, determined chiefly by the eye and ear, are recognized in part by touch, and sometimes by taste and odor. This discriminative use of the senses is an acquired one, and lies apart from the purpose which they subserve with all as avenues of enjoyment. Thus their perceptive and sensitive uses show a tendency to separation and mutual exclusion.

§ 4. A third distinct class of sensations are the appetites. These are closely united to those indicative feelings which declare the condition of an organ. They differ from these only in being more special, returning with regularity, and performing a constant and fixed service in the animal economy. The appetites are specialized and regularly returning physical feelings demanding a specific act of gratification. Both in the special senses and appetites, there are a definiteness and constancy of purpose, not found in general action, as well as a source of ever returning pleasure, almost independent of effort. While the senses are specialized to indicate external relations, the appetites are specialized to disclose internal states. Indeed, the appetite for food, as a means of enjoyment, so closely unites itself with taste and odor, as to yield with them a compound gratification incapable of practical analysis. The return in most of the appetites is at measured intervals; in others the spaces are more irregular. According to this definition, the desire for sleep is an appetite. Hunger and thirst are impulses recurring more fixedly ; sexual appetite, one that is renewed less certainly.

An appetite in its first action, as yet neither gratified nor denied, is indicative ; and indifferent as regards pleasure and pain. It is, indeed, the condition of the pleasure which is to arise from indulgence, but is itself hardly either a distinct enjoyment or a declared annoyance. One or other of these, however, it quickly becomes, according as its intimations are accepted or withstood.

Different appetites may be suppressed and modified with very different degrees of success, according to the purpose they subserve in our physical constitution. One is as imperative as the wants it indicates ; another is, in the position it holds, very much the product of intellectual and moral forces. The appetites are physical indications and guides of action, and, in their healthy indulgence, uniformly give pleasure ; in their denial, or excessive indulgence, as uniformly inflict pain. The pleasures and pains which accompany them are, carefully watched and collated, safe guides of action. They are, nevertheless, far from being sufficient, automatic forces, securing the results of physical well-being. While they are at first direct stimulants and immediate restraints, they are chiefly, in the human constitution, operative through a wise election and pursuit of pleasure, a sagacious avoidance of evil. The brute and the rational constitution seem to show an important distinction at this point; the one is wholly automatic in the restraint and control of appetite; the other leaves the checks chiefly to reason.

The purposes served by our sensations are various, frequently co-existent, and always concurrent. Of this, the special senses, the appetites and the feelings which accompany the active powers, are examples. A large circle of enjoyments are through them added to our physical organism, and a pleasurable life provided for. Immediately connected with this is a second purpose. A direct, physical stimulus is, through these feelings, administered to that nutritive and muscular action on which the well-being of the body depends. Pain abates, pleasure promotes effort. The one exhausts, the other stimulates, and, within certain limits helps to renew the strength by which it is fed.

A third purpose of our sensations is found in the knowledge, otherwise unattainable, which they impart of the states of the body, the conditions and demands of its several organs. They thus become the basis of that reasoning by which we adjust action, food and remedial agents to our real wants; make an intelligent provision, and lay down wise precepts, for our immediate and future well-being. A fourth and somewhat more remote ministration of our sensations is to general knowledge. Through them, we come in contact in a new way with surrounding objects, take cognizance of a different set of qualities, and thus make more complete and perfect our classifications. There is a tendency, in thus making our sensations means of intellectual discrimination, somewhat to abate their force and character as feelings. Of this, we have sufficiently spoken.

The relation of the physical feelings to health and activity is easily seen. Unimpeded activity is pleasurable, but the seat, the source of pleasure, is found in an original conformation of the physical man; as much so, we apprehend, as the enjoyment of a fragrant rose in the peculiar power of the special sense of smell. We are not to suppose that we have explained either pleasure or pain by referring them respectively to unrestrained, and to impeded activity. We are able to give some of the conditions, and some of the consequences of physical sensations, but their immediate causes in the organs themselves, and in the mind, we cannot give. The last and exhaustive analysis we can not make. A feeling as a feeling is ultimately and, shall we not say, sufficiently known in itself.

Before passing to the intellectual feelings, we mark some border facts which prepare the way for the transition.

What are termed natural affections, are examples of transition facts. We suppose these words strictly employed to designate feelings aroused by physical facts, physical ties; not intellectually considered, but sensationally experienced. There seems to be a small remainder of such affections in man, but they are so lost in the higher feelings, stirred by the same facts intellectually considered, that it is difficult to separate them. The animal is, for a time, passionately attached to its young. These affections seem to follow in a direct, physical way from the sensations present. The helplessness of the young apparently forms no ground of the emotion. The young of another animal may become the object of immediate and bitter attack. The substitution of another offspring for its own is successful only when the perceptive instincts of the parent are baffled and misled. Something of this direct attachment seems to appear in the human parent, though it is so overlain and modified by feelings of a purely intellectual character as to play no very important part in our constitution. Doubtless the tenderness of the mother does owe something of its quick, yearning, responsive action under the claims of the infant t the purely physical conditions of the relationship.

Irritability, which is often a physical state, and may always be more or less due to physical conditions, nevertheless does much to determine the character of the conceptions present to the mind. There are inseparably mixed with their intellectual causes, immediate physical conditions, which often make them in degree, if not in kind, what they would not otherwise be. The force of the emotions, and the fact of their presence are often determined by physical states.

# CHAPTER II.

## *The Intellectual Feelings.*

§ 1. THE intellectual are distinguished from the physical feelings by the fact of their dependence on objects and relations presented to the mind, and thus, in a secondary way, influencing the emotions. The sharp thrust of **a** weapon brings instantaneous pain; the abuse of an enemy **arouses** anger only as it is **understood and** mentally contemplated. These feelings may also be divided, as regards emotional **character,** into pleasurable, indifferent and painful; and as regards **their** relation to action, into stimulative, indicative and repressive. These two divisions—and this is especially true of the second—do not so much express intrinsic characteristics as passing relations. Essentially the same feeling which in one relation or in one degree is pleasant, may in another relation or in another degree become painful. So also the same feeling, as fear, may at **one** time quicken and at another restrain action.

The intellectual feelings are divisible into primary and secondary feelings. The secondary feelings arise from the relations which things assume in consequence of the primary feelings; while the primary feelings rest, at one less remove, on constitutional endowments. The primary feelings are of two orders, according as the relations which call them out are simply intellectual, or are also those of interest. The root of the first order is in the passing phases of the intellect, of the second order is in the intellect only as it ministers to deeper constitutional impulses. The feelings **of** the first order are those called out in connection with habit, by separation and reunion, by things or events new or unexpected, by wit and by humor; and those of the second order are desires. There are obscure feelings of comfort which attend on the habitual in action, and of discomfort which arise from the interruption of habits. There is a large mass of less obscure feelings of satisfaction and discomfort which are connected with the presence or absence of friends. Wonder is a more purely intellectual feeling, and is awakened by things new in our experience. Surprise is a yet stronger feeling elicited by that which contradicts our expectations. Both indicate the wakefulness of the intellect to a change of data. Wit is the joining of ideas apt to our purpose by an unexpected relation; humor is the joining of things or images apt to our purpose by an unexpected relation. Things are in this definition opposed to ideas in the former definition, but include persons. The unexpected relation of the first definition refers to some secondary or remote connection as opposed to the philosophical connections of thought; in the second definition, it indicates an unaccustomed, and incongruous link. Though the feelings that accompany wit and humor are of an intellectual order, they may be easily united, as in ridicule, to personal feelings. All of this order of feelings turn on the familiar and unfamiliar. In habit both mind and body are involved; in associations, the emotions and the thoughts; while in wonder, surprise, wit and humor, the thoughts are deeply concerned.

The second more intense order is composed of the desires. These may be termed the appetites of the mind, as they express its appetences, its longings, its objects of pursuit. They have been usually spoken of as directly native feelings. Herein there seems to be some confusion of ideas. If they were direct, unreasoning impulses, they could not fall into the second general class of feelings, to wit: those

which have an intellectual basis. That they are not spontaneous, immediate impulses, a little thought will be sufficient to show. As universally stated they are directed
toward abstract ideas, not toward concrete objects; they
are desires of wealth, of power, of knowledge, not for wam-
pum, for the ability to bend a bow, or to calculate an eclipse.
Now a desire directed in the outset to a generalization, to
an abstract quality, is an absurdity, since no such quality
can be present to the mind except as the result of much
comparison and many judgments. Neither should we avoid
the difficulty by saying, that these desires fasten themselves
with native, original force on specific objects under each of
the categories of desire. There are no specific objects
which draw forth universal desire, and which can stand as
concrete types, or representations of the notions of power,
wealth, honor. Specific powers become points of interest
and desire according as they are able to gratify certain
native appetites or tastes. Possession is a matter of interest to the child only as the thing claimed stands in some
relation to its sports, by which it is capable of promoting
its enjoyment.

Possession, without some connection with our pleasures,
has no significance, either in early or later life. A square
mile of territory on the frozen continent of the Antarctic
Zone, has no power to awaken desire in any man. Now this
discerning of the relation of things to our appetites, our active powers, our tastes, which makes them valuable, is an
intellectual activity, receiving constant expansion as we
grow older, and leading us to attach importance to the
ownership of an increasing variety of things. The ignorant man cares not for a book, except as he can sell it; because the mental conditions which make possession important to him have not been met.

Our desires, then, are secondary feelings uniformly

evoked by the perceived relations of objects to our primary native feelings; our appetites below, and our tastes above. Without either the lower region of animal tendencies, or the higher region of spiritual impulses, desires would not exist; because those objects now included under the term wealth, or those possessions known as knowledge, would have no value, having no power to minister to our pleasure. The statement has been made only on the positive side; of course we include the corresponding negative considerations. Objects may excite desire, because they enable us to escape pain. An action, however, which stands in no relation to either pain or pleasure, must be one to which we are wholly indifferent.

We have, then, no occasion to suppose, indeed no intelligible grounds for supposing, the presence of native desires in our constitution for certain abstract qualities, or for abstract qualities under a concrete form; because, first, the relation of wealth, power, knowledge, to our happiness is a sufficient explanation of our desires for them; because, second, these desires come and go with this relation—the miser even not being able to prize that which can not, under any conditions, be sold; and third, because there is a difficulty in supposing generalizations, arrived at by much reflection and constantly expanding, the direct object of a simple, primitive feeling.

The very notion and definition of a primitive feeling is rather the immediate action of some object or intuition on the emotional constitution. The secondary relations to our well-being, which things disclose through the intellect, are grounds of our intellectual feelings. These are all in one sense secondary, though they are so in two degrees, and may be subdivided among themselves as primary and secondary.

In classifying the desires, we are then classifying the objects which draw them forth. Desire is an emotion essentially of the same character, whatever that be to which it attaches. The mind does not remain indifferent to those things and states which it sees to concern its enjoyments. This fact is expressed in a feeling toward them which we term desire. A desire is the inclination of the mind toward things which it sees to be the direct or indirect sources of pleasure. It rests back as a secondary feeling on those primary sensibilities to which the world directly ministers. Now the variety of objects which gratify man, and the variety of their separate ministrations are so great, that it is not easy to give an exhaustive classification of them. Those general **words** which divide, **yet include the** most of the things pursued by men, are **wealth, power, honor; truth,** beauty, and virtue.

It is easy to fall into confusion in speaking **of the** desires. The difficulty arises chiefly from not keeping the words by which we express them at the same grade of generalization. A great variety of means, near and remote, general and special, separates our actions from the ultimate gratifications at which they aim. These gratifications, lying **in** the outer circle and due to constitutional appetites, passions, tastes, are the grounds of the desires, which attach to any or all of these intervening means. It **is these means** that **are** grouped under very abstract general expressions, and classified as the desires. If the classification is to be of any worth, it must take place at one grade of generalization, must lie in and cover one circle, to the exclusion on the one side of still more general terms, and on the other of more specific ones. Thus wealth, power, honor, — by honor are meant positions and circumstances of honor— beauty, truth, virtue unite to cover the **two** halves of one circle of the generalized objects **of human effort.** Knowledge is not added, because it is divided between power and truth.   As a simple means to an end it is a form of power, as in itself productive of pleasures it is truth.

Having so classified the desires, we must guard against a tendency to recognize as distinct desires any of the more remote objects to which wealth, power, honor, beauty, truth, virtue are the means.   It is accurate, if not fitting language to say, I desire revenge.   The heart also yearns for objects of affection, and that it itself should be made an object of love.   When suffering pain, we desire its removal; when fearing punishment, we desire escape.   These are not new desires under our list, but a few of the many gratifications to be reached by wealth, power, honor.

The desire of happiness is sometimes added to the list. The objection to this is, that this desire is a still broader generalization, including all the others.   This desire embraces all our desires, is the utmost stretch of analysis and abstraction.   Admit this, and there is no opportunity for further division—all impulses are grouped under one general impulse common to each.   The desire for existence is also a desire dependent for its force on those other desires which make life pleasurable.   It, too, is a common condition of them all.

We regard desire, as a feeling, as indifferent; neither pleasurable nor painful, at least in its earlier forms.   When nourished into full strength, it may assume a more positive character.   A desire for wealth that is, as yet, neither gratified nor balked, while it becomes an immediate ground of pleasurable activity, while it gives direction and concert to the feelings, can hardly of itself be called distinctly painful or pleasurable.   This is seen in the case with which desire passes into pain or pleasure with any increase or decrease of the obstacles to its gratification.   In the ordinary, familiar balance of effort and reward, desire guides rather than vexes or excites us.   When it produces pleasure, it is rather by the activity it inspires, the hopes it enkindles, than by its own nature as an impulse : when it provokes suffering, it does so by the unusual obstacles it encounters, by the disappointment of fruitless effort. A pure desire seems to be as simply indicative as any feeling can well be, to make way for the current of emotions that is sure to rush along in its channel.

The desires have different degrees of strength according to the minds in which they arise, and the objects toward which they are directed. The desire for wealth passes with a few into a passion, and becomes the most exacting of impulses, while, with others, it is so gentle an incentive as to **control** but few of their actions. Herein, again, is seen its secondary character. The mind that habitually forecasts the future, that brings coming enjoyments into clear contrast with immediate pleasures, is one in which the desires show their full strength. The conditions of their activity are fully met, and they soon come to rule with undisputed sway. One, however, in whom the primary appetites **are** exacting, and the reflective powers feeble, renders but wayward and intermittent obedience to the desires, and leaves the events of life to be fashioned by the objects in most immediate connection with the sensibilities.

The strength of desires also depends on the nature of the objects sought — a farther result of their secondary character. The pursuit of wealth, of power, of honor, may, in rare instances, settle down into an exorbitant passion in minds in which the lower circle of vigorous, primitive sensibilities is united with moderate reflective faculties, furnishing a clear, yet nevertheless limited horizon of effort. In many cases these desires are relaxed by the disappointments which attend upon them, or the unsatisfactory nature of the results when realized. The desire for wealth is likely, under the force of habit, under the momentum of the mind, either to pass into the blind passion of avarice, or to suffer abatement from the limited character of the good wealth can confer. The desires for truth, for virtue, on the other hand, grow under success with a normal, rational growth. Each acquisition is a stimulus to further acquisition, and the satisfaction of possession increases every moment with possession. The mind more and more justifies its choice to itself, and congratulates itself on that which it has accomplished. The desire for wealth is like a stream that at length finds a precipice so high that in its leap it is lost in air, dissolved again in mist, and never resumes a peaceful flow; while the love of truth and virtue, more tranquil currents, swell in volume, and roll on increasing waters to the ocean.

§ 2. On either hand, the desires give rise to a large class of feelings dependent upon them. We will speak first of those pleasurable ones which accompany success, and thus stimulate effort. They fall into four classes, those which arise from success as *being achieved ;* those which arise from success as achieved *by ourselves ;* those which arise from success as achieved by the *aid of others ;* and those which arise from success as achieved *by others.* Immediately consequent on a state of desire, are the feelings of hope and joy in view of the prospect of obtaining the object sought. Indeed, hope is resolved in analysis into the feeling, desire, and the intellectual condition, expectation. We would rather regard these as the occasion of the emotion than the very emotion, hope. Joy accompanies success, and passes through various stages lying between tranquil satisfaction and triumphant exaltation. These feelings spring immediately from a free flow of the activities called forth by a successful desire, and, in turn, greatly quicken their action. The emotional state thus becomes instantly complex, consisting of the immediate effect of an-

ticipated pleasures, and the realized pleasure of fully employed powers. This has always been regarded as one of
the most unalloyed forms of enjoyment—that evoked by
the grasp of coming good by the mind as a certainty, together with the high exercise of its own faculties in securing it. The stimulated powers and feelings not only yield
the delight of successful action, but the imagination makes
the most of the pleasure promised, and overlooks the vexa-
tions and disappointments which too frequently embitter
the actual enjoyment of it. This concurrence of the practical and imaginative faculties leads to an exalted state of
feeling, especially when neither experience has sobered, nor
age made sluggish, the emotions.

The second class of pleasurable feelings comes from the
connection of effort and success with our own action. They
are pride, vanity. These emotions are most influential over
action, and constitute a large part of its reward. Vanity,
the pleasure which the mind receives from the admiration,
the favorable notice of others, exists with various conditions
and under very different degrees of intensity. In its moderate forms, it is a quiet incentive, and only becomes ill-
grounded and foolish when it leads to a neglect of real ex-
**cellence** and solid attainments, in favor of popular powers
**and** showy acquisitions. Within its legitimate sphere, it
closely unites itself with that desire for the good opinion of
others which the good man may well cherish. There are
few feelings which sustain the inferior desires as those **for**
wealth and position, as constantly and effectively as this of
vanity. Wealth owes its attractions, with many, to its ability to captivate and dazzle the public eye, to open gaping
mouths, and bewilder feeble wits.

Pride arises from the same good opinion **of** one's self
and one's possessions that characterizes vanity. It is, however, accompanied with more independence of character, and

does not, therefore, find its gratification so much in the admiration of others as in its own admiration. Vanity loves
parade, delights in the flow of popular sentiment, floats its
gay shallop on the good opinion of others, and is stranded
when public favor, like a shallow stream, is lost on some
sand-bar. Pride, in its high opinion of itself, despises
others, receives indifferently or contemptuously their admiration, and, like an ocean vessel, rides solitary on the
heaving tide of its own conceit. Like vanity, it has a legitimate form. As just self-esteem, it furnishes strength and
independence to character. It accompanies all grades of
desire. The food which the accomplishment of our desires
affords to our own good opinion of ourselves, and our love
of the admiration of others, are the most constant and
certain, most secret and sweet, of the pleasures of success.
In a modified form, these feelings enter into our highest
moral sentiments. The various words by which we designate these feelings, derive their meanings in part from the
different degrees of the same emotions, and in part from
the supposed justice, or fitness, with which the feeling is
entertained. Conceit, self-conceit, assumption, self-compla-
cence, indicate a vanity or pride in advance of the grounds
for it in our power or possessions. Indeed, the words vanity
and pride are also more commonly used to mark these ex-
cesses of feeling, than its restrained and praiseworthy forms.
Self-confidence, self-respect, personal pride designate the
more measured and well-founded phases of feeling.

The third class of pleasurable feelings arises in view of
the relation of others to our success. We are grateful to
those who have aided us. We are sympathetically attached
to those who share our triumphs, who enjoy our pleasures
with us. Our feelings are made deeper, hence more pleasurable, by the impulse of kindred feelings on them. Emotional
states, like electric conditions, intensify each other, and a

movement once established tends to complete itself in part by the reflex influence of one mind on another. The love and complacency begotten by success **are** as manifest as the impatience and vexation that spring **from** failure. The moment of achievement is usually seized upon as propitious to those who seek either forgiveness or favor. The degree of this satisfaction in others depends on the intimacy of their relations to our success, but extends itself often in a feeble form to indifferent parties. It is expressed under various words according to its character and degree, as gratitude, good-will, attachment.

The fourth class of feelings incident to success are those called out by the achievements of others. They are admiration, emulation, honor. The highest, the chief object of admiration is character; though simple power, physical or intellectual, may draw forth the feeling. This emotion inclines to the class of pleasurable feelings, and this, we think, in proportion as it opens a line of emulative action. Wonderful powers shown in fields of effort entirely foreign to our own labors by no means bestow, in the admiration they elicit, the same pleasure as do like triumphs in the familiar paths of our daily exertions. According, then, as admiration carries us from the midway point of indifference into emulation, does the pleasure become declared and intense even. Let the feeling, by a contrast with our own weakness, discourage us, and it is painful rather than pleasant. We enjoy honors also the more fully which we can in some measure share; those which have their grounds in our own experience, and which we aid in conferring.

§ 3. The feelings which accompany the failure of desire correspond to the opposite classes, but are more intense and more varied. Those which follow directly from the prospect of failure, or from failure itself as occurring, are fear, discouragement, disappointment, despair, all tending to repress effort, and to make the effort that is put forth peculiarly exhaustive. That the activity of the mind is an independent source of strength, is necessary to the highest, most successful development of purely physical strength, is indicated by the very different physical results which accompany efforts alike in intensity, but unlike in the satisfaction which accompanies them. Hope gives strength, discouragement at once takes it away. As physical life is an independent stimulus to the mind, so mental life is an independent stimulus to the body.

The second class of unpleasant feelings, arising from the relation to our own actions of baffled desire, is limited. They are certain forms of shame and humility. We are humbled by failure; we are ashamed of the ill success which has followed our efforts; we are mortified that others should be spectators of our weakness. These emotions are disagreeable, and may become excessive, permanently weakening the incentives to effort. Humility and shame find their fullest play in the moral field. Like some of the other intellectual feelings, they are adumbrations of emotions called forth by moral relations.

The third class of painful feelings, those excited toward others by opposition and failure, is especially full and varied. Envy, jealousy, dislike, antipathy, resentment, anger, hatred, malice, rage, revenge, are some of the words which express varied phases and stages of feeling exasperated by the indirect or direct interference of others, by an opposition of attitude, or character, or effort. Envy and jealousy arise from the designed or undesigned displacing of ourselves in position, or in affection, by others. They do not necessarily imply any fault on the part of their object, but merely an entrance upon ground we had coveted for ourselves. When this entrance is an intrusion, the feelings are proportionately more bitter. Antipathy and dislike express the results of **a** sense of opposition in character which prepares us for opposition in action, and provokes in a milder form, by anticipation, feelings of repulsion.

Resentment, anger, hatred, malice, rage, revenge, mark the more violent outbursts of feeling toward **those who di-**rectly thwart our efforts, who stand astride the path of our desires. **These** feelings, in their extreme form, so blind the mind as to make it almost indiscriminate in its action ; as to lead it to give vent to the **pent-up** passion on the first ob-**ject** that offers. The mind, like an electric battery, charged to the full by the irritation and friction of chafing events, **is** ready to launch a bolt at the nearest point, to blast and splinter in mere wantonness of wrath.

It may be doubted, perhaps, **whether these feelings of** resentment are not in part pleasurable. As simple emo-tions we think not. They give rise, however, to secondary desires, desires of retaliation and revenge, and in the grati-fication of these we experience pleasure. Language recog-nizes this in such an expression as, The sweetness of re-venge. These feelings may also be blended with moral sentiments **of** indignation, and thus their true character be **somewhat disguised.**

**Some** have regarded it as a reflection on **our** constitu-tion, that we should be capable of malevolent feelings. This perhaps it might be, if they were necessary, primary emotions ; **if,** like the appetites, they found direct, inevitable expression. As secondary feelings, however, they depend for their character on the character of the person who enter-tains them. They arise under the general possibility of transgression, of wrong desires wrongly pursued, and thus are involved in the general problem of sin, and admit of the same remedy that transgression itself suffers. Right de-sires, in their method and measure right, may be attended only with right feelings. The holy will may ultimately reach to the correction of these products of the violent, the unsubmissive, the selfish will. The malevolent feelings are simply the evil outflow of an evil purpose.

The fourth class of feelings find expression toward others in their failures. They are those of contempt, pity compassion. Contempt is the direct product of a selfish spirit toward weakness. Pity involves sympathy, and leads to consideration in the mishaps of others. It is a feeling that independent spirits accept with reluctance, as it so often bears with it something of the taint of contempt. In compassion the mind goes freely forth and shares with others the burdens of failure. A contemptuous frame of mind, as a personal characteristic, reduces all the incentives to generous action. It is a painful emotion, except so far as, inflaming self-conceit, it finds in the failure of others the food of pride. A low, disparaging estimate of the powers of men, giving birth to contempt spiced with misanthropy, will, unless relieved by a marked exception in our own favor, depress action and enjoyment. Each newly discovered case of weakness increases the bitterness of the heart. This feeling slowly over-clouds the sky, and leaves the soul in a chill, benumbing, disheartening atmosphere, rendering it incapable of pleasure, and indisposing it to the effort by which the spell might be cast off. The contemptuous man takes home as guests, sarcasm, satire, unbelief, aversion. He abides in their companionship, lies down and rises with them, and suffers their corrosive breath to tarnish the brightness of every object. Contempt is the rust of the soul, which eats it up with increasing pain. Nothing can be intrinsically more diverse, or more diverse in their effects, than that intellectual contempt which feeds on the weakness of men, and that moral sentiment which scorns a mean action. The one is the recoil of the soul upward:

the other, its gravitation downward, its cynical unbelief in goodness, its despair of strength.

The most beneficent of the intellectual feelings, as good-will and compassion, are but feeble sentiments when dis. joined from the moral nature. They are still pleasurable, still indices of action, impulses to a little desultory effort, but rarely have a deeper foundation than that of sympathy, which feebly transfers to us another's feelings; and play but a secondary part among those towering and dominant passions which drink up the life of the soul. They are remote reflections, faint types of those strong affections, those profound sympathies which give **to** the higher, the moral **nature its** compass and **power, which** enable it successfully to confront the **appetites** and passions, outweighing the good they offer with a greater good.

It is the feelings **now** indicated in this second great class resting primarily on self-interest, **and** especially liable **to** excess, that are termed passions. These emotions are **frequently** so strong that we *suffer* from them, that we seem **to be** their passive, afflicted subjects rather than their responsible sources.

# CHAPTER III.

## *The Spiritual Feelings.*

§ 1. THE spiritual feelings are so called because they belong peculiarly to our higher nature. Intellectual action is spiritual action: yet that which gives guidance and government to our interior, hidden life, is found in our intuitions. The intellect is instrumental under these, and, as in the brute, is simply a means to safety and gratification. Our spiritual feelings spring up, then, in direct connection with our intuitions; those mental elements which make our life truly rational, which give to us a choice of ends, and liberty in the pursuit of them. The only intuitions which draw forth directly feeling, are those of truth, beauty and right. There is in the emotions connected with these regulative ideas the action of the intellect, yet an action different from that presented by the last class of feelings. In these, it was the observed relation of things to our enjoyments which was the ground of desire, with the attendant sensibilities. The mental action intervened between the remote appetites, tastes, passions, and pointed out the means of gratification, and called forth a variety of emotions in prosecuting the labor presented. In the present case, the intellectual action precedes the intuition. Patient inquiry reveals the grounds of belief, the truth: a careful discrimination of qualities, of the symbols of expression, of complex relations, discloses the conditions of beauty: a thorough inquiry into the nature and results of action, its reflex and progressive effects, lays open its true character, and then

the intuitive faculty comes in to complete and seal the work
in the discernment of a new and distinct quality—that of
right.    The proposition is said to be true, the statue is seen
to be beautiful, the action is pronounced right, and forth-
with there arise many sentiments which find their spring
in these ideas.    These are the spiritual feelings.    Their
immediate dependence is on the mind's intuitive action;
their secondary dependence, on our intellectual faculties.
Our intellectual feelings, on the other hand, find their immediate source in mental action, in the conclusions of experience, and their ultimate ground in the appetites and
tastes.

These feelings again are open to the same division into
pleasurable, indifferent and painful emotions.    This relation
of the feelings to happiness must necessarily be a fundamental distinction of all the emotions.    Their relation to
action may be said to be secondary to their relation to enjoyment, since action itself is undertaken or withheld in
view of its immediate or ultimate effects on the sensibilities.
The feelings can only be classified by their external relations, since, intrinsically, they are all diverse, all simple
original states, known in experience only.    Of the external
relations of the feelings, this relation to happiness is most
essential, while that to action comes next in order, both as
indicating an immediate purpose served by our sensibilities
and their secondary effects on our character and well-being.
In their connection with action, the spiritual feelings assume a more imperative character than either of the other
two classes.    In those, feelings enter to stimulate and gratify
effort, or check and discourage it; here, they go before it
as well to command as to forbid action.    They cease merely
to allure, and seek decisively to enjoin and prohibit different lines of conduct.    The middle ground of indication
seems narrowed to a point, and to be pressed closely on

either hand by dissuasives and persuasives. The spiritual sentiments may be divided into those of persuasion, indication and dissuasion. Their voice is always one of authority, though its authority need not be felt so long as it is kindly and cheerfully accepted. Actual or contemplated resistance provokes a class of penal sensibilities; and obedience elicits feelings that have the positive character of approval and reward.

The weakest of these sentiments, and those therefore which least well represent the class, are the somewhat intangible, rare, and uncertain sensibilities which accompany the discovery, the recognition of the truth as truth. Truth is the agreement of a proposition with the facts which it states. Much the majority of truths are received as truths with no emotion. Most of them are matters of interest only as they effect action—only in their relation to our desires and tastes, indicating success or failure, or revealing the line of conduct to be pursued. Truths, for the most part, are means possessed of no inherent, emotional force beyond their relation to ends.

This negative character of truth seems sometimes to disappear, and truth as truth to inspire a certain enthusiasm of mind, by which we feel that this is indeed the food of our spiritual nature. We may breathe the air ordinarily without thought, or sensible pleasure. Occasionally, we find it peculiarly invigorating; we inhale great draughts, and bring our whole physical being into a more conscious and exalted state. Thus is it with the truth,—the daily breath of our intellectual life. We ordinarily overlook it; at rare intervals we, in deep inspiration, feel its pervasive and subtile power, and rejoice in its possession. We travel along the valley, scarcely observing the objects about us, with no elation of feeling; we pass some crowning summit, take in a wider range, and the before concealed wave of emotion becomes sensible to us; we are lifted on its passing billow as if a breath from another world had stolen suddenly across our path.

This is the kind of emotion to which we draw attention —the enthusiasm sometimes felt in truth, more especially in those fundamental, far-reaching truths which seem to suddenly lift the veil of phenomena, of varied colors, and to disclose to us the frame-work **of** the universe; the purposes which are running through it, and bearing it to its goal. This on-going of a divine plan, when recognized, startles and inspires the mind, lifts truth out of its daily, dry, instrumental ministrations, and gives us the sense of a new inheritance and possession in a universe whose conception we can thus lay hold of, whose secrets we can thus penetrate, whose wisdom and love we can thus interpret and feel. I care not how little or how much of this sentiment we may have felt, how far it may be thought **to be confined** to the more poetic and penetrative temperaments; it is sufficient to draw attention to it as an enthusiasm for truth occasionally felt and avowed, finding expression in the collective use of the word truth, the truth, the truths, as if a certain concealed link and deep unity were to be found in all **facts.** We do this, too, in the face of those detestible facts, truths, which sin is forcing constantly upon our notice, as if after all, there were some profound fellowship, some one exaltation in all truths, rendering them *the truth.*

This sensibility to the truth, be it more or less clear, be it more or less deep (1) inspires pursuit, (2) leads to faith in a profound, unfolding plan, and (3) quickens the mind to discover the corrective laws, the compensatory statements for the defects and transgressions which lie on the surface of the world. This sentiment opens up a line of effort, inspires enthusiasm, sends faith in advance of reason, and rejoices in the slow displacement of accredited by appre-

hended facts, of statement by disclosure, of trust by sight,
of instinctive belief by the light of comprehensive principles. It is little more than the exaltation and joy of
our spiritual faculties as they enter on, and begin to occupy
their inheritance—an inheritance which we are pleased to
call that of eternal truth, though on the shifting surface
of changing events, everything seems most transitory—of
blessed truth, though most horrible and terrible facts are
daily evolved before our eyes. Yes, the sense and the revelation of deep principles that undergird the world with
abiding strength, and gather it up in the embrace of an exalted, a blessed purpose, are with us, steal in upon us in
our best convictions, and yield the repose which a belief in
its ultimate triumph inspires. There is inlocked in our language and our nature a belief in truth, central, adaman-
tine, giving safe, benignant support to the universe of God.

In like manner, we carry over to the false, the untrue, a
farther concentration of opposition and rejection in the
word, falsehood. We personify it as a distinct principle or
power of mischief, believe in its weakness, and rejoice in
its ultimate overthrow. No matter what may have been
their character, few of any party have ever espoused falsehood as such, few have not felt that the confession of it
would be the admission of ultimate failure. We recognize
the vague way in which these words, truth and falsehood,
are frequently used; yet, nevertheless, we claim that there
is in this tendency of the mind to recognize the inherent
opposition of the true and the false, the ultimate, necessary
victory of the one over the other—a latent belief in fundamental principles and forces, which it is the vain, temporary
effort of falsehood to cover up and counter-work. This embrace of the real, as ultimately involving the ideal, and
passing in evolution from excellence to excellence, is the
fruit of the mind's discovery of truth and error, its hearty

acceptance of the one and its rejection of the other; its satisfaction in the external plan of God.

§ 2. The next group of intuitive feelings, though of a more manifest character, and more prevalent, has yet much of the same subtlety, the same choice of persons and times. Indeed, these are features of the whole class of emotions of which we are speaking. It has, doubtless, been one reason of the difficulty with which the spiritual feelings and the intuitive ideas, on which they are immediately dependent, have been recognized, that they are not, like the physical feelings, universally present with approximately equal power, but in many scarcely seem to exist at all, and in their full, intense forms to be confined to comparatively few. Yet the reason of this is obvious. They are each of them dependent on previous culture, on a faithful, special, discriminating action of the understanding. The beauty of the world is not seen, or at least is but very partially and inadequately seen, without an inquiry into its structure and relations, without a discernment of the exquisite perfection of idea and workmanship involved in it. No more is the right understood without a broad survey of conduct, the tracing of actions to their consequences; without rising **above** the immediate current of the stream to see whence **and whither** its flow. The intuitive feelings, therefore, can **only** be strong and clear in the more penetrative and reflec**tive minds.** They do not thereby cease to be universal or **characteristic when** their appropriate conditions are met.

The esthetical emotions arise solely under the previous action of mind. Disorder, absolute and complete, can furnish no beauty, nothing to be admired, nothing intrinsically to be delighted in. Order, arrangment, is the first step toward beauty, is the first, simplest product of taste. But this order is the result of thought. This arrangement will present itself as beautiful in proportion to the number and variety of the ends it meets, and the ease and accuracy with which these separate purposes are fulfilled. A little formal order imposed by mere utility, simple convenience in the classification of material, is not sufficient, or sufficiently significant to excite and to satisfy the taste. It is not till more feeling enters into our plan, more variety, skill and precision of adjustment, that the elements of beauty begin to be clearly revealed, and the mind takes an additional delight in the work aside from each and all of the ends subserved by it. Gardening, architecture, music, are the arts least imitative—the arts in which the beauty present is most immediately the result of the combining power of the human mind. In each of these, mere order produces scarcely a sensible effect. It is not till the plan discovers high appreciation of the resources at the disposal of the artist, and great power and pleasure in combining and developing them—not till the product becomes thoroughly emotional, and in its scope and variety betrays a mind and heart alike active, that it begins in turn to command our emotion, and impress us, as the case may be, with the grace, symmetry, harmony, force of the conception.

Here, then, beauty throws us into appreciative sympathy with the thoughts and feelings of a worker; of one who executes well and powerfully, and delights in such execution—one with whom perfection is a thing esteemed, sought after, and includes far more than the immediate subordination of the means employed to a useful physical end. It is this effort of the mind, without neglecting utility, to lift each of its works out of the mere routine of labor, off from the simple plane of service into an emotional region, —to make it in its excellence, in its skillful or affectionate or grand handling, a source of independent, superior, constant pleasure, that is the source of beauty, and of its com-

mand over the heart. Not merely work, or good work, but
superior, expressive, emotional work is its aim. The esthetical feelings cause us to delight in such labor, and to
go, as far as may **be, to** every undertaking crowned with
garlands.

If **we pass to** the beauties of nature, equally do we find
that it **is** thought, aptness of arrangement, skill **of workmanship,** labor performed with infinite love and faithful-
**ness,** that **arrest** the mind and gratify the heart. In pro-
**portion** as many adaptations, many **powers are** gathered
into a brief compass, and with a perfect finish and relation
**of parts united in one** organic whole, are we climbing with
**slow gradations, with a thousand steps of varied progress,
from the lowest life to the highest, from** the plant to man,
delighted **with the goodness** of the thought, the kind and
abundant ministration **of** faculties to the **well-**being and **ex-**
cellence of the **final** product. In each advance **of** beauty,
there is more expression, because there is more and more
perfection, more **and** more beneficent labor, till, in man
**we** find the highest condensation of power and regard; ser-
**vice,** compactness, symmetry, finish, in their most perfect
forms.

Everywhere, then, it is **the labor** of mind and heart, the
**births** of thought and feeling, the rational products of high
**intelligence and** love, that arouse the sensibility of beauty;
and we **are so** constituted that we can not be indifferent to
these qualities when perceived by us. A cold, intellectual
apprehension **does not** exhaust them. They elicit a certain
regard, assume a certain relation which we designate as
beauty, and so call forth the pleasures of beauty. Such enjoyment on our part is (1) a crowning sympathy with excellence; such perception (2) an additional incentive to high
attainment. They are the thirst of **an** aspiring spirit for
that which is beyond, which is above; for that which it

knows it can grasp and enjoy. They take all barrenness, all deadness from simple intellectual movement, breathe through it desire, cause it to draw back the curtain between us and the ideal world, and fire us with the zeal of pursuit.

While the specific character of esthetical emotions is very pronounced, their minor differences are very great. The same fruits have not all the same flavor. The most exquisite and characteristic tastes complete the circle, with an endless division and change of quality. In works of nature, plants, trees, landscapes, birds, beasts, men; in works of art, painting, statues, poems; in varied objects, and in their yet more varied combinations, we find a constant change of predominant qualities, endless degrees of power, and ever shifting methods of expression. Hence arises in esthetical sentiments every shade of form and force, from impressions scarcely perceptible to those which wholly occupy the soul—overpowering emotions breaking out upon it like a flood. The flow of these enjoyments in the sensitive mind may be compared to the movement of music, now gay and cheerful, now common-place, now low and sad, now mysterious, now wild, now sublime, gliding from phase to phase of emotion with perfect ease and inexhaustible felicity. The scope, body, variety of feelings which are either in whole or in part of an esthetical character, are in sensitive, poetic temperaments very marked. A large share both of their gentler as well as more exalted pleasures springs from this source.

The form of action which these emotions prompt is manifest. They always afford a mild, often a powerful stimulus to painstaking, emulative and refined action. They promote the finish, the perfection, the beauty of every product of the hand or of the mind. They reveal themselves in the physical results of labor, and certainly not less in character. The restraints and checks of esthetic sentiments are

experienced constantly in manners and social customs, and,
if the taste is keen and just, in the more deep, personal,
spiritual traits of action. Indeed, nobility, magnanimity,
the symmetry and proportion of robust, thorough, healthy
virtue, can hardly be reached without a large infusion of
this esthetic insight, which discerns, delicately **and** completely, the formal as well as the intrinsic bearings **of** conduct. The dependent, complementary relation of the esthetic **to the** ethic sense cannot be doubtful. Some may
**strive** to make the first a detached law of action, but it only
performs safely and to the full its office, as it accepts the
higher law, and aids in its complete application. Perfect
beauty in man, its highest subject, is the strong and varied
and delicate development of moral power—the infusion
of all the members and means of life with this inner, true
life of the soul—the flowing outward in limb, **lineament,**
and language of those manifold forces and susceptibilities
that spring from wholesome, healthy, physical forces, in the
handling of a supreme, spiritual power. Taste rightly developed can no more fail to distinguish morality from immorality, to work under the one and against the other, than
it can fail to discriminate between life and death, health
and disease, exalt the first, and hide the second in its de-
**formity.** Beauty stands in the same relation to action as
right; like it, it enjoins and forbids, rewards and punishes.
It blows a more silvery trumpet, its notes are less **clear,**
penetrating **and decisive** than those which break sternly
forth from the lips of ethical law, yet they wind their way
into many remote places, and persuasively bend into **cheer-**
ful and perfect order the otherwise unpliant recruits **of**
virtue.

§ 3. We have now reached the feelings which are most
central and characteristic in the class to which they belong,
the moral sentiments. The emotions **just spoken** of would

lose much of their character were it not for their interpene-
tration by those of the moral nature.  It is this filtration of
the higher sensibilities downward which gives coherence
and authority to the recognition of truth, to esthetical feelings, which of themselves simply have little binding force.
The only imperative voice in man's nature, is that of conscience ; all other authority is but the echo and reflection of
this.  In one view of the subject our moral nature may be
said to be our entire nature ; since a moral quality and
moral relation are imparted to all thoughts and actions by
the presence of this supreme, supervisory power.  In a
more strict use, our moral nature includes those emotions
which more directly spring from it.  Conscience, the perceptive faculty, which, in an indivisible act, sees the right
and feels the sense of obligation, is the centre of our moral
constitution.  Without it, we should have no affections, no
moral sentiments ; with it, we find the whole atmosphere
of our being irradiated, and a thousand colors revealed in
objects, tangible, indeed, in the darkness ; endowed with
odor and with flavor, but with no direct avenue of approach
through the physical night to the intellectual day.  Light
does not more modify, I may say etherealize matter, multiplying a thousand fold its intelligible signs, crowding
them in from all quarters and all distances on the astonished
mind, than does a moral perception affect our estimates of
character, deepen in meaning, and broaden in time the relations of actions.

The fundamental moral feeling from which all others
spring is that of obligation.  This, as regards pleasure and
pain, is indifferent.  It may give place to one or the other
according to the attitude assumed toward the duties designated.  The blended, the indivisible nature of the intuition and the accompanying sentiment should be carefully
marked.  A sense of obligation, a mere feeling, with no con-

viction to which that feeling attaches, is theoretically unintelligible, and practically unserviceable. An intuition of right on the other hand, which does not instantly assume the force and pressure of duty, loses its character and slips from the throne of the mind. Intrinsic quality and exterior form, the rational and the emotional elements, are inseparably blended, and give us a command, whose unquestionable authority, like that of one born to rule, is in the immediate fact, in tone, attitude, outspoken power.

If obedience follows the intimations of our moral sense, there sets in a deep and deepening current of pleasurable feelings, of reward. The force and intensity of these emo**tions** will depend very much on the degree in which the judgments which sustain the action of conscience and prepare the way for its decisions have been cultivated; on the relative force which the moral sentiments have secured in our constitution by obedience. Ethical feelings, like esthetical ones, are very dependent on cultivation. The reason of this is obvious, since in neither case are we dealing, as in external perception, with a direct, immediate faculty, but with one acting on previous intellections, previous conceptions of **the** mind, and therefore limited in its scope and correctness to them. It is evident that **the character of** phenomena should be judged by instances **in which they are most man**ifest and complete, not by cases in which they are obscure and furtive. A powerful moral nature makes itself at once felt in the pleasures it pours in upon the obedient mind, of such degree and quality that the appreciative heart prefers them to all others, and purchases them at any price of suffering which can be exacted of it. Yet these enjoyments are of a tranquil rather than a violent kind; a deep sense of satisfaction in the choices made, a thorough contentment in actions done, an inner approval which anticipates a like outward acceptance on the part of the wise and just.

The feelings which follow disobedience, though more irregular and unequal in their action, often dilatory and partial, when compared with those of approval and reward, yet frequently assume a strong, clear, undeniable character. Shame, guilt, remorse, willful opposition, and sullen despair may, in turn, hold sway, and make themselves as distinct as, and more bitter than, any other feelings which the heart ever experiences. For reaching this result, more or less time may be required. Repeated disclosure of the disasters of transgression, the accumulation of physical retributions, a revelation of pervasive law, hemming in and baffling the disobedient, may be needed to instruct the moral judgments and awaken the moral sense. When, however, a pause is given to the career of sin, when reflection and the intuitive results of reflection can no longer be averted, the force and direction of moral emotion are as certain as the pains or pleasures of sense, when things bitter or sweet are on the palate. The pains of indigestion may follow more slowly than disgust from food in itself offensive; but the consequences are no less of a distinct and undeniable character. Moral sufferings may be postponed in more ways and longer than many other emotional issues of action; yet the development of causes ripens them none the less certainly to their results. The whole history of the race renders the positive character of the moral sentiments as undeniable as the physical consequences of an unwholesome diet. The fear the cowardice, the apprehension, the boldness, the approval, the confidence; self-condemnation, self-gratulation; the reproaches of conscience, the dismay, the despair attendant on wickedness achieved, the composure of assured conviction, the calm anticipation of suffering, the triumph over it, fill the records of history, are the staple of dramatic and heroic action. Heathen and Christian literature alike breathe in their more profound and earnest moods, one spirit.

Says Juvenal:

> " But tell me, why must those be thought to 'scape.
> Whom guilt, arrayed in very dreadful shape,
> Still urges, and whom conscience, ne'er asleep,
> Wounds with incessant strokes, not loud but deep.
> While the vexed mind, her own tormentor, plies
> A scorpion scourge, unmarked by human eyes."

The history of martyrs especially develops the moral forces in man, since, on these feelings, the struggle has turned. The cruel tossings of such a mind as that of Cranmer, clear, conscientious, yet timid and distrustful, between fear and conviction, discloses as clearly as any thing can disclose the nature of the forces at work, unless it be the varying sympathy, the alternate charity and condemnation of succeeding generations, in view of the momentary overthrow and ultimate triumph of the moral sentiments in the fearful, bold saint.

§ 4. Personal qualities are greatly modified by the moral nature. Meekness, humility lose all servility and are made consistent with the utmost strength ; while moral firmness softens down without weakening the outline of character.

Still more is this true of our feelings towards others. These, in the conscientious temperament, receive almost their entire force from the moral sentiments. The affections, a distinct class of sensibilities, are our emotions toward others as moral beings. Admiration, love, sympathy, benevolence, forgiveness, charity, patience, indignation, contempt, shame, are feelings which though they may bear the same name with certain intellectual emotions are very different from them. Love a passion and love an affection, the indignation of anger and the indignation of a violated moral sense, are alike diverse sentiments in their relation both to enjoyment and to action. In the first relation, they may as easily prey upon happiness as promote it; in the second, they can not fail of being productive of pleasure.

In the moral sensibilities, the sharpness and the bitterness of the selfish element disappear, and the benignity, composure and patience of a moral impulse take their place. It is the intermingling of so many kinds of feeling, and of the words applicable to them, which confound the character of action, and the classification of this department.

The direction in which the moral sensibilities find fullest play is that of religious sentiments. The relations and duties designated as religious are those which, by the feelings and the results involved, are fitted to act most powerfully on the conscience and affections. The religious emotions, therefore, seem at times to overshadow other forms of ethical action, since their intensity and scope bear some proportion to the interests covered by them—to the ennobling, greatly stimulating presentations of the divine attributes. The foundation of religion is ethics, yet the ethical form is often swallowed up in the deep, spontaneous play of the religious affections. If we consider the permanent issues of happiness, of joy and peace, as settled in our own constitution by the moral sentiments, and the relations of actions under them; if we remember that nothing in our fellow-men is of more abiding interest to us than their character, than the moral purposes indicated, and line of conduct adopted; and, above all, if we bring to mind that the deepest, the supreme play of feeling is towards God, chiefly known to us as a moral being, we shall see that the class of sentiments now presented are at once the most varied, the most full, the most central and powerful of our emotions. So pervasive are they, that they give coloring to intellectual feelings which they cannot rule, enter in a fragmentary form where completeness is denied them, and are brought in to intensify or modify or disguise sentiments intrinsically at war with them. The **exact** shades of approval and condemnation, of contentment and restlessness, of belief and unbelief in them, are as endless as are the relations which men's actions bear to virtue.

Their authority, their retributive connection with pleasure and pain, the undercurrent of fear or hope, of repose or alarm, of conscious virtue or acknowledged guilt, which **they** cause to flow through the soul, obviously assign them the highest rank in the highest class of feelings. It is a convenient use of words, and one we have occasionally employed, to designate collectively the primary incentives **of the** spiritual nature as tastes, in contrast with appetites and passions.

§ 5. In the following diagram, feelings are introduced which have not been discussed in the text, and farther **divisions** are made. The enlargements are self-explanatory.

We do not present this classification as exhaustive. **It** aims simply to define leading directions of the emotions **and** leading dependences. It serves, also, to show the complexity of the feelings, the way in which they blend with each other, modify and pass into each other, and the insufficient, shifting terminology applicable to them. Indeed the word sometimes only implies and does not express the feeling intended.

We might easily subdivide the ethical emotions, but no good purpose wou d be subserved. They would still prove too subtile and pervasive for us. The one thing we emphasize is the degree in which the higher sink into the lower feelings, and transform them. Innumerable and most complex relations spring up between men by virtue of the moral constitution, and each relation has a new combination of spiritual sentiments. The great facts, too, of religion enter to impart a new elevation and range to these emo-

**Physical Feelings.**
- General Sensations,
- Special Sensations,
- Appetites,
- Natural Affections.

**Intellectual Feelings.**

Primary.
- 1.
  - Contentment.
  - Unrest
  - Wonder.
  - Surprise,
  - Wit,
  - Humor.
- 2. Desires.
  - Wealth,
  - Power,
  - Honor.
  - Truth,
  - Beauty,
  - Virtue.

Secondary.

Incident to *success.*
- *As being achieved.*
  - Hope,
  - Joy,
  - Satisfaction.
- As achieved. *by ourselves.*
  - Pride,
  - Vanity,
  - Courage,
  - Confidence.
- By the *aid of others.*
  - Gratitude,
  - Good-will,
  - Attachment.
- *By others.*
  - Admiration,
  - Honor,
  - Emulation.

Incident to *failure.*
- *As occurring.*
  - Fear,
  - Disappointment,
  - Discouragement.
- Through *ourselves.*
  - Humility,
  - Shame,
  - Mortification.
- Through *others.*
  - Anger,
  - Rage,
  - Hatred,
  - Malice,
  - Jealousy,
  - Envy,
  - Defiance.
- *To others.*
  - Contempt,
  - Pity,
  - Compassion.

**Spiritual Feelings.**

Incident to truth.
- Pleasure,
- Enthusiasm,
- Awe.

To beauty.
- Delight,
- Grandeur,
- Sublimity.

To right.

In reference to *ourselves.*
- Obedience.
  - Self-approval,
  - Peace,
  - Courage.
- Disobedience.
  - Humility,
  - Repentance,
  - Guilt,
  - Unrest,
  - Remorse,
  - Despair.

*To others.*
- Obedience.
  - Respect,
  - Praise,
  - Love,
  - Faith,
  - Reverence.
- Disobedience.
  - Disrespect,
  - Distrust,
  - Censure,
  - Justice,
  - Aversion.
  - Patience,
  - Forgiveness,
  - Benevolence.

tions. Yet complex or grand as the results may be, their elements are the simple feelings **we** have given. We have outlined **the primary colors** of the brilliant spectrum.

The beautiful also **unites with** the **right** with **farther** transfiguring force. We **only point** the way **to these fields** of **poetry and religion,** we **do. not** paint them. **The** position **in** which we **have** put our **words of** designation **must often** define the **word;** we cannot reproduce the **atmos**pheric coloring of the spiritual heavens.

# CHAPTER IV.

## DYNAMICS OF THE EMOTIONS.

§ 1. WE have spoken of the three classes of feelings; the physical, the intellectual, and the spiritual. We wish now to see them more collectively in their relations to each other in the formation of character and the control of action. The first class spring immediately from physical conditions, and, including incidental occasions of pleasure, have primary reference to physical well-being. At points they transcend this object. Taste, touch, smell, are means of simple, intellectual distinctions; yet, it remains true, that the senses which are the avenues of feeling, the appetites, the sensations indicating special physical conditions, all have primary reference to health, to guiding action in nourishing and maintaining the vigor of the body. Even here, it can hardly be said, that "All pleasure arises from the free play of our faculties and capacities; and all pain from their compulsory repression, or compulsory activity." Much less is this generalization of Hamilton's applicable to the remaining classes of emotion.

It is the unhealthy and the healthy action, the unwholesome repression and the wholesome repression, that give pain and pleasure respectively, if not at once, as an ultimate consequence. Pain enters frequently to arrest action, and not as the consequence of arrested action. Mere activity, voluntary though it may be, does not necessarily give the conditions of enjoyment; these must depend on its relations to health. Neither does repressed exertion, involuntary though the restraint **may be,** define **the** conditions of physical suffering.    Overlooking **the** mental vexation of such constraint, the **physical consequences** may be **agreeable.** Physical **pleasures seem to** depend **on the relation which ac**tivity and repose have to health, and not **on their** relation **to** the will of the agent.    Some forms **of disease provoke** voluntary, fitful, restless, yet painful effort.    Exertion or the want of it by no means explains the accompanying pain or pleasure; we know through experience their general connection with physical well-being.    Our pain and pleasures impart a direct stimulus to appropriate effort for the maintenance of the body, still more they instruct us as to its conditions and wants, and thus, in a secondary way, guide our action.    They subserve the purposes of intellectual discrimination and of gratification.

Intellectual feelings **have relation to success, are pleas**urable and **painful in** proportion as this end is secured or lost.    Unsuccessful activity, no matter how free and spontaneous it may be, is always in the intellectual feelings which accompany it disagreeable, often intensely painful.    **Our** physical and our intellectual enjoyments may not **always** harmonize.    Effort in itself wholesome may fail of its **ob**ject and occasion disappointment, and exertion crowned with the most flattering success may bring a severe infliction **of physical penalties.**    The mind institutes its own ends, **and afterwards finds pleasure, or experiences** suffering, **by** its prosperity or losses in the pursuit of them.    As the primary relation of the **intellectual emotions is** to success in the ends aimed at, the pleasure and pain in this direction experienced act as stimuli to sagacity, and faithfulness in the choice and use of means.    This is an instrumental, an intermediate field, and its enjoyments are of a secondary, intermediate character.

Spiritual pleasures have reference to the choice of ends,

to the marking out of lines of conduct, to obedience to higher impulses. These again may often fail of concurrence with intellectual enjoyments. We have the satisfaction of success in the attainment of ends which we should never have chosen, and the moral rebuke may thus set in at the point at which the intellectual pleasure is most complete. Physical health and spiritual health are ultimate, and the secondary intellectual enjoyments can not avert the consequences of failure as regards either of them. Spiritual enjoyments and sufferings come in to enforce obedience— obedience to the law of spiritual life. They stand in the same relation to this, that physical pleasures do to the lower life of the body. They are simple, ultimate, the moral sense sustaining them. With self-established authority, the conscience legislates for the whole man, and according as its commands are wisely understood and wisely applied, the minor physical and intellectual enjoyments are gathered up in these supreme pleasures of the soul.

Our enjoyments are not thus simply the fruits of activity, they are of such a character as to define its limits, and direct it to appropriate objects. The law of life in the whole man is indicated by them. The ends to be pursued, the limits to be set to activity, even in its right directions, are pointed out, with the accompanying injunction laid upon us of a skillful choice and use of means.

§ 2. The three classes of feelings now referred to, have a successive, rather than an equal and simultaneous hold on the mind. The physical feelings are most immediate, direct, importunate in their claims. The intellectual life is awakened through the physical life, in some sense follows it. The sensations, the appetites, the states of the body, are early and decided means of good and evil—means independent of thought, with a necessary and irresistible appeal to the sensibilities. The intellectual feelings, as secondary,

involve a previous action of mind, are not strong except in
connection with considerable forethought, a somewhat broad
survey of the relations of actions. For this reason, the desires do not set in in a deep, strong current, except in more
advanced minds, or in the more civilized states of society.
In a barbarous community, the immediate impulses are
chiefly animal; in a civilized community the desires come
to rule the leading classes, while the appetites still bear sway
in the lower ranks. The spiritual feelings are yet more
tardy in their full development. For anything like broad,
decisive action of our higher intuitions, there is requisite
much previous reflection. As beauty involves the union of
inner power with perfect form, there must be, for its due
perception, a deep, discriminating insight into both. As the
universal sway of morality arises from a clear perception of
the dependence of individual and general well-being on the
form and spirit of conduct in its every manifestation, it is
not till faithful observation and protracted reflection have
disclosed the character and issues of action, that the ethical
impulse can find very complete application. In the outset,
it is likely to be confined to a few negative precepts, cutting off the individual from gross violations of the right.
Ten commandments or twelve tables expounded in the most
barren way may seem its limits. Only the latest culture
**can open** these into the pervasive precept of universal love.
The most enlightened communities, therefore, as yet present a very partial government of the spiritual sentiments.
When the artistic sensibilities have been awakened, they
have hitherto affected but limited classes, and this in a partial, one-sided form; sometimes even in direct violation of
the moral sentiment which underlies all high acts. The religious emotions also have been restricted in their action,
and fragmentary in their character. The spirit and the
force of a higher life have not, in their completeness, been

grasped, and we have had an ethics more or less at war with esthetics—an intense yet narrowed force, which could not discriminate and command all the elements requisite for its own most perfect expression.

§ 3. Were it not that communities — that successive generations of men, achieve a collective growth, which the individual is able to receive inductively from them, starting at the point they have already reached, this order of development in the feelings would make the condition of mankind comparatively hopeless. But the growth of society reveals very clearly this progress from the physical to the intellectual feelings, and in an incipient form is disclosing that farther movement by which the artistic and ethical sentiments, under the perfect, harmonious rule of the higher impulses, shall take the supreme position amid the powers and pleasures of the human heart.

When any one feeling begins to predominate in the individual or the community, many things concur to strengthen its hold. Take, as an illustration, such a desire as that for wealth. It soon becomes a strong current, plowing for itself a deep bed, walled on either hand, and not readily changed. The desire by repetition returns easily as an habitual one. Surrounding objects and pursuits are more and more contemplated in their ability to gratify this feeling, and therefore by their presence more uniformly bring it uppermost in the mind. Kindred pursuits draw together parties in whom the desire is already developed, and by emulation and the confirmation of like judgments, they inflame it in each other. Thus a large commercial city seems a very maelstrom of economic currents, and every individual, a separate particle spinning round and round under the same feverish impulse and waiting to be swallowed up by the same insatiable lust. The brood of feelings also warmed into life by a parent desire, unite at once in the same clamorous and importunate cries. Vanity, pride, the satisfaction of success, the fear of failure, all quicken effort, and occupy the heart, when for a moment the original impulse relaxes. **The** circle of secondary desires is momentarily enlarged as the means of gratification are placed within their reach, and the wealth acquired is often less and less able to meet the claims laid upon it by feelings which, without law or limit in themselves, become ravenous in proportion to the food given them. Thus external and internal circumstances are increasingly **shaped** to the ruling feeling, grow up more and more under it, institute claims in harmony with it, confirm the **judgments** which sustain it, and **weaken and remove to a** distance adverse **emotions.** From this household of dependents, from this pressure of a prevalent opinion, from these confirmed and consolidated convictions **of the soul itself,** it is difficult to find an avenue of escape. If we substitute an appetite for a desire, though there is less warping of the judgment, there is in its place a peevish, persecuting habit, not easily to be worn out or resisted. From this confirmed movement which the feelings for the time-being assume, it becomes necessary that the forces which work for progress, should find concentration, and also that long periods should be allowed them in which to possess and fortify the ground they may **be able to win.** The overthrow of one class of feelings, and their permanent replacement by another in a community, is a truly gigantic work, requiring often the slow eradication and correction of a protracted and varied experience.

This fact is especially observable in the development of the spiritual sensibilities. The social, moral law lies between persons, and is, therefore, every moment affected in its form by the parties to it. Gracious affections can not go forth toward ungracious men, any more than from them.

Hard facts demand stern principles, and stern principles call for severe enforcement. Only as each heart is softened can all hearts be softened. Only as one sees clearly the path, can he lead others into it ; and no one can see clearly lines of action far ahead of the conditions by which he is surrounded. Each movement must be conjunct with existing circumstances, and, by a series of actions and reactions, make way for the next movement. At each stage the animal appetites and the intellectual passions must receive within themselves the modifying force of the spiritual tastes. The two ultimate sources of impulse, physical and spiritual, do not remain apart under growth ; a vigorous interaction sets in ; each class softens the other and gives it new conditions. The intellectual feelings, elicited by this double play of incentives, are correspondingly purified and enriched. Time is demanded for securing the enlargement and unity of life, and its diffusion through every function. Time is the one unalterable condition of evolution.

§ 4. The feelings of the animal, if the view we have presented of his endowments is correct, are almost purely physical. His courage is physical courage ; his fear, physical fear ; that is to say, these states are imposed upon him directly by external objects. The one is the rushing in of nerve power, prompting to conflict ; the other, the desertion of the seats of strength by the energies of life—an immediate provocation, an inclination, to flight instead of attack. Memory, giving rise to association, may indeed, in the higher animals, start trains of feeling and thus of action aside from the power of the object which is more remotely their cause. Yet these feelings are comparatively limited. Little apprehension is shown except in the presence of danger, and then not according to its real nature, but its sensible form. The alarm manifested by many animals assumes a direct, instinctive character—the appropriate action evidently follows the sensitive impression without any intervention of judgment. The young of the partridge hide themselves instantly on the first intrusion. Barn-fowls are filled with immoderate and universal alarm as the shadow of the hawk glides by them. The actions of the lower creation assume generally this direct dependence on sensations, with an occasional intervention of the intellectual element of association.

Having now the emotions completely before us in their relation to the mind and to each other, we are better able to decide on the merits **of that theory** which recognizes but **two** classes, resolving the spiritual feelings into the intellectual. This will hardly seem possible, if we fairly estimate all that belongs to the intuitive emotions. These higher sentiments so percolate downward, so tinge secondary feelings, giving them a new character and value, that it is difficult to analyze out the purely physical sensibilities, and to see how far these, with the action of the intellectual faculties upon them, can be made the foundation of our rich, emotional endowments. When, with the utilitarian, we undertake honestly to construct our entire spiritual constitution from these purely physical elements, we have a heavy labor laid upon us. Not only must the primary sense of truth, **of** beauty, and of obligation, be laid aside, all the affections which spring from them must be dismissed, **and** also that esthetical or ethical quality or flavor which inevitably pervades intellectual emotions, whose staple is physical pleasure. A rogue will pride himself on a certain honor, whose fiber and force are found in single threads of morality. A clown is vain of possessions, whose excellence consists largely in beauties hidden in great part from him.

Do this work of analysis thoroughly, separate carefully out all but strictly physical feelings, and we shall find remaining very inadequate elements to be transformed by intellectual combination into the varied and profound sensibilities of a truly developed nature. The natural movement of tender sympathies must be made the means by which this vast superstructure is reared. Yet, in the powerful and growing consent of appetite and purely selfish impulses, how quickly and wholly would these feeble sentiments be swept away. How hopeless the effort to stay the actual forces of mischief **in the world, not** only with no sense of obligation in the mind, but no admiration of virtue, no perception of . **the beauty** of excellence as such, no delight in any form of intrinsic merit, but always and everywhere, a cold, gross, **sensual** judgment of actions and their results—the pleasure of compassion rated coolly at its scale-mark in a selfish mind, and with nothing farther to commend it, except as it can be shown ultimately to make way for physical indulgence.

Grade these pleasures of the **body, give them each their** numerical **value, put the occasional play of natural** sympathy with them ; let the intellect honestly, closely adhere to them ; add, subtract, involve, evolve, at pleasure ; and forecast in the long reaches of its calculations such periods as it pleases, and how infinitely short after all must these promises of sagacious action fall of those deep, instant, noble impulses which our sense of beauty and of virtue **bestow. Virtue** is useful because **it** holds in its right **hand** peculiar and unmeasured rewards, because it is virtue. **It** is not virtue because it is useful, because it is laden with baskets filled with fruits plucked from the trees of a sensual paradise.

§ 5. There are certain laws which control the feelings. in their relations to each other. The first of these is, The· more intense feelings are transient, the more moderate ones· are relatively permanent. This law is more true of physi-·

cal pleasures than of physical pains. These last usually indicate a distinct fact, and are dependent on it for their duration. Strong physical pleasures involve **a** corresponding expenditure of physical force, and so exhaust their resources. This fact is an enforcement of the law of temperance. The law holds still more uniformly in intellectual and spiritual emotions; in part, for the same reason, and also because excited feelings fall into conflict with ordinary duties, because, seeking immediate gratification in violent action, they are satisfied by that action, and because, as intense emotions, they have less sufficient occasions than more moderate ones. **A** violent temper, therefore, is wont to be a volatile one; while one slowly moved is correspondingly firm. Intense grief is followed by comparative apathy; exciting pleasures by depression of spirits, and vehement anger by relative indifference. The evenly happy life must be fed by the milder, more sustained sentiments; and the **peace, the rest** of the soul is found in the balance and correction of its feelings one by the other. The moral sentiments yield superior repose, not from their own nature alone, but also from the restraints and rule to which they subject all vexing and **exorbitant** emotions. Esthetic pleasures are among the **most** peaceful, since they are among the most harmonized and proportionate, of the sentiments. Even a spiritual feeling that is excessive does not escape the lassitude of reaction.

A second law is, Similar feelings sustain each other, dissimilar ones displace each other. Certain views and states unite easily, flow together and strengthen each other. Others stand in the opposite relation, and exist by mutual exclusion. Harmony is consistent with contrast. Indeed, this is one of the ways in which impressions are deepened and made complete. The intellectual view is made clear and decided by uniting like with like, and **opposing** like to unlike—by agreement and by contrast. The latter is often the more effective of the two methods of deepening an impression. Harmony, as a condition of feeling, includes the presence of what is concordant, and excludes objects discordant, lying in different parts of the intellectual and emotional field. It is opposed to distraction, to diverse emotions, and thus divided effects. Living facts are always struggling for equilibrium among themselves — for an organic dependence about a single centre. Hence a prevailing tendency and a strong feeling strive to subordinate all tendencies and feelings to themselves, and to put the character in harmony with its dominant force. To this law also are due the jar of interruption, and the unusual wear of distracting duties.

A third law is, New things make a strong emotional impression, old things a weaker one. Novelty not only awakens the feeling of wonder, it enhances all the impressions made by intrinsic qualities. The new is impressed upon us by our very constitution with a peculiar force, a distinct wave of sensibility, and is thus enabled to initiate a rapid, tidal flow of feeling, not otherwise possible. In early and in uncultivated life, that which is novel is sought for its immediate emotional character. The grotesque, the odd, the extravagant, the new, the news, give fresh excitement, and the intrinsic value or worthlessness of the matter offered to the mind is overlooked. When the powers are more mature or more cultivated, wonder becomes a secondary, a briefly initiatory impulse, making way for the deeper satisfaction of recognized truth; and when it fails to yield this pleasure, it drops away almost at once.

This law is connected with another law of a reverse nature. Customary things are more pleasing to us, uncustomary things less pleasing. This is the result of passive habit—of the silent adaptation of body and mind to their surroundings. This law **is** likely to gain ground, as years advance, on the previous law; and both, as arising from the accident of circumstances, need to be guarded against by a self-contained spirit. We should be servants neither of the old nor the new.

A fifth law is, The feelings of men are harmonized and greatly increased by sympathy, they are divided and intensified by repugnance. We tend decidedly to share or to reject the feelings of those about us. The one impulse is that of sympathy, the other that of repugnance. A certain contagious force belongs to emotion. The swell of sentiment among **masses,** like the surge of the ocean, is heavy, forceful, dominant. It is difficult to maintain feelings which **are not shared by** those **about** us; it is difficult to escape the influence of those which are prevalent. **The** minds of men flow into each other, and come to feel and propagate, with increasing power, the **same influences.** Sympathy, strictly so called, does not change the character of a sentiment, it only disseminates it. The inflammable nature of the feelings by which assemblies, mobs, armies are laid open to conflagration, each firing his neighbor, till all are caught up in one uncontrollable frenzy, is a very familiar fact. A less significant fact is that of repugnance. If a division already exists between men, as in classes, or in religious faith, that division is broadened by repugnance. All tyranny and cruelty are enhanced by this law. The tears of an enemy beget contempt and aversion, not pity. Laughter we do not share seems to us foolish. If we join in a joke at our own expense, its sting is lost; if we do not, the amusement of others angers us.

A sixth law is, Objects and acts have, in reference to the feelings, intrinsic quality and associative quality. The last quality, which is frequently the stronger of the two, and may be more or less in conflict with native force, is due to the part that objects have played or are playing in human history.

Our feelings become grouped in memory by repeated experience, and on each recurrence, restore by suggestive power a large class of emotions and incentives with which they have previously consorted. Like feelings are thus consolidated into varied, powerful classes, which work together on the mind, one feeling never arising alone, but uniformly having present for its aid some of its familiar companions. We shall not understand the force of certain passions without comprehending the multiplied echoes which they find in the soul. The transforming power of association is a cardinal fact in the feelings. Still association can create nothing; it simply combines and recombines in many ways the occasions of feeling, working up life into an experience of a definite order.

The animation of the feelings is also frequently dependent on the power of imagination. Our intellectual emotions arise in connection with sensible objects, and the vividness with which these are present to the mind will determine the degree of action in the accompanying sensibilities. The passionate and the poetic temperament are influenced by the images of the fancy. The clear and vivid pictures of the imagination arrest the attention, and arouse the passions, till they come baying along the trail of indulgence, like hounds in full scent.

The nature, character, and excitability of the emotions are diverse, but their activity at any one time depends, aside from direct influences, on these mental conditions. Arising out of intellectual action, they are especially affected by the circumstances and conditions of that action. While the pleasurable feelings are evolved, for the most part, in connection with successful activity, and the painful ones in connection with baffled effort, we are not to suppose that this fact explains their very nature, or identifies action with enjoyment. It only indicates the relation of our emotions to the ends of life, but leaves them each to be understood in its simple, intrinsic character by experience. The great diversity and mobility of the feelings, and the subtile way in which they act on the thoughts and are acted on by them, are the points we need most to mark.

# BOOK III.

## THE WILL.

§ 1. WE have now to speak of the power of volition—
the centre and source of free activity. Willing is distinguished from thinking and feeling in its positive and peculiar character by a reference to consciousness—to that experience in which its phenomenal nature is laid open. It,
moreover, bears a different relation to action from that of
either of the other two, and this may be pointed out. It
stands in the last, the most immediate connection with effort. Exertion is prompted by feeling, is anticipated and
guided by thought, is initiated and maintained by volition.
While the motive lies back in the emotions, the final determination and executive impulse of free action are found
in the will. The intellect is instrumental and intermediate in its office. It presents objects to the feelings, and
inquires into the means of their easiest, safest gratification.

The voluntary powers are simple as compared either
with those of thought or feeling. Our emotions present by
far the most numerous, complex and varied features of the
mind. Our intellectual faculties are relatively few, yet exceedingly subtile in their inter-dependence and action. Our
voluntary powers are yet more simple, and offer their chief
difficulty in intrinsic character, in the problem of liberty.
We shall first speak of the nervous system and of the functions of its several parts. Next we shall consider executive
volitions, and later, the highest form of volition—choice.
The first division of volitions is into primary and executive
volitions. The ultimate choice is that which presents the

more remote objects of pursuit in reference to which other
volitions are simply intermediate. The distinction of executive volition and of choice while a very real one is also a
very changeable one. Choices may have every degree of
generality; may be very near or very remote. As the
primary act becomes more inclusive, a larger number of
volitions are simply executive. As a subordinate question
becomes more independent, it assumes the character of
a choice. One may decide to build a house, and it may
still remain to him to determine where, when, with what
materials, in what style he shall build. The same volition
may be termed in one relation a choice, and in another, an
executive volition. Choices rise into more and more general purposes, and executive volitions sink into and unite
with automatic action.

# CHAPTER I.

## *The Nervous System.*

§ 1. IF it were asked, What one fact more than any other distinguishes animal life collectively from vegetable life? we should answer, a nervous system; not merely because a nervous system is confined to animal life, but because it is a controlling condition in all higher forms of that life. This nervous system, though either wholly wanting or very obscure in the lower forms of animal life, once present, assumes increasing importance with every step upward. In the higher animals it is the administrative system, whose modifications contain a record of the history of evolution.

A formal distinction between vegetable and animal life lies in the much greater freedom of motion, internal and external, which characterizes animals. The primary function of the nervous system, out of which all others grow, is the facilitating of motion. Motion is made by it more rapid, more varied, more general, more concurrent. Vegetable life, in exceptional cases, exhibits definite and somewhat rapid motion under external stimuli; concurrent movement of parts within itself for an end, and functional activity in prosecuting that end.

It thus presents, in the absence of a nervous system, a clear rudimentary expression of the primary offices of that system. But the last attainment of vegetable life becomes the first of animal life, and, as specialized in the nervous system, the means of its enlargement. This system, therefore, is the pre-eminent structural factor in the new development. By means of it, functions of many orders proceed concurrently in constant interaction within the body; every portion of the body is subject to more or less rapid change; and special members of the body and the whole body are set in motion by external stimuli. Thus motion becomes a striking feature of animal life, and different forms of motion distinguishing features. The nervous system is the means at once of the inside organizing process, and also of the extended interaction with the environment which accompanies it. A general knowledge of the nervous system, through which all these forms of activity grow up together, is necessary as a means of approaching the highest phase of development, that of voluntary action. Vital action is so closely united with the secondary forms of voluntary effort, known as executive volitions, that we shall not be able to understand these without some general apprehension of the mechanism they employ, and its methods of play under simple, vital forces.

§ 2. Life we hold to be a superior, plastic power, working pervasively, yet under one harmonious plan or impulse in all parts of the living body. This life,—this pre-eminent, peculiar and inscrutable power, whether we regard it as the immediate presence of the Divine hand, or as a distinct existence, is *the* maker — the indispensable architect of that most strange and marvelous of structures, a living thing; be it plant, shrub, tree, insect, bird, beast, or man. Molecular, chemical, electric, thermal forces are the means employed; but these as much fail to explain the form and relations of the final product, the wonderful manner of its putting up and repair, as do the stone, mortar and timber, the digging, the hewing, and the heaving, the plan and proportions of a cathedral. The exact thing to be accounted for is that on which these blind forces cast no light. How came they to work in these marvelous relations to each other; how to institute these unusual and strange condi-

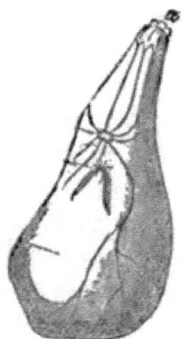

FIG. 1.—Nervous System of an Ascidian.

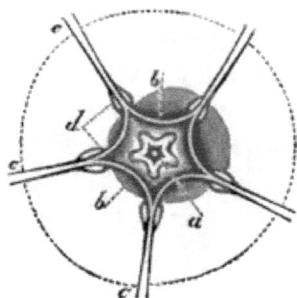

FIG. 2.—Nervous System of the Sea Urchin.

*B*

FIG. 3.—Nervous System of the Fresh-
water Clam.

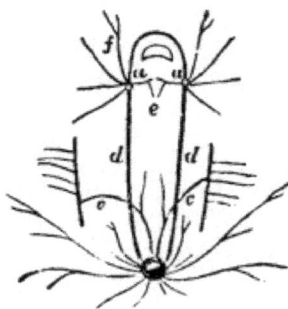

FIG. 4.—Nervous System of the Oyster.
a. a. Ganglia united about the Œsophagus.
   b. Posterior ganglion.
c. c. Gills.

tions of various and complete life, a power which they nowhere else exhibit? We explain the action within the
chemist's retort by the chemical properties of the material
present, but the retort itself, the application of the heat, the
proportion of the ingredients, the experiment as an experiment, must find a solution in a new, an intelligent agency.
Account as we will for changes that go on in the blood, that
there should be veins, arteries, such a fluid as the blood,
and the needed combination of powers to propel it; these
and like adaptations which make up the living agent meet
with no explanation in simple, molecular forces. Yet these
forces always and everywhere intervene between the inscrutable agent and the phenomenal result. Under a phenomenal form, they are the second facts which lie back of
the first—the massive product. Molecular movement is to
the living structure, what the mechanical transfer of stone
and timber is to the edifice. Many of the changes by
which the animal structure is built up and renewed take
place locally, by an action there instituted. But as the
parts of the body are reciprocally interdependent, the
changes of one part must be correlated and exactly harmonized with the wants of other parts. This transfer of
vital sympathy is affected by the nervous system.

§ 3. The essential parts of a nervous system are nerves
and a nerve centre or ganglion. It is the office of the
nerves to carry stimuli to and from the ganglia. It is the
office of ganglia to receive stimuli, and to redirect them so
as to secure fitting, harmonious action. These two portions
of a nervous system are distinct in structure and color.
The nerves are white and fibrous, the dispersive portion of
the ganglia is gray and vescicular. The gray centres are
usually enclosed in the white matter. Nerves convey impressions in two directions, and are hence termed afferent
and efferent. They also convey two kinds of stimuli, or

better perhaps are the mediums of changes which give rise
to two distinct results, one of feeling one of motion. Hence
they are termed sensor and motor nerves. Yet the action of a sensor nerve is most frequently not accompanied
with a sensation. The distinction seems to lie in the different termini of the two sets of fibres, closely united as
they are in their sheaths and indistinguishable in structure.
The sensor nerve starts in a sensor surface, and ends in the
gray matter of a ganglion ; the motor nerve starts in the
same gray matter, and ends in a muscle. The inscrutable
changes which take place in a nerve in the transfer of an
impression have no more likeness to the sensor or motor result than have the electric states of a wire of a telephone
to the sounds at the termini. The simplest action of a nervous system is termed reflex. It is the immediate response
along the same bundle of nerves to irritation, by action in
the part irritated. Thus the foot is tickled, and immediately withdrawn. The response to stimuli is usually much
more complex. A blow is aimed at the face, the attitude
is changed, the head turned aside, the arm upraised, the
pulse quickened, the eyes closed. There is a *consensus* of
actions in one end. These responses may, without the intervention of consciousness, under organic stimuli, become
very complex, the distribution being determined by that
plastic power accumulated along the entire line of development. When these actions pertain to the interplay in functions of the organs of the body, they belong to the organic
life. It is the office of this life to institute and sustain
these relations. If they pertain to movements directed
toward external objects, and still arise from organic stimuli,
they belong to the instinctive life. This life has the same
base as the organic life, and is hardly more than it. If
consciousness intervenes, stimuli pass into sensations, while
the responsive actions become still more extended and com-

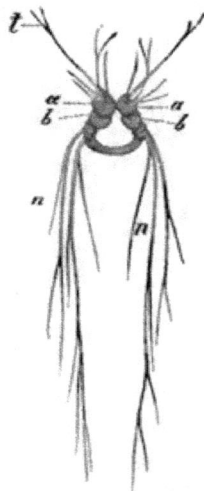

FIG. 5.—Nervous System of Nudi-
branchiate.

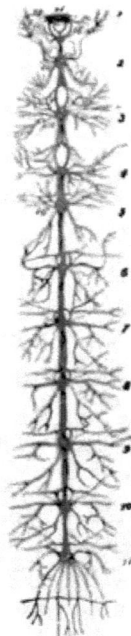

FIG. 6.—Nervous System of a Caterpillar.*

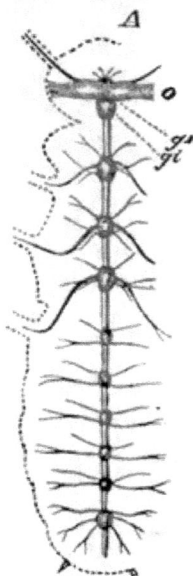

FIG. 7.—Nervous System of White Ant.

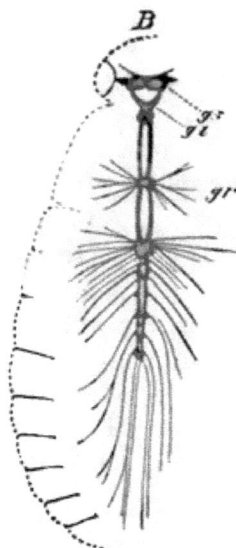

FIG. 8.—Nervous System of Fly.

* Orton's Comparative Zoölogy.

plex. This increase of complexity is due largely to the more distinct introduction of time. Sensations remain in the memory, and the experiences, also, which have arisen under them; they thus serve to combine actions through long periods. Actions and sensations united by the mediation of consciousness constitute the associative life. By the intervention of reason, still broader areas and longer periods may be included, and the complexity of responsive movement becomes incomparably greater. These combinations are those of the rational life. These forms of life do not exist by exclusion, but by the inclusion of the lower under the higher; by the building of the higher on the lower.

§ 4. The simplest form of the nervous system is that of nerves united in a single ganglion. An example of this is seen in an Ascidian, belonging to the class of Mollusks, A first step of combination is found in the union of several proximately equal ganglia, each with its own nerves, to each other by other nerves. Each stimulus thus affects not simply its own ganglion, but other ganglia, and the reaction is proportionately extended. The star-fish and the sea-urchin, belonging to the Radiates, present examples. In the star-fish, a circle of ganglia are gathered about the central opening, each ganglion being also connected by nerves with the ray to which it corresponds. Thus the stimuli of any ray act on all rays. A third form of the nervous system found in Mollusks, as the fresh-water-clam and the oyster, consists of several unequal ganglia, somewhat irregularly distributed through the body, in connection with leading functions, and united to each other by filaments or by cords. Thus the oyster has a large posterior ganglion closely connected with the great adductor muscle, with the mantle, and with the gills. It has two much smaller ganglia, situated on either side of the mouth and united above and below it.

In the farther development of this division, the ganglia about the œsophagus increase in number and size, and become the controlling nervous centres. Of this character are the nervous systems of the cuttle-fish and of the Aeolidæ or Nudibranchiates. The head thus begins to take its final relation to the nervous system. It becomes the centre of the special senses, and the chief source of stimuli. This accumulation first takes place about the mouth, the leading organ of nutrition. As the attainment of food is a primary necessity, this effort is supported by all the senses. In the vertebrates, the mouth, though it is no longer surrounded by the great ganglia, is still supported by the sense of taste, touch, smell, and less directly, by sight and hearing. While the higher life rises out of the lower, it is united to it by the old bond of service.

In the lower Articulates, as larvæ, many proximately equal ganglia corresponding to the several divisions of the body are united to each other by a longitudinal cord. The ganglia of the head only slightly predominate. To this bilateral symmetry the nervous system begins to conform, and the nervous cord and ganglia become double. In the higher Articulates, as insects, the ganglia show more subordination, and are frequently, as in the bee and the fly, gathered into the thorax and the head, the two seats of action and perception. It is here that instinctive life finds its highest development, yet, as in the white-ant, the ganglia are often markedly subdivided.

In the Vertebrates, cephilization becomes far more complete. If we start with brainless-fish, and close the series with man, we have traveled from a uniform spinal cord to a complete centralization of life, and subordination of it in all its forms to consciousness.

When we observe the great complexity and wonderful harmony of action in the nervous system of man, and also

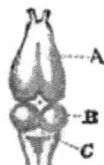

FIG. 9.—Brain of Carp.
A. Cerebral hemispheres.
B. Optic lobes.
C. Cerebellum.

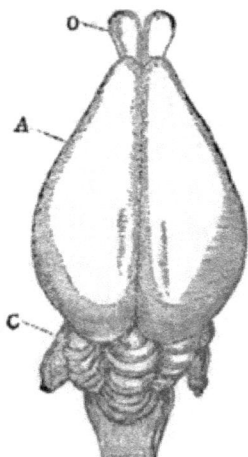

FIG. 10.—Brain of the Rabbit. O. Olfactory bulbs.
A. Cerebral hemispheres. C. Cerebellum.

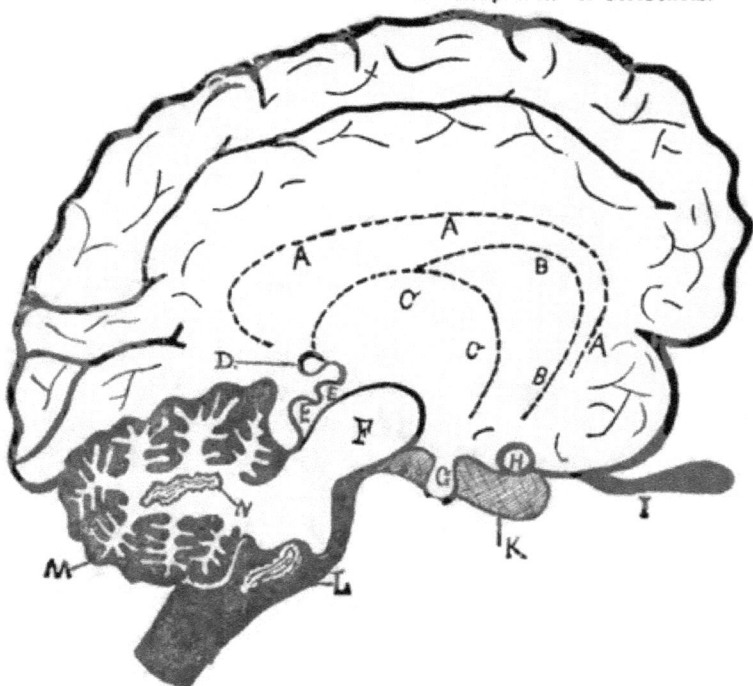

FIG. 11.—Arrangement of the Brain. The Corpus Callosum (A), the Corpus Striatum (B), and the Optic Thalamus (C) are shown in dotted outline. (D) Pineal body. (E) Corpora Quadrigemina. (H) Optic nerve. (I) Olfactory bulb. (L) Medulla. (M) Cerebellum.

observe the slow steps of progress by which this result has been reached, we shall be profoundly impressed by the fact, that all life is gathered up in man and epitomized by him. The several strata of acquisition lie one above the other and directly and·indirectly support each other, as certainly as do the several layers in the earth's crust. Organic life prepares the way for instinctive life, and the two grow together. These in turn, while sufficient unto themselves, are the needful platform for associative life, and associative life makes way for rational life, ready to use all below it.

# CHAPTER II.

## *The Nervous System of Man.*

§ 1. The nervous system, the medium of action, pervades the entire body of man. An intricate net-work of nerves lies over the surface of the body, spreads through its members, and is gathered in certain lines and centres of nervous communication. There is no pin-point on the skin that does not disclose the presence of nerves; nor an organ which does not show itself when diseased to be wrought into the nervous web.

The collective mass, made up of the cerebrum, the cerebellum, the pons Varolii, the medulla oblongata and the spinal cord, constitutes the nervous centre, the cerebrospinal axis.

" Beginning with the spinal cord,—which we have seen to be a rod or column of white matter or fibres, enclosing a slender core of grey substance—if we trace the fibres of the cord upwards, we find them continuing into the medulla oblongata, the first and the lowest portion of the brain. Of the whole mass of fibres entering the medulla oblongata, the larger portion pass up into the pons Varolii and the cerebellum, while a part terminates in the grey substance of the medulla itself; and from that grey substance other fibres take their rise and proceed onward, in the company of the through-going fibres of the cord. Thus the emerging white matter of the medulla oblongata is partly the fibres that entered it as a continuation of the cord, and partly the fibres originating in the grey central matter of

FIG. 12.—Brain of the Cat.*

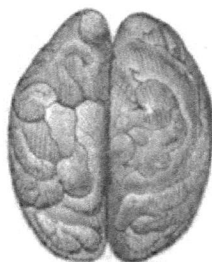

FIG. 13.—Brain of the Orang-utan.*

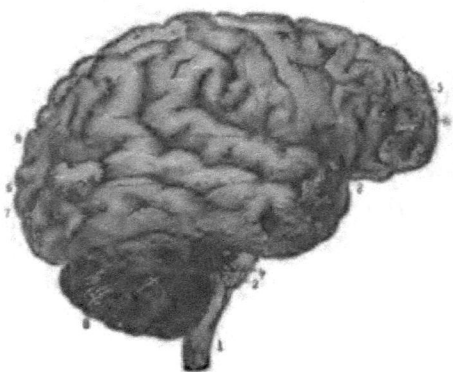

FIG. 14.—Human Brain, side view.*

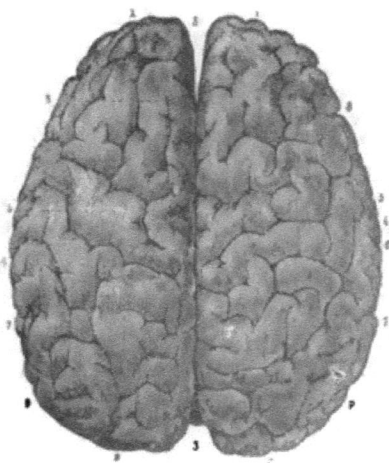

FIG. 15.—Human Brain, upper view.*

* Orton's Comparative Zoölogy.

the medulla, replacing, as it would seem, those that terminated there. From the pons Varolii, where we come next, the white fibres advance in various directions, intersecting with transverse fibres connecting the two halves of the cerebellum, and passing upwards towards the cerebrum proper. The fibres thus going upwards constitute the crura, peduncles or stems of the cerebrum, and seem destined to terminate in the grey matter of the convoluted surface of the hemispheres. But in passing through the ganglia of the brain—the thalami optici, and corpora striata—the arrangement described above is repeated ; that is to say, while part of the fibres proceed through the ganglionic masses, the rest stop short in the grey substance of those masses, which grey substance gives origin to other fibres to pass out with those that had an uninterrupted course through the bodies alluded to. Both sets together—those passing through and those originating in the grey substance of the corpora striata, or thalami optici, constitute a portion of the white or fibrous substances of the hemispheres, spreading out and terminating in the grey matter, or cortical layer of the convolutions. They are the first of three classes of fibres, described above, as constituting the white matter of the cerebrum, that is to say, the ascending or diverging class.

Whatever number of central masses we may calculate as interposed between the spinal cord beneath, and the convoluted surface of the cerebrum, the manner of communication between them is found to be as now stated. The fibres passing between one intermediate mass and another, are partly transmitted and partly arrested. Wherever grey matter exists, there is the commencement or termination of white matter. The fibres that enter the cerebellum from the medulla oblongata terminate in whole or in part in its outer layer of grey substance, and in that substance a new set of fibres originate to pass to other parts of the brain, as the corpora quadrigemina, the hemispheres, etc., and from one half of the cerebellum to the **other.** The fibres spreading out, as already mentioned, in the hemispheres toward the convoluted grey surface, will have had very various origins. Some may perhaps have come all the way from the extremities of the body, passing by the spinal cord, medulla oblongata, cerebellum, pons Varolii, thalami optici, etc.; others have originated in the grey matter of the cord, passing without a break through all the intervening centres; a third class may have had their rise in the grey matter of the pons, a fifth in the cerebellum, a sixth **in** the corpora quadrigemina; others in the thalami **optici,** or corpora striata; besides other more minute sources.

The arrangement may thus be **seen** to resemble **the** course of a railway train. The various central masses are like so many stations, where the train drops a certain number of passengers and takes up others in their stead, whilst some are carried through to the final terminus. A system of telegraph wires might be formed to represent exactly what takes place in the brain. If from a general terminus in London, a mass of wires were carried out to proceed towards Liverpool, **and** if one wire of the **mass were to end** at each station, while from the same station new wires arose, one for every station, farther on, a complete and perfectly independent connexion could be kept up between any two stations along the line."*

The nerves are divided into two classes, the spinal and **the** cerebral; the one passing into the body along the **spinal** cord, the other directly from the **brain.** The nerves go forth in pairs from the spinal cord, passing out on either side between **the vertebræ. Of** this class, there are **thirty-**one couples. Each of these nerves is divided **at its** root, **into** two portions termed the anterior root and posterior

* Quain's Anatomy.

root. These portions subserve distinct purposes. The cerebral nerves are composed of nine pairs,—sometimes divided as twelve—four of pure sensation, terminating in the special senses, and five motor nerves. Nerves from either lobe of the brain terminate in the opposite half of the body. Thus the dexterity of right-hand work involves a discipline of the left lobe of the brain. This lobe consequently tends to greater power.

§ 2. The spinal cord is the means of sensation and of movement through the entire trunk and extremities. If this cord is cut, sensation and the power of movement by the *will* are lost in the parts below the point of separation. The power of movement nevertheless remains under local irritation after the division. Superficial irritation will cause a spasmodic movement, accomplished by a reflex action of the spinal cord alone. Movements closely resembling voluntary action, of which the individual is unconscious, and which he cannot control, will, under these circumstances, take place in the limbs. The circle of nervous action is completed through the spinal cord, independently of the brain. The spinal cord, by virtue of its grey matter, is itself a nerve centre. Including in the spinal cord the medulla oblongata, continuous in structure and functions with it, we find that they, independently of the cerebrum and of consciousness originate and sustain many movements. They institute and harmonize a portion of the automatic action of the body. Of this sort are movements connected with digestion. After the food has passed the lips, been tasted and masticated in the mouth, and thus been fully subjected to inspection and voluntary action, it goes through the remaining processes of digestion, dilution, assimilation, without further consciousness of voluntary action. The contractions of the throat, the peristaltic movement of the stomach and intestines are accomplished by nervous stimuli, transmitted from the medulla oblongata. This portion of the nervous system chiefly sustains the muscular action in breathing. This is complex and rhythmical, nicely alternating in the states indicated, and in the muscular action induced. To receive and combine the indications of the actual state of the **lungs,** and to distribute to the muscles the appropriate stimuli, so far as the movement is stated and involuntary, is **a** portion of the office of the medulla **oblongata.** This action is, moreover, capable of being modified, arrested, or quickened by voluntary effort.

In the same way the support and harmonizing of voluntary muscular movements generally are referred with sufficient proof to the cerebellum. By far the larger part of this action is involuntary and unconscious, though voluntary stimuli reach and modify it. A portion of this sustaining influence of the voluntary muscles is received from the spinal cord, to wit, that which gives them always a certain tension or tone, distinguishing them from lifeless flesh, and maintaining them in readiness for instant effort. That the harmonizing and co-ordinating of muscular movement are due to the cerebellum, is shown by proof briefly presented in the following passage from Todd and Bowman, page 50.

" Animals deprived of the cerebellum are in a condition very similar to that of a drunken man, so far as relates to their power of locomotion. They are unable to produce that combination of action in different sets of muscles which is necessary to enable them to assume, to maintain any attitudes. They cannot stand still for a moment, and in attempting to walk, their gait is unsteady, they totter from side to side, and their progress is interrupted by frequent falls. The fruitless attempts which they make to stand or walk are sufficient proof that a certain degree of intelligence remains, and that voluntary power continues to be enjoyed."

The cerebrum, on the other hand, is directly connected

with all voluntary and conscious action. We present its functions in the words of Bain, to whom we are especially indebted in this connection. "Experiments have been made with a view of determining the characteristic functions of this cerebral mass, so large in the human brain, although dwindling to the most insignificant dimensions in the lowest vertebrate animals, namely, reptiles and fishes.

"The convolutions are the portions most accessible to operations. The hemispheres have been seen above to consist of an outer layer of convoluted grey matter, and an interior mass of white, fibrous, or connecting matter. When irritation is applied to the hemispheres, as by pricking or cutting, we find a remarkable absence of the effects manifested in the other centres. Neither feeling nor movement is produced. This makes a very great distinction between the hemispheres and the whole of the ganglia and centres lying beneath them.

"Pressure from above downwards, produces stupor.

"The removal of both hemispheres in an animal has the following results:

"First: Sight and hearing are entirely lost.

"Second: Consciousness, including both feeling and thought, seems utterly abolished: so that whatever bodily activity may survive, the mental life is extinct.

"Third: All power of moving for an end, all forethought, purpose, or volition, is entirely extinguished. This is an inevitable consequence of the preceding fact. For without feeling and the memory of feelings and ideas there can be no voluntary action. The simple act of seizing food implies, besides the power of sight, the feeling of hunger, and the mental association of the appearance of the food with the satisfying of the feeling.

"Fourth: The power of accomplishing many connected movements still remains. The actions of flying or walking may be sustained after the loss of the hemispheres, but in that case a stimulus from without is necessary in order to commence the action. As a matter of course, the automatic actions, those that we have seen to go on in the decapitated or anencephalous animal, may still proceed.

" Fifth : The sensibility of the skin, and taste, and smell would appear to remain in a greatly impaired form. Such sensibility, however, cannot be of the nature of true sensa-tion, for to have a sensation is to feel. It may consist in some mode of reflex stimulation, operated through the other centres. By operating energetically on any nerve of sense, we may excite reflex movements extending over almost all the muscles of the body.

" Hence it appears that the hemispheres of the brain are indispensable to the exercise of our two highest senses, and to feeling, volition, and thought."— *The Senses, and the Intellect, page* **57.**

That the higher senses, however, aside from the connection of their ganglia with the cerebral hemispheres, **act** purely automatically, is shown by facts of vivisection given by Taine in his work on Intelligence, p. 155. " Here is a pigeon, whose cerebral lobes are entirely removed, but whose corpora bigemina remain. When I suddenly put my hand near it, it makes a slight movement of the head to avoid the **threatened** danger." This fact, then, presents automatic movement through the highest special sense, entirely aside from conscious control, or conscious activity. The ordinary action of the eye in perception is therefore a state superinduced on a purely organic power, and gives a striking illustration of the descent of the conscious into the unconscious life, and its control over it.

The offices **of the** several parts of the nervous system in man may be briefly summarized as follows; all portions save the highest are mediums of general communication;

the spinal cord is a secondary centre **of muscular action ;**
the medulla oblongata is an automatic centre of organic
action ; the cerebellum harmonizes voluntary action ; the
pons Varolii is a subsidiary automatic centre to the cerebellum ; the cerebrum is the source of all conscious activity ;
the mesencephalic ganglia—optici thalami, **corpora striata,**
corpora quadrigemina, corpora geniculata — are automatic
centres subordinate **to the cerebrum.** The sympathetic
system, not included in the cerebro-spinal-axis, **serves the**
purposes of purely organic harmony in strictly animal
life.

§ 3. We are now prepared to understand that vital, nervous action which is not voluntary, but anticipatory merely.
Its first most simple form is that of reflex action—superficial irritation returned directly from a nervous centre as
motor stimulus. This, detached nervous ganglia accomplish in animal life, and the divided **spinal cord in man,**
An advance on **this is seen in continuous, vital movement**
accomplished by a special nervous centre, **like the medulla**
**oblongata,** wholly involuntary and beyond the **cognition of**
**the** mind. A farther progress is seen in that mixed action
**which** is chiefly **involuntary,** and sustained by a nervous
centre as the cerebellum, which is not the seat of conscious-
**ness, but is** intimately connected with a second nervous
centre the cerebrum, from which it receives voluntary influences. A still more intimate blending of the higher
and lower life takes place through the mediation of mesen‧
cephalia ganglia. Stimuli which come through the superior
senses as sensations are carefully united with fitting organic
actions,—as clear articulation in reading—and shortly **the**
**two** become an automatic **combination.** The highest action
**is** that which remains throughout under **the** guidance of
consciousness. That we should understand this blending of
the automatic and the voluntary is indispensable to a right

apprehension of the will. At this point, physical inquiry has been very fruitful in its influence on philosophy.

Says Bain, page, 63 : "The conducting power of nerve fibre is attended with nervous waste, and the substance has to be constantly renewed from the blood, which is largely supplied to the nerves, although not so largely as to the vesicles. If now we compare this liability to waste and exhaustion, with the undying endurance of an electric wire, we shall be struck with a very great contrast. The wire is doubtless a more compact, resisting and sluggish mass ; the conduction requires a certain **energy of electric** action **to** set it agoing, and in the course of a great distance becomes faint and dies away. The nerve, on the other hand, is stimulated by a slighter influence, and propagates that influence with increase, by the consumption of its own material. The wire must be acted on at both **ends,** by the closure of the circuit, before acting as a conductor in any degree ; the nerve takes fire from a slight stimulus, like a train of gunpowder, and is wasted by the current that it propagates. If this view be correct, the influence conveyed is much more beholden to the conducting fibres, than electricity is to the copper wire. The fibres are made to sustain or increase the force at the cost of their own substance.

"The nerve force is propagated more slowly than an electric current through a wire. The rate has been estimated at about two hundred feet a second as an average. It is to be remarked, that a nerve is not a simple conductor, but is supposed to consist of a countless number of molecules, each of which has playing round it an electrical current, or currents, which are an obstacle to the simple or direct propagation. There is always a certain delay in passing through the nerve centres ; a reflex movement occupies from one-thirtieth to one-tenth of a second under favorable circumstances, which is more time than would be required for transmitting an influence through the same length of nerve without interruption. When the stimulus is weak, a proportionately longer time is required to produce the corresponding movement. We may hence infer that what is called nervous excitement is a quicker rate of the nervous current. The obvious facts bear out this view."

These then are the means by which an external force is received, modified and distributed in centres; by which an internal **state directs and secures** the succeeding steps in vital movement; by which an inner impulse of the mind is **made in** muscular effort **to** reach the external world; or by which these vital and mental forms of effort are inseparably **blended.**

§ 4. The superiority of the Vertebrates in the animal kingdom is indicated by the presence and growing power of the cerebrum, the organ of **conscious action; and the** predominance of the voluntary life in **man is disclosed at** the same point. **The supreme relation of the cerebrum in** man to the other ganglia is seen in **its absolute size,** its relative size, its increase in relative size through all the grades of animal intelligence; in the number and depth of its corrugations, and the amount of blood it receives. Starting down no lower than the cod, we find the cerebral lobes smaller than the optic ganglia, and on a par with the olfactory ganglia. As we pass up they increase in absolute or in relative size, or in both, till, in man, they have stretched over and covered all the associated ganglia, multiplied manifold their relative dimensions,— relative in reference to other ganglia, and in reference to the size of the body— and become truly the superincumbent, overshadowing hemispheres of thought.

It is, however, in the combination of relations that man's great superiority is **found, and not in any one of** them alone. In absolute weight of brain he is surpassed

by the elephant and the whale; and in weight relative to
that of the body by many of the smaller birds. There
must be farther considered the proportion of the grey to
the white tissue.\* The four particulars combined, absolute
size, size in reference to the body, size of the cerebrum in
reference to other ganglia, the proportion between the grey
and the white matter, assign man his pre-eminent position.
We shall see the importance of the last particular when we
remember that the nervous system is an instrument of transmitting impressions, and also of thoughts : that physical activity and mental activity are dependent, the first more
immediately on the medium of transmission, the white
matter; the second on the medium of interior activity, the
grey matter.   Great muscular development, as in the bird,
may, therefore, carry with it a relatively large nervous development.

"As we rise through the mammalian series towards
man, we find not only a marked increase in the *absolute*
bulk of the *cerebral hemispheres*, and a yet greater *relative*
excess in their size as compared with the aggregate of that
of the sensory ganglia, but an augmentation of their functional powers beyond all proportion to their size, which is
derived from the peculiar manner in which their ganglionic
matter is disposed.   In all ordinary ganglia, the nerve-cells,
on whose presence their special attributes depend, form a
sort of *internal nucleus;* but in the cerebrum they are
spread out on the surface, forming an *external* or *cortical*
layer.   This layer is covered by a membrane termed the
*pia mater* which is entirely composed of blood-vessels, held
together by connective tissue ; and thus a copious supply
of blood is brought to this important part.   But, the extent of the cortical layer, and of its contact with the pia
mater is enormously increased by its being thrown into

\* Journal of Nervous and Mental Disease, Jan., 1876.   **First Article.**

folds, so as to produce what is known as the *convoluted surface* of the hemispheres." · · · "In the higher orders of Mammalia, the convolutions are well marked; but we do not find them either numerous or complex in their arrangement till we approach Man."\* "While the brain in man is about one-fortieth of the weight of the body, it receives from one-fifth to one-sixth of the whole circulating blood.† In the position of the cerebrum, superincumbent and external, in its enlarged size and greatly enlarged activity, we have a plain physical expression of the degree in which in man the conscious life overshadows, envelops, and takes in charge the organic life. "It may be doubted whether a healthy human adult brain ever weighed less than thirty-one or thirty-two ounces, or whether the heaviest brain of a gorilla has exceeded twenty ounces."‡ Yet the gorilla with a brain of twenty ounces would weigh twice as much as the man with a brain of thirty-one ounces. The largest human brain weighs sixty-five or sixty-six ounces.

That the two functions of the brain, its motor function and its reflective function, are somewhat separate from each other, and somewhat exclude each other, is plain. Great power of reflection is attended by an indisposition to activity, and great muscular activity by a like indisposition and inability for reflection. A small and active bird, like a snow-bunting, demands relatively a very large nervous system to maintain the heat and intense life needful to meet its circumstances. Such size, therefore, does not indicate corresponding intelligence. Though our knowledge is not sufficient to enable us to say, that muscular activity is always accompanied with a predominance of white matter, and reflective activity with the predominence of grey matter, yet the relations of the two parts of the nervous system

---

\* Mental Physiology, p. 93.  † Ibid p. 39.
‡ Man's Place in Nature, p. 120

seem to indicate this. The conspicuous way in which the least thought interrupts the flow of perceptions is seen in an effort to count the flying posts when a railroad train is in motion. We easily discern them as separate, and can give a tap of the finger for each one, long after the motion becomes **too** rapid for a distinct enumeration. **The** distinct recognition of each post, and its addition to the number already reached, is relatively a slow process.

# CHAPTER III.

*Executive Volition.*

§ 1. WE are to distinguish executive from primary volition. Primary volition is frequently termed choice, and there is no objection to the word, if we carefully exclude from it the intellectual weighing of reasons, the balancing of inducements, which often accompany it. The volition is not in these, but in the act which brings them to a conclusion. A choice initiates a series of acts in reference to an object to be reached by them; an executive volition regards the performance of these acts thus determined on.

The primary volition is the true seat of freedom, since subsequent acts flow necessarily from it. This choice may indeed be reconsidered, but so long as it remains in force, so long as it is a purpose of the soul, the acts included under it flow directly from it, fixed thereby in their character. An alternative is presented to the first volition, not to those later volitions by which it is completed. These may be looked upon simply as the prolonged force of the first, as much so as the repeated shocks of the ricochetting cannonball are the results of an impulse received at once and in the distance.

Executive volitions are successive points from which fresh executive impulse is given to a series of actions whose existence and purpose have already been determined. Some have striven to separate widely between volition and choice. The division is a secondary one, covered by this distinction between executive and primary volition. These secondary volitions springing out of consciousness, though properly phenomena **of** mind, **become inseparably** blended with those automatic, unconscious **movements by** which most vital action, and the larger share **even of** what is termed **voluntary** action, are sustained.

§ 2. The voluntary and conscious region **of action is** evidently very much more limited in the **lower** animals **than** in man. We might expect this from the much larger relative development of the secondary, nervous centres, as compared with the cerebrum—the seat or instrument of conscious activity—in the one case than in the other. A command of limbs, a power and discipline of muscle, which **with man are** the result of protracted training, are spontaneous **in the young of** animals. No conscious, tentative effort seems to lie back of their powers. They develop themselves spontaneously, with the precision, certainty and rhythm of automatic life. Stimuli, sensations do their work directly, and when as feelings they enter consciousnes, they seem to depart thence with an automatic, rather than with a voluntary impulse, with the decision and certainty of a self-sustained movement, rather than with the hesitancy and uncertainty of choice. With primary volitions, secondary volitions also disappear, and the conscious and unconscious feelings, or, more properly, the feelings and **unrecognized** physical states, blend with each other in securing fitting muscular action.

In man, in connection with choice, there enters into action a large element **of** both conscious and voluntary impulses, and these mingle with, and modify, and are sustained by, the involuntary action of lower nervous centres. Indeed, the acquisition of skill seems to consist in transfer**ring** the nervous impulse from the conscious to the unconscious centres, or at least in sustaining the one by the automatic action of the other. The distinct, conscious, volun-

tary impulse of each effort in the combined movement is
lost, and the changing conditions developed by the progress
itself of action, — be these recognized or unrecognized —
with increasing, self-poised force sustain it.   Here, we
would look, so far as we would look at all, for the sub-con-
scious region of Hamilton and others.   It is in the case of
the will found in purely physical phenomena which transpire chiefly in the lower nervous centres, or, if in the cerebrum, in it simply as a nervous centre and not as the agent
of mind.   Here the physical and the mental are closely
united, inseparably blended with each other, and muscular
education lies in substituting involuntary for voluntary connections—in establishing an independent movement which
the mind may at any moment modify or correct, but is not
called upon momentarily to sustain.   Thus we quicken or
check inspiration, though the ordinary action of the lungs
proceeds independently of the will.   Again, we wink when
we will, yet wink constantly also under a purely vital impulse.   The movements in walking are illustrations of this
interlacing of the voluntary and involuntary—the slow displacement of the one by the other.   A walk determined
on, the mind may busy itself with other things, and the
muscular play be unconsciously sustained.   If, however,
any portion of the way presents peculiar difficulties, attention is renewed, and a voluntary stimulus quickens the
muscles to the needed effort.   The leap made, the embarrassments overcome, the automatic movement again sets in.

There is, perhaps, no more complete example of self-
sustained action, reached as the result of protracted, voluntary effort, than that of reading.   In fluent enunciation, the
organs of speech are modified each minute so as to express
several hundred distinct sounds.   These rapid and precise
changes go on unconsciously.   There is no direct, voluntary impulse back of them.   So far is this true, that it is

entirely possible to read intelligibly with no conscious recognition, not only of the meaning of the words, but even
of the letters which compose them.   One, in moments of
abstraction, may find himself at the foot of the page, with
no proof of having passed over its contents, except the attention of others, and the point reached by the eye.   Such
reading, while it progresses, is as involuntary, as purely
automatic, as the inhalation of the breath which makes it
possible.   Nor is the sensible effect of the images present
to the eye on the muscles of the throat in guiding and impelling them any more surprising than the declaration each
instant, at the nervous centre, of the state of the lungs, and
the correlative return of stimulus.   Executive volitions,
then, are greatly modified by the interplay of voluntary
and involuntary action; by the ease with which the second
displaces the first, and yet can be restored at option to its
former character.

§ 3. That the cerebrum is the exclusive seat of consciousness, or rather, that consciousness is directly associated with its action alone, has become very plain.   Yet
in one sense it is the most dependent of the nervous ganglia, since the other centres minister to it, furnish its data,
and its connections are indirect through them.   The great
mass of action, the automatic action of the body, is sustained by lower centres, while conscious and voluntary influences alone pass out from the cerebrum.   The will-im-
pulse, striking down into this unconscious region, is blind
as to the method of its fulfillment, pushing its way tentatively through automatic connections.   We will an unusual movement, as the successive separation of the fingers
on the hand, or the articulation of a strange sound.   We
purpose the result while the means are hidden from us ; by
some these are hit on at once, by others they are reached with
difficulty.   There lies below our conscious life a measurably

complete and independent organic life, whose functions are placed partially within the reach of mind, and among whose activities may be introduced many others of a voluntary character. The mind thus executes its will through the body, much as one accomplishes his service by a servant. Nor is the mind left without the means of training this servant to increased efficiency. Its powers and tastes are slowly transferred as skill to the body, and begin to flow on in the current of inheritance as a new exaltation of physical life. Organic action precedes **the** nervous system. This system, automatic in its play, enters to enlarge these organic functions, and sustain them by a variety of muscular activity.

In this unconscious circuit appear, in a reflex automatic form, the conditions of general sensation, and, later, the organs of special sensation. At length these threads **of** unconscious relations are united still more closely by **con**sciousness, and a strictly mental dependence begins **to** appear. Sensations as sensations are associated by memory, and the new connections have the force of a judgment. On this plane, animal life, supported by a sensitive, complex organism and strong instinctive connections, develops itself. **In man, there arise, finally, the** intuitions, acting as a yet higher and more rational consciousness. The processes **which before** proceeded as feelings now transpire as thoughts and accept voluntary guidance. The rational life is put in full possession of its powers. The great mass of action in the animal kingdom lies far down in the dark region of organic effects, where most of it, even in man, still **remains, yet with** him it has assumed quite new dependencies.

In reference to the will, we may divide human actions, into four classes: involuntary, voluntary-involuntary, involuntary-voluntary and voluntary. These actions diminish in number and increase in significance in the several classes as we pass upward. The second class includes action resting on an organic basis, as breathing, but penetrated by the will. The third class covers action initiated by the will, but passed over to organic connections, as those of walking or reading. In the fourth class, the dependencies remain variable and purely voluntary. It is doubtless impossible to find any complex movement which is wholly supported by executive, voluntary effort. Even when we utter our own thoughts, though attention and purpose are constantly present, a greater share of the muscular movement, that imparting motion to the lungs for instance, is of an involuntary kind. In struggling to give a difficult sound from a foreign language, the effort seems for **a** time to approach independent, voluntary exertion, and is often for **that** reason very unsuccessful.

In reference to consciousness there are three classes: unconscious, semi-conscious and conscious activities. **Consciousness** always abides with the mind, and the different degrees in which it penetrates the physical constitution are due to the character of the special and general stimuli. Along the lines opened up by these sensations, the judgment and the will are operative, reaching indirectly much beyond consciousness.

As the intellectual world as a whole has been slowly built up on the physical, organic world, and receives support from it; so man erects his voluntary, comprehensive, and spiritual powers on the automatic forces, the nervous connections, the associative combinations, which lie beneath them. Thus in language we are often as much struck with the sort of blind help which words themselves give us, as we are with the fact that they have all grown out of a living thought-process. Indeed, the two impressions are opposite sides of the same thing; words are infused with life and so yield life. Everywhere the lower grows up to, gives way to, and enlarges the higher. The primary material of knowledge are sensations ; to these comes the new element of intuitions, and the true intellectual activity merely foreshadowed in lower relations is initiated. Sensations pass into perceptions, associations into judgments, instinctive action into voluntary life, and all into conduct and character.

The strictly physical and the organic world include facts only that are borne forward by inherent forces. Upon these are slowly superinduced the experiences of consciousness, phenomena that find no expression or measurement outside their own circle. These sensations, appetites, affections begin at once to be united by a concomitant power, new like themselves, that of memory, into a definite experience more and more taking the place of organic, instinctive guidance. Herein is a higher animal life, wrought out on its own plane, and constituting increasingly the significant feature in development. In this associative life, though its data are conscious data, its processes conscious processes, all connections are limited to sensible things, and to the combinations which have arisen among these in experience and been impressed upon the memory. This life, therefore, lies quite below the rational life that, with a marked transition, is built up upon it. The distinctive feature of this new stage of development is the discernment of relations, the penetration into the substratum of forces and powers, and the construction, out of these abstract data, of the world of thought. Sensible impressions no longer occupy exclusively the consciousness, or control its connections. The ears can be closed and the eyes shut, and the most active and productive mental processes go forward with increased advantage. Mind thus becomes spirit, enters a spiritual world, does its work among things invisible, and draws from them its most efficient motives.

But this new life must be an embodied one, must be put in relation with the world of sensible qualities, spring out of it, and return to it. The medium of this connection, the symbol of these new experiences, is language, whose controlling feature is its power to express relations, to designate and hold fast the abstract. By means of language the mind climbs out of the **world** of sensations into that of relations, and works there the great constructive labors of thought by which the phenomena about us become the expression of the ancient forces that have borne the creation **on** their bosom until now, and are sweeping with it placidly by us into the eternity before them. Spaces quite beyond the interpretation of the senses, times into which our time falls as a drop in the ocean, forces which invisibly interlace all visible facts, powers which potentially abide in this field of effort and work out there their own ends, these are the rational elements of a rational life.

§ 4. That mind is not the product of cerebral action but that cerebral action is the medium of mind in reaching the physical world, seems probable when we consider the facts of evolution simply. The vital power in many and cunning combinations precedes the nervous system. This system has been from the beginning simply **the means to** farther development in a direction previously indicated. Again, the automatic action of the nervous system has **preceded** by a long period its conscious action. Consciousness has not been an inseparable function of nervous action, but has entered as a later additional term. Consciousness has been superinduced on a system relatively complete within itself. The higher is not added for the sake of the lower; but the lower is put to the uses of the higher. So true is this that the organ of consciousness, even after it has been woven into the nervous web below it, can be removed, and **a large portion of** automatic action remains. That the last sensor state, in its passage into the cerebrum, is not united causally to the first motor stimuli, issuing from it, is probable; (1) for if this were true, the cerebrum would simply repeat the functions of lower ganglia; and (2) in that case consciousness would be a superfluous addition. Plainly consciousness intervenes between the two in a way that interrupts simply automatic connections. In this fact lies its entire significancy.

# CHAPTER IV.

## *Primary Volition or Choice.*

§ 1. WE have now reached that central point on which all volition rests, and every effect. In choice we find the home of liberty, the highest expression of power, the unconditioned support from which hangs all the chain of linked events.

Some divisions have been made in choice, which have value in practical morals, but little interest in philosophy. They mark the relation of choices to the action and character of the person whose they are, and not any inherent difference in the volitional acts themselves. Thus an ultimate choice is one which has reference to the most remote, or at least, the most general and inclusive ends of action. Thus a choice of virtue is of this nature, since it at once sets a limit and law to all other volitions, made secondary in their relation to this. A choice of pleasure to be pursued directly and everywhere is also of this character. Such choices have more frequently a theoretical than an actual existence. The pursuit of pleasure usually arises under detached, limited choices fastening to some object at no great remove in advance. The universality of such volition is of a *quasi*, not of a formal character. Even the choice of virtue is often made by a specific surrender to a given duty, rather than by a broad forecast of the entire field of effort — is the settling the struggle of life under an example, instead of a principle.

Desultory volitions are also spoken of; that is, volitions which spring up one side of the leading line of action and are directly or indirectly at cross purposes with it. **Thus one whose** general pursuit is that of pleasure, gives way transiently to the claims of right, and one usually **obedient** to duty, for a time, turns aside under some **peculiar temptation.** Of these choices, practically there are **many ; and** while their moral bearing is most important, as choices they present **no points of particular interest.** Life is more frequently **expended under** the impulse of general **choices,—** not assuming the **character** of a single, ultimate choice, **though as certainly as such** a choice, throwing action into one direction—and under **desultory** choices, bending without **reversing the current of the soul.** Thus actions flow onward, submitting to a gravitation they may not have recognized, and yet, in never-ending circuits and **turnings,** betraying the influence of the passing hour.

§ 2. Passing, then, these distinctions in the relations **of** volitions rather than in their character, we have only to consider simple choice, **the primary act of the will, the chief ex-** pression of spontaneous power. We shall speak first of what is involved in this notion of free-will, and later, of the proof of its existence. As liberty is a primary, simple relation, we must define it by cutting it off from other things, by denying of it those qualities which have become attached to it from abroad, reflected upon it from the physical connections of the world below it, and then leave it to be understood and accepted by the intuitive grasp of the mind itself.

Liberty is not, as some would have us believe, **found** in the absence of outside coercion. If this were liberty, the plant would be free in its growth ; **since this proceeds** under no mechanical, external impulse, is the result of **the** action of inner forces. When we say that man is free, we do not, in the higher use of the word, mean to affirm that he is not bound or imprisoned. The ordinary significance of language makes this point sufficiently plain.

By the word choice, we intend to cut off all efficient forces, that is all physical forces, external or internal, mechanical or vital, from any control over, or direct effect upon the action which is so designated. The commencement of the line of effort which springs from a primary volition—a volition, as we shall concisely term it—is absolute and complete.

We do not affirm hereby anything concerning the exact manner in which the train of physical forces is set in motion by volition, but only that it does, of its own power, initiate the physical movements which follow. These energies may lie in store for it, ready to be used, but the will liberates and controls them. The will, then, in the first place, stands above and beyond the range of causation, even in its most subtile forms as presented by nervous energies and influences. It descends upon and **uses these,** is not evolved by them.

By the limitations now given, all reflex action, all automatic action, under the play of the senses and appetites, are as physical states excluded from the realm of liberty, are but the higher forms of physical action. Equally are those executive volitions which have received their impulse from above, those acts which follow directly an intellectual weigh**ing of** means, a balancing of probabilities, a deliberative movement which is simply the **gathering** and eddying of executive force looking for a new avenue, the best avenue for advance, cut off from the freedom which attaches to choice. Having reached a point wholly unaffected by physical force, we are to inquire what are the conditions of liberty. The inducements to action in the will lie before it, not behind it; they are motives, not causes. There is no opportunity for choice, unless there are two or more of these,—and as by successive rejection they at length assume the typical form —unless there are two motives or lines of action. Neither is there properly opportunity for choice unless these two are distinct motives, subordinate to distinct ends. If the relation is one of means simply, it does not involve an **act** of choice, but one of intellectual estimates, of judgment. As the word **choice** is applied both to selection and election, both to the purely mental act deciding on adaptations and to the **volitional act deciding between courses of** conduct with different **and independent** moral characteristics, we easily **confound the two.** These motives, then, must be present, **and so present as to** furnish a true alternative of action—**not a** seeming one. Five dollars as opposed to ten **dollars, as** detached, single considerations, constitute no true **alternative.** They are exactly of the same kind, and, in ordinary states of mind, there is no basis of action on which the less can be preferred to the greater, since that which gives value to five dollars gives double value to ten dollars; and to feel the first inducement without feeling the **greater** force of the second is simply to disclose a defective estimate, or an abnormal state **either of the** mind or of social wants. In all cases **of which this is a type,** there is no proper freedom. The mind can only choose the less valuable, the less desirable of things, like in kind, by adding to the smaller inducement a distinct, factitious consideration, as that of evincing independence, or the exhibition of eccentricity. If, then, all motives are resolvable at bottom into impulse, and measurable on one standard, we assert that there is no real liberty, but only that semblance presented by an intellectual inquiry into the intrinsic value of things not bearing their sale-mark on them.

§ 3. There is necessary, then, to liberty not only two motives, but motives unlike in kind, resting back ultimately on different principles, revealing different forms of good and phases of character. In other words, there is no choice without the moral element which can alone oppose itself to all varieties of physical good, and present a distinct ground of action, a reward incommensurable with any sensual pleas**ure.** The esthetical element indeed, as infused with ethical sentiment, may furnish a secondary feature in that contrast of action which gives a basis of choice.

Two such motives being present, the question returns, What **is** their relation **to choice?** We answer: They influence the will without **in** any sense controlling it; here **we** have reached the final, inexplicable thing, liberty. The **will can,** by its own power, take either of the two lines of action to the rejection of the other; can feel motives to any degree, yet refuse to yield to them. The will, with spontaneous independent power, initiates the one or the other of the two courses of action before it. Here is neither **fatality nor** chance, causation nor fortuity. The will feels, without submitting to motives, and discloses in itself a true beginning of action.

§ 4. There is one view of liberty which needs to be guarded against, and, in the rejection of it, we shall have defined sufficiently the conditions of choice. It is this. The will always does yield to the strongest motive, not of necessity, but as a fact. **In** the first place, this theory incurs all the difficulties of the view, that the will yields to **either of the two** motives by an impulse or decision resting in **itself** alone, without its advantages. By motives in this discussion, we understand not simply the outward, objective element, but the inner, subjective one as well, all in short that makes them motives. Influences are influences only through the susceptibilities on which they play, the desires they evoke. The one theory affirms that these motives may be spoken of as stronger and weaker, and that in each case of choice that motive prevails, though not necessarily, which is the strongest. **The other** theory asserts such a distinction of motives is impertinent, and the will itself, in its freedom, is the sufficient and entire reason of the volition that follows.

The mind, in the act of choice, is no more ruled by its own states than by external conditions. If it were, liberty would as certainly disappear, as if, in the outset, we placed the will within reach of physical forces. We should do with two steps what we had refused to do with one. The present state of the sensibilities would be determined by previous states, and these by constitutional endowments and external circumstances, and thus the threads of influence, the lines of causation, be at length lodged elsewhere than in the will. Each volition would be the fruit of conditions which it itself had not determined, and thus be as certainly interlocked with the flow of forces as is the mill-wheel which revolves in the stream. The one theory evades this result by saying, that the stronger motive does control the will, yet not necessarily. The choice may be, though it never is, against it. The other denies the applicability of the conception, greater and less, and affirms an absolute, unqualified freedom, finding and seeking no explanation in forces expressed in motives.

This admission, that the will may choose the line of action supported by what is termed the weaker motive, involves philosophically all the difficulties of the view which represents it as alike independent of both incentives, and making either a true alternative to the other. There is no philosophical obstacle to supposing that the will *does* sometimes do what it is admitted that it *may* do. The statement of an action as possible involves the concession of grounds sufficient to render it intelligible, if it should actually occur. No law of mind can be violated by the happening of that which these laws suffer us to regard as possible. We must rely on special reasons, not on general principles, to establish the impossibility in given cases of that which we have granted to be a theoretic possibility. We can find, therefore, in philosophy alone no sufficient reason for saying in the same breath, that a thing may be, and denying that it ever will **be**. The last assertion must rest on some special, empirical reason; since the first assertion sweeps the ground of philosophy and says, that there is nothing to prevent it. Our philosophy, then, as philosophy, is no more encumbered with the assertion, that the will does choose, than with the declaration, it may choose, either alternative. The general principles which admit the one statement, will cover the other. The fact, that an admitted possibility never does become actual, must be established, if established **at** all, on special reasons peculiar to the case. If there were a general principle or law against the action, it would not remain possible.

Moreover this theory establishes an inductive law, of the strongest possible character, against itself. Admittedly, the weakest motive, so termed, never is chosen. There is an absolutely uniform line of action in innumerable and most diversified cases. No law of induction is established on stronger **grounds**. Yet, when we are just about to reach the conclusion, that what, under no circumstances, is or ever will be done, is an action excluded by the very nature and method of the forces at work, we are suddenly bidden to face around by the very unexpected assertion, the choice under discussion is one that may constantly be made. On what ground does this odd inversion rest? Not on that of induction, for this line of argument prepares the way with well-nigh irresistible power for exactly the opposite statement. Not on philosophical principles, for, as previously shown, these principles would show that what may at any time happen, probably, under the inexhaustible variety of circumstances presented by human life, will happen. This assertion, then, that the will may, but never does, choose the weaker motive, grounds itself neither on experience nor philosophy. It is an ill-grounded affirmation under either view of it.

§ 5. Again, to what a mere shadow does it reduce liberty. We are free by virtue of a power never put forth. If we could not accept the rejected alternative, we should not be free; yet, one of the two alternatives always, before choice, stands in such relation to the will, that it never accepts it. The action of the will is practically as fixed by antecedent conditions as any line of causation. One might as well claim that a python should walk because of certain rudimentary limbs hidden under its skin, as to annex all the fearful consequences of sin to such a hypothetical power as this—a power that has never found exercise, subserves no practical purpose, and is only possessed of a metaphysical existence. To sustain the ponderous chain of sin—its interlocked links reaching through all eternity, its galling weight crushing the life of myriads—by so theoretical and fanciful a support, can certainly never subserve the purposes of actual moral government.

Farther, a will of this sort, is wholly superfluous. If motives have superior efficiency, and this efficiency is always yielded to, why should any volition intervene? There is a power present able to secure action, and that does secure the action that actually follows. Why should not this surplus of power, this over-balance of influence, be left in an immediate, precise, inevitable way to reach its own results. Are we to insert another wheel, itself with no practical connections, only that we may band to it the moral universe, and assert responsibility? If so, let us, in the name of virtue and honesty, give it some other office than that of simply bearing inward a power already existing in completeness in the motive. To deal thus subtly with one's moral judgments, to practise upon them with these evanescent distinctions and cunning subterfuges of words, itself approaches wickedness.

§ 6. Whence springs this distinction of motives into stronger and weaker but from a false analogy with the forces of the physical world? We are not to attach to the word influence a definite, measurable power, capable of numerical comparison with like powers. If our pleasures were all referable to one sensorium, something of this sort might be admissible. But they are not. A moral gratification can be expressed in no terms of greater and less with a sensual indulgence. Were it not for our moral, our rational nature, were we wholly physical, the conditions of liberty would indeed disappear. We might weigh the claims of the senses, assign a numerical value to indulgences, and trace the rise and fall of motion along this new meter of the appetites and passions. But nothing of this is possible, no approximate estimates of pleasure are possible when the moral nature enters into the calculation; when the supreme claims of conscience afford a full and fair alternative to every degree and form of self-indulgence. We should have no occasion for freedom, were it not for the self-imposed law of the moral nature, and in issuing a command it also gives the conditions of that liberty which enables us to obey it. There is no such final reference of motives to the same or like sensibilities, by which we are able to pronounce them greater or less. There is no common term or point between mere pleasure and duty. We cannot take the pleasure of a glass of wine from a sense of obligation, and give a numerical remainder.

But if there is no antecedent standard by which motives may be measured, it is a mere circle of words to call that the strongest motive which does prevail, and then to repeat the assertion in the form, the will always chooses the strongest motive. There must be antecedent measurement,

—and there is no such measurement—or our language means nothing.

This view overlooks the office of the moral nature, the transcendent purchase and power that it gives to choice. It confounds simple, intellectual discrimination between enjoyments, or, still worse, a certain automatic adjustment and balance between animal impulses, with choice. Liberty keeps aloof from this lower region. It reposes on extended wing in the upper air of our rational, intuitive powers and emotions. There is, and of necessity must be, a moral character to every true act of choice, since the higher impulses must enter to break up and rule out these estimates of greater and less, these automatic adjustments of influences essentially one.

The sense of guilt which accompanies a moral struggle sustains the view we have presented. If the guilty party could feel that he had yielded to the strongest motive, that a balance had been cast up between motives, and he had accepted the largest sum proffered, the sense of condemnation and shame would be very different from what it now is. In proportion, however, as the transcendent, unmeasurable character of virtue is present to the mind, are the accompanying moral struggle and the subsequent sense of guilt strong and bitter. The more declared the sin, the more clear the knowledge of the high nature of the things rejected. It is the increase of light and motive, not their decrease, which evokes the forces of moral retribution. The mind is not allowed to console itself with the assertion, that at the time and under the circumstances, it actually chose the strongest pleasure, the highest good. Its infinite folly, its unaccountable guilt are enforced upon it, not its sad mistake, its grave misjudgment.

§ 7. Against the notion of liberty, absolute and complete, now presented, it may be urged, that it admits of no control, that its action can not be anticipated, and hence provided for. Now liberty is limited **to the** alternatives before **it.** It can not choose anything, but only one of two things ; and it is unsafe to give the opportnnity of choice, when we are not ready for the acceptance of either of the things offered. Liberty is simply a larger field of activity, the opening of two lines of effort instead of one, and this is often found very easy even for a man in his control and management of his fellows. It does, indeed, make of government a higher art, but does not in skillful hands take away its perfect efficiency, all the efficiency contemplated.

Liberty provides for less, recognizes less of a certain sort of control than does slavery. The inevitable, mechanical movement of necessary forces is, indeed, lost ; but there is substituted a nobler movement, because it is a freer one, manageable in a different measure, and on different principles. Those who prefer the clang and ceaseless on-going of machinery may not be pleased ; but the product itself, nevertheless, is every way superior.

Moreover, will is constantly declaring itself under its own liberty, establishing a movement and revealing a character more and more manifest to those who have to deal with it. The virtue of a virtuous man does not cease to be free, nor the vice of a vicious man, because the choice of each is not momentarily altered. A free action remains free, no matter how far pursued, and those impulses of the rational life once revealed become more and more declared and fixed in their directions. The conduct of a perfectly virtuous being is among the most calculable forces in the whole universe, and this without the least loss of freedom. We manage events readily which turn on moral evidence, yet the connections are not absolute, are not seen by us to be certain. There is the same difference between causation and liberty as between demonstration and evidence, proof and argument. Each subserves a feasible, practical purpose.

It may be farther objected, that liberty so defined is synonymous with chance. It is not. The ground of action—and there remains a most adequate and complete ground—is simply transferred from the motives to the will, from the outside to the inside, from secondary and causal agents to a primary and independent one. We must, indeed, give up all hope of conceiving this under forms of the imagination, or, of the understanding through analogical judgments; but let alone, it is just as intelligible as red, or sweet, or hard, or as causation itself, which, for some inscrutable reason, seems to be thought by many to be so perfectly translucent a notion as to be the only proper solvent for everything else. If we could get over the futile feeling that everything must be like something else, a habit of mind confirmed by physical inquiry, we should have no more theoretical, than we have practical difficulty with liberty, claiming hourly its fullest consequences from child and adult, from friend and foe.

§ 8. What are the proofs of the existence of the power of choice as now defined? Our analysis, our rejection of this and that explanation as insufficient, have proceeded on the claims of an intuitive notion. We have denied the conclusions which seemed incompatible with perfect freedom, which furtively subjected the mind once more to the same forces which drive the world. Our proof of the existence of this power is not found directly in consciousness. If it were, the question would hardly admit of dispute. The evidence of consciousness is negative rather than positive. We are conscious of the presence of motives, we are conscious of volitions, these are phenomenal; we are not conscious of the connection between the two, this is not phenomenal. We are negatively, indeed, aware of no restraint;

our volitions seem to be, what we affirm they are, free. But consciousness does not directly settle **this** question, for the sufficient reason that freedom is not a phenomenon, but the condition or form of **phenomena,** and **hence** it does not immediately arise in consciousness, but is only **suggested** from what is there present.

The occasion of this suggestion is found **in our moral** nature. Laws are constantly imposed on our actions **by** ourselves, by others, and our moral sense justifies them. The record of history and of individual life everywhere **presents** them, and hourly, momentarily demands them. Now no law, no command can be imposed on a being that is not free. The only law to which such a being can **be** subjected is a physical law, **working in and through it. A** moral law **above it, before it, is an absurdity;** and, if followed by punishment is most cruel.

Hence those who logically accept **the consequences of** their own doctrines utterly subvert the phenomena under consideration, the facts of the moral world, and give an entirely **new** rendering of them as a consequence of their denial of liberty. Says Bain, in *The Emotions and* **The** *Will;* "Under a certain motive, as hunger, I act in a certain way, taking the food that is before me, going where I shall **be** fed, or performing some other preliminary condition. The sequence is simple and clear when so expressed; bring in the idea of freedom, and there is instantly a chaos, imbroglio, or jumble. What is to be said, therefore, is that this idea ought never to **have come into the theoretical** explanation of the will, and ought now to be summarily expelled." Again, " the word choice is one of the modes of designating the supposed liberty of voluntary actions. The real meaning, that is to say, the only real fact that can be pointed at in correspondence with it, is the acting out one of several different promptings. When a person purchases

an article out of several submitted to view, the recommend-
ations of that one are said to be greater than of the rest,
and nothing more needs really be said in describing the
transaction. It may happen for a moment the opposing attractions are exactly balanced, and decision suspended thereby. The equipoise may even continue for a length of time,
but when the decision is actually come to, the fact and the
meaning are that some consideration has arisen to the mind,
giving a superior energy of motive to the side that has
preponderated. This is the whole substance of the act of
choosing. The designation, liberty of choice, has no real
meaning, except as denying extraneous interference." In
the same vein, he continues, " The term responsibility, is a
figurative expression of the kind called by writers on rhcto-
ric, ' metonymy,' where a thing is named by some of its
causes, effects, or adjuncts, as when the crown is put for
royalty, the mitre for episcopacy, etc. Seeing that in every
country where forms of justice have been established a
criminal is allowed to answer the charge made against him,
before he is punished, this circumstance has been taken up,
and used to designate punishment. We shall find it con-
duce to clearness to put aside the figure, and employ the
literal term. Instead, therefore, of responsibility, I shall
substitute punishability ; for a man can never be said to be
responsible, if you are not prepared to punish him, when
he can not satisfactorily answer the charges made against
him." In another passage, he gives concisely his notion
of the method of moral suasion. " There is one form of
stating the fact of ability that brings us face to face with
the great metaphysical puzzle. It not uncommonly happens that a delinquent pleads his moral weakness in justification of his offence. The school-boy whose animal spirits
carry him to a breach of decorum, or whose anger has made
him do violence on a school-fellow, will sometimes defend

himself by saying he was carried away, and could not restrain himself. In other words, he makes out a case closely allied to physical compulsion. He is sometimes answered by saying, that he could have restrained himself if he had chosen, willed, or sufficiently wished to do so. Such an answer is really a puzzle or paradox, and must mean something very different from what is apparently expressed. The fact is, that the offender was in a state of mind such that his conduct followed according to the uniformity of **his** being, and if the same antecedents were exactly repeated, the same consequent would certainly be reproduced. In that view, therefore, the foregoing answer is irrevelant, not to say nonsensical. The proper form, and the practical meaning to be conveyed, is this: It is true, that as your feelings then stood, **your conduct resulted as it did**; but I am now to deal with you in such a way, **that** when the situation recurs, new feelings and motives will be present, sufficient, I hope, to issue differently. I now punish you, or threaten you, or admonish you in order that an antecedent motive may enter into your mind, as a counter-action to your animal spirits or temper on another occasion, seeing that, acting as you did, you were plainly in want of such a motive. I am determined that your conduct shall be reformed, and therefore every time that you make such **a** lapse, I will supply more and more incentives in favor of what is your duty."

Here is consistency. Mr. Bain has determined that there is no freedom, that the notion is an absurd one, and hence he pushes his theory right over the convictions of men expressed in the most unmistakable, universal and constant use of language. He says to himself, the line of my road lies through yonder hill, and he buries his engine up to the furnace in the soil in his effort to drive it through. **As we** have undertaken only the easier and more modest task of explaining, instead of overthrowing, the universal facts of mind, we must needs believe that the world, wise and ignorant, have not whistled to the wind in talking about freedom, choice, responsibility, and in constructing the frame-work of private, social and religious life upon them. In the above theory, there is the entire transformation of the very familiar facts of hourly life that seek our explanation. The language we apply to them is found to be all wrong. There is no proper guilt or punishment, virtue or reward. There is no law, as we use the word in social and ethical discussions; all is ultimately resolvable into physical force. The man indeed, like the brute, can be reached on two sides instead of one. He can be pushed, guided from behind, and, through the mirror of the mind, can be invited, influenced by things yet before him. As, by ingenious reflection, rays that do not directly fall upon the object are thrown upon it, so forces not yet realized are flung by anticipation on the mind, and become present powers working vital results in the brain. To lay a command, therefore, as conscience does, and furnish, for its execution, no forces, promise no pleasures, threaten no pains, as the immediate results of obedience or disobedience, is, according to the above view, absurd, is to furnish the plan of a noble edifice, and provide no workmen to put it up. There is, on this theory, no other moral law than when I flourish a whip in the face of a restive ox, or apply it to his tough hide. The actions are essentially one; the first brings the anticipation of pain, and the second, actual pain.

In the passages quoted, there is an undersigned confession that the author can make nothing of the true moral phenomena of moral law, and has, therefore, put in their place a gross caricature, at war with the form and language of our daily life. We do treat the brute and the man very differently, and the more diversely, as we are the more intelligent.

We furnish an influence, an incentive for the one, we claim its existence in the other. We provide for obedience **here, we demand it** there; we give the sharp intonation here, we simply state the law in its imperial power there. We accept as complete the service which fear has brought here; **there** we despise it, as no solution of the claims of right **on the** soul. Bain gives the theory of brute life, we **are** striving to give that of rational life. He takes his examples promiscuously from the causal and the free side of human action. While recognizing the way in which the two laws blend with each other **in** conduct, we assert the radical distinction between them. If a true, moral command is ever uttered from within, **or** from without, rightfully to man, liberty, the power to obey it, is implied **therein.**

The second portion of the proof **of liberty, without** which the first would be incomplete, is the fact, that the mind does spontaneously, inevitably place this notion of liberty back of human, responsible action as its explanation. Our conclusion is the conclusion of the race; just as certainly, universally, inevitably as is any judgment whatever. We no more necessarily refer an effect to a cause, than we **do** responsibility to liberty; and responsibility we universally claim of others. It remains to be shown that any man **has ever lived,** who has not believed in the guilt of his neighbor; it is axiomatic **in practical** morals, that guilt **is** commensurate with power. Every excuse and apology pre-**suppose it.** The full form, then, of the proof of the existence of freedom is found in the double fact, that we universally lay moral claims upon others, and that we justify ourselves in so doing by attributing liberty to them. There is a large class of familiar and undeniable facts which the mind pertinaciously explains by an assertion **of** its power of **choice.** The difficulty of philosophers in analyzing it, their perplexities over it, their escape by denials of it, are no more proofs against it, than the like treatment of the mind's action in a dozen other directions. The spontaneous, ever-recurring action of the mind is the proof we have of liberty, and the only proof we have for anything our faculties offer us. We see and see again, till we believe that we see. We think and think again, till we accept our thought.

§ 9. Liberty, as a primary power, calls for a broader basis in our constitution than we have thus far assigned it, or than is usually seen to belong to it. If one act only, that of choice, is spontaneous, then this act can accomplish nothing, enclosed as a single term in the on-going processes of the mind. A volition must have at its disposal spontaneous powers to execute its purposes, powers that can be rescued from the current of previous causes, and be opened up to a new impulse. If the thoughts and feelings are ever moving forward under sufficient and independent forces or causes, then neither can the antecedent conditions of volition be secured, nor the subsequent ones. Antecedently volition would fail, because each state of thought and feeling being fixed by forces alien to the will, there would be no opportunity for independent inquiry on any topic; the will would be found in the midst of intellectual and emotional conditions alien to every other than the established drift of thought. The volition would fail subsequently, because an act of choice is nothing unless previous tendencies can be checked by it and new ones established; unless spontaneous powers can be brought forward for its execution. One may stand in a mill, its busy wheels revolving everywhere about him, and choose this or that result; the choice does not avail unless he can put his hand on the machinery and modify its action. So far as this is complete within itself, and driven by its own forces, it goes forward heedless of volitions. If one is to oversee men, his oversight avails not if he finds them all occupied in their own ways, and is unable to divert them from their labors, and convert them to his purposes. In other words, an act of will must go deeper and extend farther than itself and lay hold of a whole circle of modifiable powers in the execution of its plans. Unless the thoughts and feelings are spontaneous, unless they are potential, and hold themselves at the beck of the will, in whole or in part, the will remains impotent, having no service because it has no servants. Spontaneity, then, must belong to our intellectual constitution or freedom cannot belong to our voluntary life. Origination at single detached points avails nothing. The will can not be operative if out of harmony with our other powers. It must be able to act by anticipation, to accumulate and modify motives; it must be able to rally to its choices the forces of the mind, and carry protractedly forward its processes; it must be profoundly in sympathy with the entire constitution, and pervade its powers as a life-giving law.

Dr. Carpenter, unwilling to abandon liberty, though it is a notion quite out of keeping with his general system, regards volition "as exerted in augmenting the nervous tension of the part of the cortical substance of the cerebrum which is concerned in the formation of the idea of the thing to be done. · · · It consists in an intensification of the hyperæmic state of the ideational centre." (Mental Physiology, p. 425). This voluntary increase of the blood in the brain is open philosophically to all and more than all the difficulties of complete, proportionate freedom, and is most impotent in accomplishing its purposes. If one could at will increase or diminish the steam in the cylinder, and so modify the motive power in any branch of manufacture, this fact would not avail to alter the processes in progress. It would quicken or retard the movement, but not re-direct it. This very narrow volition would be so enveloped in previous states, that it would have no real control. An act of will, to be efficacious, must so pervade the mind as to give new starting-points and new directions.

All pure intellectual action is spontaneous, beyond causation, and ready to be played upon by the will. The feelings, intellectual and spiritual, are also spontaneous, that is, referable to powers of mind and not to physical forces. These, however, stand in such dependence on the thoughts that they are only indirectly reached by the will. The actions of the mind, though free, first through its spontaneous powers, and second through its choices, none the less stand in determinate constitutional relations, and remain to be operated under their appropriate laws. Thought does not cease to be spontaneous because it is logical, truthful; because the premises contain the conclusion. No more do the feelings lose their spontaneity because they are united to the thoughts, and follow after them. It is not the nature of the will to set aside all relations, it is its office to work under them. There is order that is not causal order, to wit, thought-order, emotional order. Will means the power to guide and propel the mind, and this power is no more lost because the mind moves in definite ways, than is the control of the engineer because the engine requires a track. The mind works for the truth, not against it, or at random in reference to it.

If, then, we deny liberty, our denial will reach proportionately deep, and the spontaneity of our intellectual action will go with it. Our thoughts, as a coherent movement of powers, will be dissolved apart. The conclusions will no longer inhere in the premises, and be taken thence by the *mind*, but impression will follow impression without direct connection, as the shadow of one car pursues that of another in the same train. Intellectual relations thus become the relations of shadows; dependence is found only between things, is exclusively physical and causal.

In strict consistency, however, **we cannot** hold fast to causation, since the link of force, like the link of liberty, **is** one supplied wholly by the mind, is one of its notions; and no verification falls to a single idea which is **not** common to them **all**. Nothing can be affirmed of causation **as** proof which can not also be asserted of liberty.

**By** the disappearance, therefore, of liberty, not only **are** all the social, civil, moral, and religious facts of the world dissolved, the coherance of thought also disappears, every connection is illusory, and every joint dislocated. We are **in** a world of films and shadows. Our moral actions first **shake** off responsibility; then our thoughts slip their logical connections and pass into shadows; last **of** all the visible **world** becomes a dream. We dream that we dream, and there is no awaking. To come to **ourselves, is the** very pregnant phrase of all right-mindedness. **When we** possess in confidence our own powers, then we comprehend other things. Will is germinant, the only germinant thing in the universe; all else is flow. Is it marvellous, then, that liberty as an idea must be the norm of constructive thought? Liberty is spontaneity exercised in choice. Spontaneity is self-centered power as opposed to transmitted power. On spontaneity rests the potential—what may be as opposed to what must be.

**We cannot** go as far as Martineau and others desire to, and extend this dependence of force on will into an identification of them, making an alleged consciousness of force exercised in volition the source of the notion of causation. The subphenomenal power as truly escapes us in mental experiences as in physical ones. The mind is alike penetrative and constructive in both. What we should learn to do is not to distrust and struggle against our intuitions, but to call them forth and guard them. We shall everywhere **lose** the substratum of real being, unless we can penetrate **to it by** special insight.

§ 10. **As the proofs** of liberty are of the utmost moment, and as they arise from a **variety** of scattered considerations as well as from central facts, we will for their better apprehension, epitomize and group them.

(1) **Pure** mental facts, more particularly those of thought, must lose their quality without spontaneity. The mind, in its search for truth, must be free to follow it. If secret causal forces control the movement, the distinction **between the true and the false is lost; since every** effect is equally necessary and real, the one termed false as the one termed true. If this argument is well taken, it is final; for an overthrow of this distinction abolishes all denials and affirmations, and among them those of the necessitarian.

(2) **The** moral facts of the world **can** not maintain their ground as simply causal facts. The distinction as a primary one disappears; all facts **are** of one grand order, all are necessary facts. Any **division that** may remain is one of form simply. **The discussion has swept away** the phenomena that provoked it.

(3) Physical **facts, as united by** forces and understood through forces, have no basis of knowledge firmer than that which has just given away in morals. The notion of force **is one** supplied by the mind, and applied for the same rea**sons** and in the same way as that of liberty, to wit, to explain certain facts. If the one notion is without proof, so **is the** other; if the one has proof, so has the other. If we substitute succession for causation, succession is more allied to liberty than to necessity. And if we strip away dependencies, thought must go with **them, as** thought is one **of** them, and each instant **involves them.** If there **are no** connections there are no thoughts, and **nothing for** thought to pursue. Either the links of thoughts or the links of things must be allowed; and if one is allowed both must be.

(4) The two dependencies involved in necessity and

liberty must remain **as** the rational correlatives of each
other in all knowledge. Necessary movement is not a
movement to be known by itself, since such a knowledge
would be a **superfluous** adjunct, a waste of energy. Knowledge, on the other hand, being present, must have an element of freedom, or the simply necessary will remain alien
and inapproachable to it. It is along the line of interaction
between the fixed **and** the flexible that rational life is developed.

(5.) Language, the most complete and permanent image
of mental facts, includes fully **the notion of** liberty. We
refer not merely to the words of moral action and of intellectual and political **freedom,** — though these forms of
liberty are so wrought into speech, **directly** and indirectly,
that the most careful expression can not **shun** them, that a
consistent utterance of the doctrine of **necessity** becomes
impossible—but to the presence of such **moods as the poten-**
tial and the subjunctive and the imperative, and the constant overshadowing of the actual by the possible and the
ideal. This perpetual tenor of speech is illusory, if the
world is covered in all its parts by one inflexible movement.
Language again, like life, lies **in** the interplay of the possible and **the actual.**

(6) **If pure** mental action is not spontaneous, it is the
product **of realized** forces; **no distinct seats of these forces**
can **be given** without involving materialism. **Motives lie**
before **the mind,** and the objects expressed by them may
not as yet even **exist.** Motives are images of possibilities,
they are not forces in **the mind moving it.** The only
imaginable seat of forces, efficient **in a** present process
of thought or volition, must be brain tissue. But nervous forces working nervous effects bring no explanation of thoughts, unless these effects and thoughts are
**identical.** Forces must **be physical and** must occasion

physical effects, and these alone are what the theory of necessity expounds.

(7) Nor does physical investigation disclose any term in the circle of forces which can be regarded as a thought-force. Though we can not trace exactly the circuit of the forces that play into and through the brain, we regard them as complete within themselves on a purely physical basis; there is no opening, no transition stage, at which to insert a new force, a thought-force. The forces active in the telegraph stand on terms of complete equivalence among themselves; the mind of the operator is not included in them. No more is thought embraced as a recognized part of the nervous circle. We have chemical, thermal, electric nervous forces, but no known thought-force. Not the first fact of this order appears in physical inquiry. Yet will expresses itself in forces of great energy, and if it does this by virtue of itself being a force, the fact should be a palpable one. Quite the reverse seems to be the case; we have a complete circuit of physical forces, with no hint of any deficiency.

(8) Nor do motives combine like forces. Forces are not lost in the effects, whether they give apparent form to them or not. Adverse motives are lost. Single lines of action are taken. Mind does not move along the combining diagonal.

(9) If the theory of necessity were correct there could be no successful resistance to it. It is entirely simple, and if it were true, there would be an end. It is its inadequacy which stirs the mind to perpetual resistance.

(10) Nor would the necessitarian, if his view were a sound one, be led so often into fatal concessions. There is no midway ground, we must accept necessity or liberty. Few have the boldness to take necessity, and to consistently defend it. Most, like Dr. Carpenter, are tempted just at

the end to claim something, or to concede something which undoes all their work.

(11) The palpable evasions of the necessitarian lead to the same conclusion. Thus Bain explains the action of the school-boy by transferring attention to the teacher, and allowing on his part the introduction of new motives. But this involves liberty. If the boy is in the chain of existing motives, the teacher is also, and the committee also, and the community also, and the generation as well. We can not by going backward find a point of modification. The action of the boy may not be altered, for the motives are not alterable.

(12) If there is liberty, and only if there is liberty, can there be a beginning. Causation knows no beginning, no change of direction, no possibilities. Simple facts without ultimate reasons, inflexible and inexplicable movement, are all that remain to us. If we seem to see **reasons in this** on-going, something addressed to a rational comprehension, the vision is a mirage of the mind itself. New facts **are all** that we have. Our vessel sails under bare poles, we know not whither, before an invariable wind. Inquiry is futile, superfluous, a mere accident of the motion itself.

The first five of the reasons now offered spring from the very nature of mind. These are followed by three others which show that the doctrine of necessity can gain no clearness of conception without embracing materialism. Three more arguments spring from the weak way in which the doctrine is centered in itself, and the last argument turns on the relation of liberty to ontology.

# CHAPTER V.

## *Dynamics of the Will, and of the Mind.*

§ 1. The will is so nearly single, that little is to be said of the form of its activity. There is but one line of exertion, executive volitions resting back on a choice. This endures as a permanent impulse, and finds execution in mingled voluntary and vital action. From what has been said, it is evident that animals are destitute of all proper power of choice. Their action is the unconscious or the involuntary resolution of physical states and feelings into muscular impulse. The feelings which arise in consciousness are as directly connected with action as those physical states which never there present themselves, but, in the darkness and concealment of a purely vital force, accomplish their purpose.

The will is strengthened chiefly by use, and that not alone by its own activity, but even more by the restraint and check thus imposed on the appetites and passions. These, allowed control for any length of time, assume so domineering and persistent a form, that the will regains only with the utmost difficulty the ground that it has lost. This anarchy of the soul is, of all forms of confusion, the least susceptible of a remedy, as aid cannot come from abroad, and the chronic weakness of the powers that offer resistance to the mob of impulses, and establish authority over them, speedily passes beyond all cure. Some sudden shock of the moral nature, in rare cases the awakening of a strong desire, is the only spring of hope.

In speaking of the activities of the mind as a whole, we

are to remember, that these bear by no means the same proportion to each other in different individuals. Not only are specific, intellectual endowments and feelings diverse in power, the three classes of activities present various degrees of development. In one, intellectual effort absorbs the mind; in another, the emotions are the chief seats of action; while a third is possessed of a will that lapses into stubbornness, through the inefficiency of the thoughts in its guidance. Moreover, different temperaments cause essentially the same faculties to exhibit very different degrees of force. The nutritive and the nervous systems are most intimately associated with the mind. Great impressibility and power in the nervous organization; a preponderance of the nutritive functions giving a full animal life; nervous power well-balanced and well-sustained by the nutritive system, constitute the nervous, phlegmatic and sanguine temperaments, which greatly modify the measure, hopefulness, and satisfaction of intellectual efforts, even when the natural endowments of mind are nearly the same. As the body is at once the medium by which impressions reach the mind, the source whence the strength for their consideration is secured, and the instrument by which its practical and theoretical conclusions concerning them are expressed, the importance of the physical conditions of mental activity cannot easily be over-stated, nor be too carefully inquired into. These researches, however, pertain chiefly to physiology. It is our task to trace the strictly mental interplay of the faculties, a dependence, not primarily the result of physical connections.

§ 2. Thought, feeling and volition, express the order in which action ordinarily occurs, the line along which any influence brought to bear on the mind passes through its faculties.

Yet these three steps, though usual, are not all necessary. Through sensation, feeling may be directly occasioned, and activity immediately follow from it, yet this is of an involuntary character. Thought, also, unites feeling and volition, points out the present relation of things, and guides the mind in the right use of means. While the first movement is in the direction now indicated, there are reflex influences of an opposite character. The feelings affect strongly the thoughts. They direct attention to pleasing objects, fasten the faculties upon them, and thus intensify the emotions already established. The candor and fairness of the judgment are lost through this influence of the feelings, withdrawing attention from facts displeasing to them, and minutely and laboriously searching out those which maintain and justify their action. Unusual intellectual and moral development is required on the part of one possessed of strong feelings to reach even ordinary impartiality, and to give any considerable weight to reasons for action opposed to the inclinations. The intellect thus becomes the instrument of the feelings, using all its acuteness, its power of presentation and argument in behalf of conclusions already reached by the heart. When the intellect is thus the sagacious counsellor or the cunning attorney of the emotions, the distortions of truth are proportioned to its strength, and the most powerful thinking is productive only of misleading sophisms.

The feelings in the same way frequently engage the will, and the man becomes headstrong and willful in the line of action indicated by them. There is no defence against this but that quick moral sense, which responds with an adequate alternative to the selfish suggestions of the mind, and introduces a calm consideration of the claims of duty in each case. The only sufficient resistance to this domination which strong feelings are sure to assume over the intellect and the will, through the one evoking all the imagery which influences passion, and the reasons which justify it, and through the other imparting a haste and momentum to action which at once clear the way of all ordinary obstacles, and render the onset easy and retreat difficult, is afforded by the moral nature, calming feeling, soliciting candor, and holding the will in the leash of duty.

Government in the mind is not then self-evolved, is not the spontaneous inter-action of forces graded to their tasks, but is found in the direct, authoritative claims of a law-giving power. The order of the mind is moral, not natural; one of command and obedience, and not of self-poised powers; one to be discerned and pursued, not one to be developed simply. The disorder of transgression discovers itself, not in faculties lost, not in addition to, or subtraction from the original powers of the mind, but in that disproportionate development among them which is the fruit of anarchy, of usurpation on the one side, and overthrow on the other.

§ 3. If we look at the influences at work on any one character at any one time to make it what it is, there seems to be in it very little power of resistance or modification. **The** thoughts take such partial and justifying views of action, so blind themselves to the future results and even **the** immediate consequences of conduct, so misrender and misinterpret **facts; the** feelings so reward and maintain indulgence, cast such disfavor and so repulsive an atmosphere over every form of restraint, choke up the path of reform with so many imaginary difficulties, and find the accustomed way so open, so easy, so inevitable; the will submits so easily where it is wont to submit, is so reluctant to open a new conflict, and so weak to resist the impatient, persistent and domineering passions and appetites, that swarm in troops around it at every suggestion of change, that much modification of character established in its **springs and** conditions of action **seems** to us **impossible.** Indeed only the breaking in of an earthquake-power is able to alter and redirect the channels in which the activities of the soul are flowing.

If, however, we look at long periods, we see that there is a supreme control of the **will over character. Single** changes that **in the outset** are alien to the general movement prepare the way for others. New thoughts give **rise** to new feelings, and these slowly displace the old ; the **ac**tivity induced in fresh pursuits establishes and strengthens the will, and sets gradually at work varied reflex forces, giving different external and internal conditions, new feelings, motives and rewards of effort. At length, the mind accepts spontaneously the changed form of life, and a complete transformation is achieved. There is a momentum in mind which prevents its movements from becoming wayward and fitful, and yet there **is present a force which can** slowly and certainly bend them **in any direction it chooses.**

" There are a thousand microscopic motives," says Mallock, "too small for us to be actively conscious of, which according to how they settle on us, will really decide the question."* This is true only when we leave ourselves to the drift of life. Nothing is provided for, circumstances accumulate, push toward one issue, and make every other issue increasingly difficult. A firm and comprehen**sive** purpose anticipates such results, evading them before **they** are reached. If to such a purpose we add active, broad and candid judgment, pouring into the mind new light, new incentives, and the suggestions of new methods, we have the conditions of a character ripening in strength and in self-guidance. The key of the movement lies in apt and growing knowledge, bringing to the mind fresh terms of activity, and putting a sober will constantly at the helm.

* Is Life Worth Living, p. 259.

§ 4. The feelings are plainly most central and important in the constitution of the mind. Here is the seat of enjoyment, of all good. Thence spring the motives which influence the will, which offer its alternatives, and thither return the fruits of choice—fresh gratifications with accompanying incentives to effort. The intellect is scarcely less instrumental to the emotions. It multiplies its resources that these may be nourished; it fills its canvas with figures that these may be profoundly moved. The emotions are sooner or later endowed with all the treasures of thought, and the painter, the poet, all who can accomplish this transfer most quickly, skillfully, perfectly, become the chief artists in human society. The merchant, the inventor, labor for grosser forms of transmutation, the artist for higher, the true hero, for the highest. He alone lifts thought into the moral sublimity of an actual life, that is integral with the triumph of order—the ample victory of the law of freedom in the universe of God.

As the impulses to action spring from the feelings, and the fruits of action return to them, it is evident that happiness must depend on the predominant emotions. Out of the heart are the issues of life. The physical feelings, the appetites, are primitive sources of pleasure; yet they are necessarily intermittent, and can be made safely to occupy but a small part of the time which falls to us. Moreover, their permanent enjoyment depends on physical vigor, and this must be maintained by that temperance, by that well-regulated activity which sets these enjoyments still further limits. It is only on the condition of making the appetites secondary, incidental sources of good, that they can at all maintain their position as safe and just means of pleasure.

The intellectual feelings are, indeed, capable of incessant activity, yet fail of conferring a sufficient and permanent good. There is not that repose in them, that perfect reaction of gratification on the appetitive desire which arrests it in complete indulgence. These intellectual impulses become rather increasingly exorbitant in their claims, fling us ever forward in search of the unattained, and leave us restless and unsatisfied with every acquisition actually secured. If we check the desire, we are immediately thrown back on other sources of good; it fails any longer to maintain our active powers and call forth our hopes. We must once again put to ourselves the question. What are those grounds, those sources of independent pleasure, of which at length, with the means in our hands that wealth, power, and rank confer, we are to avail ourselves in reaching complete and permanent happiness? If, on the other hand, we steadily inflame and expand the desires, we are fed on promises never realized, we are driven from one round of activity to another. We spread a feast, but have no time to partake of it, or, beginning to partake, are disappointed in its quality. The good is not in it we thought to be there, and we are driven to the hopeless expedient of still farther enlarging our board, enriching our service, and multiplying our viands. It thus not unfrequently happens, that the appetites decrease in the ratio in which the means of their gratification increase, and, at length, under this ever-returning experience, we discover that desires are wearing us out with unrequited labor; that the coin is indeed paid into the hand, but that it has lost its purchasing power; that we have served for Rachel, and that Leah has been given us.

The spiritual feelings, on the contrary, yield adequate and supreme pleasure for several reasons. The higher intuitions call forth emotions which are of a primitive and permanent character; unlike the appetites, they may accompany our every action with subdued pleasure, or with the swell of buoyant emotion. They may give way to outside, incidental enjoyments, and yet return to us as the undertone of a steady and protracted harmony. Moreover, there is repose in them. The mind is filled with the satisfaction which truth, beauty and virtue afford; without stimulating an **excessive activity,** they momentarily reward it. It is not merely a good in advance, but one in possession, that gives to the contemplation of beauty, of physical and moral excellence, a supreme and abiding pleasure. The concurrent reward and stimulus of the faculties take from **them** the intense thirst of desire, the restless, insatiate longing of intellectual emotions, expanding the circle each instant, and finding it forever made up of the same futile pleasures in greater multiplicity.

Again, the rational gratifications increase in scope and in purity of tone. They arise from intellections which, with the growth of mind, become broader, more varied and more just. They **yield,** therefore, to the **esthetical and** moral sense more extended, harmonious, and profound impressions. No one exhausts art, no one measures the **re**sources of virtue, nor makes barren to the contemplation those plans and that providence which are working the **world** up, with all its stubborn and refractory materials, **into a** perfect and permanent product of religious art.

These pleasures owe their high character also to **the ex**tent in which they combine and blend all the activities of the triple powers of man. The intellect is most active in preparing the conditions, in giving the grounds of esthetical and ethical intuitions, while the intuitions combine inseparably perception and emotion. To see the true, the beautiful and the good is to feel their power. Nor is the will inactive. Under the surface of the mind, fully occupied with these noblest objects of contemplation, there flows a steady purpose to conform all action to them, never to mar them, **to** win them by becoming a part of them. Here is doubtless **the secret of** the repose, the rest of truth, art and virtue, that they remove all conflict from our powers, and blend them in satisfied and indivisible activity. This is not asserted of art as divorced from virtue, but of art as the highest embodiment of rational life, of virtue.

The chief difference between play and labor seems to be that the one gives vent to a superabundant power and life in a direction in which it spontaneously flows, and the other demands, in view of a reward, exertion to which the physical or intellectual state does not prompt. Labor approaches play in its character in proportion as the effort becomes spontaneous. Now success stimulates the feelings, and the quickened feelings arouse the active powers in the direction of their gratification. Hence it happens, that those whose labor is abundantly rewarded often take so keen a delight in it, as scarcely to be willing to turn aside for so-called play. The true amelioration of labor is success, the success which expresses power and enhances it, making realization easy and sportive. Drudgery is not so much labor as poorly requited labor. Hence labor that is undertaken under the prompting of strong and gratified desire, is much more easily endured than the same exertion when coerced. Self-directed and prosperous labor will, in proportion as these elements of liberty and power enter into it, assume the character of play, and the ultimate lifting up of the burden of toil will be found in a more spontaneous and successful movement, that is, in one more thoroughly spiritual. Exactly in the degree in which higher power is present and prevalent, do we already see the servitude of labor removed. Beauty and virtue must assume this easy, irrepressible character which belongs to the physical putting forth of animal life, before they can lay aside the harsh aspect of toil and struggle, and present the beauty of angelic strength —strength that is no more burdened by the load laid upon it, than the hero of the ring with his own muscle.

# CHAPTER VI.

*The Relation of the System here offered to the Prevalent Forms of Philosophy.*

§ 1. THE inquiries of broadest outside and inside interest as regards any system of philosophy are: How does it unite the intellectual to the physical world? Which, if either, does it absorb in the other? What are with it the pregnant, ontological principles? The philosophy now offered strives **to** maintain, so far as man is concerned, physical and **mental** phenomena on an independent basis; so far as God is concerned, it centres and absorbs them both in Him. It thus endeavors to explain the familiar facts of experience, not as a vision, delusive in its form; but as the substantial, sufficient frame-work of knowledge. It does **not** by thought abolish that which called forth thought, but retains entire the phenomena it seeks to expound. Indeed, it is difficult to see on what ground the reasoning of a few **is** to be accepted, while it overturns fundamentally the con**clusions** of the many concerning facts of which each is independently cognizant. To yield our faith to such theories seems to be a surrender of the trustworthiness of our faculties, since with almost perfect unanimity and endless reiteration they have reached results exactly opposite to those thus offered. Nor is it an answer to this statement to say, that such a submission of the philosophical to the common mind precludes progress. It does not preclude the addition of new facts, **a** more careful analysis of old facts, with the correction **of** opinions **that is** sure to follow. It does cast suspicion on a movement, that it pre-supposes the entire error and deceptiveness of all spontaneous convictions, denies the validity of every conclusion but its own, and will not go to the common mind for the facts even that seek statement and explanation ; for the facts without which there could be no philosophy. Such theories shake centrally the structure of knowledge, and lead to a complete distrust of those faculties which have been so signally, so universally, so completely wrong in directions wholly open to their action. To make one, two, three mistakes, and retain confidence is possible, to affirm that everything thought hitherto has been a mistake, is to reflect the most gloomy uncertainty on our present conclusions, which have no other verification than that they are the last results of faculties hitherto always at fault.

That a system of philosophy lies, in the main, in the line of recognized conclusions, gathering up, harmonizing and expounding them, furnishes the same evidence of its truth as that afforded to a physical theory by the fact, that it easily includes and explains the facts under discussion ; or to a social theory by the fact, that it recognizes and makes clear events of hourly occurrence. Nor is it sufficient to give alleged reasons why men have been mistaken; universal and complete mistake is an impeachment of the mind whose consequences cannot be evaded.

We postulate in the system now presented, the trustworthiness of all our faculties in their careful, corrected, legitimate exercise; and accept as proof of a faculty or power, steady, reiterative action in any direction, yielding fruits of knowledge. What we see and hear, we accept as seen and heard, because our faculties are self-consistent and persistent in the affirmation. They renew the impressions in the same form on each like occasion. For a like reason we accept the conclusions of judgment. If we reached a different result each time we reviewed the proof of a proposition, we should trust no one of our conclusions. We believe what we believe, because the mind, on repeated inquiry, arrives again and again at the same convictions. Thus is it with memory. We are uncertain when we find inconsistent and changeable impressions; we are certain when the faculty restores the same image on each occasion. We start with no *a priori* theory as to what faculties the mind can have. We recognize as a fact that it does do what it seems to do, and take as a sufficient and ultimate proof of its power to impart and impart correctly any knowledge, the observed fact, that it does do this repeatedly and consistently. We cannot, therefore, accept the existence of the notion of causation, and recognize the constant use which the mind makes of it, and at the same time affirm it to be illusory. The admitted fact establishes a power of mind to discern and employ this notion, and is thus a sufficient proof of the correctness of such a notion. We should as soon say, the mind insists that it sees, but the vision is fanciful; as to say, the mind persists in assigning causes, but it has no ground for such assignment. The simple fact, that it does persistently assign them, is all the proof we are resting on in any department of knowledge.

We postulate, then, the assertions, that the mind does what it does by virtue of a power of doing it, and that the habitual conclusions of a power are sufficient evidence, and the only possible evidence of its existence and their own truth. If the mind supplies ideas, in a uniform way, ideas which the senses alone can not reach, then this fact is satisfactory proof, that these ideas rest back on a distinct faculty, and are sufficiently verified by that faculty. The philosophy here presented bridges the chasm between mind and matter, not by direct sensation, but indirectly, by intuitive ideas, whose presence gives occasion to the discussion, and makes it intelligible to us. In pronouncing so

authoritatively, as some do, that matter is cut off hopelessly
from mind, that there can be no communication between
them, they seem to contradict their **own** statement; since
the mind is dealing with matter in the very affirmation by
which it declares matter to be unapproachable. It **is not,**
then, with the idea of matter, that the mind finds difficulty.
This it works with in all its theories, and discovers nothing
in it self-destructive, or destructive to the notion of mind.
Whether, however, this idea, so manageable within the
**mind, has** any outward thing that corresponds with it, is a
question of simple proof, and, if such proof be present,
yields no new perplexity. If the mind can in thought
handle things so unlike itself as natural objects, it can also
recognize their actual being on sufficient evidence. But it
is said, there can be no such evidence, for such evidence
implies not an ideal, but an actual influence of matter on
mind. Is there, then, a **clear** *a priori* impossibility, that
there should be found in the phenomena of mind such
traces of the influences of matter as to furnish the grounds
for an inference of its existence? To the ordinary mind
this question presents not the least difficulty. To it, sensations, perceptions, are plainly such traces. But, says one
who has longer contemplated the problem, is not space the
condition of all material being, and is not this the one form
which has no actual relevance to acts of mind? Is not consciousness the essential characteristic of thought, and does
not this in turn exclude altogether physical forces? How
then shall a material force strike within consciousness, or
how shall a mental activity leave it to appear in space?
Here undoubtedly our powers of explanation are at fault.
The inquiries put us lie too deep in the secret nature, the
unphenomenal nature of things to admit of that phenomenal
statement or explanation which is sought for. Indeed, in
**the** very language in which our queries are urged, we have

over-leaped the limits of clear thought. In speaking of a
mental activity as *leaving consciousness*, or a physical force
as *entering it*, we have subjected to the conditions of space
that which is wholly foreign thereto. Yet these embarrassments should be no ground of disquiet, since, sooner or
later, whatever path we take, we reach the unphenomenal,
and thus the ultimate. The how of pure thought is as unintelligible as the how of pure matter, and the inter-dependence of the two is no more obscure than the manner of the
existence of either. The nature of thought is as unknown
to us as anything can be. We discover easily the relations
of things that lie in its light, but what that light is in which
they are seen, what is the sub-phenomenal nature of the activity whose product we retain as a judgment, is wholly inscrutable in the sense of being capable of any other phenomenal rendering than that through which we actually know
it. When we reach the bounds of events, we also reach the
limits of a certain form of explanation. Yet we cannot deny
the forms of existence that lie beyond, since such a denial is
itself the source of greater perplexities than those it seeks
to escape. Moreover, that space is not directly or indirectly penetrable by the activities of mind, is a proposition
whose conditions are too obscure to suffer it to be ranked
as an *a priori* conception. Were it not for our belief in the
actual existence of the external world, and our connection
with it, there would be no problem, since ideally the mind
deals freely with space. If matter did not exist, if powers
to apprehend it did not belong to us, there would be nothing to call forth the question which perplexes us. The very
query itself thus becomes proof of the fact.

We are not alone in an inability to solve ultimate problems, pertaining to matter beyond the bounds of experience.
Indeed an experience that should commence with a complete knowing, that should even know how it knew, would

be an eye that saw itself, an ear that heard itself. Mind is not such an organ. It reveals thought, not the nature of the thinking powers ; its phenomenal, formal character, not the very essence of the act itself. All that we claim is, that there is no *a priori* impossibility discoverable by **us**, making a transfer of influence from mind to matter, from matter to mind, **an** absurdity, Our last traces of **physical** force in the movement inward are found in the brain, our first traces in the movement outward are also met with at the same point. Thus far only can the eye follow material changes ; here is it first able to pick them up. How the last nervous impulse is linked to the play of consciousness, or how a pure volition breaks forth and liberates a physical force without itself becoming such a force, we cannot explain. We only affirm that our ignorance is so complete as to cut us off **as** perfectly from a denial of the possibility of such a transfer, as from an exposition of it. We simply do not see that the realms of space and consciousness anywhere over-lap, or even touch each other. We are profoundly ignorant of the nature of any connection between the two. We therefore satisfy ourselves with denying the existence of any *a priori* proof against such a dependence ; while experience, under the spontaneous interpretation which the human mind everywhere gives it, constantly affirms it as a fact.

In the ideal world, the mind freely contemplates physical being and forces. It moves at liberty among them, regards them as modified by its own activity, and is, in turn, modified in its thinking by them. It thus far recognizes no incompatibility between the two realms ; but is prepared to accept those actual relations which give occasion to these **ideal ones.** If an *a priori* necessity, ingrained in mind, divided the two fields, how could the mind so easily escape it in its own spontaneous movements ? It does not, can not regard lines as at once parallel and intersecting; a relation of space as equivalent to one of time; how, then, can it practically accept the communicability of matter and mind, and theoretically pronounce it impossible?

§ 2. An increasingly prevalent form of philosophy, held crudely by some and subtily by others, is materialism. In its most logical, yet most naked and repulsive forms, it re-solves all thought into the mere action of nervous centres, induced in a purely physical way by physical forces. This system is for the most part the product of scientific inquiry, a study of the laws of the material world simply. While affecting great contempt for *a priori* systems, and claiming experience as the only source and test of truth, in its phil-osophy—by courtesy so called—it presents an example of the most unreasonable *a priori* method anywhere found in the progress of knowledge.

The entire organum, the scheme of inquiry and instru-ments of thought, with which it approaches the intellectual world, have been gathered in departments utterly alien to the one to be contemplated. Far from being ready to ac-cept new facts under their own laws, philosophers of this school approach the science of mind, with the antecedent conviction, that physical laws reign everywhere, that there is the same fixed dependence of events in the realm of thought as **that** which **they have found** in matter. They thus, with the blindness of a limited system, push up the stream of causes as far as they can go, and then deny there is anything new beyond. As this theory fails, not merely to explain, but even to accept, the new and diverse phe-nomena of consciousness; and feebly substitutes for them some connected, but very different phenomena, to wit, those of the nervous centres, we feel at liberty, giving its scien-tific inquiries due praise, to pass it very lightly as a philoso-phy. It deals with the external conditions and accompaniments of mental activity, and not with the inner forms and laws of those activities. Under that fatal certainty which causes equivalent errors to follow each other at opposite extremes, it strives to stand outside in space and expound consciousness, as formerly the hasty philosopher inclosed in consciousness constructed his outside facts.

The last gate which this school suppose themselves to have opened, at which the powers of the physical world are to rush in and submerge those of mind, is that known as the correlation of forces. All material forces are convertible and indestructible. Hence it is concluded, that those which are at play in the living nervous organism mutually replace each other, and evolve from within themselves all the most subtile and the most palpable of the activities of rational life. Accept this relation of forces in the body, and we yet need the independent, spontaneous power of mind. The mind avails itself of a stream of forces that flow incessantly through the physical organization; into this it dips its wheel, and with it works out its purposes. This admission by no means closes the argument. We have here a telegraph, we discover that the electric, chemical, thermal, mechanical forces liberated are so far equivalent as to induce us to believe that they are perfectly so. We stand in an office; we behold an intelligible cypher rapidly appearing on the ribbon before us; does the equivalence, the indestructibility, the convertibility of the forces in the mechanism we have investigated, explain the message we have received? We may say, that nothing has been lost or added to the sum of forces concerned in the transfer of these words. Very well, the words in their intelligibility still seek solution. These are explained by the constant interference of a higher power, a remote operator, above the circle of self-balanced forces which have transferred the motion from the indicating to the inscribing index.

I may never see the hand that plays the remote key, but I cannot fail to believe in its existence, nor in the independent, intelligent character of the force that presides there. I know not how the key is touched by which the self-poised, nervous forces of the brain are set in motion; but in the product wrought out, I do see unmistakably the evidence of such initiation, guidance, arrest. The continuity and equality of the forces in the nervous circuit, if fully established, do not weaken or embarrass the conviction. They simply leave us where they found us, ignorant of the way in which the mind employs the current of material forces; these still yield the clearest evidence of being at some point of their circuit intersected by another and higher circle of influences. To say that the only force which can modify physical forces must itself be a physical force, betraying its presence among them as a new, additive power, **is not** merely to affirm what we do not know, but is **to make the** assertion that the intelligence of the products momentarily evolved by these nervous centres does not indicate a like quality in the ultimate agency, an assertion in flat contradiction of the principles of reasoning on which we habitually proceed.

How little this form of philosophy can accomplish is **evident** from the fact, that it itself must admit, that some kinds of matter are intelligent, self-conscious, spontaneous, and others are not. Thus having laboriously swallowed up mind in matter, it is compelled to re-include under matter, distinctions in every way as perplexing and inscrutable as those displaced. The facts remain, and either matter is self-conscious, or that which is self-conscious is mind. Words, rather than ideas, are thus offered as explanations in this deceptive resolution of two distinct elements into one. If an adversary of this theory chooses to add the farther affirmation that this self-conscious matter is also free, the point can only be fairly settled by re-opening the entire discussion; for it is antecedently no more improbable that matter is free, than it is that matter is conscious, and intelligent. The forces concerned in intellectual action are either conditioned from within to all the facts of mind, and we are remitted to consciousness to determine what these facts are in their entire complement; or these forces are conditioned to their action from without. If we accept the first statement, we have recognized two kinds of forces or activities utterly distinct from each other; if we accept the last, we have used two words, and called one set of forces appearing in space, material; and the same forces arising in consciousness, mental; thus overlooking the distinctions between them. What possible explanation is there in this? Do not the fundamental differences between matter and mind, open to all our faculties, remain as before? It would be well for philosophers to remember that theories can not reflexively wipe out facts, and that those of mind are of the most primitive and undeniable order. If either of the two classes of facts is to be merged in the other, physical ones necessarily yield to those of mind, as in their nature secondary, being known only as they affect consciousness. As the material world is at best reached inferentially, it can not logically displace the very faculties that know it. The knowing must have precedence of the thing known. If either is to be found to contain the other, it must be the first the second, not the second the first.

Materialism does not always assume the crude form now controverted. It has sometimes a more mixed and subtle character, one in which it is partially blended with idealism. Mr. Mill, while deriving all knowledge from experience, and declining to recognize any intuitive elements, nevertheless leaves the existence of matter in doubt. Sensations and perceptions are accepted in an ideal form, and the outside world of realities, which lies back of them, is left unapproached. Such a system is beset with more difficulties than either materialism or idealism. Sensations, whose existence and influence lie wholly within the mind, can with less reason be made to control and give form to the mind, than matter conceived as wholly outside and independent of the intellectual powers. Indeed it is not easy to see how a perception can occupy this anomalous position, on the one side giving law to the mind, on the other, cut off from all known, exterior dependence, and resting back on the very faculties whose form it controls.

This system exhibits the same defective analysis which belongs to all materialism. Space and time are evolved from experience, though they are the conditions of experience. They are made to spring from sensations, though themselves utterly beyond sensation. **Those** ideas on the other hand, that are admittedly in the mind, yet admittedly beyond experience, are pronounced delusive. Of this character is that of causation. Breaking this cord of connection, the external world swings loose from this philosophy. There lies against it concisely these difficulties. Claiming experience to be the source of knowledge, it elaborates a system far removed from ordinary conviction, and subversive of many of its most cherished opinions. It knows nothing of matter, while mankind knows this chiefly. It gives sensations, perceptions control over the mind, while the opinions of men divide control between outside and inside conditions. While employing it makes illusive, in **its** intellectual basis, the notion of causation, which above all has universal sway in the practical world.

It denies moreover necessity to any ideas whatever, while the whole history of pure mathematics shows the contrary. It is compelled to refer to experience the recognition of such facts as this, that straight lines, parallel through a portion of their extent, are so through their whole extent. Its analyses are inadequate, and it rejects without reason the ideas for which it can find no place in its system. That is to say, it makes its method the test of the facts, and not the facts the test of its method. There are two forms or tendencies in materialism; the one is found in the identification of the phenomena of matter and mind, and the other in the identification of the laws of matter and mind. The last is the method of Mill and Spencer, and is not less destructive of the facts than the first.

§ 3. The next system of which we shall speak, is a mixed one, that presented by Hamilton. Its most striking feature is, that it makes matter itself the direct object of perception, and thus, losing one occasion for intuitive ideas, accepts a part of them, perverts a part, and neglects a part. Among those resolved into powerlessness, are causation, liberty and the infinite. We need only to speak of its central characteristic, the direct perception of matter. Against this there holds, we believe, the very generally accepted axiom that nothing can act save where it is. The introduction of the adverb where, shows this statement to be limited to physical forces, since these alone appear in space, alone have locality. Physical forces must be where they are exercised. This will hardly be denied by any one. For a force to show itself as a force where it is not, would be for it to be and not to be at the same point at the same time. Mind, thought, have no reference to space, and hence it conveys no very intelligible idea to say, that the mind must be, a thought must be where it acts. Their objects of consideration may come from any quarter, and any distance; conclusions may strike out into the most remote regions, and such words as come and go, near and distant, have only a figurative signification. Now perception, till the brain is passed, is a thing of physical forces, and each organ and

nerve can only be affected by that within it, not by that
without it. It is against the above axiom to say, that I feel
the stone, meaning thereby that the sensation is outside the
organ — conversant, less or more, with the very essence of
being in the stone. The organ is affected by what is within itself; till the contour of its own states is penetrated, the
object might as well be miles, as inches, or fractions of an
inch distant. Physical effects lie as content in each **organ**
of sense, and are as localized within it as is the object with-
**out it.** If, then, these physical changes which accompany
perception, sensation, were perceived by the mind, the very
object, the source of these, would not thereby be directly
**known.** But these states are not perceived, we know nothing about the states either of the eye, the ear, or tongue, in
seeing, hearing, **tasting.** Sensations enter consciousness,
and lose at once their special organic grounds. When we
have reached the last physical change in our nervous organism, we have not reached the first thing that the mind is
conscious of in sensation. No organ of sensation is revealed
by its own sensations, but by other sensations of other organs
**of** which it is made an object. If, then, the mind knows
the object in perception, it is not by the movement inward
from the object, since this finds change, when from it, as a
cause, there arises a nervous affection in an organ of sense;
**and this** again meets with a second inexplicable change,
when there is a transfer to consciousness, and the true content of the mind lies within it, divested of physical qualities. We might as well say, that the first ball is in the
second ball moving after concussion, as to say, that the very
object of perception, or any portion of it, is in this its latest
effect. No, the second and third ball move through a
change within themselves; the organ becomes a condition
of perception—itself distinct—through a distinct condition
of its own nervous substance.

**It is, then,** by an outward movement of the mind, that matter is known, and this is not perception but inference, the interpretation of sensations. Through the notions of existence and causation and space, the mind establishes the external world. Sensations, till interpreted and expounded by judgment, are the crudest possible conditions of knowledge.

If it be said, that the act of perception itself is the result of an outward, not an inward movement, that it takes place at the exterior tip of the nerve, and not as the consequence of physical effects traced to the nerve centres; we say, that the mind must either pass perceptively beyond the sensational organ, or the perceptive act is still within the human body, and thus removed from the object perceived. Moreover such a theory neglects the obvious ministration to perception of all the chain of nervous influences passing inward. If these are means to sensation, they must intervene between the presence of the object and the perception of it. The inscrutable transition from a nervous state to a feeling is the last result of the inner current. Of an outer nervous current, there is no proof. The mind has no further perceptive connection with the object than that in which these several conditions of the organ intervene between the mind and the object. The last nervous condition remaining, the sensation remains.

§ 4. The last system of which we shall speak, is idealism. Idealism has peculiar excellences and defects. It seizes the most fundamental element of the universe, and evolves all else with consistent logic from it. It does not humble mind under the laws of matter, but makes it the source and law of all things. As all known existences must in some way enter consciousness, or be productive of phenomena there, it is evident that idealism has no occasion to lose or overlook any part of knowledge. Neglecting that inferential action of the mind by which it recognizes the objective validity and relations of the various sources of its perceptions and sensations, idealism is able, by limiting the attention to the phenomena of the internal world alone, to trace the inherent relations among these, and develop a purely ideal system of purely ideal objects. Herein there is opportunity for great subtlety, profoundity, consistency, and even breadth of thought; since everything, outer and inner, finds representation here. If the images of all the objects and events of the external world were brought to the eye of a spectator on a transparency, it is plain that he might form a very inclusive, and, in some of its aspects, correct philosophy concerning them. Consciousness is such a screen, and the philosopher, confining his attention to this, may evolve a very harmonious system.

Idealism more signally than most other theories fails of being a science, a knowing as actual that which is conceived of as theoretical. It matters little, that the inherent connections are necessary, unless the premises from point to point of the argument are verified as real. The difficulties of idealism are much the same as those of the *a priori* proof of the existence of God. An ideal conclusion is evolved from ideal premises, but as the last do not take hold of the world of facts, no more does the first. Philosophy is not merely philosophy, but science as well. It possesses inductive, united with deductive, elements. It resembles mixed rather than pure mathematics. It does not start with definitions of ideal objects, but with facts. Idealism, on the other hand, while contemplating thought, contemplates it as thought merely, in its formal relations rather than in its actual, phenomenal character and force. It deduces the individual from the general. It inquires not so much what is given actually and practically with independent testimony by the several faculties of mind, as what can be evolved from the mere fact of thought.

The result is, that no system is as far removed from general belief and faith as idealism. None **so** signally fails to recognize and expound the phenomena **of mind** under the form they actually assume in experience. It seems rather a field of intellectual gymnastics than of sound, sober inquiry concerning things, corrected and guided each instant by an observation **of facts.**

Idealism starts with assuming the least possible. It would commence with nothing if it could. **It accepts only activity known in** consciouness. It must not even say "an action," lest there should thus be implied something which **is active.** From this it proceeds to develop matter and mind, **activity and divided activity;** recognizing itself inconsciousness by opposing to the naked knowing the consciousness of knowing. Thus it moves onward, spinning a world out of its own bowels, and with little more of actual **correspondence** of results to the notions **of men than there exists** between the threads of **a spider's web and the** actual forces which hold the world together. Yet the idealist relishes his own system none the less for being so stuffed with the *ego*.

Scientific philosophy does not inquire how little it may assume, but how much it may consistently accept; at how many points it has reached ultimate facts. If the idealist **is** at liberty **to** regard the connections of thought not as fanciful and chimerical, but, as they seem to be, logical and coherent; in short to accept thinking as a valid and reliable act; **if he** is at liberty to assume memory, these necessary. assumptions involve the fitness of still farther assumption. Are not these, portions of a set of powers, and if the philosopher avails himself **of two, can he do better than to** avail himself of all? **Does he** trespass any more **on sound** principles in using the **entire** group than in using a part? Indeed, does he not act absurdly in employing thus adroitly **a part, and** neglecting the remainder, equally fitted for another and specific purpose? Should it be one's object to see how much can be done with the least possible means, or to see how much can be accomplished with all available means? Having a clue ought he not as a thinker to follow it as far as it will carry him, and does it not carry him logically to a faith in all his faculties, since he must have a faith in a part of them? Possibly, one can hop a little distance painfully on one foot; is it, therefore, wise to sling up the other? The scientific philosopher at once sets to work to determine by observation and analysis all his faculties, and accepts the testimony of them all, as each necessary to the right understanding of the peculiar and independent facts rendered by it.

Thus the idealist and the less **cunning but more wise** inquirer begin at once to diverge. The **one constructs a** system of remarkable connections, subtile and sagacious, but altogether airy and unsubstantial; the other acquires classified knowledge, with many lines of causation and deductive relations in it; often presenting, indeed, inscrutable points, yet always having the ring and firmness of facts. Idealism is ideal; science, the philosophy we seek, is actual.

§ 5. The system we have now presented aims fully to recognize the different, independent kinds of knowing. Each of these is ultimate, and, therefore, inexplicable under other forms of knowing. To carry one faculty into the province of another, is to displace that other, and with it the information it is fitted to give. Knowledge, in its last analysis, has always a certain mystery about it for the very reason that we can go no farther. There is a mystery in a color, as green; in a taste, as sweet; in an odor, as fragrant; in a judgment, pronouncing the stone to be hard; in every intuition, as that of a cause, of liberty, of the infinite. We **must** not expect to expel mystery, but to reduce it to a minimum, and place it at the right **points**.

One of the chief labors of the philosopher is to keep independent faculties, so recognized on adequate grounds, from devouring each other; from making incursions into fields alien to them, from refusing to accept what has not been submitted to themselves, and received their peculiar seal. The imagination and the understanding belong especially to these intrusive faculties, while the intuition of cause, having swept through the entire physical world, is ever bent on a raid into spiritual realms. To be ready to recognize, in their unrestricted forms, the facts of consciousness as revealed in the mind, in language, in history; to analyze these cautiously, without bias and perversion, for the discovery of the simple activities or faculties they reveal; and afterward to hold fast to every affirmation of these faculties, is the duty of the wise cultivator of mental science. We have a love for science above that for philosophy, because of this inductive element it so obviously includes.

The confusion which arises from undue emphasis laid upon a single faculty is seen in our knowledge of the thing-in-itself, of mind-in-itself. These, we are said, not to know, because we can not conceive them. To wish to conceive them is the futile desire to put a second circle of phenomena below the first circle. Such a movement could admit of no pause. The noumena must either be resolved into phenomena, or always escape the imagination. But do we not know the noumena, things-in-themselves? Do we not know the whole circle of effects which express them? What more could we wish to know; unless forsooth, we we are dissatisfied with our circle of senses and wish a larger one? To desire to know a thing in one way, when its very nature only allows us to know it in another way, is certainly an irrational impulse.

The independent validity both of causation and of lib-

erty has been recognized. Each idea is present to the mind
in the spontaneous explanation which it offers to a certain
class of facts. They divide the universe of events between
them. In the one moiety, we have necessity, in the other,
liberty; in the one, movements already conditioned by the
forces at work, in the other, movements then and there
conditioned by the power that initiates them. In their
relations to each other, liberty is primary, and causation
is secondary. Causation marks dependence, a dependence
which, on its own level, can find no arrest, no matter how
far we trace it. Events, follow them backward, forward,
on either hand, are conditioned one upon another; forces
are already at work accomplishing the tasks assigned them.
But a first, an independent, an unconditioned force nowhere
appears. Causal action, therefore, necessarily presents a
fragmentary and partial character. Of it alone, there can
be made up no whole, no universe ; since the more we have,
the more we demand to explain what we have. The events
before us, like the section of a river, must flow into and
flow out of the horizon. We can reach no beginning and
no conclusion, nor even find diminution as we go backward,
or increase as we go forward. The boundaries of our vision
enlarge themselves in all directions, but are always illusory.

Liberty, on the contrary, to the extent of the events
which spring from it, affords a complete commencement.
We need go no farther back. An arrest is found in it, and
the events which flow thence are explained by the form,
impetus, and direction which it has imparted to them.
Causation is necessarily finite in its manifestation; since it
inheres in a power already put forth, and is conditioned to a
given number and form of products. Liberty rests back on
the agent, never goes forth from him, and partakes, in its
possibilities, of the breadth and the limitations of his faculties. It commands more than the actual, to wit, the poten-

tial of being. Infinite power can inhere in a free personality, and in no other form of existence.

Causation is closely connected with space. It may be questioned whether it ever acts in any other connection. It inheres in forces, and these are put forth into separate, spacial existence. The phenomena of mind which involve cause and effect do so through material dependencies. The mind's own action would seem to be always either spontaneous or free, that is its spontaneity is revealed under the three forms of thought, feeling and volition. Liberty, in contra-distinction, remains always in connection with consciousness. We can only choose consciously. Matter can only be the source of causative action. Mind is the source of spontaneous and of free action; of spontaneous action, that is action springing independently from it, though often evoked by conditions not supplied by it; of free action, that is action held within the conditions which are its occasion but not bound to any one of them.

Liberty, again, lies back of all causation, because the whole flood of forces with which human liberty plays springs from the choice of God, is but the executive power with which he momentarily sustains and accomplishes his purposes. Here we reach another ultimate fact. We know not how the mind affects these secondary physical forces, that in the human body play beneath its touch. No more do we understand how these imperishable and uniform forces on which the universe is buoyed, of which it is fashioned, go forth from the will of God. Their wholly finite, yet rational character compels the reason thus to refer them to an independent, self-sufficient and wise Source; and therein to complete the conception of the universe in time as in space. A cord of great length is no more self-supporting, no more explicable in itself, than a shorter one. The only idea which is, as it were, spherical, self-centered, demanding nothing, suffering nothing outside of itself, is that of an Infinite, Personal God, a sufficient source of all things; whose spontaneity and liberty require no explanation, and bring explanation to all beside. On this ground, and on this alone, the reason accepts the idea, as one by which it does see—as a sun that does spread its light through the whole heavens, leaving nothing which is not sought out by its rays. The final proof of truth is the fact of light, the very fact of light admitting no controversy and no denial to those who receive it—to whom it gives the power to become the sons of God. The real efficiency of every word is found in the disclosure **of** itself as the light which comes down from heaven.

§ 6. While the division of schools of philosophy into materialistic, realistic and idealistic is simple and fundamental, it does not express with any fullness **and exactness** the very variable facts before us. We offer, **therefore, a** second division more suggestive of this complexity.*

Constructive Idealism.
Idealism.

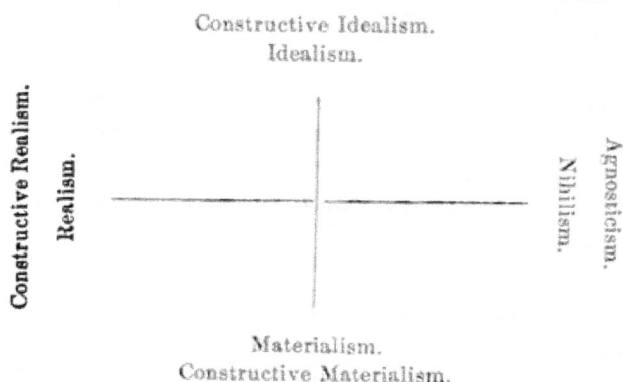

We draw attention to the direct contrasts **of** the inner **circle, of** realism **to** nihilism, of materialism to idealism;

* **Consult recent British Philosophy.**

and also to the relations of the outer circle. This circle turns, in its divisions, on the force given to intuitive ideas.

By realism we mean what is sometimes termed natural realism. It is the realism of Reid and Hamilton. Each act of perception is said to include, as an indivisible constituent, the direct knowledge of both matter and mind. Materialism is the identification of matter and mind as two forms of the same experience; this is the method of M. Taine. Idealism is the absorption of all being into processes of mind, after the manner of Fichte and Hegel. Nihilism is the denial of all knowledge, phenominal and constructive. The impressions we call knowledge are merely impressions afloat with other impressions, reflections in a stream which may disappear at any moment.

Constructive realism is realism reached as the result of the combined action of our perceptions, intuitions and judgments. It is the realism offered in this work. Constructive materialism is the materialism of Spencer. It gathers the constructive laws of thought from the phenomena known as physical, and builds the universe, both physical and intellectual, by means of them. It affirms nothing as to ultimate, substantial being; but phenominal being it puts exclusively under the laws of matter. Constructive idealism declares that all the forms of knowledge are purely mental, and cannot be said to be forms of matter. Thus matter, when its existence is allowed, is not known under its own types. Substantially and phenominally it is hidden from us. Constructive idealism rests chiefly on the works of Kant.

A measure of agnosticism is involved in opposite directions in both constructive materialism and constructive idealism. When these two incapacities are united, we have agnosticism; and agnosticism may easily lapse into nihilism —the antithetical point to realism. Hume is the best expo-

nent of nihilism.   The circuit on either hand through idealism **or** materialism involves a decay of power, and so leads
**on** to nihilism.   Pure Positive Philosophy is agnosticism.
**It directs attention** wholly to phenomena.

A ninth central school might be added, that of identification ; but it has not gained, **and** can not readily gain, any
clear expression.   Matter **and** mind are to be united in one
concurrent line of **evolution.**   This is the goal of Hegel.

**It has been our purpose** to draw cardinal lines firmly,
and this farther division is added simply as provocative of
historical inquiry.

# INDEX.

## A.

Abstraction, 153.

Actions as voluntary, 395 ; as conscious, 396.

Affections, 311 ; natural affections, 320 ; affections, 350.

Analysis, 153.

Animals, their powers, 295 ; tricks, 298 ; training, 298 ; language, 300 ; manner of judgment, 300 ; character, 301 ; sagacity, 302 ; feelings, 361 ; actions, 392.

Appetites, 317.

Association, subconscious facts, 43 ; **memory, 133, 138, 175 ; laws, 172,** 174 ; beauty, 240 ; power of mind, 291 ; animals, 301 ; feelings, 366.

Attention, **what, 291 ; to more than one thing, 291.**

Automatic action, **385, 395.**

## B.

Bain, Prof., imagination, **143, 144,** 147 ; judgment, 162 ; existence, 181 ; space, **196 ;** cause and effect, 210, 213 ; right, 228, 233 ; feelings, 314 ; nervous system, 383, 386 ; liberty, 412, 424.

Beauty **as an** idea, 240 ; **feelings, 342.**

Bentham, J., **morals, 239.**

Berkeley, Bishop, perception, 111.

Brain, relations to mind, 56 ; functions, 383 ; superiority in man, 387, 394.

Bridgman, **Laura, 276.**

## C.

Carpenter, **W. B., unconscious cerebration, 50, 53 ;** brain, 388 ; will, 418, 423.

Cause and effect, an idea, 209 ; nature of, 210, 218 ; growth of mind, 281 ; relation to liberty, 420, 421, 451.

Cerebration, 49, 55.

Chance and liberty, 411.

Choice, 31, 346.

## 458 *INDEX.*

## P.

Perception, nature, 80 ; organs, 82 ; objects, 82 ; judgments, 84, 101, 104 ; statement of doctrine, 92 ; consciousness, 94 ; data, 97 ; not direct, 99 ; eye, 101, 103 ; ear, 104 ; importance, 107 ; history, 108 ; relation to philosophy, 113, 445.

Philosophy, advantages, 2 ; progress, 8 ; postulates, 13.

Phrenology, 29.

Plato, 158, 185.

Play and labor, 433.

Postulates, 13, 435.

Power of mind, 145, 436.

## Q.

Quain's anatomy, 380.

Qualities of matter, 116.

## R.

Realism, 158 ; as a system of philosophy, 435, 451, 453.

Reason, 176 ; what it gives, 179, 397.

Reasoning, 281 ; kinds, 286, 288.

Reid, 13 ; perception, 87.

Relation as an idea, 260.

Relativity of knowledge, 114.

Resemblance as an idea, 185 ; growth under, 279 ; science, 280.

Right as an idea, 224.

## S.

Sagacity in animals, 302.

Science and resemblance, 280.

Sensations, 80 ; growth, 269 ; feelings, 312.

Sight, 101.

Sleep, 67.

Somnambulism, 67.

Space as an idea, 188.

Spencer, mind and brain, 63 ; judgment, 162 ; association, 173 ; space, 186, 191, 196, 198 ; time, 205 ; causation, 212 ; right, 288 ; infinite, 251 ; ideas objective, 257 ; inheritance, 260 ; dynamics, 268 ; feelings, 315 ; systems, 455.

Spinal cord, 378, 381.

THE END

**A History of American Literature.** By Moses Coit Tyler, Professor of English Literature in the University of Michigan. Volumes I and II, comprising the period, 1607-1765. Large 8vo, about 700 pages, handsomely bound in cloth, extra, **gilt top, $6.00**; half calf, extra, . . . . . . . . . . **$11 00**

The History of American Literature, now offered to the public, is the first attempt ever made to give a systematic and critical account of the literary development of the American people. It is not a mere cyclopædia of literature, or a series of detached biographical sketches accompanied by literary extracts: but an analytic and sustained narrative of our literary history from the earliest English settlement in America down to the present time. The work is the result of original and independent studies prosecuted by the author for the past ten years, and gives an altogether new analysis of American literary forces and results during nearly three centuries. The present two volumes—a complete work in themselves—cover the whole field of our history during the colonial time.

"An important national work."—*New York Tribune.*

"The literary event of the decade."—*Hartford Courant.*

"A book more interesting than half the new novels."—*The Nation.*

"A work of great and permanent importance."—*New York Evening Post.*

"One of the most valuable publications of the century."—*Boston Post.*

"A book actually fascinating from beginning to end."—Prest. J. B. Angell.

"As the work stands, it may rightfully claim a place on the library table of every cultivated American."—*New York Times.*

"No work of similar scope and magnitude and erudition exists, or has been attempted in this country."—*New York Evangelist.*

"A unique and valuable work."—*Chicago Tribune.*

"A work which will rank with those of Sismondi, Ticknor, and Taine."—*New York Evening Express.*

"It is this philosophical character of the work which brings it not far distant from the works of Taine, of Buckle, and of Lecky."—*Buffalo Express.*

"One can hardly speak too strongly in praise of these conscientious, careful and successful volumes, which deserve to be studied alike by scholars and patriots."—*Rev. Henry Martyn Dexter, D.D,*

"But the plan of Professor Tyler's book is so vast and its execution so fearless, that no reader can expect or wish to agree with all its personal judgments. It is a book truly admirable, both in design and in general execution; the learning is great, the treatment wise, the style fresh and vigorous. Here and there occurs a phrase which a severer revision would perhaps exclude, but all such criticisms are trivial in view of so signal a success. Like Parkman, Professor Tyler may almost be said to have created, not merely his volumes, but their theme. Like Parkman, at any rate, he has taken a whole department of human history, rescued it from oblivion, and made it henceforward a matter of deep interest to every thinking mind."—T. W. Higginson, in *The Nation.*

"The work betrays acute philosophical insight, a rare power of historical research, and a cultivated literary habit, which was perhaps no less essential than the two former conditions, to its successful accomplishment. The style of the author is marked by vigor, originality, comprehensiveness, and a curious instinct in the selection of words. In this latter respect, though not in the moulding of sentences, the reader may perhaps be reminded of the choice and fragrant vocabulary of Washington Irving, whose words alone often leave an exquisite odor like the perfume of sweet-briar and arbutus."—George Ripley, in the *Tribune.*

"Professor Moses Coit Tyler's 'History of American Literature,' of which the first two volumes have just been issued, will take rank at once as a book of lasting value, even though the author should advance no further than he has already done in the scheme of his work. We are not unmindful of the eminent historians this country has produced, when we express our opinion that his history is the best study of American historic material that has been written by an American. There has been manifestly no limit to the enthusiasm, conscientiousness and industry with which he has possessed himself of the entire body of the literature of which he treats, and at the same time he has displayed the qualities of a true literary artist in giving form, color and perspective to his work."—David Gray, in the *Buffalo Courier.*

**VAN LAUN. The History of French Literature.**

By HENRI VAN LAUN, Translator of Taine's "History of English Literature," "the Works of Molière," etc.

Vol I. FROM ITS ORIGIN TO THE RENAISSANCE. 8vo, cloth extra . . . . . . . . . . **$2 50**

Vol. II. FROM THE RENAISSANCE TO THE CLOSE OF THE REIGN OF LOUIS XIV. 8vo, cloth extra . . . . **$2 50**

Vol. III. FROM THE REIGN OF LOUIS XIV. TO THAT OF NAPOLEON III. 8vo, cloth extra . . . . **$2 50**

The set, three volumes, in box, half calf, $15.00 ; cloth extra, **7 50**

"We have to deal with a people essentially spirited and intellectual, whose spirit and intellect have been invariably the wonder and admiration, if not the model and mold of contemporary thought, and whose literary triumphs remain to this day among the most notable landmarks of modern literature." * * *—*Extract from Author's Preface.*

"Mr. Van Laun has not given us a mere critical study of the works he considers, but has done his best to bring their authors, their way of life, and the ways of those around them, before us in a living likeness."—*London Daily News.*

"This history is extremely interesting in its exposition of the literary progress of the age, in connection with the social and political influences which helped to mould the character and the destinies of the people."— *Boston Daily Globe.*

"It is full of keenest interest for every person who knows or wishes to learn anything of French literature, or of French literary history or biography. Scarcely any book of recent origin, indeed, is better fitted than this to win general favor with all classes of persons."—*N Y Evening Post.*

**THIERS** (LOUIS ADOLPHE) **Life of.** By FRANCOIS LE GOFF, Docteur-ès-lettres, Author of a "History of the Government of National Defense in the Provinces," etc. Translated, from the author's unpublished manuscript, by THEODORE STANTON, A.M. Octavo, with Portrait, cloth extra. . . . . **$2 00**

This book is written especially for the American public by M. Francois Le Goff, of Paris, a French publicist of the Conservative-Republican school, who knew Thiers personally and who is thoroughly conversant with the history and politics of France. Besides the biographical narrative, which is enlivened by many fresh anecdotes, the writer attempts to present such a connected view of French political history for the last fifty years, as will throw light upon the present crisis in France, so incomprehensible to most Americans. The work will also be interesting as an able defense of the unity of Thiers' political life, a position rarely assumed by even the most ardent friends of the great statesman. It is illustrated by a fac-simile of his handwriting and autograph, a view of his home, etc.

**BRIEF BIOGRAPHIES. First Series. Contemporary Statesmen of Europe.** Edited by THOMAS WENTWORTH HIGGINSON. They are handsomely printed in square 16mo, and attractively bound in cloth extra. Price per vol. . . . . . . . **$1 50**

Vol. I. ENGLISH STATESMEN. By T. W. HIGGINSON.
" II. ENGLISH RADICAL LEADERS. By R. J. HINTON.
" III. FRENCH LEADERS. By EDWARD KING.
" IV. GERMAN POLITICAL LEADERS. By HERBERT TUTTLE.

These volumes are planned to meet the desire which exists for accurate and graphic information in regard to the leaders of political action in other countries. They will give portraitures of the men and analysis of their lives and work, that will be vivid and picturesque, as well as accurate and faithful, and that will combine the authority of careful historic narration with the interest attaching to anecdote and personal delineation.

"Compact and readable * * * leaves little to be desired."—*N. Y. Nation.*

www.ingramcontent.com/pod-product-compliance
Lightning Source LLC
Chambersburg PA
CBHW031812270326
41932CB00008B/389